The Illustrated Encyclopedia of

PISTOLS & REVOLVERS

**An illustrated history of hand guns
from the sixteenth century to the present day**

The Illustrated Encyclopedia of

PISTOLS & REVOLVERS

An illustrated history of hand guns
from the sixteenth century to the present day

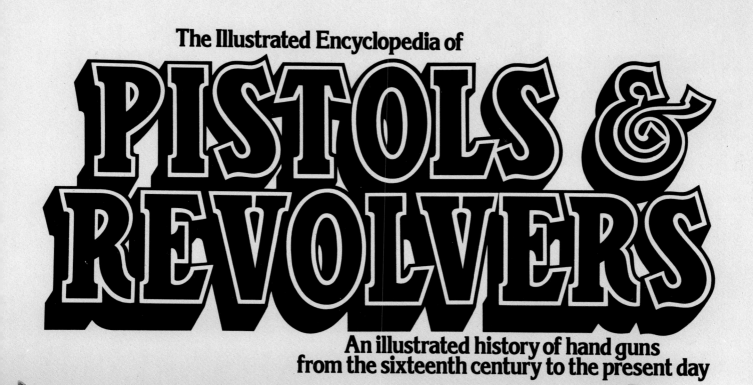

Major Frederick Myatt M.C.

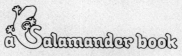

a Salamander book

Published by
CRESCENT BOOKS
New York

A Salamander Book

© Salamander Books Ltd 1980
Salamander House
27 Old Gloucester Street
London WC1N 3AF
United Kingdom

Library of Congress Catalog Card
Number: 80-67515

ISBN 0-517-321246

Editor:
Richard O'Neill
Designer:
Barry Savage
Picture research:
Diane Rich
Line diagrams:
Terry Hadler
© Salamander Books Ltd
Photography of weapons:
Bruce Scott
© Salamander Books Ltd
Filmset:
Modern Text Ltd, England
Colour reproduction:
Tempus Litho Ltd, England
Printed by:
Henri Proost et Cie,
Turnhout, Belgium

The Author

Frederick Myatt is a retired officer of the Royal Berkshire Regiment, British Army, into which he was commissioned in 1940. He was seconded to the Royal West African Frontier Force for most of World War II and won the Military Cross in Burma. He retired from the Army in 1969 and immediately took up his present position as Curator of the Weapons Museum and Librarian at the School of Infantry, Warminster, Wiltshire. He is a regular contributor to such well-known journals as *American Rifleman*, *Guns Review* and the *British Army Review*. His previously published books include *The Golden Stool*, *The Royal Berkshire Regiment*, *The March to Magdala*, *A Short History of the Small Arms School Corps*, *The Soldier's Trade*, *Peninsular General* and the Salamander titles *Modern Small Arms* and *Nineteenth Century Firearms*.

Introduction

Anthony Taylerson was born in 1924 and educated at Oundle School, at St John's College, Oxford, and in the RAF. He was called to the Bar in 1950 and now works as an "in house" lawyer for a chemical company. An acknowledged expert on revolving arms, he is the author of *The Revolver 1865-1888* (London, 1966), *Revolving Arms* (London, 1967) and *The Revolver 1889-1914* (London, 1970), and co-author of *The Revolver 1818-1865* (London, 1968) and *Adams Revolvers* (London, 1976).

Contents

Author's Foreword

In their various forms, pistols and revolvers are probably the most familiar of all firearms, and they appear to be of some considerable interest to people who are not otherwise concerned with weapons. The reason for this, I feel, is that although relatively few people — in Great Britain, at any rate — ever actually see pistols, and fewer still are able to handle them, they are nevertheless very much a part of life from our earliest days. In fiction, most of us are conditioned from childhood to the highwayman, the pirate, the duellist, the cowboy and the secret agent, all of whom tend to bristle with hand guns — while the average cinema or television screen seems to be the scene of almost endless gun battles.

Even more to the point, perhaps, is the increasing incidence of pistols and revolvers in real life, in the hands of terrorists and criminals. From this, it inevitably follows that hand guns are increasingly carried and used by the forces of law and order. This is particularly true of Great Britain, where, until a few years ago, an armed policeman was a rarity. Now he is a relatively common sight, and is likely to become more so. As a result of publicity, both fictional and real, the hand gun has acquired an aura of glamour — if, indeed, this is the proper term to apply to an instrument designed specifically to kill.

This book does not set out to moralize, but to explain. Hand guns are part of our past, our present and our foreseeable future, and a great many people have a perfectly healthy and legitimate interest in their development and use. It is, however, becoming increasingly difficult for most private individuals in Great Britain to own hand guns: antique specimens have become very expensive, while modern arms are the subject of so many legal restrictions that they are, for all practical purposes, unobtainable except by a relatively few members of pistol clubs. In fact,

it is often quite difficult even to see modern hand guns, since most gunsmiths no longer display them, for security reasons. All this is regrettable from the point of view of the enthusiast, but the present state of the world makes it inevitable. In the circumstances, therefore, it may be that good photographs with detailed captions are the best substitutes—and that is the main purpose of this book.

As we have aimed at size and quality of photographs, rather than mere quantity, the selection of arms for illustration has been quite difficult. There are thousands of different hand guns in existence; but it is hoped that those we have chosen to illustrate present a reasonably representative cross-section of the more common types, together with a leavening of rarities. In general, real oddities have been omitted in favour of weapons which have seen some general use; nor does this book attempt to cover the various highly-specialized types, such as air pistols, free target pistols, signal pistols, and the like.

The data provided are the best available, and in most cases have been taken fron the actual weapons shown. Manufacturing variations do exist, however, and must be taken into account. Typical cartridges have also been included; but here, again, it must be remembered that some weapons, notably cartridge revolvers, will handle a variety of cartridges with differing bullet and charge weights—and this naturally has an effect on the assessment of muzzle velocity. Although the various sections are arranged chronologically, it has proved difficult strictly to maintain this rule in the case of the arms themselves, because of the desirability, in some cases, to group them by category.

Most of the arms illustrated in this book are in the Weapons Museum at the School of Infantry, Warminster, and I am grateful to Colonel A. J. Adcock, OBE, Commandant of the Small Arms Wing and Chairman of the Museum Trustees, for his permission to photograph them. The remainder of the specimens are from the Armouries of H.M. Tower of London or from the Pattern Room of the Royal Small Arms Factory, Enfield, and I thank the authorities concerned for allowing them to be photographed. In particular, Miss R. R. Brown at the Tower and Mr H. Woodend at Enfield were most helpful in providing facilities for the production team. I am also grateful to Gunmark of Fareham, to Major George Shears and to the Curator of the Regimental Museum of the Duke of Edinburgh's Royal Regiment for assistance of various kinds. Mr F. Davie, assistant curator and technician of the Weapons Museum has, as always, been extremely helpful, and Mrs P. Kedge has coped very efficiently with the very large volume of paperwork involved. Lastly, I must thank Mr A. W. F. Taylerson for writing the Introduction; his name is too well known in the world of hand firearms to need any introduction from me.

F.M., Warminster, Wiltshire 1980

Introduction

A faded anti-gun gibe that "only a man who has a pistol needs it" sits not uncomfortably here, for both Major Myatt's excellent pictures of civilian and service hand guns, and his remarks upon them, will indeed often raise the question: "Who needed this particular pistol?" Consider, briefly, how difficult it is for most of us to shoot well, even with a modern hand gun, at just 7 metres (23 ft), and under stress no greater than that of competition. Consider, further, how badly most of us would shoot with the same weapon in combat. Extend the scenario to using a single-shot percussion pistol against an adversary who will cut or ride you down if you miss — and the need will seem to be for a blunderbuss rather than what you hold.

Indeed, in that last scenario, you may have fired only ten practice rounds of ball ammunition *annually* in the pistol you are using. Moving the time-frame forward into the 1930s, and substituting the current Enfield revolver, will not assist you greatly, for the scale of ammunition then laid down to be carried in the British Army was twelve rounds on the man, with six more in Regimental reserve.

Now try that legendary American West. "I would call that very good shooting myself, if I took careful aim and did my best." The speaker? Sheriff Pat Garrett of Lincoln County, New Mexico, who killed Billy the Kid. The shooting? To hit a 1·5in (38mm) mark twice out of five shots, at a range of 15 or 20 paces.

Yet, *faute de mieux,* the householder, the soldier, the sailor and the traveller have all had, or have felt that they had, a need for these difficult weapons — and that for almost as long as firearms have existed. Equally important, those who were responsible for arming the fighting services of their countries also accepted that need.

One obvious "need" for a hand gun may be shortly dismissed. From the very earliest days of small arms, some were carried as personal ornaments or as a sign of their bearer's rank or affluence. Such arms still appear today, as they did then, and still bear little relevance to real need. The rich man's status symbol may be a watch or a hand gun — but, if the latter, it is only incidentally a weapon.

If a real need for civilian or military hand guns for self-defence seems difficult to establish, against my view of their likely efficacy in ordinary hands, nevertheless, that particular need was, from the outset, their *raison d'être*.

Leaving aside criminals and duellists, there have been legitimate, if fairly rare, offensive roles for the hand gun in hands and times as distanced as 16th-century European cavalry, caracoling to break pikemen's ranks with pistol fire; German "storm troop" NCOs of World War I, using long-barrelled Luger self-loaders with "snail magazines" in attack; and US Army anti-tunnelling forces in Vietnam during the 1960s. However, the bed-rock use intended for most pistols, revolvers or self-loaders has been defence of their bearer's function, whether as civilian householder or traveller, or as military officer, senior NCO or non-combatant specialist.

With quite rare exceptions, and into living memory, civilian makers of hand guns set the pace of design, when filling civilian defensive needs, and the armed services followed that lead — usually at some distance — in the light of available finance and the nature of the military or naval tasks before them.

The users of the earliest small arms, in the 15th century, had muzzle-loading, single-shot weapons, fired by a match, as described by Major Myatt. We do not know if such weapons, fired while butted against breast or belly, developed a variant fired in one hand, ie, the pistol, but if such a variant did appear, it can only have emphasized the unreliability of the match for ignition and the disadvantage of a single-shot weapon. As Major Myatt indicates, users in the 16th and 17th centuries found answers to these problems, in the surer ignition of wheel- or flintlocks and in revolving chambers or the simple multiplication of loaded barrels. Even conservative service interest, concerned with hand guns for use by cavalrymen and sailors, had accepted the improved ignition systems by the 18th century, although it disregarded multi-barrelled arms and breechloading or magazine alternatives.

As a generalization, it may be said that this pattern was followed through the 18th and 19th centuries, with civilian demand leading the way in the development of percussion pistols, revolvers, magazine arms to use self-contained ammunition and self-loading pistols. Military and naval concern was largely with the improved ignition systems resulting from these developments, and was only reluctantly turned towards any quicker-loading, faster-firing hand guns embodying such systems. It was felt that the function of an officer or NCO was to lead his men, of the cavalryman to strike home in formation with sword or lance, of the trumpeter to call his signals, and so on. Although each might have a legitimate need to defend himself, he should have no need of a quick-firing weapon, which might tempt him to the offensive and away from his true duties.

There were, of course, many exceptions to that pattern of reluctance in adopting more effective, civilian-developed hand guns — and they bear mention, in order to dispel any implied adverse judgement upon the relevant official decision. Thus, the Royal Navy made extensive use of Colt revolvers as early as the Crimean War; the French Navy adopted a breechloading "Pistolet-Revolver Mle 1858" a full 15 years before their Army colleagues took a similar step; and the Austro-Hungarian Army adopted a Roth-Steyr Model 1907 self-loading pistol, for cavalry use, before any other major power took up such a weapon.

The pattern — of civilian development picked over by service committees — has been distorted in the present century: firstly, by huge government purchase or manu-facture (of obsolete revolvers and self-loading pistols) arising from two World Wars; secondly, by the increasingly-fashionable legislation against the private possession of firearms. The first of these factors seriously delayed hand gun development, while the second eroded (and, in Britain, eventually destroyed) the West European civilian market that formerly supported exotic revolver or self-loading pistol developments. (In Eastern Europe and the Soviet Union, of course, the same end was achieved by nationalization of the gunmakers.)

The United States of America stands, fortunately, as an exception, and it seems no accident that so many hand gun developments since 1945 (as alloy frames, high-velocity cartridges, stainless steel weapons and improved lock mechanisms) have come from the USA — while other major powers seem to proffer only such exotica as the fully-automatic pistol, in silenced form, as their contri-bution to the art.

Now read on, to learn the technical steps and stages by which we came to this pass.

You have an excellent guide.

Anthony Taylerson   Kea, Greece   May 1980

Early Pistols: the Wheel-lock and Flintlock

Few inventions have had a greater effect on mankind than that of gunpowder; yet in spite of its importance, its origins are still largely shrouded in mystery. Over the years an odd mixture of folklore and speculation has to some extent come to be accepted as fact, but so little of this knowledge is subject even to basic proof that it must all be more or less suspect. It is probable that like fire, the bow or other fundamental advances, gunpowder was discovered independently in several locations and at various times—although this again is mere conjecture. Roger Bacon, the English monk and natural philosopher, certainly knew of the existence of gunpowder by around the mid-13th century; but only, it seems, as a curiosity, a kind of noisy firework. Bacon did not claim to have invented gunpowder and did not attribute its discovery to any person or place. Nor did he mention its use as a propellant; which was, of course, where its real importance lay.

All that may be said with some certainty is that basic cannon were in use in Europe in the first half of the 14th century—and that by about 1450 they had been joined by portable, one-man firearms, recognizable as such to the modern eye. These weapons were all discharged by the direct application of fire to gunpowder. This process entailed the use of match: a piece of loose cord impregnated with chemicals to make it burn. When action was imminent, the end of the cord was ignited and allowed to smoulder slowly: the gunner blew on it to produce a hotter spark when it became necessary to discharge his weapon. This system, primitive though it was, worked well enough with a musket; but it was of less efficacy in the case of a hand gun. A pistol is, above all, an arm for quick shooting at close quarters—which necessarily implies that it should be carried ready for more or less instant use in pocket, belt or holster. This naturally precluded its use when the matchlock was the only known type of ignition, for a glowing match could hardly be carried in such close proximity to the priming without great danger of accidental discharge. Some matchlock pistols are to be found, but they are all of relatively modern Eastern origin and thus very much an aberration in terms of the development of hand guns.

THE WHEEL-LOCK

The need to produce ignition as and when required was apparent to gunsmiths for many years. As the traditional, and indeed the only practical, way of achieving this in everyday life was by striking flint or iron pyrites against steel, it was natural that the same system should be applied to new gun locks. The wheel-lock probably came into use during the first few years of the 16th century and may have been invented—in theory, at least—by Leonardo da Vinci. It made its first practical appearance either in Southern Germany or Northern Italy, and soon

Above: *An illustration of 1590 shows German "Ritters" (heavy cavalry) armed with wheel-lock pistols and lances. Note that they wear full armour and that the horseman at (4), having discharged his pistol, resorts to his lance.*

Left: *A German cavalryman with a wheel-lock pistol, 1601. The ball-butt facilitated drawing from a saddle-holster and prevented the hand from slipping.*

Top: *The equipment of King James II at the Battle of the Boyne, 1690. A flintlock pistol (one of a pair) is carried in a saddle-holster. The increasing power of firearms had made battlefield armour obsolete: the King's armour is largely ceremonial.*

Right: *Dated 1594 and attributed to the Flemish painter Gheeraerts, this portrait of Captain Thomas Lee shows the British soldier with his arms, which include a finely-ornamented snaphance pistol, apparently held by a belt-hook.*

Facere et pati Fortia

Ætatis suæ 43
An. Dñi 1594

Henry Lee of Ireland

became popular within certain clearly defined limits. As the mechanism is described in detail on page 16 (and in the accompanying diagram), it is only necessary to say here that it worked in much the same way as a modern wheel-and-flint cigarette lighter—although it was, of course, much larger and its wheel had to be spun mechanically. This made it a very complex mechanism —in its time, perhaps second only to the clock—and it is not surprising that it should have made its first appearance in an area already well known for its skilled clockmakers.

The wheel-lock was obviously an expensive arm to manufacture, and its initial use was thus restricted to those who could afford to lay out a considerable sum of money. Indeed, the possession of a wheel-lock weapon soon became something of a status symbol, and many of them were so highly decorated with gold, silver, ivory and horn, that they came to be regarded more as works of art than as practical weapons.

As manufacturing techniques improved, cheaper and more practical arms began to appear in greater quantity. Although hand guns were never really numerous in the 16th century, several countries became alarmed at the prospect of their use by criminals and attempted to ban them. Emperors, kings and other great men disliked hand guns because of the advantages they gave to potential assassins: a would-be murderer with a dagger might be stopped by alert guards before inflicting mortal injuries, but a killer with a small and easily-concealed firearm was more to be feared. Like most new inventions, however, hand guns soon gained general acceptance and, as time went by, were made in a variety of styles. These included double-barrelled models and guns with single, sliding locks which could be adjusted to serve several touch holes in succession. Some were even made to fire multiple charges on the principle of a roman candle, although these must have been more spectacular than dangerous—except, perhaps, to the firer.

The main military importance of the wheel-lock was that it could be used by a mounted man. For a short time, wheel-lock pistols had some effect on military tactics—something which no other pistols ever really achieved. By the 16th century cavalry were becoming increasingly impotent when pitted against infantry armed with matchlock muskets; so for a time they virtually abandoned shock tactics and sought instead to demoralize their opponents by advancing in successive ranks and firing volleys of pistol bullets. It was hoped also that this demoralization would cause the enemy to break ranks, and so give the cavalry a chance to use swords and lances. Horsemen's pistols soon developed into characteristically

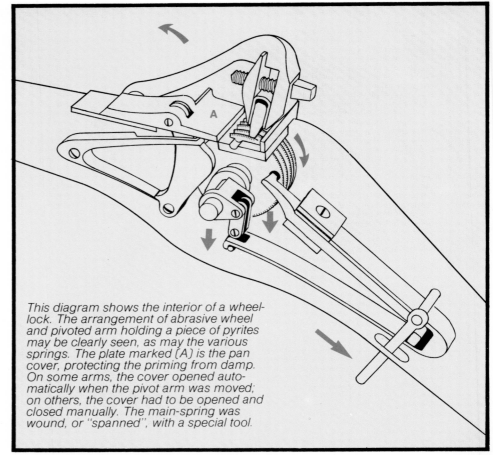

This diagram shows the interior of a wheel-lock. The arrangement of abrasive wheel and pivoted arm holding a piece of pyrites may be clearly seen, as may the various springs. The plate marked (A) is the pan cover, protecting the priming from damp. On some arms, the cover opened automatically when the pivot arm was moved; on others, the cover had to be opened and closed manually. The main-spring was wound, or "spanned", with a special tool.

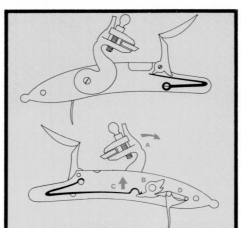

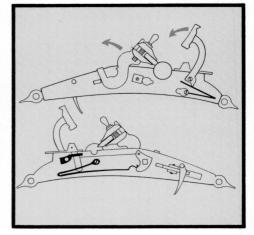

ball-butted arms, often known as "puffers". But in the long term, pistol volleys from restless horses could never prove a match for steady fire from the muskets of infantry—so the cavalry had to seek other means of re-establishing its traditional domination of the battlefield.

THE FLINTLOCK

Having established a reasonably reliable, if complex, system of producing ignition as required, gunmakers naturally sought to simplify the process; a search in which they were supported and encouraged by soldiers. In the 16th century, men struck flint against steel to light a fire, candle or pipe—so it was, presumably, a relatively short step to devise a mechanism which would perform this action. It is probable that a primitive but reasonably effective

Above: *Snaphance lock. The upper view shows the cockerel's-head shape which gave the "cock" its name. The cock is forward and the steel, on its spring-operated pivot arm, is in the "safe" position. When the pistol was primed and ready to fire, the cock was pulled back to its full extent and the steel drawn down until it was over the pan, where it was struck by the flint. Below is the reverse of the lock, showing the springs.*

Above left: *Flintlock mechanism. When the cock (A), holding a piece of flint in its jaws, was drawn back, it rotated the tumbler (B), thus compressing the main-spring (C) by forcing its longer arm upward. At the same time the nose of the sear (D) engaged the half and full-cock notches; then pressure on the trigger released the sear and allowed the cock to spring forward. The flint struck the vertical steel and simultaneously knocked open the pan, allowing sparks to reach the priming and ignite the charge.*

lock on the flint-and-steel principle had been produced by as early as 1550; and all the indications are that this happened in the same area that had seen the origination of the wheel-lock.

In the earliest flintlocks, a piece of shaped flint was held in a pair of pivoted jaws which were often known as a "cock", from their not altogether fanciful resemblance to the head of a cockerel. A spring device actuated by a trigger caused the flint to "peck" forward and strike sparks from a piece of steel set at the proper angle above the pan; the shallow, spoon-like container that held fine priming powder. A hole in the barrel linked the pan to the main charge: once the priming had been ignited by the sparks, flame flashed through the hole and fired the main charge. The steel on which the flint struck was on a hinged arm so that it could be moved away from the pan when the weapon was not required for immediate use—a simple but effective provision for safety. It is said that the "pecking" action of the flint gave rise to the Dutch name of *snap-haans* for the weapon, which soon became corrupted in English to snaphance (or snaphaunce).

The next stage in development, which probably was reached in the first half of the 17th century, was to combine the steel and the pan cover in such a way that the process of striking sparks and opening the pan was practically simultaneous. The combined steel and pan cover, often called the

frizzen, was hinged at the front and its opening was controlled by a separate spring. The accompanying diagram explains the system—but a diagram cannot express the extreme care which had to be taken to get both springs and the angle of striking in the proper balance, so as to give almost instantaneous fire. Once established, the principle remained unchanged—so it was very largely the skill of the individual maker that led to considerable variation in efficiency between one lock and another. The flintlock was in use until well into the 19th century.

In Britain, although relatively few people habitually carried firearms after the 18th century, a great many people appear to have owned them; and with the possible exception of sporting guns, most of these privately-owned weapons were pistols of one kind or another. The methods of law enforcement were not then highly effective, even in the major towns, and most people of substance considered it prudent to take steps for their own protection. In particular, travellers of the better class—ie, those apparently prosperous enough to be worth robbing—usually carried a pair of pistols, unless they were rich enough to be accompanied by a retinue of armed retainers. Likewise, many householders kept a pistol in some convenient place in their sleeping quarters. Thus, the civilian demand for arms was quite considerable and pistols were made in a great variety of shapes and sizes, ranging from elegant little models to fit into a

Above: *The American privateer John Paul Jones shoots a member of his crew who had attempted to surrender during the engagement between Jones's* Bonhomme Richard *and HMS* Serapis, *23 September 1779. Obviously expecting a fierce fight at close quarters, Jones carries several flintlock pistols in his belt.*

Above left: *Lieutenant Stephen Decatur, US Navy, leads a boarding party against a Barbary pirate ship: an incident during the Tripolitan-American War of 1801-05. Flintlock pistols were useful weapons at close quarters, but in such a mêlée there was, of course, no time to reload: having fired a single shot, the pistol wielder had to resort to cold steel.*

Top right: *This illustration from the English artist Thomas Rowlandson's "Doctor Syntax" series, dated 1813, shows a horseman attacked by footpads, two of whom are armed with flintlock pistols. Lawless conditions prevailed on many highways before the establishment of efficient police forces, so wealthy travellers often went armed.*

waistcoat pocket, or even a lady's muff, to so-called "traveller's pistols" which, while reasonably compact, fired a ball weighing about one ounce (28·35gm) with a fair charge of powder.

Apart from its early use by cavalry, described above, the pistol never became a significant military arm—but nevertheless it was very often carried by soldiers. Mounted men usually had one or two pistols in holsters on their saddles, and although hand guns remained secondary to the sword they proved useful in the close-quarter mêlée which often developed after a cavalry charge. It was, of course, impossible to reload pistols in the thick of a hand-to-hand fight; for this reason, some combatants favoured double-barrelled arms, although the need for an extra lock tended to make these bulky. The Royal Navy used pistols to equip boarding parties and the like, and some naval officers favoured brass-barrelled pistols with bell mouths, since these were somewhat easier to load in a pitching boat and were also less liable to corrosion.

DUELLING PISTOLS

One highly-specialized type of pistol was that used for duelling. Until the end of the 18th century, gentlemen habitually carried swords, which were then the standard arms for affairs of honour; but around the turn of the century swords went out of fashion and were replaced by pistols. Any man "going out" at the risk of his life naturally wanted the best possible arms, and many leading British gunsmiths began to specialize in the production of weapons suitable for duellists. These tended to fall into a fairly distinct category, with a barrel about 10 inches (254mm) long and of 0·5-0·6 inch (12·7-15·2mm) bore. Great care was taken with their balance and, in particular, with their locks, which had to be both fast and reliable. Rifled arms were generally considered to be unsporting, although some are to be found, and most duelling pistols were severely plain, with no more than a touch of fine engraving on the lock-plate, for they were looked upon as deadly weapons rather than works of art. However, the quality of workmanship in these arms and the combination of blued or polished metal with fine wood gave them a certain rather sinister beauty. They were usually cased in pairs with various accessories and, in view of their role, were usually most carefully maintained. They are, in consequence, still relatively common—but extremely expensive.

Right: *The English caricaturist George Cruikshank (1792-1878) neatly sums up the circumstances of many duels. Inflamed by drink, the adversaries scuffle and a challenge ensues—but in the cold light of dawn their combative ardour has cooled!*

Blood-Heat and Freezing-Point.

SCOTTISH PISTOLS

Another interesting variation was the Scottish all-steel pistol, which was made throughout the greater part of the 18th century. Although these vary in detail, they are easily recognizable as a species. Most have ball triggers and many have butts with bottoms shaped like a pair of ram's horns, with a pricker for cleaning out the touch hole screwed in between them. The men of the 42nd (Royal Highland) Regiment carried pistols of this general type when the regiment was first raised in the later 18th century, usually in an arrangement of straps near the left shoulder, so that the pistol could be readily drawn, across the body, with the right hand. As the soldiers already carried musket, bayonet and claymore, these pistols were really more ornamental than useful: many were Birmingham-made arms of relatively poor quality, presumably purchased at a low price by some frugal colonel. Highland all-steel pistols are still to be found—but like most old

CALIBRATION

A system of describing the calibre of small arms developed soon after their appearance. It was based on the number of spherical balls which could be cast for the individual arm from one pound (0·45kg) of lead. A 16-bore (16-gauge in America) thus fired bullets weighing exactly one ounce (28·35gm) each, while bullets for an 80-bore ran at five to the ounce. The smallest ball regarded as having any sort of stopping power was about 120-bore. The various tables by which lead bullets to the pound could be converted to the diameter of the bore in inches varied slightly from maker to maker; the representative figures given in the accompanying table are from Baker's *Remarks on the Rifle*.

arms they now command a price which would have greatly surprised their original buyers.

BREECHLOADING

The concept of loading a weapon from the breech end was well understood almost from the earliest days of hand firearms, but the need for the direct application of fire to the charge, and the problem of producing a simple yet gas-tight breech mechanism, made it difficult to achieve. A number of experimental breechloading pistols were made, many with loading apertures closed by screw plugs, but it is highly unlikely that they became even remotely popular. Somewhat later, arms in which the entire barrel could be screwed off were also developed, and these achieved a measure of success. It was, however, the percussion system, which is discussed on pages 36-41, which really made breechloading firearms possible, by allowing the use of a metallic cartridge which effectively sealed the breech at the moment of firing.

Above: *As the "Fateful Dawn" approaches, the duellist has been setting his affairs in order. His second checks the action of one of a cased pair of full-stocked, flintlock duelling pistols.*

Top right: *A gunsmith at Williamsburg, Va., USA, works on the restoration (or replication) of a flintlock pistol. The shape of the butt is typical of early 19th-century American pistols.*

Below: *Although the Duke of Wellington discouraged duelling, honour compelled him to "call out" Lord Winchilsea, a political opponent. The exchange of shots was a formality: neither man attempted to inflict injury.*

Bore	Weight of Ball	Diameter of Ball
1	16oz (454gm)	1·67″ (42·4mm)
8	2oz (56·7gm)	·837″ (21·3mm)
10	1·6oz (45·4gm)	·777″ (19·7mm)
20	·8oz (22·7gm)	·614″ (15·6mm)
32	·5oz (14·2gm)	·524″ (13·3mm)
50	·32oz (9·1gm)	·451″ (11·4mm)
80	·2oz (5·7gm)	·385″ (9·8mm)
120	·13oz (3·7gm)	·32″ (8·1mm)

At first sight, some of the figures seem surprising; as, for example, the fact that a 16-ounce (454gm) ball is only about twice the diameter of a 2-ounce (56·7gm) ball. It must be remembered, however, that the volume of a sphere is based on the mathematical formula $\frac{4\pi r^3}{3}$, which in practice means that quite a small increase in r (radius) leads to a very considerable increase in volume. It will also be seen from the table that some of the round-figure sizes had bore diameters which remain virtually unchanged to the present day; although modern bullets, being elongated, naturally weigh more than their spherical counterparts of earlier times.

Italy
WHEEL-LOCK PISTOL

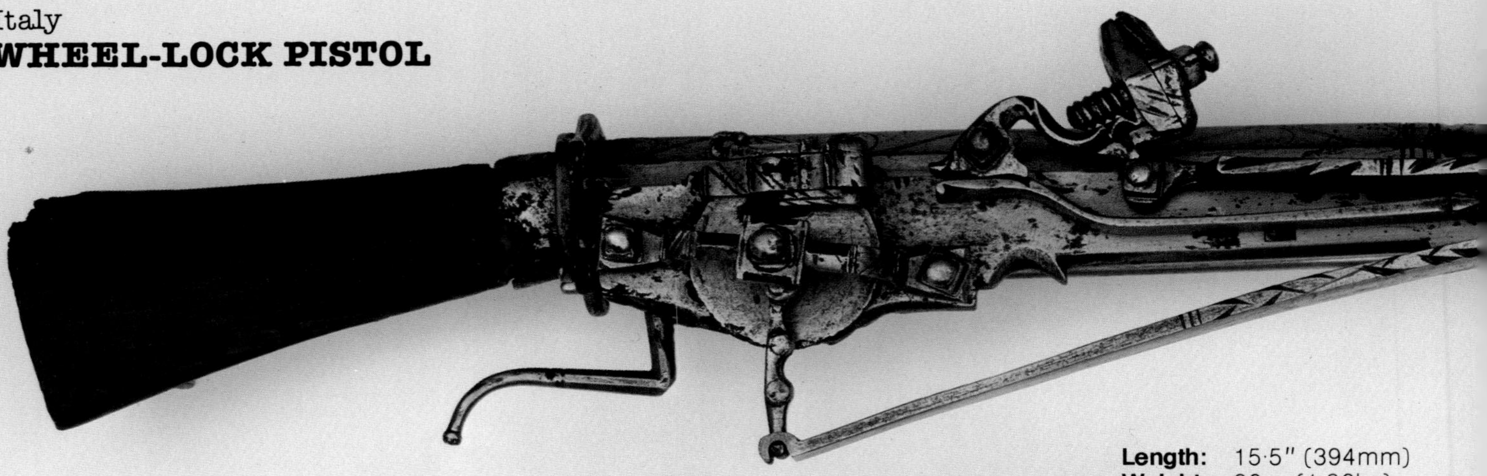

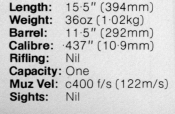

Spain
FLINTLOCK PISTOL

Length: 20·5" (521mm)
Weight: 36oz (1·02kg)
Barrel: 13·4" (340mm)
Calibre: ·665" (16·9mm)
Rifling: Nil
Capacity: One
Muz Vel: c400 f/s (122 m/s)
Sights: Nil

Length: 15·5" (394mm)
Weight: 36oz (1·02kg)
Barrel: 11·5" (292mm)
Calibre: ·437" (10·9mm)
Rifling: Nil
Capacity: One
Muz Vel: c400 f/s (122m/s)
Sights: Nil

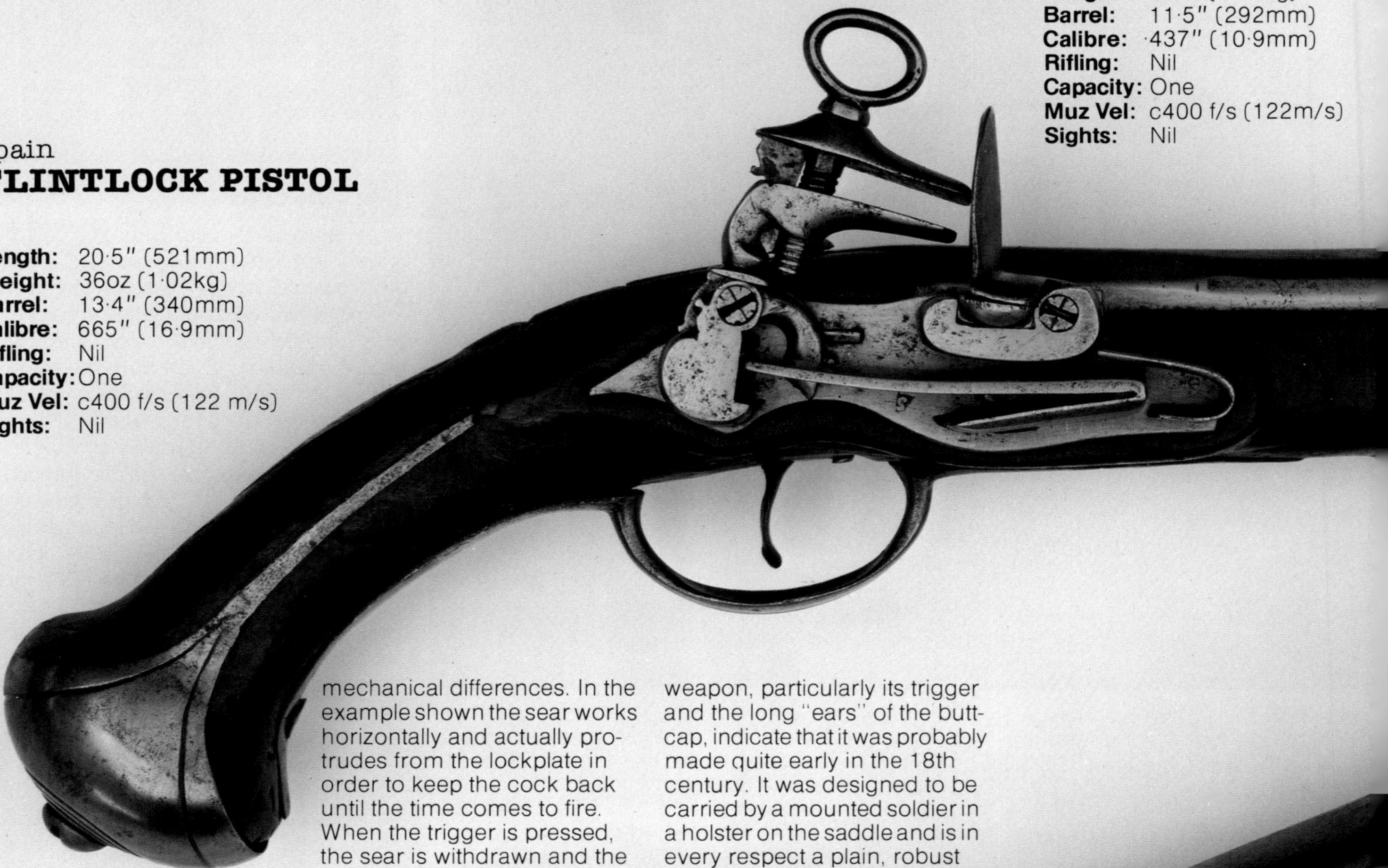

The flintlock represents the last development in the use of flint and steel to ignite a charge, and remained in use until the introduction of the percussion system early in the 19th century. In the Spanish pistol seen here, the barrel is round, except for about two inches (51mm) of rounded octagonal at the breech end, and is slightly swamped (ie, opened out) at the muzzle end. The pistol has no sights of any kind. The lock is of the pattern now usually known as miquelet (or miguelet), a type which is believed to have originated in the Spanish province of Catalonia some time early in the 16th century. In terms of operation it works like any other flintlock, although there are mechanical differences. In the example shown the sear works horizontally and actually protrudes from the lockplate in order to keep the cock back until the time comes to fire. When the trigger is pressed, the sear is withdrawn and the cock falls, the flint in its jaws striking the vertical steel and knocking it forward; taking forward also the horizontal pan cover—an integral part of the steel. This allows the sparks from the blow to ignite the priming and fire the charge. The mainspring (which, it will be seen, is on the outside of the lockplate) is necessarily a very strong one; and for this reason a top ring is fitted to the cock to provide a firm grip. The trigger and trigger-guard are of orthodox type, the tip of the trigger being turned back on itself; and the butt has a steel cap with long spurs reaching almost the whole way up the butt. The ramrod (missing in this case) was held in a groove on the underside of the stock by a brass loop and tailpipe. The style of this Spanish weapon, particularly its trigger and the long "ears" of the butt-cap, indicate that it was probably made quite early in the 18th century. It was designed to be carried by a mounted soldier in a holster on the saddle and is in every respect a plain, robust arm, well suited to the cavalry service for which it was originally designed.

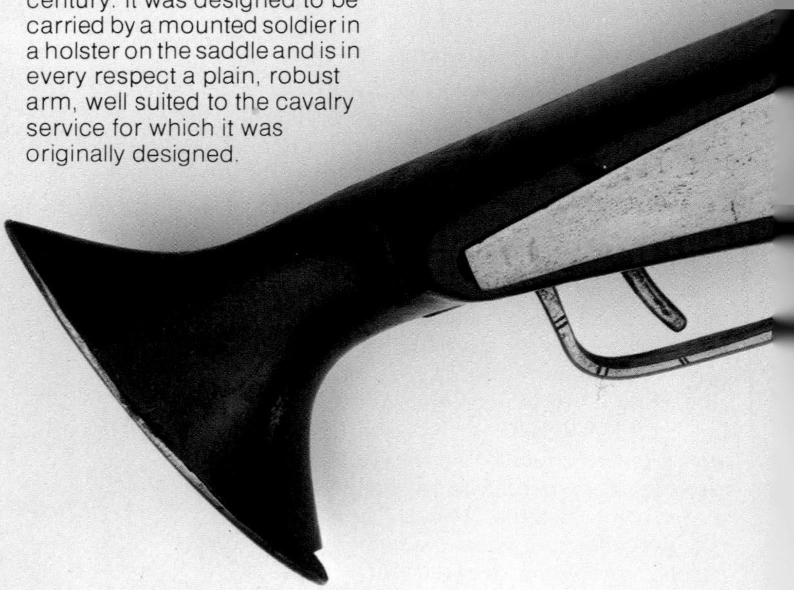

It was the invention of the wheel-lock, probably in the earliest years of the 16th century, which at last made the pistol a practical proposition by providing it with a lock which produced fire only when required to do so. Although some of Leonardo da Vinci's early drawings show a lock of similar type, and thus suggest Italian origins, it is probable that the wheel-lock was, in fact, invented in Southern Germany. At that time it was, with the possible exception of the clock, probably the most complex piece of mechanism ever invented by man, so it is perhaps no coincidence that it appears to have originated in an area already known for the mechanical skills of its clock-makers. The general principle on which the new lock worked was quite simple in theory, although remarkably difficult to put into practice. The wheel, which gave the lock its name, was spun mechanically by a spring, so that its roughened edge rubbed briskly against a piece of pyrites and caused sparks. The upper part of the wheel protruded through a close-fitting slot in the pan, which was connected to the barrel by a touch hole. Once the arm was loaded and the pan primed, it was necessary to wind the wheel, usually about three-quarters of a turn, by means of a key; open the pan (unless this was also done by mechanical means); and pull down the hinged jaws holding the piece of pyrites until it was held firmly against the wheel. Pressure on the trigger then allowed the wheel to spin against the pyrites, thus striking sparks and igniting the priming. This mechanism, when well made, was reasonably reliable in dry weather, although the relatively poor quality of temper of the springs made it advisable not to leave it wound (or "spanned", as it was often referred to) for longer than was necessary. The arm illustrated was made in Italy in about 1530, and is a plain but well-made weapon, apparently intended for use rather than ornament. Note in particular the straight grip, presumably a legacy of the mace. This certainly gave a good hold on the arm but must have made it virtually impossible to direct the ball with any real degree of accuracy, except in action at very close quarters.

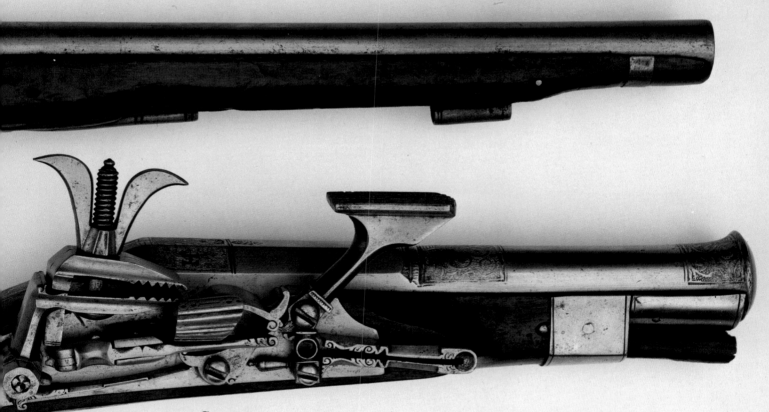

Germany
SNAPHANCE PISTOL

Length: 15·75" (400mm)
Weight: 59oz (1·67kg)
Barrel: 8·2" (208mm)
Calibre: ·675" (17·1mm)
Rifling: Nil
Capacity: One
Muz Vel: c450 f/s (137 m/s)
Sights: Nil

In terms of development the snaphance (or snaphaunce) pistol seen here falls between the other two specimens illustrated on this spread. Although the name given to this arm is of Dutch derivation, there is no evidence that the type originated in the Low Countries; and the lock on this example appears to be of Franco-German origin. The pistol, which was made in about 1575, has some gold damascening on the barrel but is otherwise plain, although well made. Soon after the invention of the wheel-lock, many European gunmakers began to seek ways of incorporating the principle of flint and steel— then the only practical way of ignition known—into a weapon better suited to the primitive manufacturing facilities then available. Instead of a complex wheel mechanism, this pistol has a "cock" (oddly reptilian in appearance, although supposedly resembling the head of a cockerel) which "pecks" forward when the trigger is pressed. The piece of flint held in its jaws strikes a steel plate positioned over the shallow priming pan, from which the touch hole leads into the breech. The steel is situated at the end of a pivoted arm, which can be held either safely forward (as in the photograph), or backward, over the pan. The steel is usually linked to a sliding pan cover, which thus opens automatically when the steel is pulled back preparatory to firing. The cock has a short throw, so a strong spring must be fitted to give it sufficient impetus to strike a shower of good hot sparks. The long wing-nut on the jaw screw, holding the flint firmly in position, therefore has the secondary function of allowing a good grip to be taken in order to cock the arm.

Spain
PAIR OF FLINTLOCK PISTOLS

Length:	21·25" (540mm)
Weight:	49oz (1·39kg)
Barrel:	14·1" (358mm)
Calibre:	·625" (15·9mm)
Rifling:	Nil
Capacity:	One
Muz Vel:	c500 f/s (152 m/s)
Sights:	Fixed

By the end of the 15th century, matchlock muskets were being made in large numbers in Spain, where development of an arms manufactory had doubtless been greatly stimulated by the final drive to oust the Moorish invaders who had been in possession of much of southern Spain for well over seven centuries. The Moors were finally driven from their last strongholds in Granada during the reign of Ferdinand and Isabella, in 1492, a date which marks the beginning of modern Spain. The wheel-lock was introduced from Germany in about 1530 and manufacture of arms with locks of this type was well under way within 30 or 40 years. The main centre was

Madrid, but they were also made at Ripoll in Catalonia. The snaphance pistol replaced the wheel-lock in due course, and was in its turn ousted by the miquelet lock, manufacture of which started as early as the middle of the 17th century. As some description of the miquelet lock has already been given (on page 16) it is only necessary to add that the Spaniards considered it superior to any other type of flintlock and continued to make it until the introduction of the percussion system. This said, the reader may wonder just why such a fine pair of what may be termed orthodox flint-locks came to be made in a country apparently dedicated to a different type. The explana-

tion is somewhat lengthy. After the Treaty of Utrecht in 1713-14 had given the Spanish crown to a French Bourbon, King Philip V, there was an upsurge of French influence in Spain. However, this was largely confined to the capital, Madrid; the remainder of the country remaining obstinately Spanish. The very fine arms illustrated were made by Juan Fernandez (sometimes spelt Fernandes), a famous maker who worked in Madrid from 1717 until 1739. This was at the height of French influence and fashion, so it is not surprising that Fernandez, like most other makers, should have abandoned the indigenous miquelet lock and made instead arms of the type type shown. The barrels,

18

which are well blued and heavily decorated with gold inlay, are round for two-thirds of their length, the breech ends being octagonal. This was considered to give a much stronger breech. The locks are of the usual French type and the lockplates, the tails of which droop slightly to the rear, are beautifully ornamented with battle scenes in gold and silver damscene. The cocks are of the graceful type known, for obvious reasons, as "swan-necked". Both are fitted with flints seated in small patches of leather; this was considered desirable not only to hold the flints rigid but also to cushion them against the repeated shock of striking the steels. The combined steels and pan-covers (later often known as frizzens) are decorated with rearing horses; these appear to be mainly ornamental, although they also prevent the pans from opening too far by exerting pressure (as seen in the lower of the pair) on the frizzen springs. The triggers have curled-back ends and there are long spurs on the highly ornamented butt-caps, which, together with the shape of the lockplates, indicates a date of manufacture not later than about 1720. The stocks are of a wood not immediately identifiable—walnut, cherry and pine were all in use at the time—and are elaborately carved, with caps at the muzzles matching the ends of the ramrods, which in each case are held by a single pipe and a tailpipe. These are in every respect beautiful pistols and were presumably made either for royalty or for some rich nobleman. Although it is difficult not to regard them primarily as works of art, they would nevertheless have been excellent weapons for anyone extravagant enough to use them. They are fitted with adequate sights and, once loaded, they would have been effective enough by the standards of the day. As we have seen they were exceptional in that they were made at a time when all except the most fashionable Spaniards still preferred their miquelet locks. This period was probably the greatest in the history of Spanish-made arms: there was, thereafter, a slow but appreciable decline in overall quality. By the beginning of the 19th century the miquelet lock had at last begun to lose favour, perhaps because of the great influx of French and British arms during the Peninsular War, but before its decline became absolute the percussion system had supplanted it. In more modern times, Spain's output of arms was largely disposed of in her erstwhile colonies in South America: her arms were cheap by European standards and the South American republics were short of money. Many Spanish-made arms of World War I were of very poor quality, and the reputation of Spanish makers then suffered accordingly.

Great Britain
PAIR OF HOLSTER PISTOLS

Length: 14·75" (375mm)
Weight: 32oz (·91kg)
Barrel: 8·5" (216mm)
Calibre: ·62" (15·7mm)
Rifling: Nil
Capacity: One
Muz Vel: c500 f/s (152 m/s)
Sights: Nil

The Georgian period, and perhaps particularly the second half of it, was a time that saw British gunmaking at its greatest. The country was peaceful and prosperous (although, to be sure, prosperity was not necessarily universal) and the first stirrings of the Industrial Revolution were beginning to point the way towards new and better techniques of manufacture—without, however, seriously affecting the individual quality which was the trademark of

Great Britain
SCOTTISH ALL-STEEL PISTOLS

Length: 12" (305mm)
Weight: 22oz (·62kg)
Barrel: 7·4" (188mm)
Calibre: ·556" (14·1mm)
Rifling: Nil
Capacity: One
Muz Vel: c500 f/s (152 m/s)
Sights: Nil

Pistols of a type peculiar to Scotland were being made all over that country by the mid-17th century, but within about one hundred years Lowland gunmakers had turned to making weapons of English type. However, Scottish pistols continued to be produced in the north of Scotland, and they are thus often referred to as Highland pistols. Some of the earliest specimens had snaphance locks, and a few had

wooden butts, but in general the main characteristic of Scottish pistols was their all-metal construction—sometimes of brass, sometimes steel, and sometimes gunmetal, and quite often with gilded decorations. In the very early days they were made in pairs, with one left-hand lock and one right, and were frequently fitted with belt-hooks, flat steel springs, attached parallel to the barrel on the opposite side from the lock, which could be slipped inside the waist-belt so that the pistols were carried ready to the hand without holsters. The early models frequently had butts shaped like fish-tails. These were followed by butts with oval or heart-shaped protuberances; and later still by pistols

with so-called "rams-horn" butts, of the type seen here. This pair of pistols was made in about 1770 by Murdoch of Doune, a small town near Stirling which was a noted centre for manufacture of pistols. They have round steel barrels, with slight flares at the muzzles, and elegant locks, the plates of which are marked "To. Murdoch, Doun". The butts terminate in the pairs of incurved horns which gave the type its particular name. The small knobs between the horns are the handles of prickers, which can be unscrewed from the butts and used to remove fouling from the touch holes. The triggers are of the universal button type (which changed slightly in shape but never in principle) and there are no

trigger-guards, a characteristic which may also be regarded as universal in the type. Almost every part of the weapons is covered with fine engraving. When the Royal Highland Regiment was first raised in the middle of the 18th century, every one of its soldiers carried a musket, bayonet, broadsword and Highland pistol, the latter being worn in an arrangement of straps, not unlike a modern shoulder holster, under the left arm. It was soon found, however, that the pistol was of no military value to an infantryman, so these arms became purely ornamental. Frugal colonels, anxious to save money, then bought cheap Birmingham-made versions, usually from the maker Isaac Bissell, until pistols fine craftsmen. Society moved, moreover, in a leisurely fashion; so that rich customers were happy to give those same craftsmen enough time to produce their best. The fine pair of pistols seen here was made in 1780 by a gun-maker named Memory, who worked in Southwark, London, in the last quarter of the 18th century. Although he is not generally regarded as having been among the really top-ranked English pistol makers, it will be clear from the illustrations that Memory's products were of very high quality and finish. The barrels are of brass, the front two-thirds being round and the breech ends octagonal, a most favoured style during the period under discussion. The breech ends are highly ornamented, while the muzzles, although by no means to be described as blunderbusses, are slightly swamped. The barrels are held to the stocks by flat keys passing through loops on their undersides, the ends of these being visible. In later years it became customary to inset a small plate round these keys, so that they could be tapped out without any risk of bruising the stock. The locks are of typical English type, the plates being beautifully engraved and bearing the name "MEMORY" within small ornamental scrolls. The cocks, also decorated, are of swan-necked type, the angle of the edge of the flint to the steel being carefully calculated to ensure the combination of a good shower of hot sparks with the fastest possible opening time for the pan, rapid ignition being an essential requirement for accurate shooting. The pan speed naturally depended also on the frizzen spring; and it will be noted that the frizzen springs on these pistols have small semicircular projections on their upper surfaces. When the pan is closed (as in the upper pistol), the tail of the pan cover is forward of the projection and snaps down on the other side, thus helping to accelerate opening time. The stocks are of fine walnut and the butt-caps, which have long spurs, are finely chiselled and gilded. The ramrods are of ebony with brass tips and each is housed in one pipe and a tailpipe; the ends of the pins holding the pipes in position can be seen in the stocks above them. The original owner of these pistols is not known, but the brass barrels indicate a naval connection, for brass was thought to be less susceptible to corrosion. In a sense, these arms represent the end of an era in pistol making, since from the time of their manufacture onwards ornamentation was progressively reduced and pistols became severely plain—although often none the less handsome for that.

ceased to be worn by the rank and file in 1776. Although officers continued to carry pistols, this marked the beginning of the decline of the Highland pistol, except as an item of ornament. The weapons experienced a brief resurgence in the first half of the 19th century, when Scotland had a period of romantic popularity (largely inspired by the novels of Sir Walter Scott). A few were even made with percussion locks, but these were little more than toys compared with the handsome arms of the previous century, and the fashion was short-lived. Fine Scottish pistols are rare, and although many Scottish museums and castles have impressive displays of them, specimens do not often come on to the market—and when they do, they command extremely high prices.

Great Britain
ANNELY FLINTLOCK REVOLVER

Length:	12" (305mm)
Weight:	46oz (1.3kg)
Barrel:	5.375" (137mm)
Calibre:	.400" (10.2mm)
Rifling:	Nil
Capacity:	Eight
Muz Vel:	c400 f/s (122 m/s)
Sights:	Nil

Although the invention of the wheel-lock made the pistol a viable weapon, it was in a sense a dead end, since it was very difficult indeed to make a hand gun which would fire more than once without reloading. This was a very slow process;

Great Britain
MORTIMER REPEATING PISTOL

Length:	19" (483mm)
Weight:	62oz (1.76kg)
Barrel:	10.125" (257mm)
Calibre:	.500" (12.7mm)
Rifling:	Nil
Capacity:	Seven
Muz Vel:	c450 f/s (137 m/s)
Sights:	Fixed

Repeating weapons probably originated in Germany and Italy, and were known as early as the 16th century. The diarist Samuel Pepys recorded seeing a repeater, probably made by John Dafte or Harman Barne(s) of London, in 1664; but although the theory of making such weapons was sound enough at that time, the tech-nical problems of producing accurately-fitting parts with crude hand-tools were so considerable that very few were made. By the end of the 18th century, however, manufacturing techniques had improved considerably and one or two London makers again turned their attention to repeating weapons. Among them was H.

Great Britain
COLLIER FLINTLOCK REVOLVER

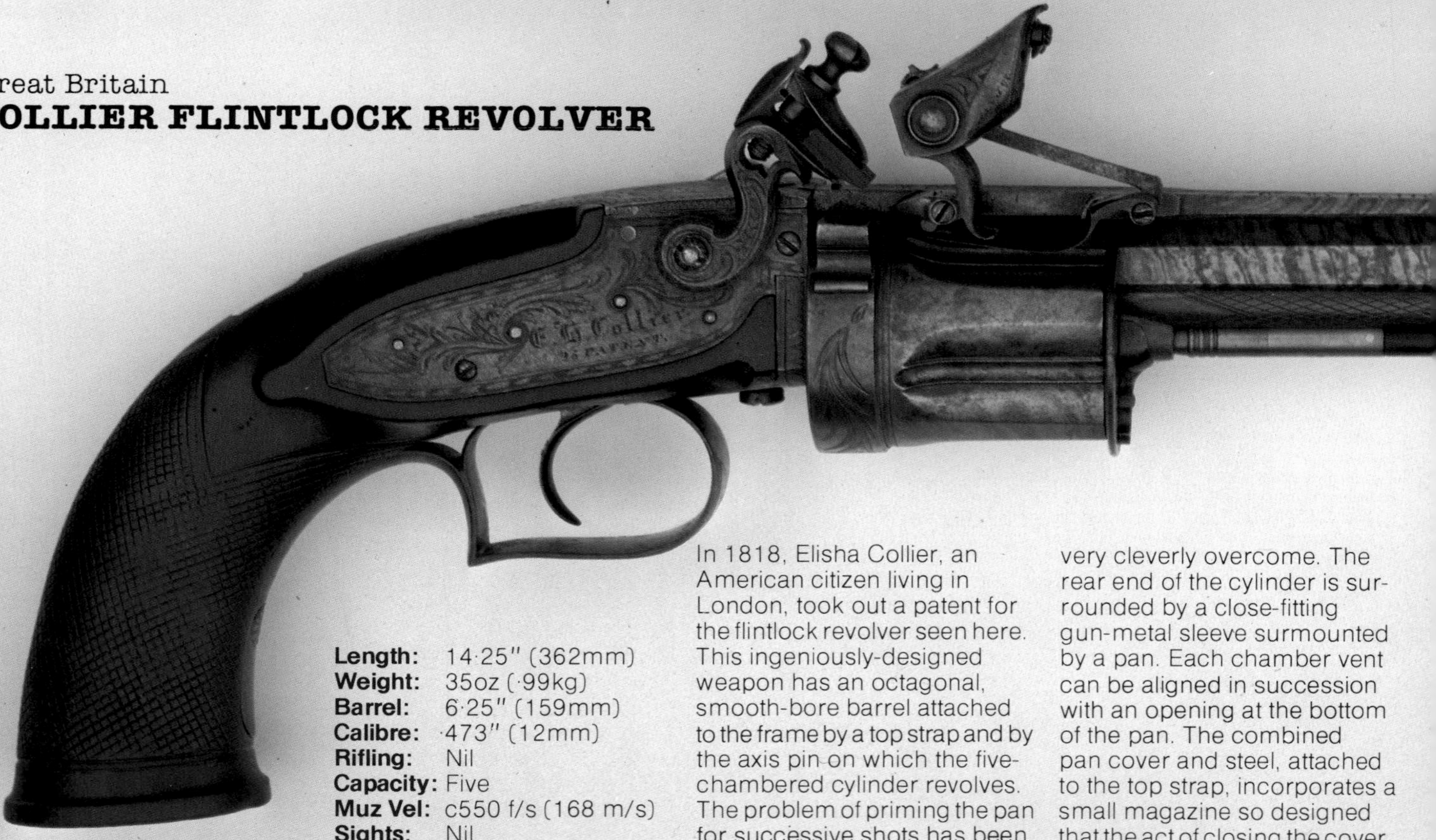

Length:	14.25" (362mm)
Weight:	35oz (.99kg)
Barrel:	6.25" (159mm)
Calibre:	.473" (12mm)
Rifling:	Nil
Capacity:	Five
Muz Vel:	c550 f/s (168 m/s)
Sights:	Nil

In 1818, Elisha Collier, an American citizen living in London, took out a patent for the flintlock revolver seen here. This ingeniously-designed weapon has an octagonal, smooth-bore barrel attached to the frame by a top strap and by the axis pin on which the five-chambered cylinder revolves. The problem of priming the pan for successive shots has been very cleverly overcome. The rear end of the cylinder is surrounded by a close-fitting gun-metal sleeve surmounted by a pan. Each chamber vent can be aligned in succession with an opening at the bottom of the pan. The combined pan cover and steel, attached to the top strap, incorporates a small magazine so designed that the act of closing the cover indeed, it may be said to have been almost impossible for a mounted man—to whom the pistol was most useful. Thus, for some years, all that a pistol user could hope for was two shots: one from each of a pair of single-shot weapons. How-ever, the development of the snaphance lock made some sort of repeating arm a practical proposition, and by the early years of the 17th century a number had been produced. The system of having a cylinder pierced with chambers which might be successively aligned with a barrel had already been tried on carbines, so this offered a starting point for further experiment. Most of this took place on the continent, mainly in Holland and France, and there is no evidence that revolvers were made in Britain before about 1650. The flint-lock revolver seen here was made by T. Annely; and although it dates from the earliest years of the 18th century it may be taken as being reasonably typical of its kind. It has a round, cannon-type barrel of brass (most of the remaining metal is of the same material), which is fastened to the frame by means of the cylinder axis pin. The brass cylinder has eight chambers, each with its own pan and touch hole normally covered by a sliding pan cover. The hinged steel is mounted on an arm which is attached to the barrel lump, and the neck of the cock is therefore bent over so that the flint will strike it. The lock is of back-action type, and its plate (which may not be the original one) is engraved with the maker's name. The action of cocking the lock causes the cylinder to rotate by means of a pawl and ratchet; when the cock falls, a lever attached to it pushes open the cover of the pan in line with the barrel. The butt has a rounded plate bearing a Tudor rose. The weapon has no trigger-guard. Weapons of this type were reasonably effi-cient, but they were very difficult to make; the drilling of the chambers presented a parti-cular problem. The relative softness of the metals used also led to rapid wear. Such arms are now very rare.

W. Mortimer (a pair of whose duelling pistols are illustrated on page 34), who produced the arm seen here. This pistol has at its breech-end a horizontally revolving block into which two recesses are cut, one for powder and one for a ball; and there are two corresponding tubular magazines in its butt. In order to load the weapon, it is held muzzle downward and the loading lever is pushed for-ward. This brings the recesses in the block into line with the magazine, and one ball and one charge are fed into them by gravity. The action of pulling the lever backward causes the block to counter-rotate. As the recess holding the ball passes the breech, the ball rolls in; the recess holding the charge then moves into position behind it to act as a temporary chamber. This second motion of the lever also cocks and primes the arm. Although most ingenious, such arms never became popular, mainly because of the prob-lems of obturation; ie, the escape of burning gases. Any minor discrepancy in fitting the various parts could lead to the explosion of the powder in the magazine—with disastrous results to the firer. It was not until the advent of the percus-sion system, with the use of gas-tight metallic cartridges, that the problems involved in making efficient repeating pistols (as opposed to revolvers) were finally solved.

causes the correct amount of priming to be deposited in the pan. When the trigger is pressed, the flint acts against the steel in the normal way, and the flash from the priming passes through the aligned vent and fires the charge. It is then necessary to re-cock, re-close the pan and cover, and rotate the cylinder manu-ally in order to bring the next loaded chamber into position for the next shot. The breech end of the barrel is coned, the mouths of the cylinders being counter-sunk to fit over it, so that when rotating the cylinder it is necessary to draw it back a little against a spring to dis-engage it. The forward action of the cock thrusts a steel wedge against the rear end of the cylinder, to hold it rigidly in position while the shot is fired. This device not only ensured that the barrel and chamber were aligned at the critical moment, but also helped to prevent the escaping gases from acci-dentally igniting the charges in the adjacent chambers. Al-though Collier's revolver was by far the best of the flintlock repeaters, it came too late for success, for the percussion system with all its advantages had already entered use. The Collier could have been converted to percussion (in fact, some were) but the inventor, who was a mechani-cal engineer rather than a gunsmith, lost interest and turned his talents elsewhere.

EMPEROR NAPOLEON I's PISTOLS

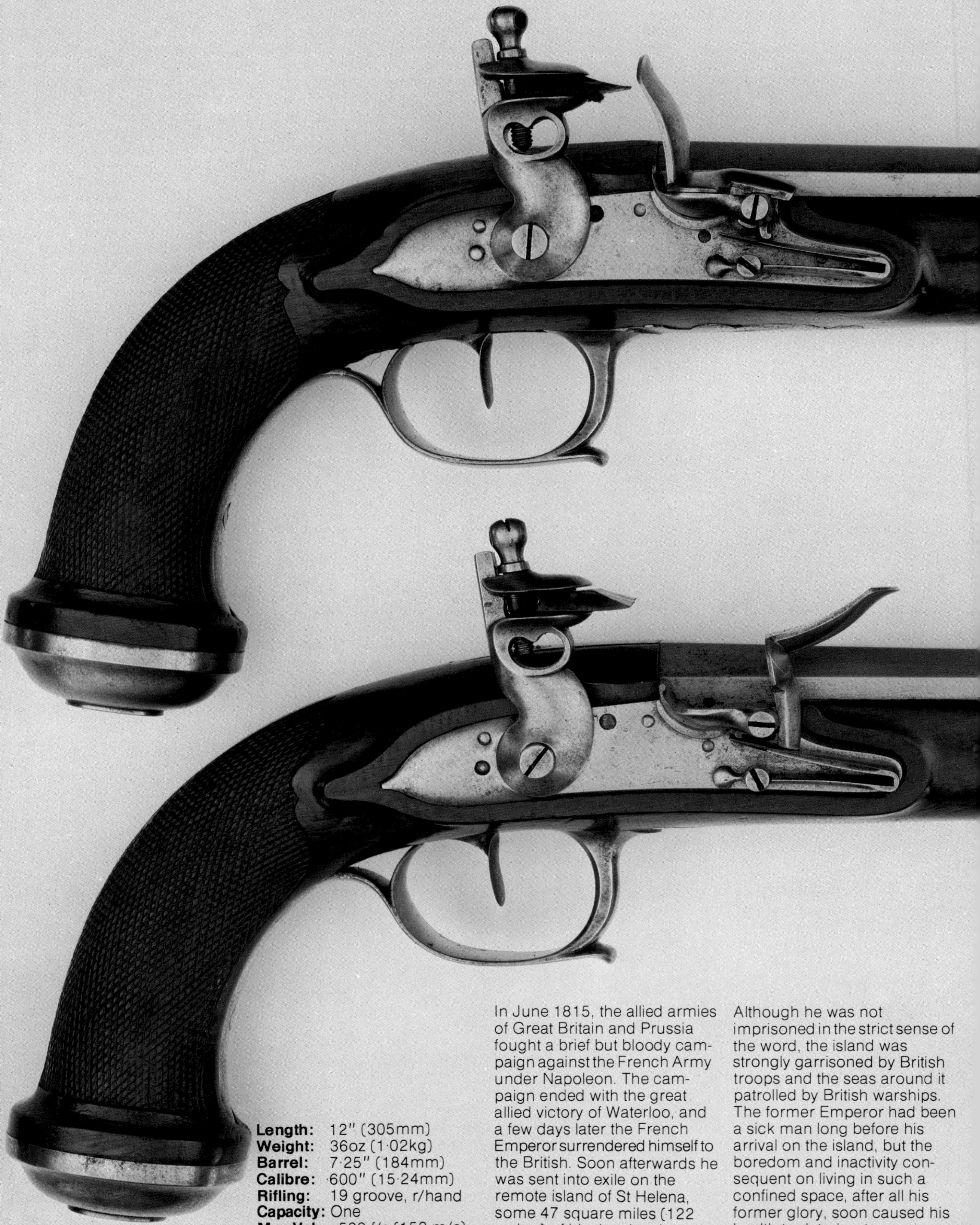

Length:	12" (305mm)
Weight:	36oz (1·02kg)
Barrel:	7·25" (184mm)
Calibre:	·600" (15·24mm)
Rifling:	19 groove, r/hand
Capacity:	One
Muz Vel:	c500 f/s (152 m/s)
Sights:	Fixed

In June 1815, the allied armies of Great Britain and Prussia fought a brief but bloody campaign against the French Army under Napoleon. The campaign ended with the great allied victory of Waterloo, and a few days later the French Emperor surrendered himself to the British. Soon afterwards he was sent into exile on the remote island of St Helena, some 47 square miles (122 sq km) of bleak volcanic rock rising from the South Atlantic.

Although he was not imprisoned in the strict sense of the word, the island was strongly garrisoned by British troops and the seas around it patrolled by British warships. The former Emperor had been a sick man long before his arrival on the island, but the boredom and inactivity consequent on living in such a confined space, after all his former glory, soon caused his health to deteriorate even further. At some stage towards

The pistols have a velvet-lined, wooden case—probably not the original one—with this inscribed brass plate inside the lid. Another plate (not shown) states that the pistols were presented to the School of Musketry by Major Adams in 1870.

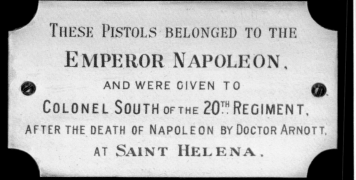

THESE PISTOLS BELONGED TO THE
EMPEROR NAPOLEON,
AND WERE GIVEN TO
COLONEL SOUTH OF THE 20TH REGIMENT,
AFTER THE DEATH OF NAPOLEON BY DOCTOR ARNOTT,
AT SAINT HELENA.

the end of Napoleon's life, Dr Arnott, medical officer of the 20th Regiment (later the Lancashire Fusiliers), which then formed part of the garrison, was called in to treat him, effecting at least a temporary cure. Napoleon was grateful and gave Arnott a number of presents, including a gold snuffbox on which he had scratched the single initial "N"—and the fine pair of holster pistols seen here. These are handsome weapons, very characteristic of their maker, Lepage of Paris, whose name is engraved on the top flats of their octagonal barrels. They are, of course, flintlocks, and are somewhat unusual in that they have multi-grooved rifling, which would have conferred the capacity to throw a ball of about 0·8oz (23 gm) to a considerable distance with great accuracy. They are strictly service arms, plain and unadorned, but a fine pair of pistols of their kind and well worthy to have been carried by one of the world's greatest soldiers. Fortunately, it has been possible to ascertain their subsequent history. Dr Arnott was then a veteran of more than a quarter of a century of the kind of active service which fell to soldiers during the Napoleonic Wars. He had served against the French in the earlier campaigns in Holland, Egypt and Italy and had been through much of the Peninsular War as medical officer of the 20th Regiment. He was an old friend of Colonel Samuel South, also of the 20th, a fine old warrior who had enlisted as a private soldier in the late 18th century and had worked his way up by sheer ability to the command of his regiment. It is, therefore, understandable that Arnott should have presented these pistols to South, probably in about 1826, when the doctor returned from service in India. Colonel South had a son, Charles, who inherited the pistols in due course. Charles, who was commissioned into his father's regiment in 1844, served continuously for 39 years thereafter, mainly as Paymaster. After

service in the Crimea he became Paymaster at the Royal Military Academy, Woolwich, the establishment which then trained cadets for the Artillery and Engineers. He collapsed and died very suddenly in 1874, when the pistols passed to Major G. H. Adams of the 86th Regiment (later the Royal Ulster Rifles). Adams had originally been commissioned into the 20th and had served with it in 1846-52 before transfer; although there is no direct proof, it seems likely that he knew the younger South well—certainly, well enough to be nominated as his executor. He also received the balance of South's estate after the payment of various legacies and, although not specifically stated, the pistols presumably formed part of it. Major Adams (who eventually retired as a Major-General) had been a Captain Instructor and District Inspector at the School of Musketry, Hythe—which he joined in 1865, only 11 years after its oficial establishment—so it is, perhaps, natural that he should have presented the pistols to the School in the same year that he inherited them. It must, of course, be understood that it is not in any sense claimed that these pistols are the only ones to have been owned by Napoleon. Emperors do things on a lavish scale—and it is certain that Napoleon owned numerous pairs of pistols of various kinds. A great many of these were made for him, often in complex sets that included sporting guns by Boutet of Versailles, who was probably the bestknown of all French gunmakers of the period. Many weapons made for Napoleon were, however, so heavily ornamented with precious metals and enamels that they must be regarded primarily as works of art—very much in the same way as some of the ornate wheellocks illustrated earlier in this book. The pistols seen here, on the other hand, are essentially functional arms of the highest quality; they now form a valued exhibit in the collection of the Weapons Museum at the School of Infantry, Warminster, Wiltshire.

Great Britain
CANNON-BARRELLED FLINTLOCK PISTOL

Length: 14.75" (375mm)
Weight: 28oz (.79kg)
Barrel: 9.25" (235mm)
Calibre: .65" (16.5mm)
Rifling: Nil
Capacity: One
Muz Vel: c450 f/s (137 m/s)
Sights: Nil

Weapons of this type took their name from the obvious resemblance of their barrels to those of the type of cannon then in use. As an alternative, they are frequently known as "Queen Anne pistols", although this suggests a date that is really a trifle early; Anne died in 1714, at a time when arms of this type were only just beginning to appear. They continued to be made thereafter until at least 1775—and possibly very much later. The pistol seen here bears no maker's name, but it was almost certainly made in England in about 1725. Its size shows it to be a holster pistol and it was probably originally one of a pair. It is of medium quality, of the kind which would have been carried by the guard on a coach or by a mounted servant escorting his master on a journey (a very necessary precaution in the 18th century, when footpads lurked on most highways). The pistol has no butt-cap and the butt itself is of slightly unusual shape: generally, butts of this type had more bulbous ends, as may be seen from the butt of the screw-off pistol illustrated on the opposite page (above). It has a swan-necked cock (from which the top jaw and screw are missing), and the slight roughening on the surface of the jaw was to ensure that the flint, which was often seated in leather, was held firmly. The tail of the combined pan cover and steel (now often known as the frizzen) bears on a characteristically-shaped curved spring which governs the degree of resistance to the falling flint: it was necessary for the pan to open quickly and smoothly, while still offering enough resistance to ensure good sparks. Some weapons of this type had ramrods held in a pipe or pipes below the barrel.

Russia
CAUCASIAN FLINTLOCK PISTOL

Length: 13.75" (349mm)
Weight: 16oz (.45kg)
Barrel: 8.9" (226mm)
Calibre: .400" (10.2mm)
Rifling: Nil
Capacity: One
Muz Vel: c400 f/s (122 m/s)
Sights: Nil

This is a good representative specimen of a type of pistol which appears to have been manufactured with little or no change throughout most of the 18th and 19th centuries. These arms take their name from the fact that they were made and carried in the general area of the Caucasus mountains (now called Bol'shoy Kavkaz), a range extending from the Black Sea to the Caspian, and are sometimes also known as "Cossack pistols". They were probably assembled by local craftsmen, although the locks and barrels were frequently imported from Spain, Italy and elsewhere. The barrel of this specimen is decorated with an elaborate pattern of silver inlaid with black, in the Italianate style known as niello.

The lock is of characteristic miquelet type, a form which originated in the Spanish province of Catalonia. In this type the sear projects horizontally from the lockplate and acts directly on the projection at the bottom of the cock, the jaws of which have a distinctly reptilian appearance. The sear can be seen just above the button trigger, which is practically universal on pistols of this kind. The pan cover and steel are combined and the face of the steel is scored with eight vertical grooves to ensure a good spark. The entire lock—and, indeed, all the metal parts except the barrel and lanyard ring—is damascened in gold. The stock is of the orthodox slim design and has a thin covering of black leather with an ivory tip and a large, ivory, ball-butt, designed to prevent the weapon from slipping from a greasy hand. Ramrods for these arms were carried separately, often on a cord or ribbon around the user's neck. In spite of their regional title, weapons of this kind seem to have been made, or at least used, over much of Russia. They also bear a resemblance to a variety of arm known as Turkish, Balkan or Albanian pistols, although these often have orthodox locks and slim, rat-tailed butts. All arms in these categories appear to be somewhat fragile for the sort of rough handling inseparable from service use: it is possible that they were to some extent status symbols, like early wheel-locks.

This photograph shows the pistol barrel screwed off for loading. The powder chamber is contained within the male screw and has a concave top. The chamber is loaded vertically; the ball is balanced on top; and the barrel is then screwed on again with the key described in the main caption. This was a slow process, but the system allowed for the use of a tight-fitting ball.

Great Britain
SCREW-OFF FLINTLOCK PISTOL

Length:	11·75" (298mm)
Weight:	27oz (·76kg)
Barrel:	5·5" (140mm)
Calibre:	·62" (15·7mm)
Rifling:	Nil
Capacity:	One
Muz Vel:	c450 f/s (137 m/s)
Sights:	Nil

This is a cannon-barrelled pistol of broadly similar type to the one shown opposite (above), but with the important difference that this specimen has a removable barrel, and thus can be loaded from the breech end. The general method by which this was done is shown in detail in the inset picture (above). In order to remove the barrel, a circular key was slipped over it and locked near the breech end by means of a stud (visible in the photograph), which fitted a corresponding notch cut into the inner circumference of the key. This enabled the barrel to be made a good, gas-tight fit with the breech. The somewhat abrupt swell at the bottom of the butt is more characteristic of the general type than is the butt of the pistol on the preceding page, as is the cast-brass butt-cap with its simple design of foliage and the brass escutcheon plate just visible above it. Screw-off barrels, which originated a few years before the so-called Queen Anne type, made possible the use of a carefully measured charge and a tight-fitting ball. This eliminated the need for ramming and was particularly useful in rifled barrels. This specimen, which was made by the London gunsmith Bumford in about 1755, is of medium quality. Many of the finest specimens had elaborate silver furniture and ornament; such features, being hall-marked, are of considerable help in dating these arms.

Great Britain
POCKET SCREW-OFF PISTOL

Length:	6·6" (168mm)
Weight:	12oz (·34kg)
Barrel:	3" (76mm)
Calibre:	·500" (12·7mm)
Rifling:	Nil
Capacity:	One
Muz Vel:	c 350 f/s (107 m/s)
Sights:	Nil

This weapon is of similar type and period to the one seen above, but it is a much smaller, pocket version, made by the well-known London gunsmith Barbar in about 1740. During the 18th century, the streets of London were dangerous places at night; and although most gentlemen then habitually carried swords, many liked to have a pair of pistols handy also. These were usually carried in the capacious flapped pockets of the long waistcoats then worn, where they were available for instant use. The weapon seen here (which was originally one of a pair) is a good example of the type. It is a strictly functional piece, without ornamentation of any kind, but its quality is excellent—as is only to be expected from a maker of Barbar's repute. Because it has a screw-off barrel, it could be loaded with a tight ball which would stay in place: a common enough problem with muzzle-loaders was that the ball, unless held in position by an over-wad, would move forward if the arm was jolted. The very short barrel would, of course, reduce the pistol's power at anything more than point-blank range—but this would constitute no disadvantage in the sort of close-quarter brawl for which the weapon was designed.

Great Britain
BRITISH CAVALRY PISTOL

Length: 21·75" (552mm)
Weight: 50oz (1·42kg)
Barrel: 14·5" (368mm)
Calibre: ·625" (15·9mm)
Rifling: Nil
Capacity: One
Muz Vel: c500 f/s (152 m/s)
Sights: Nil

The 16th century saw the temporary ascendancy of the pistol as a cavalry arm, an innovation forced upon mounted troops by their increasing inability to charge steady infantry armed with the more reliable muskets coming into use. It was eventually found, however, that pistols fired from restive horses were no match for volleys of musket balls: whereupon the cavalry reverted to shock action with the sword, relying on light, unarmoured troops on swifter horses to achieve at least some degree of surprise. Nevertheless, most cavalry continued to carry either pistols or carbines. The weapon seen here is a pistol of the type carried by British heavy cavalry regiments. Although it is not dated, the cypher "GR" indicates that it must have been made after the death of Queen Anne in 1714; and its general style — notably its length; the back-curled tip of the trigger; and the long ears on the brass butt-cap — indicates that it was probably made very soon afterwards, perhaps in about 1720. The lock, with its swan-necked cock, is of typical Tower type, and it will be noted that the tail of the frizzen rests upon a very different type of spring from those found on the cannon-barrelled weapons shown on pages 26-27. Just over one-third of the breech-end of the barrel is octagonal, such a configuration then being considered likely to produce a breech more robust than a cylindrical one. The calibre of the weapon means that it could fire spherical lead balls weighing about 0·8oz (23gm) each; this, in conjunction with its long barrel, which allowed a fair-sized charge to be consumed before the ball was clear, gave it a reasonable initial velocity. Cavalrymen then wore heavy clothing and sometimes even a light breast-plate, so that a fair degree of penetrative power was desirable. A loose-fitting bullet bouncing down a smooth-bored barrel would, of course, lose both its velocity and accuracy very quickly — but that factor was not considered to be of much importance: the principal arm of the cavalryman was the sword, and the pistol was usually only resorted to in a mêlée, when the first impact of a charge had been dissipated. From the crescent-and-star decoration of its butt, this particular specimen appears to have passed through the hands of a native gunsmith, probably in the Middle East.

Germany
RIFLED CAVALRY PISTOL

Length: 19·5" (495mm)
Weight: 40oz (1·13kg)
Barrel: 13·25" (337mm)
Calibre: ·55" (13·97mm)
Rifling: 7 groove, r/hand
Capacity: One
Muz Vel: c500 f/s (152 m/s)
Sights: Fixed

This pistol was probably made in about 1715, at a time when the cavalry had largely reverted to shock action. Even so, pistols were usually carried, and in some European countries it was the custom to arm a few men of each troop with weapons of superior precision, so that they could in some degree hold their own with enemy skirmishers. The weapon illustrated is of this

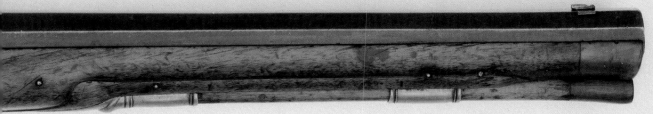

Great Britain
OVERCOAT POCKET PISTOL

Length: 8·25" (210mm)
Weight: 19oz (·54kg)
Barrel: 3·2" (81mm)
Calibre: ·75" (19mm)
Rifling: Nil
Capacity: One
Muz Vel: c500 f/s (152 m/s)
Sights: Fixed

Flintlock pistols tended to fall into two broad categories: belt or holster pistols, which were bulky and were often carried on the front arch of a saddle; and pocket pistols. The latter were again often sub-divided into very small, waistcoat-pocket arms, and heavier types designed to be carried conveniently by a traveller in his overcoat pocket. In the early years of the 19th century, many English highways—particularly, perhaps, those in the vicinity of London—were much troubled by footpads and highwaymen; so anyone who carried valuables usually provided himself with some means of self-protection. Stage coaches always had armed guards, but many individuals also liked to have a personal weapon as well, and as the sword had gone out of fashion, this was usually a pistol. The example shown here is by John Rigby of Dublin and was probably made in the first quarter of the 19th century. Like most British arms of the period, it is severely plain, with no more than a trifle of engraving on cock and trigger guard—but well-made arms had little need of ornament to point up their quality. It has a horn-tipped, wooden ramrod and is fully stocked, with a neatly chequered butt. The elegant lock is of the type often found on duelling pistols. Perhaps its main characteristic is its stubby, octagonal twist barrel, the yawning muzzle of which might prove a deterrent to would-be robbers. It fired a lead ball of 12-bore—ie, 12 bullets aggregated one pound (·45kg) of lead—and would have been a most formidable arm at close quarters. It is fitted with both foresight and backsight; but these would hardly have been necessary at the range at which it was most likely to be used.

type, and although completely unmarked was very probably made in Germany. Although severely plain (apart from a little shallow engraving on the trigger-guard), as befits a service arm, it is of excellent quality. The lock is of standard type, with the slight down-droop at the rear characteristic of the period, and it is well stocked in some hard wood which is not immediately identifiable. Its ramrod, also wooden, has a horn tip and is held in position by one pipe and a tail-pipe. The octagonal barrel is very sturdy, which is not surprising in view of the fact that it is rifled with seven rounded grooves. Rifled barrels necessitated tight-fitting bullets, and these, in turn, led to increased pressures at the breech. The pistol's foresight is square in section, while the backsight (which is just visible behind the steel) has a shallow V-notch. The flat metal plate which is seen at the back of the butt incorporates a keyhole: it was clearly intended to serve as the attachment point for a further butt (unfortunately missing in this case) which would convert the arm into a carbine. When used in this way, with a carefully-measured charge and a well-cast ball wrapped in an oiled patch, it is probable that it would have shot fairly well up to about 150 yards (137m), a range well outside the accurate capacity of a smoothbore musket. Well-trained flankers armed with such a weapon could thus give a good account of themselves; it is probable that cavalrymen acting in this role were trained to dismount in order to fire from below suitable cover.

France
FRENCH ARMY PISTOL OF 1777

Length:	13·25" (337mm)
Weight:	46oz (1·3kg)
Barrel:	7·5" (190mm)
Calibre:	·700" (17·8mm)
Rifling:	Nil
Capacity:	One
Muz Vel:	c500 f/s (152 m/s)
Sights:	Nil

This is one of the last of the new weapons that equipped the French royalist army before the country was overwhelmed by revolution in 1789. It was made at St Etienne, and is a plain, robust weapon, well-suited to service use and quite capable of being used as a club without sustaining significant damage. As may be seen, it is built on a solid brass frame and is fitted with a walnut butt with a heavy brass butt-cap, the top strap being of iron. The cock is of the common ring-necked type which, although perhaps less elegant than the swan-necked variety, gave much greater strength at the point where a fracture was most likely to occur. The tapered barrel, firing a ball about 1oz (28·35gm) in weight, has no sight of any kind. The complete lack of any stock in front of the trigger-guard necessitated special arrangements for the ramrod (which is here shown at full length below the arm). It was normally housed in a hole in the front of the frame, which is just visible in the photograph. This hole is angled slightly, so that when the ramrod is in position its front end just touches the underside of the barrel. This arrangement presumably was necessary to reduce the risk of the ramrod catching on the edge of a holster. This pistol is of particular interest in that it was the pattern for one of the earliest military pistols to be made in the United States. France supplied many arms to the American colonists in their War of Independence, and in 1799 and 1800 Simon North, a famous American maker, received contracts to make very similar pistols in partnership with his brother-in-law, Cheny. Such arms are rare.

Great Britain
SEA SERVICE PISTOL

Length:	16·25" (413mm)
Weight:	49oz (1·39kg)
Barrel:	8" (203mm)
Calibre:	·58" (14·7mm)
Rifling:	Nil
Capacity:	One
Muz Vel:	c500 f/s (152 m/s)
Sights:	Nil

Although this weapon is specifically classed as a Sea Service pistol, it may be taken as broadly representative of British martial pistols in the period 1740-1840. This one was made in about 1790 and differs from earlier models chiefly in the fact that it has a somewhat shorter barrel and lacks the long ears on the butt-cap (examples of which may be seen on pages 28-29). As might be expected, it is of very plain and robust construction, fully stocked in walnut with a very heavy cast brass butt-cap which would have been more than capable of cracking a skull—a use to which it may

This shows the pistol with the barrel removed for reloading. The powder chamber, which is of smaller diameter than the barrel, is contained within the male screw. The breech is slightly enlarged so as to allow the use of an oversized ball. This gave a tight fit in the barrel.

Great Britain
BOX-LOCK PISTOL

Length: 7·4" (188mm)
Weight: 10oz (·28kg)
Barrel: 2" (51mm)
Calibre: ·400" (10·2mm)
Rifling: Nil
Capacity: One
Muz Vel: c400 f/s (122 m/s)
Sights: Nil

This is another example of the small, screw-off, pocket pistol and somewhat resembles the arm shown on page 27 — although a comparison of the two will show that they vary a good deal in detail. The principal difference is that the weapon seen here is fitted with what is known as a box-lock. This type of lock was probably introduced in the late 17th century, but only became popular in the mid-18th century, mainly because it was a somewhat more compact lock for pocket arms than the

orthodox side lock. As may be seen from the photograph, the breech is made with two parallel side-plates, between which the cock is mounted centrally, with its own separate, flat, plate cover incorporating a rear tang for fixing the butt. The trigger has a similar plate, incorporating the butt tang. No tumbler is fitted in this type, since the bottom of the cock itself is notched to hold the sear. The arrangement necessitates the placing of the pan on top of the breech, with a flat frizzen spring inset into the breech in

front of it. The butt is of the flat or slab-sided variety, having been cut from a plank and its edges chamfered off. The screw-off mechanism is similar to those shown earlier, and a key must be used to remove the barrel. Specimens are sometimes found with a hinged key permanently attached below the barrel, but these are relatively rare. The pistol is lightly engraved and bears private Birmingham proof marks, indicating that it was made before the establishment of the official proof house at

Birmingham in 1813; the likely date of manufacture is about 1800. The left side-plate is marked "E Taylor", which could be a retailer's name: the weapon is of fair quality and is typical of the numerous arms of this type turned out by small makers in Birmingham and elsewhere in the earliest years of the 19th century. Such weapons are clearly intended to be close-quarter, self-defence arms, and if carried in pairs would be useful enough in a brawl. Some were even fitted with miniature spring bayonets.

occasionally have been put in the days when hand-to-hand fighting was a much more common feature of warfare than it later became. The lock-plate is of the usual type and bears a crown with "GR" beneath it and the word "TOWER" across the tail. This indicates that the weapon was

assembled in the great armoury at the Tower of London; although its parts would almost certainly have been manufactured elsewhere by various government contractors. The small crown and arrow below the pan is a lock-viewer's mark. The cock is of the ring-necked type, popular in military

weapons because it added greatly to the strength of what had formerly been their most fragile part. The bottom end of the screw holding the top jaw can be seen protruding into the aperture. The barrel, which is of course smoothbored, and is without sights of any kind, also bears proof and view marks at the breech end. It is held on to the stock by a tang screw (barely visible in the photograph) and by two pins which pass through loops brazed on to the underside of the barrel. The ends of these pins are clearly visible, as is the third, centre, pin which holds the ramrod pipe. It should be noted that this is made in one piece, tail pipe and front pipe being connected at the upper part; although this is not apparent in the illustration. The ramrod itself is of plain steel with the usual slightly domed

head. The weapon is also equipped with a belt-hook (which is situated on the other side of the barrel and thus is not visible in the photograph, although similar features may be seen on weapons illustrated elsewhere in this book). It consists basically of a flat spring, the rear end of which is screwed firmly through the brass side-plate and into the stock, the spring itself lying along the stock. Thus, the hook could be slipped on to the inside of the wide leather waistbelt usually worn by sailors at that period, so that it was firmly held in a position whence it could be drawn and fired without delay. This was essential in a naval arm, because the sailor carrying it, usually on a boarding party, would also be armed with a cutlass—and he needed to have at least one hand free to steady himself.

TURKISH BLUNDERBUSS PISTOL

Length:	17·5" (444mm)
Weight:	46oz (1·3kg)
Barrel:	9" (229mm)
Calibre:	c ·65" (16.5mm)
Rifling:	Nil
Capacity:	Slugs
Muz Vel:	Not known
Sights:	Nil

The commonest form of blunderbuss is the relatively short, carbine-like arm with a bell mouth, which became popular in Europe in about the middle of the 17th century and spread widely thereafter. The name, which is believed to be a corruption of the German *dunderbuchse*, "thunder gun", suggests its probable country of origin, although it is sometimes said to have been invented in Holland. The blunderbuss pistol obviously developed from it, as a horseman's weapon, and was widely distributed in the Caucasus, Persia and other parts of the Middle East. More refined versions were fitted with miquelet-type locks (a specimen of which is shown on page 26) and were often heavily ornamented with mother-of-pearl, gold damascene or silver

IRISH BLUNDERBUSS PISTOL

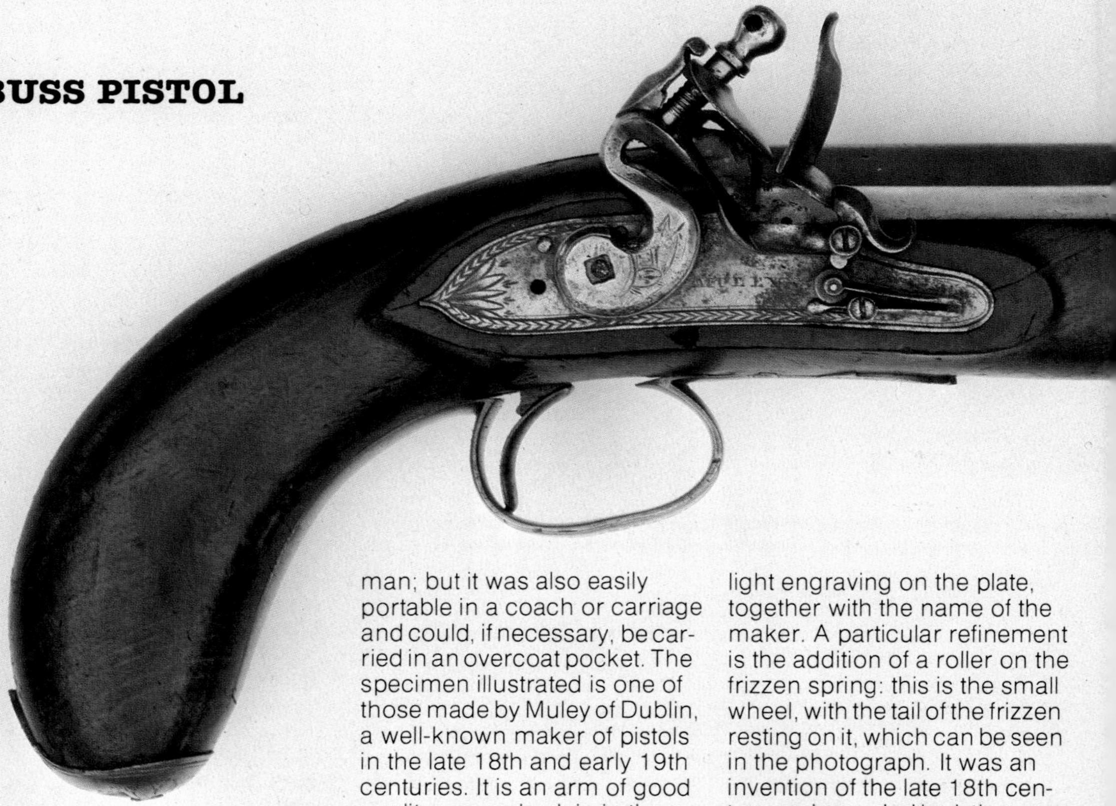

Length:	13·5" (343mm)
Weight:	38oz (1·08kg)
Barrel:	8.25" (210mm)
Calibre:	·62" (15·7mm)
Rifling:	Nil
Capacity:	One
Muz Vel:	c500 f/s (152 m/s)
Sights:	Nil

The general development of the blunderbuss has been traced in the caption to the Turkish weapon illustrated above, so it is not necessary to repeat it here. The British blunderbuss pistol, sometimes referred to as the musketoon pistol, was a natural development of the heavier, carbine-like arms produced from the 17th century onwards for both military and civilian use. Its main advantage was that it could be used one-handed by a mounted man; but it was also easily portable in a coach or carriage and could, if necessary, be carried in an overcoat pocket. The specimen illustrated is one of those made by Muley of Dublin, a well-known maker of pistols in the late 18th and early 19th centuries. It is an arm of good quality, severely plain in the best tradition of British arms, but fabricated of good materials and well-finished. The lock is of orthodox type, with a graceful swan-necked cock and some light engraving on the plate, together with the name of the maker. A particular refinement is the addition of a roller on the frizzen spring: this is the small wheel, with the tail of the frizzen resting on it, which can be seen in the photograph. It was an invention of the late 18th century and speeded lock time very considerably by reducing friction to a minimum. Since speed of ignition was vital for accurate shooting, this refinement was very soon to be found on

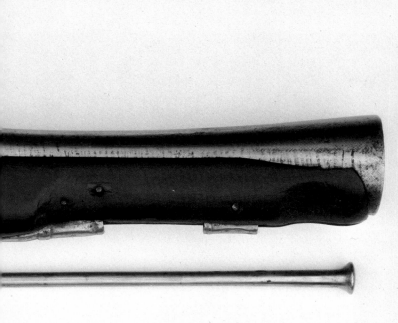

niello. The specimen seen here is a plain, crude, and in many ways ugly little arm: parts of it, or perhaps the entire weapon, were probably made in Europe in the first quarter of the 19th century, for export to the Middle East. The lock is plain, with a brass pan, and the cock is of the ring-necked type commonly found on European military arms of the period. The furniture is of plain cast brass without ornament of any kind, while the stock, with its characteristic chequered, dwarf butt, is of walnut. A rectangular brass loop is attached to the side-plate on the left-hand side of the stock, indicating that it was intended to be carried on a crossbelt by a mounted man. By far the most interesting part of the weapon is the barrel, which is narrowest at its mid-point; its external diameters are: breech 1·2in (30·5mm); centre ·95in (24mm); and muzzle 1·5in (38mm). There are distinct signs that the barrel was originally of octagonal section and that the muzzle was then beaten out to its present circular, bell form. Somewhat unusually, it is fitted with a ramrod. This may be a further indication of its European origins, for many weapons of indigenous manufacture were used with a separate rod, carried slung around the neck. It will be of value to give a brief account of blunderbuss arms generally, since they tend to be the subject of many misapprehensions. They were originally used mainly as naval weapons, sometimes of large bore, and when equipped with swivel mountings must have had an obvious value for repelling boarders. The general system of nomenclature of arms was, however, so imprecise in those days that it is difficult to discern whether the classification referred always to bell-mouthed weapons or simply to weapons of large, shot-gun type. Smaller versions, which were certainly bell-mouthed, were also made for civilian use, either by householders or by guards on coaches; these are often of better finish than their military counterparts. The usual projectiles were either pistol balls or buckshot, depending on calibre, and their effect must have been deadly at short ranges, although the projectiles inevitably lost velocity very quickly. Contrary to general opinion, the bell mouth had no effect on the spread of the shot; and if the bell was cut off at the point where it became a cylinder, this had no effect on the ballistics. It was a long time before this was fully realized, and as late as the 19th century these weapons were being made with oval muzzles on a horizontal axis, in the belief that this would assist lateral dispersion of the charge. The bell mouth was, however, a useful aid when reloading on a swaying coach or ship; and, of course, its morale effect on an opponent must have been considerable. Comic-strip suggestions that such arms were customarily loaded with gravel, broken glass or scrap iron, are, of course, absurd: jagged projectiles of this nature would have quickly torn the bore — particularly when it was made of brass, as was not uncommon. in arms of this type.

View of the muzzle end of the blunderbuss pistol. The internal diameter of the bell mouth is 1·2in (30mm) and would have been a frightening sight to any intended victim.

pistols, sporting guns and even, in some cases, on military muskets — although in the latter case it was usually limited to those weapons purchased privately by the richer Volunteer units of the Napoleonic period, which could afford to equip themselves with the best available weapons. The barrel, which is of brass, is part octagonal and part round; it will be noted that by this time (the weapon was probably made in about 1800) the trumpet-type barrel of the earlier arms had given place to a much more restrained variety, incorporating quite a narrow muzzle with moulded rings for ornament. On the breech plug there is a hook which fits into a corresponding socket on the steel standing breech; and the front end of the barrel is held in place by a flat key passing through a loop. The top flat is marked "MULEY, DUBLIN", but there are no other visible marks. The remaining furniture is of brass, the ramrod pipes being held by pins in the usual way. The ramrod (which may not be the original one) is of wood with a brass tip. The stock is of walnut and, like many service-type arms of the period, the pistol is sufficiently robust to be used as a club without undue risk of damage. The brass barrel suggests that this weapon may have been made for a naval officer: the Royal Navy favoured brass-barrelled weapons because they were less likely to corrode in salt air or salt water. It cannot be said with any certainty whether a naval officer would have used buckshot, or whether he would have preferred a bell-mouthed arm firing normal bullets, as being considerably easier to reload in a rocking boat. This was quite an important consideration — although it is probable that in close-quarter fighting the user would only have a single shot before resorting to sword or cutlass.

MORTIMER DUELLING PISTOLS

Length:	16" (406mm)
Weight:	37oz (1·05kg)
Barrel:	10·25" (260mm)
Calibre:	·62" (15·7mm)
Rifling:	Nil
Capacity:	One
Muz Vel:	c550 f/s (168 m/s)
Sights:	Fixed

Great Britain
MANTON DUELLING PISTOLS

Length:	14·75" (375mm)
Weight:	40oz (1·13kg)
Barrel:	10" (254mm)
Calibre:	·500" (12·7mm)
Rifling:	Nil
Capacity:	One
Muz Vel:	c550 f/s (168 m/s)
Sights:	Fixed

that the inebriated state of the combatants frequently saved them from serious injury. By about 1800 the sword had largely gone out of fashion as an article of everyday dress, to be replaced by the pistol. As a result, quarrels were not so frequently settled on the spot. Duels had to be arranged for a set time and place, usually early in the morning, in some remote spot where no innocent passersby were likely to be

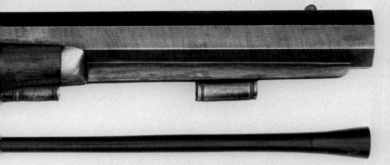

Duelling, the formal settlement of personal disputes by combat, is a very old custom, but until almost the end of the 18th century the weapon usually employed was the sword, which every gentleman carried as a matter of course. Quarrels, which frequently arose in the evening through drink, were then often settled on the spot—and it is probable

injured by stray bullets. As soon as the pistol was established as a duelling weapons, gunsmiths began to develop highly-specialized arms particularly for that purpose. A great many duelling pistols were made, almost invariably in pairs, and usually handsomely cased with a variety of accessories. The pistols seen here were made soon after 1800 by the well-

known London maker H. W. Mortimer and are the highest quality. The locks are fast and reliable, as might be expected, with cocks carefully angled to give good ignition. Note in particular the ingenious way in which the narrow necks have been incorporated into the lower jaws in order to reduce the possibility of fracture. The pans are deep and narrow to ensure the provision of ample priming, and there are rollers on the frizzen springs to ensure both smooth, fast opening of the pans and, at the same time, sufficient resistance for the flint to make a good shower of hot sparks. The heavy, octagonal, damascus twist barrels are extremely carefully bored and attractively figured. They are discreetly ornamented with gold inlay at the breech-ends and the touch holes are lined with the same metal, as are the pans, because gold was said to resist corrosion better than almost any other metal. Both barrels bear on the top flat the proud inscription: "H. W. MORTIMER AND CO LONDON, GUNMAKERS TO HIS MAJESTY". The sights are simple but adequate, consisting of a front bead and a deep U-backsight, with top ears which curve inwards so that the sight becomes almost an aperture. A long groove is cut

along the top of each stock to guide the eye quickly to the line of sight. On the breech plugs of the barrels are hooks which engage into slots on the standing breeches, the front ends being held in position by flat keys passing through loops in the barrels. The thin ends of the keys are surrounded by oval steel plates inset into the stock, so that it is possible to tap out the keys without risk of the tool slipping and gouging a piece out of the stock. The stocks themselves, which are of fine walnut, are in many ways the most interesting features of the weapons. They are the type known as "saw-handled", from their obvious resemblance to that tool. On each pistol, the back spur is designed to fit neatly over the fork of the thumb, so as to help keep the muzzle down. The spur below the trigger-guard, which was held by the second finger, also helped to achieve this important end, as did the heavy barrel. As the pistols are half-stocked, the front parts of the barrels have lower ribs along which the ramrods lie; these are made of wood with horn tips. Duelling had virtually ended in Britain by 1830, but many fine pairs of pistols survive. They are greatly sought after by collectors and, inevitably, are extremely expensive.

There were two Manton brothers in the British gun trade at the beginning of the 19th century, both well known. Joseph, the elder, was particularly famous and may well have been in his day the finest maker in England (which, in the great days of British gunmaking, meant that he was the finest in the world).

The pair of pistols shown here may be taken as representative of some of his best work, although it is probable that they were made at the end of the 18th century, when he was only just beginning to achieve fame. The locks are of fine quality, with graceful swan-necked cocks and deep pans with flash guards behind them to protect the firer from back-blown sparks. The tails of the frizzens are fitted with small

rollers which bear on the small projections visible on top of the frizzen springs. The lock plates, which are lightly engraved, bear the inscription "JOSEPH MANTON, LONDON"; the small studs near the tails of the locks are sliding safeties, by means of which the cocks can be firmly locked in position at

half-cock. The octagonal barrels are of excellent quality and the handsome twist figuring may be clearly seen. The walls of the barrels are 0·2in (5·08mm) thick. Barrels like these, which were usually known as "twist" or "damascus" barrels, were made by a process which may be unfamiliar to the reader. Thin rods of iron and steel were first twisted and then welded side by side into long flat ribbons. These were then twisted around iron mandrels of the required diameter and hammer-welded until they were solid, after which the mandrels were removed and the barrel finished. This process gave the barrel considerable strength, because the long fibres of the metal were twisted round it. However, great care had to be taken to ensure that the welding was complete, for any weakness between the edges of the twisted ribbon might cause the barrel to open under pressure or even partially untwist. For this reason, cheap damascus barrels were never very reliable. Barrels of good quality were usually attractively figured. The

pistols are fitted with Manton's patent breeches, which not only ensured good ignition but also allowed the pans to be more closely inset, thus reducing bulk. The touch holes are lined with platinum which, like gold, was very resistant to corrosion. The breeches of both pistols are inset with small, rectangular, platinum plates bearing the words "JOSEPH MANTON PATENT" and a crown. The sights consist of a front bead, which could be adjusted laterally, and plain U-backsights. The walnut half-stocks have chequered butts with a butt-cap and a horn tip at the front. The wooden, horn-tipped ramrods are held in a pipe and a tail pipe, the barrels having the usual half-ribs to ensure a neat fit. The pistols are heavy but well balanced and come up easily. They are slightly muzzle-heavy, but this counters the natural tendency for the barrel to rise. Duelling pistols were usually loaded with a small charge, just sufficient to flatten the bullet against an iron plate. This made for accuracy, but reduced the stopping-power of the ball.

Percussion Pistols

The flintlock arm had a very long life indeed, for it seems certain that, even if we exclude the wheel-lock as being a distinct and separate type, a basic form of flintlock was in existence by about 1550. Once invented and improved—a long and leisurely process which entailed few if any fundamental changes—the flintlock remained in use as a military arm until at least the 1850s. Even then, although it rapidly became obsolete in the more advanced parts of the world, it remained in service in remote areas, where some are probably still in use. Flintlock guns were certainly being manufactured in and exported from Belgium at least up to World War II, and in much of Africa they were probably the commonest type of arm known up to that time. The survival of the flintlock made sense in primitive communities with little or no system of cash economy, for flints and projectiles could usually be improvised locally and black powder was cheap.

But in spite of its long and honourable history, the flintlock had several serious limitations. It was susceptible to damp, particularly in the priming; its flints needed regular renewal, often as frequently as every 30 shots; its steel needed regular retempering in order to obtain a good hot spark; and even under the most favourable conditions there was always some risk of a misfire. In addition, the flintlock was slow, and the appreciable time lag between pulling the trigger and the firing of the charge made accuracy difficult to achieve. All this was known for a long time—indeed, from the flintlock's first appearance; but at that time science was still in its infancy, with the result that no significant changes could be made for many years. The real problem was to find a safe, reliable and instant method of obtaining ignition. This problem was not confined to firearms: the application of flint to steel was for a long time the most common method of kindling fire—and a slow way it was, for sparks had first to be struck on to a piece of tinder (usually charred cloth) and then coaxed into flame by judicious blowing.

The method which, in theory at least, seemed to offer the best hope of improvement was the use in some way or other of the chemical compounds generally known as fulminates. These were then known as unstable metallic salts which would detonate under a blow or when subjected to friction; they did not burn in the sense that gunpowder burns—ie, at a very fast but nevertheless measurable rate—but were converted almost instantaneously into gases, with great and apparently uncontrollable violence. Fulminates were known, and their properties respected if not actually feared, in the 17th century: the famous diarist Samuel Pepys recorded in 1663 that he had been told of a substance—which he called *aurum fulminans*; better known by its modern name, fulminate of gold—a grain of which, detonated in a spoon, would blow a hole through the metal.

Count C-L Berthollet (1749-1822) carried out many early experiments with fulminates.

Many of the early experiments with fulminates were carried out by the noted French scientist Count Claude Louis Berthollet (1749-1822); and it is clear from his writings that he was familiar with their manufacture and with their rather alarming characteristics. The first impact of what was to become the Industrial Revolution was then making itself felt in some degree all over the civilized world: in particular, men were seeking sources of power more effective than the traditional wind, water and muscle. Thus, they were attracted to fulminates, which appeared to develop at least six times the power of gunpowder. Unfortunately, they were for a long time unable to overcome the treacherous element of instability which was the chief characteristic of fulminates.

One of the major problems was that almost all those involved were mistakenly trying to use fulminates as a *substitute* for gunpowder, so that manufacture, even at the experimental stage, tended to be on an unnecessarily large and dangerous scale. The result, not surprisingly, was disaster after disaster. Factories were rent by the most fearful explosions in which workmen perished and buildings collapsed, until at last all attempts at large-scale manufacture ceased and fulminates were, once again, largely regarded as chemical curiosities, to be experimented with very carefully, in laboratories rather than factories.

One of the more surprising features of these experiments was, perhaps, that no one appears to have grasped fully what the probable effect of the detonation of a quantity of fulminate in a firearm would be on its metal. Gunpowder burns quickly, but its combustion takes a measurable time, with a steady build-up of pressure which can be absorbed by the natural elasticity of the metal: the effect of the instant detonation of fulminate, on the other hand, would be comparable to the explosion of a modern grenade.

The problem was finally solved in the early years of the 19th century by Doctor the Reverend Alexander John Forsyth, a Scottish minister of religion, who in 1791 succeeded his father as the incumbent of the small Scottish town of Belhelvie, a living he was to retain for 52 years. It may seem strange that one of the most important advances in the history of firearms should have been made by a clergyman; but so it was. Forsyth was an unusually intelligent man, of good education and wide interests. One of his main indoor recreations was chemistry, while his chief outdoor occupation was shooting; and it was the combination of these two diverse hobbies which led to his discovery. While shooting duck with his flintlock fowling piece, Forsyth observed that his sharp-sighted quarry saw the flash of the priming in time to jink, dive

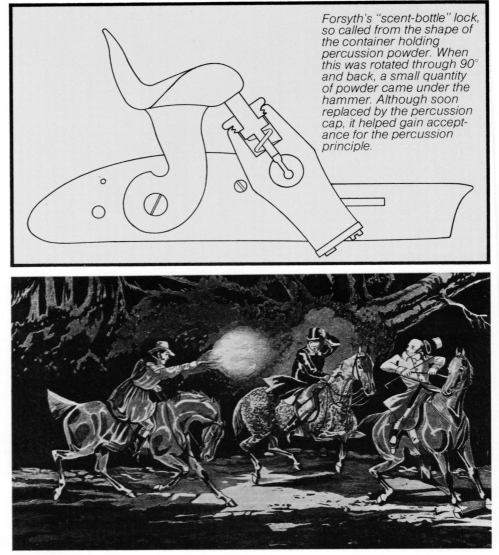

Forsyth's "scent-bottle" lock, so called from the shape of the container holding percussion powder. When this was rotated through 90° and back, a small quantity of powder came under the hammer. Although soon replaced by the percussion cap, it helped gain acceptance for the percussion principle.

Above: *"Stand and Deliver!"* — a contemporary artist's impression of an incident not uncommon on the un-policed roads of Britain in the early 19th century.

(shooting at flying birds was then not so much practised) or otherwise evade the charge of shot. He set to work to remedy the situation by means of his expertise in chemistry.

Forsyth knew about fulminates, but, unlike his predecessors, he seems to have understood very quickly that they could never replace gunpowder as a propellant. He realized, however, that they might be brought under sufficient control for use in very small quantities — just enough to replace the flash of flint and priming as a means of igniting the main charge. His experiments were eventually successful, and by 1807 he had taken out letters patent for igniting a charge of gunpowder by a revolutionary method. The specification stated:

"I do make use of some one of the compounds of combustible matter, such as sulphur or sulphur and charcoal with an oxmuriatic salt; for example the salt formed of dephlogisticated marine acid and potash (oxmuriatic of potassium), or of fulminating metallic compounds, as fulminate of mercury or of common gunpowder, mixed in due quantity with any of the afore-mentioned substances or with an oxmuriatic salt as aforesaid."

This carefully-worded description covered and protected Forsyth's entire process, without divulging too much to potential rivals. What it amounted to, in practice, was to use a minute quantity of fulminate, mixed with some other quick-igniting but more stable chemical, to produce sufficient heat to ignite gunpowder. A great deal of experimentation must have been necessary to establish the proper balance of the various ingredients, in order to reduce sensitivity to reasonable proportions without inhibiting ignition.

Forsyth's first lock was the so-called "scent-bottle" (from its shape), in which the rotation of a container of his fulminating powder deposited a measured charge in a position where it could be ignited by the blow of a pivoted hammer, thus firing the charge. The scent-bottle lock was never used for military arms but soon became popular with sportsmen. It could also be applied to pistols.

As early as 1805 — Britain then being at war with France — the patriotic clergyman offered his services to the Master General of Ordnance, the cabinet minister mainly concerned with the production of warlike material of all kinds. The offer

was promptly accepted, and Forsyth was set up in a workshop at the Tower of London, a locum tenens for Belhelvie being paid for by the government. But then a new Master General was appointed—and he at once sent Forsyth packing. Although the reasons for this are not wholly clear, it is more than probable that the new official knew something of the fearful reputation of fulminates and feared lest he should sponsor a disastrous explosion that would destroy or damage Great Britain's principal armoury.

Forsyth, having patented his invention in the meanwhile and being determined to make something of it, set up a successful London business for the manufacture of sporting guns. They were immediately popular, and it is probable that by around 1820 many sportsmen were using percussion arms—although not necessarily arms with locks on Forsyth's original pattern.

Once the system was proved reliable, many people naturally set out to improve on it. The original scent-bottle lock made use of loose powder in sufficient quantity for a number of shots, which naturally increased the risk of accidental ignition. Forsyth himself realized this,

Left: *The French politician Georges Clemenceau fights a duel with the journalist Paul Déroulède, early in January, 1893. Clemenceau's duelling pistol is of a characteristic French type, with a flared butt.*

Below: *During the Indian Mutiny of 1857, an English lady defends herself with a double-barrelled (possibly four-barrelled) over-and-under percussion pistol.*

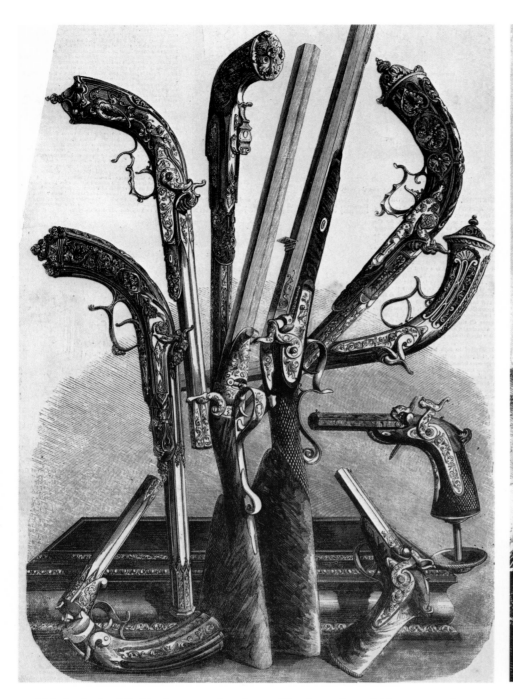

and his locks had light plugs so placed that they could easily be blown out, thus at least canalizing any accidental blast. Nevertheless, some risk remained; so the first broad line of experiment was to form the detonating compound into pills or pellets with the aid of gum arabic or some similar adhesive. These pills could be used one at a time while the rest were kept well away from the gun, in the shooter's pocket or pouch. Slim metal tubes of the compound were also devised—to be placed in the touch hole and detonated by the hammer—and these had some success. Then, in about 1820, the percussion cap as we know it today was invented; a tiny copper cup into which the required quantity of detonating compound, held by adhesive or varnish, could be placed. The cap was placed over a nipple pierced with a hole leading to the main charge. Ignition by means of a simple hammer was practically instantaneous.

The inventor of the percussion cap cannot be positively identified. Colonel Peter Hawker, a well-known sportsman and writer of the period, seems to have laid some claim to the idea, as did the gunmakers Joseph Manton and Joseph Egg; but on balance it seems likely that the best claimant is an English artist named Joshua Shaw, who, having apparently been advised that his invention was not patentable in the United Kingdom, departed forthwith for the United States, where he registered it in 1822. The final chemical improvement had come about a little earlier, with the perfection by an English chemist, Edward Howard, of a method for the manufacture of fulminate of mercury. This, when properly handled, proved both stable and reliable and very soon became by far the most widely-used compound in the manufacture of percussion caps, but was eventually found to have an adverse effect on brass.

Once perfected, the percussion cap system conferred great advantages. Guns with locks working on the new system were reliable and, if sensibly used, were very much more weatherproof than the flintlock, with its vulnerable priming. The lock action was much faster, which improved accuracy, while the jet of flame that lanced from the cap into the charge caused it to burn rather more rapidly, thus improving muzzle velocity. A good many flintlocks were converted to the new system—and a few guns naturally failed under the increased strain. Most of these were sporting guns: it does not seem likely that many pistols were converted.

The removal of the somewhat bulky flintlock made it possible to streamline weapons to the stage where double-barrelled arms became a practical proposition. The disappearance of the pan made possible the use of the back-action lock, in which the mainspring was

located behind the hammer: this further facilitated the streamling of arms—and was particularly useful so far as pistols were concerned. Very small single- or double-barrelled pistols, capable of being carried concealed in a pocket, soon became popular. Nor did the process stop there: if two shots were better than one, four were clearly better still—although care had to be taken not to increase the pistol's weight and bulk overmuch. Probably the most practical of these multi-barrelled arms were those with two pairs of barrels, one top and one bottom, each with their own nipples but able to be pivoted quickly and simply by hand, so that they came under the hammers in succession. A number of makers still had a lingering fear that an overpowerful cap might cause an accident: thus, one often finds pistols with a circular platinum plug just in front of the nipple. The plug blew out if the pressure developed was too high and thus, with luck, prevented the barrel from bursting.

A notable aspect of the percussion lock was the relative speed with which developments occurred, as compared with the flintlock. In the early part of the 19th century, with the Industrial Revolution well under way, both knowledge and manufacturing techniques improved very rapidly. Although, perhaps, no one realized it immediately, the adoption of the percussion system was probably the greatest single advance in the development of firearms: it was to lay the foundations of modern small arms. Paradoxically, it seems, the last to realize this were the armies of the world, which stuck to their well-tried flintlocks long after sportsmen were firing salutes to the genius of Dr Forsyth. But this caution on the part of the military was to some extent forced upon them by the almost universal need for military economy after the vast expenditure of the Napoleonic Wars. Another factor in the delay was the need to establish a considerable degree of certainty as to the new system's reliability under combat conditions. Men's lives, and perhaps the fate of their countries, depended on the right decision; so it is perhaps understandable that military leaders wished to be rid of any element of doubt before taking such a revolutionary step.

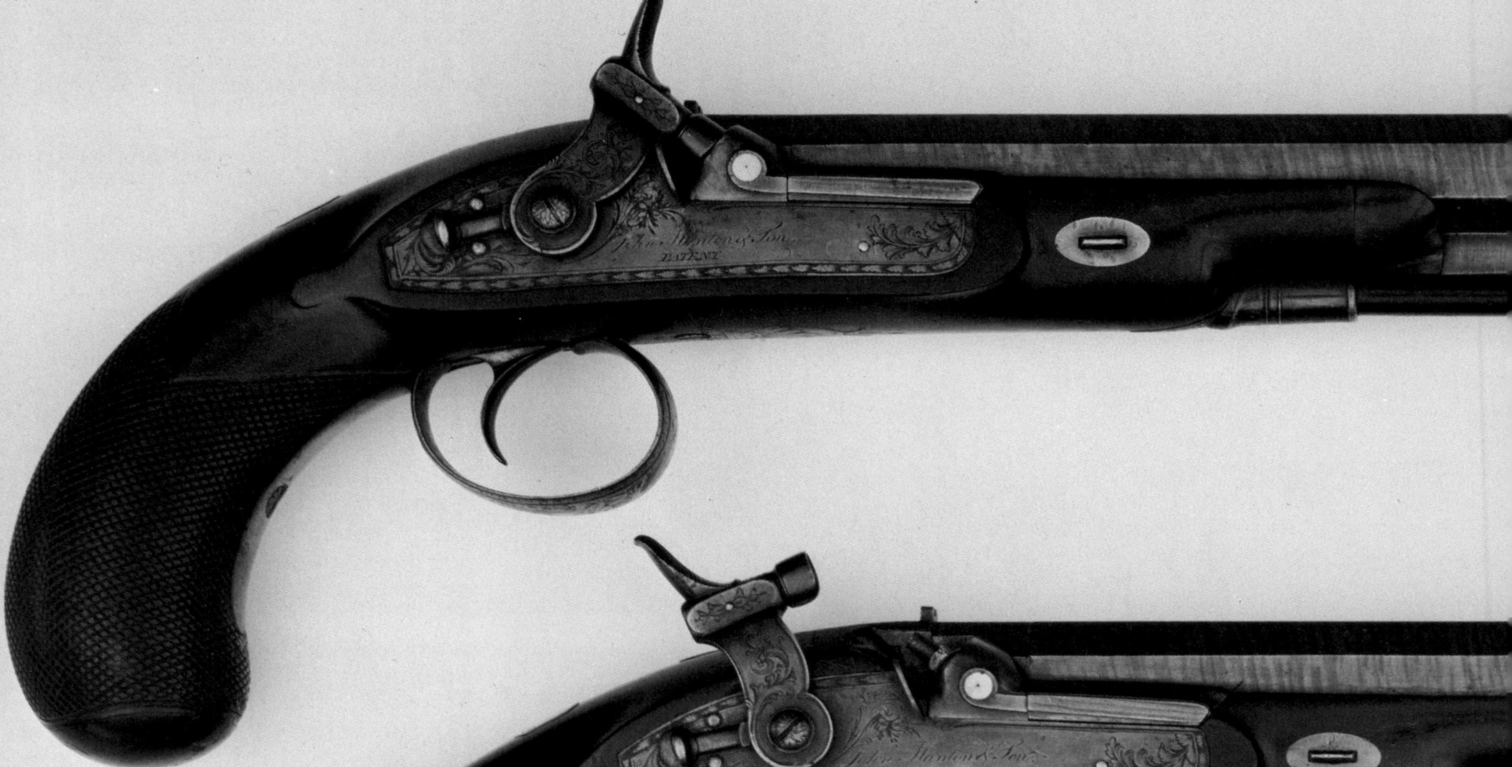

Length:	14·75″ (375mm)
Weight:	38oz (1·08kg)
Barrel:	9·25″ (235mm)
Calibre:	·42″ (10·7mm)
Rifling:	30 groove, r/hand
Capacity:	One
Muz Vel:	c600 f/s (183 m/s)
Sights:	Fixed

Of the two Manton brothers, both well known as gunmakers, the elder, Joseph (a pair of whose duelling pistols are shown on pages 34-35) was the more famous. The younger, John Manton, was, however, a fine craftsman—a fact well illustrated by the pair of percussion pistols shown here. The percussion system was first used on firearms by Doctor the Reverend Alex-

Length:	15″ (381mm)
Weight:	36oz (1·02kg)
Barrel:	9″ (229mm)
Calibre:	·700″ (17·8mm)
Rifling:	Nil
Capacity:	One
Muz Vel:	c500 f/s (152 m/s)
Sights:	Nil

Although British cavalrymen, like most others in the world, regarded the sword or lance as their principal weapons until well into the 20th century, it had long been customary for mounted men to carry firearms. These were usually

PERCUSSION DUELLING PISTOLS

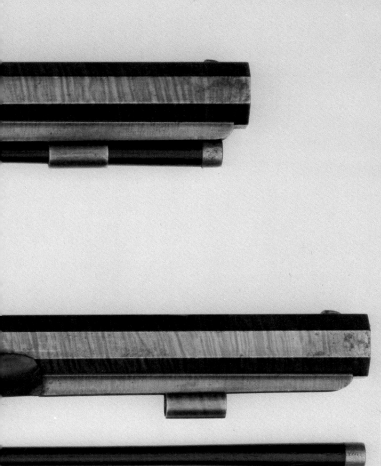

ander Forsyth in the very earliest years of the 19th century and, after experiments concerning detail rather than principle, had been fully accepted. The best way of implementing the system, so far as muzzle-loading arms were concerned, was found to be the use of the copper percussion cap. This pair of pistols was produced by John Manton in about 1823, when he would presumably have been attempting to meet the large demand for weapons made on the new system. These pistols have octagonal twist barrels with unusually thick walls — the top flats being engraved: "JOHN MANTON AND SON, DOVER STREET, LONDON" — and although they are clearly duelling pistols they are somewhat unusual in being lightly rifled. This was not generally considered to be a sporting practice in the case of such arms; but it may be that their owner was not too particular in this respect. Alternatively, and more charitably, it is possible that he also intended to use them as general holster pistols: naturally, no one objected to the use of rifled arms against the King's enemies or against highwaymen. The barrels are screwed into breech plugs about 0·7in (17·8mm) long, and are fitted with hooks which lock into recesses in the standing breeches. The top flats of the breech plugs are inset with rectangular gold plates (each bearing a crown and the words "MANTON, LONDON") and the nipple bolsters are fitted with circular platinum safety plugs. These were intended to blow out if the internal pressure was too high, to prevent the bursting of barrels: this was a sensible precaution in the days when the power of the fulminate placed in the caps was liable to vary considerably. The half-stocks are of fine walnut with horn tips, the butts being finely chequered to give a secure grip, and the barrels are held to them with single flat keys (and by the hooks already described). As the pistols are half-stocked, the lower flats of the barrels are fitted with half ribs, each equipped with a single pipe, to hold the ramrods; and these are of ebony with brass tips and ferrules. The trigger-guards have the almost universal pineapple finials, together with long rear tangs let into the butts. Probably the most interesting features of these pistols are their locks, which are fitted with flat hammers. These have hollow noses to accommodate the strikers, which have deep recesses that completely cover the nipples. The reason for fitting detachable strikers, which are held in position by pins and are of a beautiful deep blue, is partly because no one really knew what the effect of repeated blows might be, and partly to localize the damage that might be done by an overpowerful cap. The lockplates have sliding safety catches which engage in recesses in the hammers when the latter are at half-cock. At first sight it appears that these pistols were purpose-made as percussion arms, but a careful inspection shows conclusively that they are, in fact, flintlock conversions. The pans of the original flintlocks have been removed, the cocks replaced with hammers, and the lockplates reshaped; but so skilfully has the work been done that it is barely perceptible. However, the blocked-up holes where the frizzen springs once rested are just visible. The most probable explanation is that these pistols were converted from stock in Manton's workshop before they were ever used as flintlocks. They are beautiful weapons, plain and austere as befitted their role but of unmistakeable quality, and almost certainly extremely accurate at the short ranges at which duels were normally fought.

MILITARY PERCUSSION PISTOL CONVERSION

either short carbines or pistols, or sometimes both, and they were of limited use for mounted skirmishing, dismounted action, guards, picquets and similar duties. Like most firearms of the time, they were highly inaccurate except at point-blank range and lacked any great power. The weapon seen here was originally a flintlock and was made, or at least assembled, at the Tower of London in about 1796, for use by the Light Dragoons. As may be seen from the photograph, it is in rather poor condition, but it has been included because it provides a good example of one of the methods used in the first half of the 19th century to convert flintlock arms to the new percussion system. The advantages of the new system were considerable: it made no difference to accuracy and very little to power (although the new fulminate caps tended to make the charge burn somewhat faster), but it gave reliable ignition, particularly in bad weather when there was little or no chance of persuading a flintlock to produce a spark — and even less of damp priming actually igniting. It also made the arm less bulky by doing away with the relatively clumsy cock and pan. The method used in the case of the pistol shown here was simple. A hollow metal tube, closed at one end, was screwed into the touch hole. This tube, usually known as the drum, was threaded on its upper side to receive a screw-in percussion nipple on to which the cap fitted. The old flint cock was replaced by a simple hooded hammer, and the conversion was then complete. The pan and frizzen were, of course, removed: the plugged screw holes are clearly visible on the lock-plate. The simplicity of this method made it both quick and cheap and it was very widely used by civilian gunsmiths. In general, however, it was not employed in military conversions, where the favoured method was to weld or braze a nipple lump into the required position and then drill it for a military nipple — unless, indeed, the whole barrel was replaced. The new nipple lumps were usually shaped in such a way as to fit into the hollow left by the pan.

POCKET PERCUSSION PISTOL

Length: 6" (152mm)
Weight: 9oz (·25kg)
Barrel: 1·5" (38mm)
Calibre: ·500" (12·7mm)
Rifling: Nil
Capacity: One
Muz Vel: c400 f/s (122 m/s)
Sights: Nil

Pocket pistols were introduced as soon as the early gunsmiths had learnt to make weapons small enough for the purpose, and they retained their popularity in Britain into the 20th century, by which time the country had generally become so well-policed that firearms for self-defence had largely become unnecessary. The advent of the percussion system in the early years of the 19th century made it simpler to produce compact weapons suitable for the pocket, for it then became possible to do away with the bulky cock, pan and frizzen, and substitute a simple hammer and nipple. The specimen illustrated is of quite good quality and probably dates from about 1835. It is of the box-lock type, in which the hammer and trigger mechanism are fitted centrally behind the barrel in a box-like compartment. Its short, stubby barrel is of the screw-off variety and is of large enough calibre to take a lethal ball, although the pistol's small charge would make it ineffec-tive at anything above the point-blank range for which it was designed. There is a fence behind the nipple to deflect any fragments of copper that might fly from the cap; the nose of the hammer is deeply recessed for the same purpose. The hammer is fitted with a sliding safety, of which the flat bar and knob are visible behind the hammer in the photograph. The mechanism is so designed that when the hammer is down, the trigger folds forward into a recess in the bottom of the breech: cocking the action causes it to pop out in readiness for firing. The charac-teristic rounded butt, often referred to as "bag-shaped", has a small silver escutcheon plate let into it. The curved scroll visible on the breech bears the word "SUNDER-LAND", while a similar scroll on the other side is inscribed "R. D. BOOTH". This may be the name of the maker; although it was not unusual for retailers to have their names placed on arms manufactured by unknown makers in Birmingham and elsewhere.

LANG PERCUSSION PISTOL

Length: 8·25" (210mm)
Weight: 15oz (·42kg)
Barrel: 3·25" (83mm)
Calibre: ·600" (15·2mm)
Rifling: Nil
Capacity: One
Muz Vel: c500 f/s (152 m/s)
Sights: Fixed

This is another example of a rather specialized type of pistol, similar in essentials to the pocket pistol illustrated on the facing page (below). It was made, probably in about 1830, by Joseph Lang, a very well-known London gunsmith who later became famous for his early gas-seal percussion revolvers (see page 65 for an example) and his shotguns. The octagonal barrel is of the usual damascus type; but for some reason it has been cleaned bright, thus destroying the attractive markings brought out by the careful use of acid on the twisted metal. The barrel itself is screwed into a patent breech about 0·8in (20·3mm) long, the powder chamber being of much smaller calibre than the bore itself. Such an arrangement was often con-sidered desirable in a pistol of reasonably heavy bore, since the powder was concentrated in a relatively compact mass and was therefore much more likely to be quickly and com-pletely ignited by the jet of hot flame produced by the detona-tion of the fulminate in the cap. A small screw beneath the nipple can be removed to give access to the chamber for the purpose of cleaning it. This was desirable, for deposits of ful-minates had a corrosive effect very much stronger than that of plain gunpowder fouling, which could be flushed out with warm water. The top flat of the barrel is marked "LONDON" and carries the marks of the London proof house. The frame of the weapon, includ-ing the patent breech, hammer and trigger guard, is lightly engraved, the top butt tang also bearing the inscription "J. LANG". The butt is of very finely chequered walnut with an oval escutcheon plate let in 0·5in (12·7mm) behind the tang screw, and its base incor-porates a spring-lidded com-partment for percussion caps such as is often found in pistols of good quality. The ramrod, which is of swivel type, is held in a rib with a single pipe below the barrel. Rather unusually for a pistol of this size, the arm is fitted with a belt hook, a flat metal spring intended to slip inside a belt so that the pistol could be carried ready for use. As is usual, the belt hook is screwed on to the frame on the left-hand side. Its existence makes it seem probable that, in spite of its relatively small size, this pistol was intended for ser-vice use, perhaps by an officer of the Royal Navy. It was prob-ably originally one of a pair: there was no time to reload such pistols during combat at close quarters, so two were usually carried.

Great Britain
POCKET PERCUSSION PISTOL

Length:	5·8" (147mm)
Weight:	9 oz (·25kg)
Barrel:	1·5" (38mm)
Calibre	500" (12·7mm)
Rifling:	Nil
Capacity:	One
Muz Vel:	c400 f/s (122m/s)
Sights:	Nil

This is another example of the kind of small pocket pistol turned out by the thousand by makers of all grades, from the great names of the London trade down to the anonymous makers in small backstreet factories in Birmingham. Until the later 19th century, the streets of most cities were considered dangerous places, particularly at night, and many respectable citizens considered it prudent to go armed: the rich in their coaches with armed retainers, the less wealthy on foot, with a stout stick and the comforting weight of a pair of pistols in their overcoat pockets. The pistol illustrated is fairly typical of its kind, small and compact but of man-stopping calibre if used at close quarters and probably adequate to deter the average footpad. It is of the common box-lock pattern, with the mechanism retained between two rear projections from the side of the breech and enclosed by top and bottom plates. Like the arm seen on page 44 (above), this weapon has a sliding safety; when the pistol is at half-cock, the safety can be pushed forward until it engages a notch at the rear of the hammer, thus holding it immovable until the safety is withdrawn. There is no pop-out trigger in this case, the weapon being fitted with a trigger-guard of orthodox pattern. Probably the most interesting feature of this particular specimen is the provision of a device to prevent the percussion cap from falling off the nipple while the arm is in the user's pocket. As may be seen, there is a spring-loaded ring round the nipple: once the hammer has been placed at half-cock, this ring is raised by forward pressure on the vertical lever against a small spring, which allows a cap to be placed in position. The ring is then lowered again, and holds the cap firmly in place without in any way interfering with it being struck by the falling hammer. The pistol is lightly engraved and bears the name "PHIPPS" on the left-hand side of the lock; this may refer either to the maker or to the retailer.

Great Britain
BLANCH PERCUSSION PISTOL

Swivel ramrods were especially useful on service pistols, when speed in reloading was important, since they could not be dropped accidentally. The collar of the swivel on this ramrod fits into the semi-circular notch on the rib when the rod is in place. Swivel ramrods for double-barrelled pistols had to have a rather more flexible type of linkage, so that they could be equally easily used in either barrel.

Length:	11" (279mm)
Weight:	24oz (·68kg)
Barrel:	5" (127mm)
Calibre:	·69" (17·5mm)
Rifling:	Nil
Capacity:	One
Muz Vel:	c550 f/s (168 m/s)
Sights:	Fixed

By about 1830, the perfection of the percussion system had made it possible to streamline pistols very considerably, and this specimen provides a good example. It is an arm of excellent quality, made by J. Blanch and Son of Gracechurch Street, London, a well-known manufacturer of pistols and revolvers during the 19th century, whose name appears on the top flat of the barrel. The octagonal barrel is of damascus type, in which previously-twisted threads of iron and steel have been flattened into a ribbon, twisted spirally round a mandrel, and welded into a tube, before being finished and filed to shape. The barrel was then often treated with acid to bring out the figuring, which is clearly visible on this arm. It is fitted with a patent breech of the type originally developed by Joseph Manton, with a rear fence to protect the eye of the firer from flying fragments of the copper cap. The flat hammer has a deep recess in the nose with a slot at its forward end. Unfortunately, the comb of the hammer has been broken off, a not infrequent casualty in arms produced in the days when metallurgy was still not far advanced. The butt, which is well shaped and fits comfortably into the hand, is finely chequered overall, except for an ornamental, diamond-shaped portion at the rear with an inset rectangular escutcheon plate. The butt-cap incorporates a small compartment for carrying percussion caps; this has a close-fitting lid, which is held in place by a spring and may be opened with a thumbnail. In the absence of any stock in front of the lock, the swivel ramrod lies against a metal rib attached to the lower flat of the barrel (and as this is described in the inset, no further reference to it is required here). The weapon, which is of somewhat unusual style for an English-made arm, is of beautiful finish and quality with restrained engraving of characteristic type. It is essentially a service weapon, well sighted and firing a heavy ball of musket bore with a reasonably large charge of powder; probably one of a pair.

France
FRENCH SERVICE PISTOL

Length:	13·75" (349mm)
Weight:	45oz (1·27kg)
Barrel:	7·9" (201mm)
Calibre:	·700" (17·8mm)
Rifling:	Nil
Capacity:	One
Muz Vel:	c550 f/s (168 m/s)
Sights:	Fixed

Like the products of most nations with their own weapon industries, French arms developed certain easily recognizable characteristics which make the origins of arms like the pistol seen here quite clear (The reader may find it of

interest to turn back to the French Army pistol illustrated on page 30 to see, by comparison, how certain essential features persisted over a long period.) The pistol seen here is plainly made and of sound and robust construction, well-suited to service use. The slightly tapered barrel—which is, of course, smooth-bored—has both foresight and backsight; the tang is marked "Mle (ie,

"Model") 1842" and bears the date "1855", and the letters "MI" may be seen just in front of the nipple lump. There are further markings on the left-hand side of the breech. The lockplate, which is severely plain, bears the (abbreviated) inscription "Manufacture Imperiale de Châtellerault", marking its origin in one of the great French factories. The hammer, with its near-vertical

chequered comb and its massive, in-turned nose is at once recognizable as French. The solid brass cap holding the barrel to the front of the stock has a rearward projection on the left side with a retaining screw, and connects up to the

sideplate on which the heads of the lock screws rest. The steel ramrod is retained in a recess running through the brass cap and into the stock. The stock is of walnut, the top and bottom of the butt being reinforced with steel strips: the top strip just touches the massive brass butt-cap with its swivel lanyard ring. The trigger passes through a slot in the bottom strip, which also helps to secure the brass trigger-guard. This pistol, which bears a certain resemblance to American weapons of the period, was probably intended to be used by a mounted man. Its heavy bullet would have done a good deal of damage.

Great Britain
TURN-OVER PISTOL

Length:	5·9" (150mm)
Weight:	11oz (·31kg)
Barrel:	1·6" (41mm)
Calibre:	·31" (8mm)
Rifling:	Nil
Capacity:	Two
Muz Vel:	c450 f/s (137 m/s)
Sights:	Nil

This is a small, pocket percussion pistol, sometimes known as an "over-and-under" because of the relative position of its barrels. It is of good quality and was made by Pinches of London in about 1830. The barrels are of screw-off type: their muzzles have deep, star-shaped indentations to take a key of similar section, so that they could be removed. Such indentations are often found on weapons of this kind, and may give an initial but quite erroneous impression that they

are rifled. The barrels are screwed into a standing breech and, like those of many pocket pistols, are chambered. The pistol has a single hammer with a pop-out trigger and a strongly-made sliding safety, the front end of which engages over a projection on the back

of the hammer when the latter is set at half-cock. The top barrel is fired first; the pistol is then placed at half-cock and the barrels rotated manually through 180° so as to bring the second barrel uppermost. The standing breech is provided with a simple spring device to prevent any accidental rotation. The hook-shaped device in front of the trigger is intended to ensure that the cap does not slip off the lower nipple (which is missing from the weapon in the photograph) when the

pistol is drawn. The finely chequered, bag-shaped butt has a butt-cap, apparently made of German silver; but there is no cap compartment within it. This pistol is an elegant little weapon: the arrangement of the barrels makes it flat and compact, and thus most suitable to be carried inconspicuously in a waistcoat pocket, or even in a lady's bag or muff—a useful companion, in fact, for any traveller in the lawless world of a century and a half ago, without effective police.

Great Britain
FOUR-BARRELLED PISTOL

Length: 8·5" (216mm)
Weight: 37oz (1·05kg)
Barrel: 4" (102mm)
Calibre: ·500" (12·7mm)
Rifling: Nil
Capacity: Four
Muz Vel: c500 f/s (152 m/s)
Sights: Nil

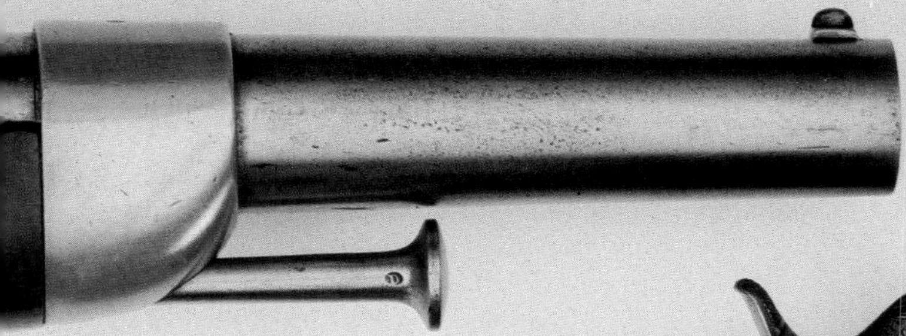

Almost from the discovery of gunpowder, men had desired firearms which would produce as many shots as possible without reloading. This was considered to be particularly desirable in the case of pistols, which were essentially weapons for use at close quarters, when there was no time to go through the complex process of reloading. Multi-barrelled arms went some way towards solving this problem. The weapon seen here is a very handsome example of a four-barrelled pistol, with some similarity in principle to the arm illustrated on the facing page (below). It was made by Blanch of London and bears the maker's name on the left-hand side of the breech, below the hammer. The barrels have been bored out of a solid piece of metal, and the damascus-type figuring on them must therefore be a later ornament, etched on with acid. Each has its own nipple with a screw plug beneath it to facilitate cleaning. The barrels are held in position by a spring catch; when it is desired to rotate them, it is first necessary to release this catch by pressing back the squared front of the trigger-guard—hence its somewhat unusual shape. There are two hook-like projections on the lower part of the frame to hold the lower pair of percussion caps in position. The hammers are gracefully shaped and have deep hoods which completely enclose the nipples. The latter, rather unusually, are lightly threaded, presumably to help keep the caps in position. The pistol has sliding safety catches which hold the hammers securely at half-cock. The chequered walnut butt is of essentially modern shape, looking forward to the revolver rather than back to the pistol. The ramrod below the weapon is normally screwed upwards into the butt. All in all, this is a most elegant pistol, although rather bulky.

Belgium
DOUBLE-BARRELLED POCKET PISTOL

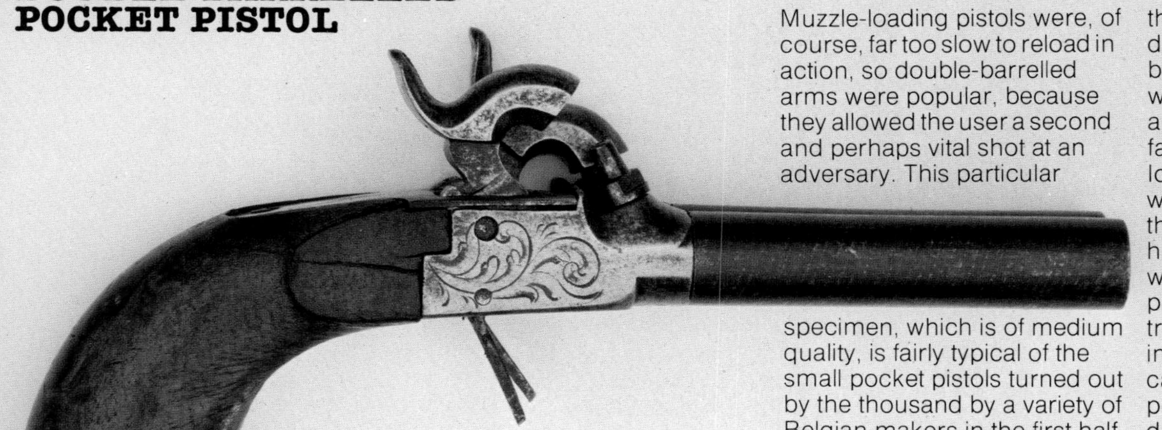

Muzzle-loading pistols were, of course, far too slow to reload in action, so double-barrelled arms were popular, because they allowed the user a second and perhaps vital shot at an adversary. This particular specimen, which is of medium quality, is fairly typical of the small pocket pistols turned out by the thousand by a variety of Belgian makers in the first half of the 19th century. The barrels are of the screw-off variety and fit over male screws of about 0·3in (7·6mm) diameter, containing the chambers. The muzzles each have four deep notches, equally spaced round the circumference, which at first sight appear to be rifling but which are, in fact, intended to take a key. As will be seen, the barrels have a very marked damascus-type spiral figure; but this was probably etched on with acid to improve their appearance, for they are, in fact, solid metal tubes. The two locks have folding triggers which are extruded only when the hammers are placed at half-cock, a common device which made it possible to dispense with the somewhat bulky trigger-guard, while still avoiding the risk of the triggers catching in the lining of a pocket when the weapon was drawn. The butt is of common bag shape without a cap, and the width of the double breech makes it rather wide and clumsy, in distinct contrast to the weapon shown (below) on the facing page. Pistols of this kind were commonly sold for a few shillings and a good many are still to be found, tucked away in drawers and cupboards of old houses.

Length: 6·5" (165mm)
Weight: 12oz (·34kg)
Barrel: 2·65" (67mm)
Calibre: ·400" (10·2mm)
Rifling: Nil
Capacity: Two
Muz Vel: c500 f/s (152 m/s)
Sights: Nil

TOWER CAVALRY PISTOL

Length:	15·5″ (394mm)
Weight:	52oz (1·47kg)
Barrel:	9″ (229mm)
Calibre:	·75″ (19mm)
Rifling:	Nil
Capacity:	One
Muz Vel:	c500 f/s (152 m/s)
Sights:	Nil

By 1838 the pistol had been abolished as a general issue to British cavalry regiments. There were, however, certain exceptions: Lancer regiments were allowed to retain one pistol per trooper, and all sergeant-majors and trumpeters also continued to be armed with them. The weapon illustrated is the Model 1842, designed by George Lovell who was then Inspector of Small Arms and well known for his work on percussion weapons. Lovell was a great believer in the virtues of strength and simplicity in military arms, and he also introduced a common calibre to facilitate the supply of ammunition in the field. This is a very solid, robust arm with a rather short butt, which detracts somewhat from its general appearance. It has a smooth-bored barrel of full musket bore, held on the stock by a long screw and one flat key. Its swivel ramrod is retained by a combined nose-cap and pipe of cast brass. The lock is unusually large, being of the standard type used in the Pattern 1842 musket, and is held in position by two screws, the heads of which rest on small brass cups. The full stock is walnut; the butt-cap and trigger-guard are brass. Instead of the usual ring in the butt, a steel sling swivel is screwed into the front of the trigger-guard.

DUELLING PISTOL

Length:	16·5″ (419mm)
Weight:	32oz (·91kg)
Barrel:	10·25″ (260mm)
Calibre:	·52″ (13·2mm)
Rifling:	Nil
Capacity:	One
Muz Vel:	c550 f/s (168 m/s)
Sights:	Fixed

This is a plain but well-made weapon manufactured at St Etienne, probably in about 1835. Although described as a duelling pistol, it may rather have been intended for general target use. The barrel, which is smooth-bored, is of damascus type, but appears to have been made with single twist only, so that the attractive figure usually found on fine-quality guns is absent. The appreciable swamping, or thickening, at the muzzle end is clearly visible in the photograph. The pistol has a patent breech, the nipple being inset into a fence, and is fitted with a bead foresight and a simple V backsight. The barrel is held on to the stock, which appears to be of walnut, by a very long top tang which reaches almost to the bulbous butt, together with a second, lower, tang incorporating the trigger-guard; the two are connected by a screw running through the butt. In addition, a single flat key passes through a loop below the barrel; its end, in its protective oval plate of German silver, can be seen in the photograph. The lock is of the type known as back-action, in which the mainspring is behind the hammer. This allows the lockplate to be set farther back towards the butt and helps to keep the breech narrow. Such an arrangement is acceptable in pistols, but when used in muskets it tended to weaken the butt at its narrowest point. The ramrod, which passes through a hole in the steel nosecap and into a recess in the stock, is of steel with a brass end. The pistol is well balanced and its large chequered butt provides a firm grip; the large knob, with its steel cap, appears to be somewhat superfluous, although it may perhaps help to balance the weapon and thus make an important contribution to accurate shooting. If loaded with a tight-fitting and well-cast ball and a carefully-measured charge of powder, it is probable that this pistol would have shot well at normal duelling distances. Duelling continued in France for many years after it had become illegal in Great Britain.

Great Britain
SEA-SERVICE PERCUSSION PISTOL

Length: 11" (279mm)
Weight: 36oz (1·02kg)
Barrel: 5·9" (150mm)
Calibre: ·56" (14·2mm)
Rifling: Nil
Capacity: One
Muz Vel: c500 f/s (152 m/s)
Sights: Nil

This is another of the new range of percussion pistols produced by George Lovell in 1842, and there are certain similarities in style between it and the cavalry weapon shown on the facing page (above). It has a smooth-bored barrel profusely marked with proof and inspection stamps and, being a sea-service arm, is of smaller calibre than musket-bore. The barrel, which has no sights of any kind, is held to the butt by a long screw and a single pin passing through a loop about 3in (76mm) from the muzzle. Like many of the new percussion pistols, this one was made up from the large stocks of flintlock parts remaining in store. This practice, although highly desirable from the point of view of the Treasury, imposed some limitations on design. The fact that this arm is a conversion is obvious from the shape of the upper edge of the lockplate: it has an arc-shaped depression, originally intended for the pan but now filled by the nipple lump, which appears to have been welded on to an original flintlock barrel. The hammer is of basic Lovell type, although the neck is flat rather than rounded, as may be seen by comparison with the cavalry pistol opposite. The swivel ramrod is held in a single tail-pipe. The butt-cap and trigger-guard are of cast brass, the former having a steel lanyard ring. As this arm was for naval and coastguard use, it is fitted with a long belt-hook, screwed to the left-hand side of the stock. Thus it could be carried ready for use on the cutlass belt worn by sailors and coast-guards, leaving both hands free. This was of considerable advantage to men scrambling about on pitching vessels.

France
GENDARMERY PISTOL

Length: 9·5" (241mm)
Weight: 23oz (·65kg)
Barrel: 5" (127mm)
Calibre: ·600" (15·2mm)
Rifling: Nil
Capacity: One
Muz Vel: c500 f/s (152 m/s)
Sights: Nil

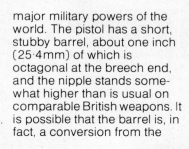

Reference has already been made on page 46 (above) to the strong national characteristics exhibited by service weapons, and this pistol is no exception to that general rule. It is of French manufacture and was made at the great Royal Factory at Châtellerault in 1845; three years after this particular model was first produced in response to the need for change to the new percussion system—a process then being carried out by all the major military powers of the world. The pistol has a short, stubby barrel, about one inch (25·4mm) of which is octagonal at the breech end, and the nipple stands somewhat higher than is usual on comparable British weapons. It is possible that the barrel is, in fact, a conversion from the earlier flintlock variety; but it is difficult to be sure of this. There are the usual tang screws, the front end of the barrel being secured to the stock by a steel collar with its long lower tang inset into the woodwork, where its rear end meets the front end of the trigger-guard. The hammer, which is of characteristic shape, is mounted on a back-action lock neatly in-let into the stock, where it is retained by a screw with its lower end sited in a small plate. The tail of the lock is held in position by a second small screw, the head of which hooks over it. The stock, which appears to be of walnut, has a steel cap, and the trigger-guard is made of the same metal (there is, in fact, a complete absence of brass on this weapon). The ramrod, the front end of which is badly corroded and blackened in this example, passes through the collar and into a hole in the stock. This is a very neat and compact arm, suitable for service use, but portable in a pocket if necessary.

DOUBLE-BARRELLED HOLSTER PISTOLS

Length:	13" (330mm)
Weight:	36oz (1·02kg)
Barrels:	6·2" (157mm)
Calibre:	·700" (17·8mm)
Rifling:	Nil
Capacity:	Two
Muz Vel:	c550 f/s (168 m/s)
Sights:	Fixed

Although pistols had largely gone out of use as British military weapons by 1838, a great many officers continued to carry them as a supplement to their swords. This was, perhaps, particularly true of mounted general and staff officers, who often had to move through hostile territory with little or no escort and who therefore needed some sort of firearm readily available. So far as an officer on foot was concerned, weight was, of course, a limiting factor; but a mounted officer simply carried his pistols in a pair of holsters, one on either side of the forepeak of his

saddle. These holsters were of leather but usually had cloth covers, sometimes elaborately embroidered, to protect their contents from the weather. The pair of pistols seen here may be regarded as fairly typical of the type of arms usually considered suitable. Although severely plain, as befits service weapons, they are of superb quality: this is not surprising when we find that they were made by Joseph Lang, 7 Haymarket, London, a famous maker of the time (a percussion pistol by Lang has already been illustrated, on page 144 (below), and more of the maker's arms may be seen in the section devoted to percussion revolvers). The pistol is double-barrelled, an improvement much facilitated by the introduction of the percussion system; although double-barrelled flintlock pistols were made, the need for two bulky flintlocks made them somewhat clumsy. The smoothbored barrels are of damascus

type with a most attractive figure, and are of a calibre to take a musket ball, making them formidable weapons. Both pistols have a bead foresight mounted on the top rib between the barrels; the backsight consists of a shallow V-groove on the standing breech. The chambers are also equipped with platinum plugs which would blow out if the arm was seriously overloaded, thus preventing damage to the barrel. The nipples are placed on top of the breeches and have shields to protect the eyes of the firer from flying fragments. The locks are of back-action type and fit neatly on to either side of the carefully-tapered stock, so that the hammers do not protrude beyond the outside line of the barrels; this ensures that the pistols are reasonably narrow across the breech. The locks are equipped with sliding safeties, which engage in slots in the hammers when the latter are in half-cock position. In

each pistol, the barrels are held to the stock by a hook at the breech end and by a single flat key, the end of which may be seen in its oval silver plate. The pistols have ingenious swivel ramrods (that of the upper weapon is seen swung out in the photograph): both barrels may thus be loaded without running any risk of dropping the ramrod, an important consideration for a mounted man attempting to re-load on the move. The stocks are of fine walnut, and the chequered butts both have cap compartments (that of the upper weapon open in the photograph). The locks, hammers and trigger-guards are all discreetly engraved; fitting finishing touches for a fine pair of pistols. It will be noted that the combs of the hammers are missing on the lower pistol: these were inevitably fragile and might snap off if the pistol was accidentally dropped; although this did not usually put the weapon out of action.

Great Britain
FOUR-BARRELLED TURN-OVER PISTOL

Length:	9" (229mm)
Weight:	37oz (1·05kg)
Barrel:	4" (102mm)
Calibre:	·500" (12·7mm)
Rifling:	Nil
Capacity:	Four
Muz Vel:	c550 f/s (168 m/s)
Sights:	Fixed

This is another very fine weapon by Joseph Lang, who also made the pair of holster pistols on the facing page. In a very real sense, it is intermediate between the double-barrelled type and the early "pepperbox" revolvers illustrated on pages 58-61. The four barrels of this weapon are bored out of a solid block of steel and the attractive damascus effect has been etched on later with acid. Each barrel has its own nipple and shield, and each is equipped with a platinum safety plug to reduce the risk of damage from either an overcharge of powder or an unnecessarily powerful percussion cap. The two hook-like projections on the standing breech are intended to prevent the caps on the lower nipples from being blown off when the upper barrels are discharged. Each pair of barrels has a small bead foresight on the rib between them, the ramrod being carried in two pipes in the third rib, while the fourth rib bears the proof marks. The butt is finely chequered and has the usual butt-cup, with a compartment for carrying spare caps. The hammers are gracefully shaped; both have deeply-hooded heads with front slots and both are fitted with sliding safeties to lock them at half-cock. Unfortunately, the thumb-piece of the one visible in the photograph has been broken off, but the principle is still clear. The system of firing the pistol is simple. Once the top pair of barrels has been discharged and the hammers re-cocked, the cluster of barrels is turned clockwise (from the firer's point of view) through 180° on its central spindle, thus bringing the second pair into position. The barrels are held by a simple spring catch in order to prevent any accidental movement.

Great Britain
OVER-AND-UNDER PISTOL

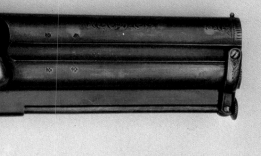

Length:	9·75" (248mm)
Weight:	30oz (·85kg)
Barrel:	4" (102mm)
Calibre:	·500" (12·7mm)
Rifling:	Nil
Capacity:	Two
Muz Vel:	c550 f/s (168 m/s)
Sights:	Fixed

As has already been noted, it was the advent of the percussion system in the first quarter of the 19th century which first made it possible to produce double-barrelled pistols of reasonably large calibre, without at the same time making them unacceptably bulky. Even with the use of the percussion system, however, a double-barrelled, side-by-side pistol of musket bore would be about 2in (51mm) wide across the breech. Gunmakers therefore developed weapons with one barrel set above the other, which, if it did not reduce the actual bulk, at least ensured that it was better distributed, thus resulting in a somewhat more compact weapon. The pistol seen here is a good example of the type. Although of good quality, it has no maker's mark: this is rather surprising, but since it bears Birmingham proof marks it may well be one of the many pirated copies of fine arms, which were turned out in large quantity, and in widely varying quality, by a number of small Birmingham makers. The barrels are bored out of a single block of steel, with a flat top rib, complete with fore- and back-sight, and concave side ribs. The lower barrel has a separate rib to accommodate the swivel ramrod, which is held securely in place by a small spring catch situated inside the end pipe, in front of the trigger-guard. The breech ends of the barrels have flash shields, the right-hand one being longer than the left because of the lowness of the nipple on the under barrel. This also necessitates the long, trunk-like (and rather ugly) nose on the right-hand hammer. The chequered butt, which is of modern shape, contains the usual cap compartment, and all the metalwork is lightly engraved. The left-hand side of the pistol is fitted wtih a belt hook, a fairly certain indication that the weapon was intended for use by an officer of the Navy or Army, who expected to see active service.

Percussion Revolvers

After the introduction of the percussion system in the earlier 19th century, the next logical step in the development of multi-shot pistols was a relatively simple one. Arms with two pairs of barrels, revolved manually through 180° so as to bring successive pairs of nipples under double hammers, soon led to arms with a cluster of four, five or six barrels, revolving mechanically under trigger pressure so as to bring each nipple in turn under a single hammer. Many of these weapons had ring-triggers operating a horizontal, rear-hinged bar hammer, the nipples being arranged radially (ie, at right-angles to the axis of the barrels). Others had striker-type firing arrangements, working on horizontal nipples (ie, nipples that were a direct prolongation of the barrels).

Weapons of this type made their appearance by the 1830s and very soon achieved considerable popularity. They were generally known as "pepperbox pistols", because of the similarity of their cluster of barrels to that household utensil. Their manufacture was, however, largely confined to small-calibre pocket models, because otherwise the bulk and weight of their barrels made them clumsy and heavy.

SAMUEL COLT

The next significant step in development was made by a citizen of the United States, Samuel Colt, whose name was to become a household word not only in his own country but also over most of the world. Colt was born in Hartford, Connecticut, in 1814, and showed an early interest in explosives and firearms. While little more than a boy he conceived the idea of a new type of revolving pistol, in which the long and clumsy cluster of barrels of the pepperbox was reduced in length to a cluster of chambers brought successively into line with a single barrel. The idea was, of course, not really new: flintlock weapons working on this principle had been known for some 200 years, but the complications caused by the need for flint and frizzen had kept them from general acceptance. It is not known whether young Colt had any knowledge of these earlier arms—although, because of his interest in firearms, he must at least have heard of the last of the kind, the ingenious Collier revolver of 1824 (see page 23). He certainly never claimed to have originated the revolver principle, but simply to have improved it until it became a viable proposition—a step only made possible by the recent perfection of the percussion cap. As a young man, Colt went to sea, and it is popularly supposed that he gained inspiration from observing the movement of the ship's wheel. It is certain that during this period he made detailed drawings and wooden models of the arms he had in mind. These were in due course translated into actual firearms by Anson Chase, a local gunsmith with

Above: *Following the end of the American Civil War in 1865, the small US Army was largely occupied with opening up the territories of the West and keeping in check Indian tribes displaced from their traditional lands by settlers. In this dramatic depiction of men of the US Cavalry "Defending the Stockade" against hostile Indians, the artist, Charles Schreyvogel, shows troopers armed with Springfield carbines (although the scout, on the extreme left, has a Winchester) and, in some cases, with Colt revolvers.*

Right: *George Armstrong Custer, as a cadet at West Point, holds a Colt New Model pocket pistol of 1855. This arm, commonly called the Root's-Colt, incorporates Root's patent side-hammer mechanism (visible here). The cylinder is held in place by a centre-pin, the rear of which protrudes behind the hammer. The pistol has a sheathed trigger, without a trigger-guard.*

Far right: *French sailors at revolver drill, c1870. Their arms appear to be Lefaucheux pinfire revolvers (fully illustrated on page 90, above) of the type adopted by the French Navy in 1856, after extensive field trials during the Crimean War. The pinfire revolver was highly favoured on the European continent, but never achieved wide acceptance in Great Britain or the United States.*

Samuel Colt (1814-62)—an inventor of genius and the father of the modern revolver.

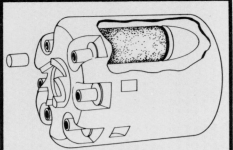

A typical percussion cylinder, showing the arrangement of the nipples in the same axis as the chambers, thus ensuring reliable ignition. The detached object to the left is a percussion cap. The chambers were often slightly tapered so as to ensure a tightly-fitting bullet, which was forced into place by a powerful rammer.

Above right: Colt's factory at Hartford, Conn., in 1862. Samuel Colt's Patent Arms Manufacturing Company was originally established at Paterson, N.J., in 1836, but Colt expanded his activities and moved to Hartford, his birthplace, in 1848, after the impetus given to arms manufacture by the Mexican War and the opening-up of the West. Although Colt himself died prematurely in 1862, his firm was boosted by Civil War demand and continued to prosper, until the name of Colt became a household word.

Right: The Patterson-Colt revolver, Samuel Colt's first production model, took its name from the factory at Paterson, N.J., where it was made in various models from 1836 until 1841. This one is a pre-1839 model with no rammer; in order to load it, it is necessary to remove the cylinder. The end of the axis-pin is so shaped that it can be used to force the bullet home.

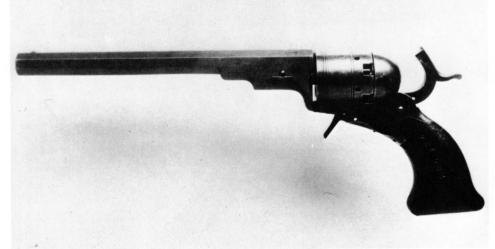

whom Colt's interest in arms had presumably already brought him into contact in his earlier years.

Once these prototypes were available, Colt was able to make material improvements by a process of trial and error — and he was soon convinced that he was on the right lines. There were two major requirements for the system's success: the appropriate chamber must be held rigidly in line with the barrel at the moment of discharge; and partitions of some kind must be placed between the nipples so that the flash from one should not set off a chain reaction round the cylinder. Colt made good progress, and by 1836 he had taken out patents and set up a factory at Paterson, New Jersey, to produce his new arms. But then things went wrong: Colt's pistols were, demonstrably, perfectly good weapons; but even so there was little demand for them, perhaps because of the Americans' traditional allegiance to their tried and trusted rifles. The business failed and by 1841 Colt was bankrupt — although still determined to persevere.

Perhaps fortunately for Colt, the probability of war with Mexico in 1845 led to a greatly increased interest in his arms; especially as the revolvers made at the Paterson factory had proved very successful in various small-scale conflicts with Indians. They were particularly suitable for mounted men, who found it difficult to reload a percussion arm on horseback and thus greatly appreciated the advantage of having six shots available before this became necessary. Acting on the advice of men with practical experience, Colt produced a series of new arms, paying particular attention to heavy-calibre models, with or without detachable stocks, for use by mounted men. Although it is probable that not many of these were produced in time for use in the Mexican War of 1846, this did not prevent their success: the reputation of Colt's arms was established and the progressive opening of the vast territories of the West and South kept the demand steady until the outbreak of the Civil War in 1861. This provided the final boost for Colt's weapons; and although he himself died prematurely in 1862, the arms bearing his name went from strength to strength.

As well as pistols, Colt made a number of revolving rifles and carbines; these are significant in the present context because of their mechanical similarity to revolvers. They were used in some quantity during the Civil War, but never became popular; partly because of the user's aural discomfort when firing from the shoulder, and partly because of a certain tendency to a chain-fire reaction, caused by the flash from the front of the cylinder igniting adjacent charges.

ROBERT ADAMS

In 1851 Colt displayed a large and impressive collection of revolving arms at the Great Exhibition held in Hyde Park, London. The intrinsic merit of his arms — with, it must be added, his excellent public relations — quickly made his pistols sufficiently popular to justify his setting up a factory in London. But he had a serious rival in the United Kingdom in the person of Robert Adams, who, having developed a revolving pistol of his own, entered into partnership with the Deane father and son and soon began to produce revolvers of excellent quality. Colt's arms were built up from a number of machine-made components, a method made essential by his modern system of mass-production by a relatively unskilled labour force, consisting largely of machine minders supervised by a few craftsmen. This made the arms somewhat heavy, particularly the large-calibre models. The frames and barrels of Adams' weapons,

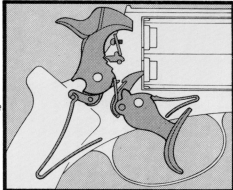

Right: *The mechanism of a Beaumont-Adams revolver. The top diagram shows the lock in the "fired" position. The centre one demonstrates how pressure on the trigger causes the vertical lifter at the rear to engage in a notch on the hammer and forces it back until the bulge of the hammer breast pushes it away and (bottom diagram) lets the hammer fall on the cap. This is a double-action revolver; the hammer may also be cocked manually.*

Left: *James Butler "Wild Bill" Hickok (1837-76), the famous frontiersman, was photographed in c1865 with a holstered pair of Colt 1851 Navy percussion revolvers, carried butt-forward in the "reverse draw" position.*

Below right: *The British gunmaker Robert Adams loads the self-cocking percussion revolver which he invented before 1850, and which bore his name.*

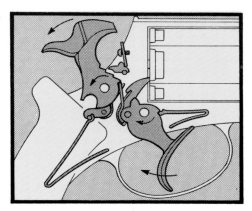

WILLIAM TRANTER

In 1853, William Tranter, a noted Birmingham gunsmith, did something to overcome the necessity for a heavy trigger pull in self-cocking revolvers by producing his so-called double-trigger model. In this revolver, a second, lower trigger—which was, strictly speaking, a cocking lever—protruded through a slot in the bottom of the trigger-guard so that it could be operated by the second finger. Pressure on the lower trigger brought the hammer back to full cock, ready for firing with a relatively light pressure on the upper trigger. When really fast action was needed, both triggers could be pressed simultaneously, giving a very high rate of fire indeed—if no great accuracy.

TRANSITIONAL REVOLVERS

At some time after about 1835 there began to appear, particularly in Great Britain, a type of revolver which has been categorized by J.N. George as "transitional"; ie, transitional between the early pepperbox and the more sophisticated percussion arms of the mid-century. Later research, by A. Taylerson and others, suggests that George dated these arms too early, and that they in fact represent little more than cheaper substitutes for the arms of Colt, Adams and others. There seem to be good grounds for accepting a later dating for transitional revolvers.

The transitional arms have a strong family resemblance both to the pepperbox and to each other. Most have radial nipples—ie, set at right angles to the line of the barrel—and many have bar hammers, often with spurs. Many have practically no frame in the modern sense of the term, the barrels being simply attached to the front end of a stout cylinder axis pin; although some do have a basic lower frame. Their construction was generally not good enough to make them sufficiently robust for service use, but they were often well made within their limitations and were probably quite adequate household de-

on the other hand, were forged from single pieces of iron. This gave great intrinsic strength, but at the added expense of employing skilled workmen.

The locks of Colt's and Adams' arms also differed. Colt's were single-action—ie, the hammer had to be drawn back manually for each shot—which slowed down the action but gave a lighter trigger pull and thus made for greater accuracy. Adams' revolvers were self-cocking; ie, they were fired simply by pressure on the trigger, which made the combless hammer rise and fall. Although this gave a heavy trigger pull, it was a decisive factor in the weapons' popularity in Great Britain, where much of the relatively limited demand for pistols came from Army officers. In those days of close-quarter fighting, officers often found themselves in hand-to-hand combat with only a light sword and, possibly, a single pistol—and what they needed above all was speed of fire. Therefore, although Adams' pistols had only five chambers and Colt's had six—hence the famous term "six-gun"—the former rapidly outsold the latter in the United Kingdom; whereupon Colt very sensibly closed his London factory and concentrated on the huge market in his own country.

fence weapons. It is not known how many were made; but so many survive that the total production must have been very large indeed.

OTHER MAKERS AND DEVELOPMENTS

Once the basic principles of the percussion revolver had been established, improvements were made quickly. So far as British revolvers were concerned, one of the most important was the general adoption of the rammer. Almost from the first, Colt had incorporated in his arms powerful rammers which securely seated slightly oversized bullets, kept the powder dry and virtually eliminated the risk of chain fire; but Adams had initially relied upon slightly oversized, tapered chambers into which bullets were forced by thumb pressure. This speeded reloading but, if the arm was jolted, entailed the risk of a bullet slipping forward and preventing the free rotation of the cylinder. Rammers were thus seen to be essential. Tranter and other makers patented several types and a considerable variety entered use. Some of the earliest could be detached from the arm and carried in the pocket of the user.

A second, very important, development was the invention of a new lock by Lieutenant Frederick Beaumont, a serving officer in the Royal Engineers. In Beaumont's lock the arm could be fired either by simple trigger pressure or by the preliminary cocking of the hammer. Patented in 1856, this double-action lock was incorporated into Adams revolvers and soon became almost standard in Great Britain and the rest of Europe—although it was many years before it achieved more than limited popularity in the United States.

Soon after the appearance of Beaumont's lock, the partnership of Deane, Adams and Deane was dissolved, but manufacture on a fairly large scale was continued by the London Armoury

Company. The superintendent of this new firm was a talented gunmaker, James Kerr, who soon produced a revolver of his own. This had a detachable, back-action lock, essentially similar to those of some sporting guns, which could easily be removed for repair by relatively unskilled mechanics who would have found it hard to strip and reassemble a more orthodox type of lock.

Many other revolvers appeared in Britain, notably those made by Webley, Lang, Daw and a number of smaller (but not necessarily inferior) makers in London, Birmingham and elsewhere. Most of these had solid frames, on the lines of Adams' original patent. An exception was the arm invented in 1858 by William Harding, who had at one time been an employee of the Deane family. His frame was in two parts, held together by a hook and a pin; but although ingenious, strong and easy to clean, it never became popular.

One slightly odd early development was the gas-seal revolver. This, as its name implies, was designed so as to prevent any escape of gas between the

front end of the chamber and the breech end of the barrel. The latter was coned and the front ends of the chambers were correspondingly opened up, a reciprocating cylinder mechanism being employed to ensure the actual seal at the moment of discharge. Revolvers of this type—many of which fall into the broad "transitional" category—were made for several years by Daw, Lang, Baker, Parker Field and others, which suggests some degree of acceptance. A few revolving rifles were also made by such British firms as Adams and Webley, but they appear to have achieved little popularity.

THE REVOLVER IN USE

Once loaded, these percussion revolvers were little if at all inferior to their modern counterparts in range, accuracy and speed of manipulation—but once the contents of the chambers had been fired away, reloading took an appreciable time. First, powder and ball had to be placed into each chamber in turn and rammed home; then caps had to be placed on each nipple. This was difficult enough, in the heat of battle, for a man

Right: *This sequence of photographs shows some of the procedures necessary to load and fire a Colt Navy percussion revolver. The hammer is first placed at half-cock and the revolver is held vertically to allow a charge of powder and a bullet (either spherical or conical) to be placed in each chamber. As the bullets are tight-fitting, it is necessary to force them down with the rammer. (Right) The lever of the rammer is released and drawn downward. (Centre left) The bullet is rammed down. Although not shown here, it was quite usual to place a blob of lubricant on top of it. This helped to keep the fouling soft and facilitated the cleaning of the revolver. (Centre right) Percussion caps are placed on the nipples: once this is done the loading process is complete. In order to fire the revolver (far right), it is now only necessary to place the hammer at full-cock and press the trigger. The re-creation of the "Old West" by enthusiasts armed either with weapons of the period or with modern replicas is now increasingly popular in many countries.*

on foot, and almost impossible for a mounted man, to whom the revolver in other ways represented a significant increase in firepower. The result, apparent during the American Civil War, was that many cavalrymen carried two or more revolvers apiece, in the hope that this would see them through the average action. Various attempts were made to produce made-up cartridges of powder and ball wrapped in some combustible material, but most of these proved too fragile to be of use on active service. Calibre, which was still generally expressed by the number of spherical balls aggregating one pound of lead, varied according to the particular needs of the individual. Military men almost invariably made stopping power a priority: they preferred an arm firing a bullet, either spherical or conical, of something approaching 0·5in (12·7mm) in diameter. At the lower end of the scale, pocket arms of 0·32in (8mm) calibre were popular; anything smaller was considered relatively ineffective because a small bullet, propelled by a small charge, lacked stopping-power.

Great Britain
COOPER PEPPERBOX PISTOL

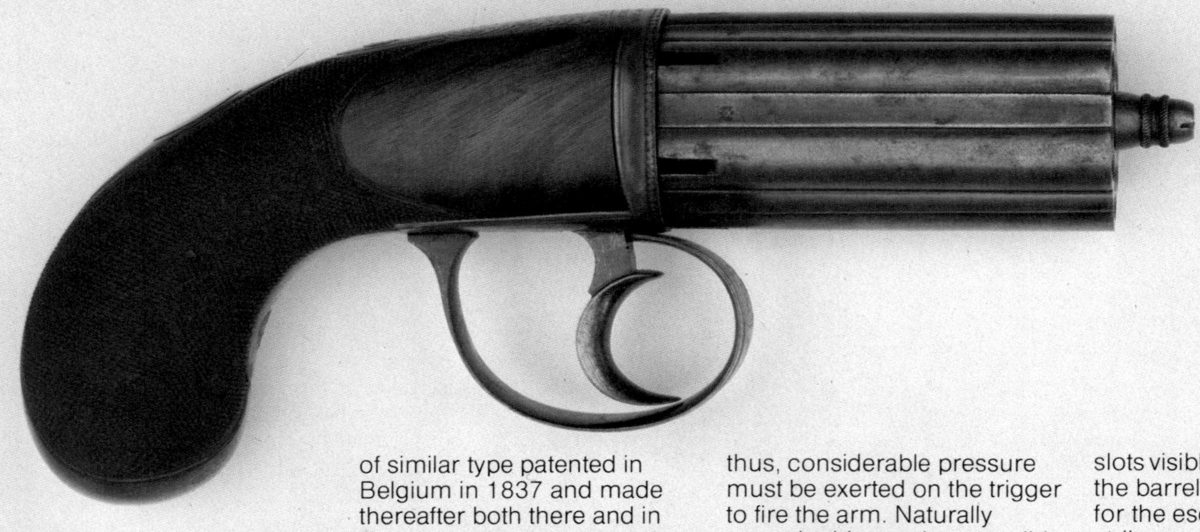

Length:	7·75" (197mm)
Weight:	17oz (·48kg)
Barrel:	2·5" (63mm)
Calibre:	·400" (10·2mm)
Rifling:	Nil
Capacity:	Six
Muz Vel:	c400 f/s (122 m/s)
Sights:	Nil

This weapon was made by the British gunsmith J. R. Cooper, who produced a large number of pepperbox pistols in the period 1840-50. Many of them were closely based on an arm of similar type patented in Belgium in 1837 and made thereafter both there and in France, under the name of Mariette.. This example, however, is of more distinctly British type. The top tang of the frame bears the inscription "J R COOPER, PATENTEE", although it is not known if it was, in fact, ever patented in England. The weapon is well, if plainly, made: its six barrels have been bored out of a solid block of metal and the grooves between the barrels bear Birmingham proof marks. The firing mechanism is internal and is of double-action only; thus, considerable pressure must be exerted on the trigger to fire the arm. Naturally enough, this requirement did not make for accuracy at anything above point-blank range. The barrels may be loaded while attached to the weapon (a separate ram-rod being provided in the case, which is not shown here), but in order to cap the nipples it is necessary to unscrew the front cap and remove the cylinder from the pistol. The nipples, which are placed in line with the axis of the barrels, are set in deep, circular recesses, in order to reduce the risk of a multiple discharge; the slots visible at the breech end of the barrels are mainly to allow for the escape of gases. As the striker comes forward to fire the top barrel, a cylinder-stop also emerges from the bottom of the standing breech and engages in the lowest slot, thus preventing any rotation of the cylinder at the moment of firing. The butt of the pistol is of chequered walnut and the top tang bears the inscription "SELF-ACTING CENTRAL FIRE REVOLVING PISTOL". The weapon, although plain, is a robust arm of good quality and is provided with a neat, baize-lined case.

United States of America
ALLEN AND THURBER PEPPERBOX

Length:	7·5 (190mm)
Weight:	23oz (·65kg)
Barrel:	3" (76mm)
Calibre:	·31" (8mm)
Rifling:	Nil
Capacity:	Six
Muz Vel:	c400 f/s (122 m/s)
Sights:	Nil

This pistol was made in Worcester, Massachusetts, by the well-known American firm of Allen and Thurber. Ethan Allen set up in business as a gunmaker with his brother-in-law in the late 1830s and thereafter made a variety of civilian arms, including rifles. He was, however, best known for his pepperbox pistols. These were for some years by far the most popular repeating arms in the United States, until they were finally displaced by the more modern percussion revolvers of Colt and others. The weapon seen here is neat, compact and of the quality traditionally associated with the firm of Allen and Thurber. Its six barrels are bored out of a single block of steel, with ribs between: two of the ribs bear the inscriptions "PATENTED 1837, CAST STEEL" and "ALLEN & THURBER WORCESTER". The subject of the patent referred to was, in fact, the double-action bar hammer mechanism. Steady pressure on the trigger causes the rear-hinged hammer (which is inscribed "ALLEN PATENT") to rise until the lifter hook disengages, allowing it to fall and strike the cap. The action of the trigger also rotates the barrel cluster by means of a pawl and ratchet. Access to the lock mechanism is gained by removing a plate on the left-hand side of the breech. The nipples, which are set at right-angles to the barrels, are covered by a close-fitting shield; an aperture to the right of the hammer nose gives access to them for recapping. Light pressure on the trigger lifts the nose clear of the nipple and allows the barrels to be rotated clockwise for recapping. The butt consists of a continuous metal strap made integrally with the body; both of its two wooden side plates, held by a screw, bear small, oval, escutcheon plates. The body of the weapon is ornamented with rather crude engraving, but the arm is otherwise strictly utilitarian. Although the combination of heavy trigger and obscured sight-line reduced the accuracy of arms of this type, they were nevertheless widely carried as pocket pistols in the United States — where, in those days, most men carried a firearm as a matter of course — and they would have proved fast and formidable arms in a close-quarter brawl. They appear to have been quite widely used even after Colt's revolver had become popular, and continued in production until about 1871.

Belgium
MARIETTE PEPPERBOX

Length: 7·25" (184mm)
Weight: 24oz (·68kg)
Barrel: 2·8" (71mm)
Calibre: ·38" (9·6mm)
Rifling: Nil
Capacity: Six
Muz Vel: c500 f/s (152 m/s)
Sights: Nil

This is an example of the Mariette-type pistol, made to a design patented in Belgium in 1837 and manufactured widely thereafter in both that country and in France. This specimen is of Belgian manufacture and bears the Liège proofmarks. It is of the orthodox design of the type, in that its barrels, instead of being bored from a single block, are screwed separately on to six chambers, into which the nipples are fixed. Each barrel has four rectangular slots at 90-degree intervals round the muzzle, to facilitate its removal with a special key, and each barrel is also numbered, as is each chamber. The cluster of barrels is screwed to a spindle on the standing breech, access to which is gained by way of the central space left in the cluster of barrels. As may be seen, the nipples are in the same axis as the barrels; this reduced the chances of a misfire and made the arm neat and compact. Pressure on the ring-trigger causes the barrels to rotate, bringing each in turn into line, and also draws back and releases the internal hammer, which strikes the nipple on the lowest barrel. There are partitions between the nipples, and in addition a further shield (visible in the photograph) rises as the hammer falls to guard completely the nipple being fired. Re-capping is achieved by pressing the trigger sufficiently to allow the barrels to be manually rotated: a small slot is exposed in the right-hand side of the frame, allowing the caps to be slid into place. The butt is of ebonised plates, on a strap inscribed "MARIETTE BREVETTE".

Great Britain
TURNER PEPPERBOX

Length: 9·25" (235mm)
Weight: 32oz (·91kg)
Barrel: 3·5" (89mm)
Calibre: ·476" (12·1mm)
Rifling: Nil
Capacity: Six
Muz Vel: c500 f/s (152 m/s)
Sights: Nil

This weapon was made by Thomas Turner of Reading, a well-known provincial gun-maker of the 19th century, and is of excellent construction. Its six smooth-bored barrels are drilled from a single block of steel in the usual manner; but somewhat unusually, each is numbered at the breech end, the ribs between them being stamped alternately with either a view mark or a proof mark. The nipples are at right angles to the axis of the barrels and, as may be seen, there are no partitions between them. This must have increased the risk of the barrels chain-firing, an event likely to be disconcerting to the firer—and even more so to his proposed victim. The breech also incorporates a nipple shield to prevent the percussion caps from being brushed or shaken off; however, by canalizing the flash from the cap, this must also have contributed to the risk of more than one barrel firing from a single cap. The bar hammer is of standard double-action type and requires considerable pressure on the trigger to operate it. The trigger action also activates a pawl and ratchet to rotate the barrels. These rotate on an axis pin screwed into the standing breech; they are held in place on the pin by an engraved, brass-headed screw which fits flush with the muzzles. Access to the nipples is gained through an aperture in the flash shield just to the right of the hammer, and slight pressure on the trigger raises the hammer nose from the nipples sufficiently to rotate the barrels manually in anti-clockwise direction. The hammer and frame are both lightly engraved, with the inscription "THOMAS TURNER, READING" in an oval on the left-hand side. Rather unusually, this weapon is fitted with a sliding safety catch (visible behind the hammer). When this is drawn back, it locks the hammer in the down position; it can be easily released by thumb pressure. The finely-chequered walnut butt is held between two tangs. It has a small, shield-shaped, escutcheon plate just behind the top tang screw and is fitted with a spring-lidded cap compartment. This is an unusually large arm: possibly a naval boarding pistol.

COGSWELL PEPPERBOX PISTOL

This photograph gives some indication of what it must have been like to face a pepperbox pistol; obviously, it would have been a frightening enough sight. Even worse than the prospect of six single shots would have been the possibility of being on the receiving end of a multiple discharge.

Length: 7·6" (193mm)
Weight: 28oz (·79kg)
Barrel: 3" (76mm)
Calibre: ·476" (12·1mm)
Rifling: Nil
Capacity: Six
Muz Vel: c500 f/s (152 m/s)
Sights: Nil

This pistol may be considered representative of arms of its type made in London for the upper end of the market. It was made, probably in about 1850, by B. Cogswell, a well-known London gunmaker, and is a well-finished arm of good quality. Its six smooth-bored barrels have been drilled out of a single steel cylinder, with the intervals between the barrels machined out into plain but elegant grooves. Unusually — and perhaps somewhat unnecessarily — each barrel is neatly numbered at the breech end, while the grooves are stamped alternately with view marks and proof marks. The chambers are in a cylinder of somewhat smaller diameter than the barrel cluster, and the nipples are screwed into the chambers at right-angles to the axis of the barrels. There are no partitions between the nipples, and this must have increased the risk of multiple discharge; a risk made greater by the fact that such pistols usually employed especially sensitive caps to compensate for the relatively weak blow struck by the type of hammer fitted. Unlike a revolver cylinder, there was, of course, no obstruction in front of any of the muzzles;

thus, multiple fire exposed the user to no danger — except, perhaps, the shock of a massive discharge. The breech mechanism is of German silver and is discreetly engraved in the English style. The left-hand side bears the inscription "B. COGSWELL, 224 STRAND, LONDON", while on the right-hand side are the words "IMPROVED REVOLVING PISTOL". The breech includes a nipple shield: the advantages and disadvantages of such a provision roughly balance out, for the protection afforded to the caps was offset by the increased risk of several barrels going off together. The butt consists of a continuous strap of German silver, with walnut plates held in position by a screw. The action is of typical bar-hammer type with a normal trigger and guard; as is usual with such an action, considerable pressure is required to fire a shot. This, together with the difficulty imposed on taking aim by the position of the hammer, made all arms of this type inaccurate, except at close quarters — when their rapidity of discharge made them formidable weapons indeed. At this stage it will be of value to summarize the development and progress of the pepperbox pistol, as typified by the illustrations on these and the two preceding pages. Repeating weapons with a cylinder or a cluster of revolving barrels are almost as old as hand-held firearms, although technical problems naturally limited their scale of manufacture. All the early arms were, of course, flintlocks, with the problems inseparable from their kind.

Most were manually rotated, although a few were turned by mechanical means. As in other aspects of the development of firearms, progress was at first slow; but the general introduction of the percussion cap in the first quarter of the 19th century led to a sudden acceleration of development — and, indeed, to firearms as we know them today. Some early percussion arms had four, or sometimes even six, barrels which could be rotated manually so as to be brought in pairs under two hammers; from that stage, it was a relatively short step to reduce the system to one single-action hammer and a mechanically-rotated barrel cluster, the latter usually worked by means of a simple pawl and ratchet. Because such improvements were rarely patented, their dates of introduction cannot be stated with certainty: however, we

shall not be far wrong if we date the system described above to 1836-37. Double-action locks with bar hammers soon made their appearance, as did partitions between nipples, but there the mainstream development stopped. A few pistols were made with up to 24 barrels, as well as some with bayonets, but these were freaks. The pepperbox was eventually superseded by the true revolver, probably towards the end of the 1850s; although the American firm of Ethan Allen and Co apparently continued to make a few up to 1870. They had been especially popular in the United States where, presumably, some of their older users remained loyal to them. A very few large-calibre pepperboxes are found; they were often for naval use and thus, like other service weapons, were usually, but not invariably, fitted with belt hooks.

France
MARIETTE FOUR-BARRELLED PEPPERBOX

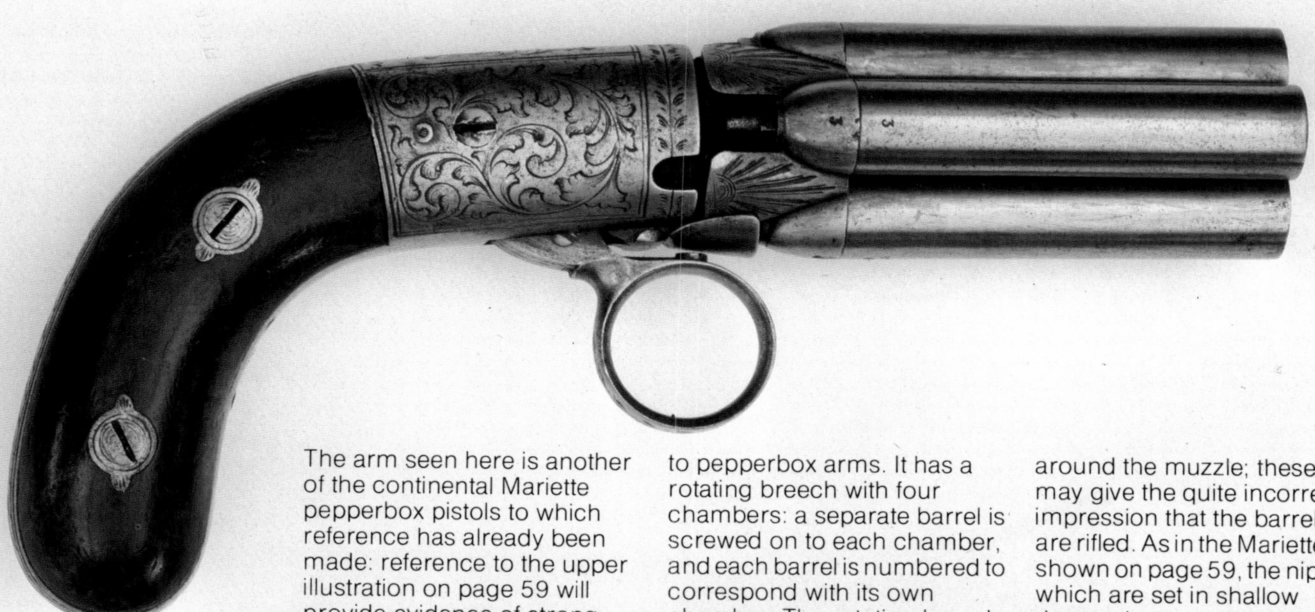

Length:	7" (178mm)
Weight:	18oz (·51kg)
Barrel:	2·5" (63mm)
Calibre:	·35" (9mm)
Rifling:	Nil
Capacity:	Four
Muz Vel:	c450 f/s (137 m/s)
Sights:	Nil

The arm seen here is another of the continental Mariette pepperbox pistols to which reference has already been made: reference to the upper illustration on page 59 will provide evidence of strong basic resemblance between the two weapons. This particular arm, which has four barrels, is one of the immediate successors to the four-barrelled, double-locked, turn-over pistols described in the section devoted to percussion pistols (see page 47); but with additional refinements peculiar to pepperbox arms. It has a rotating breech with four chambers: a separate barrel is screwed on to each chamber, and each barrel is numbered to correspond with its own chamber. The rotating breech is screwed on to a spindle in the standing breech, to which access may be gained—with some difficulty—by way of the narrow space between the barrels, which very nearly touch each other. The barrels may be removed individually by means of a squared key, which fits into four slots equally spaced around the muzzle; these slots may give the quite incorrect impression that the barrels are rifled. As in the Mariette arm shown on page 59, the nipples, which are set in shallow depressions, are in prolongation of the axis of the barrels; they may be capped by way of the U-shaped aperture seen on the right-hand side of the frame. The ring-trigger rotates the barrels and activates the hammer, and also incorporates the usual hood which masks completely the nipple which is actually being fired.

Great Britain
COOPER PEPPERBOX PISTOL

Length:	7·75" (197mm)
Weight:	26oz (·74kg)
Barrel:	3" (76mm)
Calibre:	·400" (10·2mm)
Rifling:	Nil
Capacity:	Six
Muz Vel:	c500 f/s (152 m/s)
Sights:	Nil

This is another pepperbox pistol by J. R. Cooper, a specimen of whose work has already been illustrated on page 58 (above). Cooper was well known for the production of arms of this type; but although he seems to have produced a number of good-quality arms of his own design—with adequate triggers and guards and often handsomely cased like the pistol shown on page 58—most of his pistols were more or less closely based on the design of the Mariette range of arms, patented in Belgium in 1837 and widely manufactured thereafter both in that country and in France. In the arm seen here, the left-hand side of the breech bears a scroll containing the inscription "J R COOPER, PATENT", although it is not certain that it was, in fact, so patented. The barrels are bored out of a solid cylinder of steel, with shallow grooves between each; each groove bears a Birmingham proof mark. The nipples are in the same axis as that of the barrels and have flat, rectangular shields between them to reduce the risk of multiple fire. A V-shaped groove on the right-hand side of the frame allows the caps to be placed in position. Pressure on the ring-trigger draws back an under-hammer—basically similar to a normal hammer, but combless and working upside down—and a spring on the trigger releases the hammer at the right moment, allowing it to strike the cap on the lowest nipple. The butt consists of a continuous strap, with a pair of side plates held in position by a single screw. The weapon is lightly engraved. This pistol may be said to be reasonably typical of most of Cooper's Mariette-type arms: there is little elegance about it and the finish may fairly be described as rough. Nevertheless, it is robustly made and mechanically reliable, and provides a fair example of a weapon produced for sale at the lower end of the British market.

61

TRANSITIONAL REVOLVERS

Length:	11·5" (292mm)
Weight:	35oz (·99kg)
Barrel:	5·6" (142mm)
Calibre:	·44" (11·2mm)
Rifling:	14 groove, r/hand
Capacity:	Six
Muz Vel:	c500 f/s (152 m/s)
Sights:	Fixed

Reference has been made to arms of the "transitional" type in the introduction to this section (see page 55) and, as was stressed there, there remains some element of doubt as to the earliest date at which the weapons thus classified were made. Colt's new revolvers must have been known to gunsmiths, if not to the general public, by the mid-1840s, and it is possible that a few so-called transitional arms were manufactured at that time, using components made for pepperbox pistols, to which transitional arms bear a fairly strong family resemblance. It is probable, however, that most were made in the early 1850s, after the percussion revolver had become generally known. The revolvers shown here were made by T. K. Baker of London and are close to being a pair, although, as may be seen, the upper one has been cleaned bright at some time, while the lower arm retains most of its original blue. A somewhat old-fashioned look is given to the rifled barrels by the fact that they are octagonal for just over half their length. The cylinders are deeply rebated at the rear to give a seating for the nipples which, in orthodox pepperbox fashion, have no partitions between them; a factor increasing the risk of a chain-fire discharge. The rear faces of the cylinders are cut to form a ratchet, with a further, outer row of six slots for the cylinder stops. On each weapon, the hammer, although similar in some respects to the bar-type hammers encountered on some of the earlier pepperbox pistols, is in fact of single-action type and must be cocked for each shot; hence the provision of the long hammer spur. The action of placing the hammer at half-cock causes the cylinder to make a very slight rotation in an anti-clockwise direction; pulling the hammer back to full cock brings the next chamber into line and also locks the cylinder in such a position that the top chamber is in line with the barrel. Although positioned so as to strike centrally on top of the frame, the hammer is slightly angled, so that when the arm is cocked the foresight can be aligned with a shallow V backsight on the hammer itself. The frames of these revolvers are of German silver and incorporate nipple shields; the butt-plates, which are held by a single screw, are of walnut. Arms of this type had three basic weaknesses as compared with the later percussion revolvers: the nipples are placed at right-angles instead of straight into the charge, which increased the chance of mis-fires; there are no shields between the nipples; and the method by which the barrel is held in place, screwed to the axis pin without any secondary brace to the frame, is unsatisfactory. In the latter case, although the pin is robust and is firmly seated at the breech end, there must be a tendency for the barrel to work loose, which would lead to loss of power, to inaccuracy and, possibly, to real danger to the firer if the chamber and barrel are actually out of alignment at the moment of firing. The arms' far from robust qualities probably led to their rejection for service use: most officers preferred to retain their comparatively old-fashioned double-barrelled pieces — or purchase one of the new revolvers produced by Colt or Adams. (The latter were both widely used in the Crimean War and the Indian Mutiny.) Revolvers of the kind seen here were, however, probably quite adequate self-defence weapons for house-holders and travellers; certainly, the large number still in existence suggests that they were originally turned out in very considerable quantities. However, in civilian use these arms would probably have spent much of their lives in a convenient drawer, being used rarely if at all; this may account for the surprisingly large number of extant examples of arms which were only manufactured for a relatively short period during the 19th century.

TRANSITIONAL REVOLVERS WITH BAYONETS

Length: 12" (305mm)
Weight: 32oz (·91kg)
Barrel: 5·8" (147mm)
Calibre: ·42" (10·7mm)
Rifling: 9 groove, r/hand
Capacity: Six
Muz Vel: c500 f/s (152 m/s)
Sights: Fixed

These are both interesting arms of their type and together show the lines along which the transitional revolver developed in the mid-19th century. The lower arm is almost certainly of slightly earlier date, and a reference back to the pepperbox pistols — particularly the lower example on page 61 — will show very clearly the influence which those earlier arms had on later developments. The lower revolver here has an octagonal, blued barrel and the top flat bears the inscription "IMPROVED REVOLVER", but there is no indication as to its maker. The cylinder is of orthodox type and, from its general appearance, could well be a cut-down cluster of pepperbox barrels (although it is not suggested that this is the case). The nipples are at right-angles to the axis of their chambers and there are no partitions. The cylinder bears Birmingham proof marks, which at least indicates its origins. The lock is of double-action type with bar hammer and orthodox trigger; as is the case with most arms of its kind, considerable pressure is required to operate the trigger. The frame, including the shield, is of German silver, quite nicely engraved; the butt, with side plates of some hard, black composition, is well-shaped but somewhat too small for a normal hand. The weapon is fitted with a folding bayonet, details of which are shown in the inset below. This is a fairly well-made and well-finished weapon which suffers from the usual defects of its type: notably the angle of the nipples and the lack of partitions between them; and, perhaps, more importantly, the fact that the barrel is attached only to the axis pin, without any additional bracing. It has the further defect that the rising hammer completely obscures the line of sight, although this was probably not a serious disadvantage in the close-quarter action for which the weapon was presumably intended. The upper revolver is similar in its main essentials to the arm already described; it, too, has a folding bayonet, part of which is just visible above the barrel. It will, however, be seen that there is a strong projection below the cylinder to which a corresponding projection below the barrel is firmly screwed, thus making a very considerable contribution to the strength and rigidity of the weapon. The frame of this revolver is made of iron and the butt is of a more handy size than that of the lower arm; thus, all in all, in spite of its general similarity to the lower one, it is in most respects a more robust and more serviceable arm. The exact function of arms like these cannot be defined with certainty: as has been stated, they were largely intended to be for self-defence; but the presence of the bayonets (although of little larger size than pen-knives) suggests at least some degree of offensive intent. The upper of the two may possibly have been of the naval type often referred to as boarding pistols; but this is mere speculation. (The data refer to the upper weapon of the two. It is 0·75in (19mm) longer in the barrel than the lower example, but otherwise of similar dimensions.)

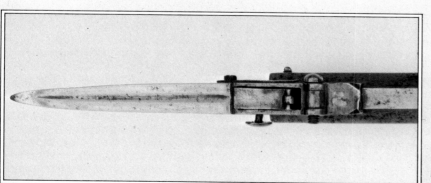

This photograph shows the folding bayonet in place. In order to fix it, the stud near the muzzle was pressed; then a helical spring flicked the blade into the fixed position. The blade, although short, would have been quite sufficient to inflict a serious or even mortal wound.

BAKER GAS-SEAL REVOLVER

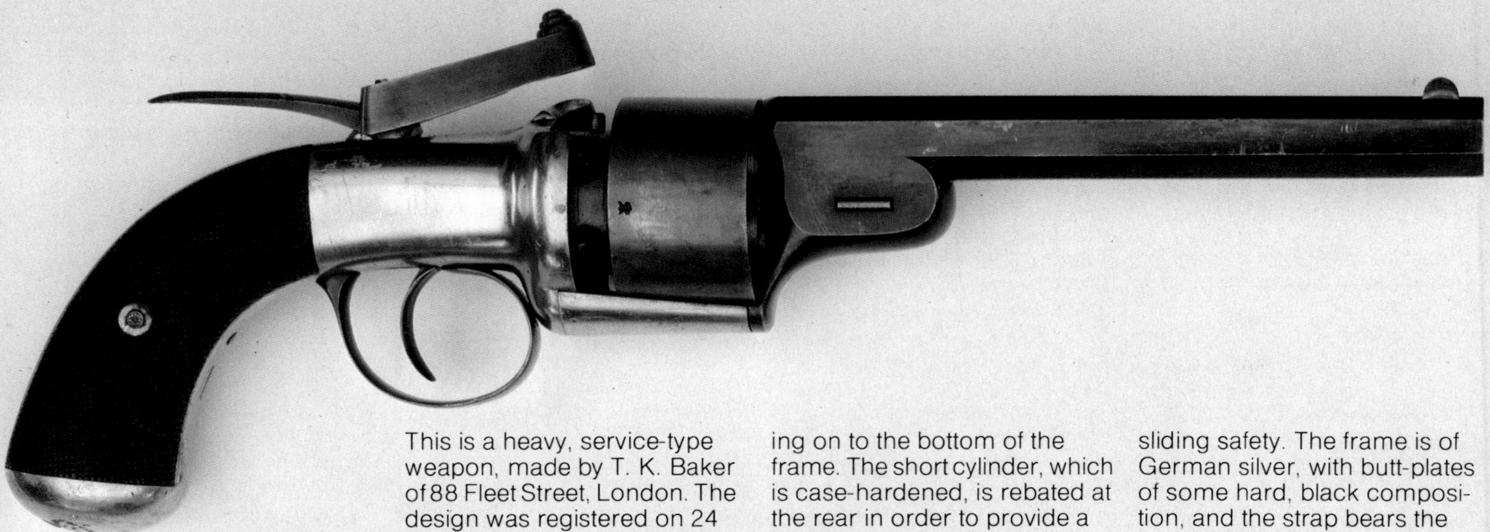

Length:	13·25" (337mm)
Weight:	49oz (1·39kg)
Barrel:	6·5" (165mm)
Calibre:	·577" (14·6mm)
Rifling:	16 groove, r/hand
Capacity:	Six
Muz Vel:	c600 f/s (183 m/s)
Sights:	Fixed

This is a heavy, service-type weapon, made by T. K. Baker of 88 Fleet Street, London. The design was registered on 24 April 1852, nearly one year after the Great Exhibition had made the revolvers of Colt and Adams well known in England. This arm has an octagonal, blued barrel with multi-grooved rifling. The barrel is held rigidly to the weapon by the combination of a key through the axis pin and a lower extension locking on to the bottom of the frame. The short cylinder, which is case-hardened, is rebated at the rear in order to provide a seating for the nipples, which are at right-angles to the barrel axis and without partitions. The hammer is of the bar variety already noted, but it is of single-action type, with a long, rearward spur for cocking; it is slightly angled, so that the sights can be aligned when it is cocked and is fitted with a sliding safety. The frame is of German silver, with butt-plates of some hard, black composition, and the strap bears the number "2151". The pistol is of the type known as gas-seal, in which the cylinder reciprocates so that each chamber is locked securely to the barrel at the time of firing. The system is described in full in the caption for the Lang gas-seal revolver which is illustrated on the facing page (below).

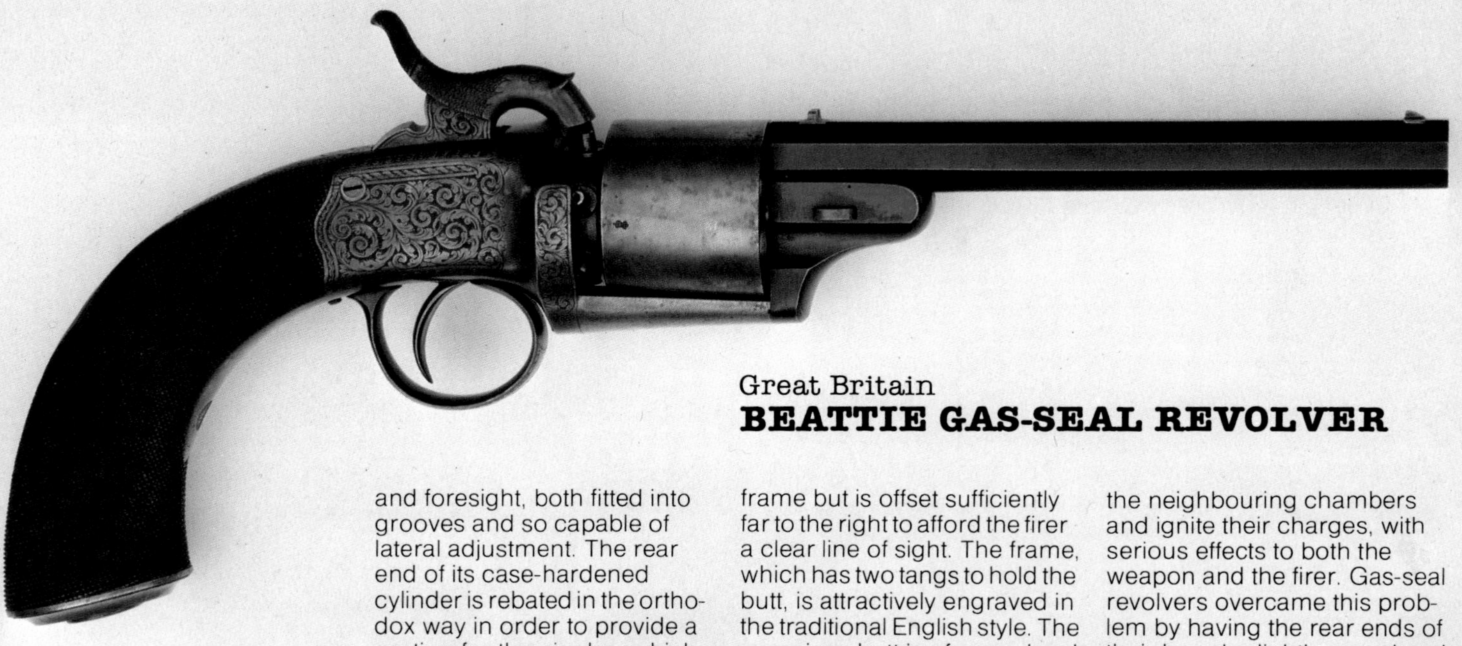

Great Britain
BEATTIE GAS-SEAL REVOLVER

Length:	13" (330mm)
Weight:	40oz (1·13kg)
Barrel:	6·25" (159mm)
Calibre:	·42" (10·7mm)
Rifling:	30 groove, r/hand
Capacity:	Six
Muz Vel:	c600 f/s (183 m/s)
Sights:	Fixed

This gas-seal revolver was made by Beattie of London. The browned barrel is octagonal and the top flat is engraved with the inscription "J. BEATTIE, 205 REGENT STREET, LONDON"; it has multi-grooved rifling and is fitted with back- and foresight, both fitted into grooves and so capable of lateral adjustment. The rear end of its case-hardened cylinder is rebated in the orthodox way in order to provide a seating for the nipples, which are, as usual, as right-angles to the axis of the chambers and are not separated by partitions. Each chamber bears a proof mark. The barrel is securely wedged to the axis pin by means of a flat, sliding key with a retaining screw; it also has an extension which engages with the lower part of the frame to give a secure, rigid join. The hammer is of single-action type; thus, it is necessary to re-cock it for each shot, an action which also rotates the cylinder by means of a pawl and ratchet. The hammer, which is of the shape commonly found on earlier single- or double-barrelled percussion arms, is mounted on top of the frame but is offset sufficiently far to the right to afford the firer a clear line of sight. The frame, which has two tangs to hold the butt, is attractively engraved in the traditional English style. The one-piece butt is of some hard composition, finely chequered, and the metal butt-cap contains a cap compartment with a spring-loaded lid. However, the most interesting feature of this weapon is the fact that it is (like all those illustrated on this spread) of the type usually known as "gas-seal". One of the defects of early percussion revolvers was the absence of a rammer, which meant that the bullets could be no more than finger-tight in the cylinders. In consequence, that part of the burning gases which was inevitably deflected downwards, into the gap between the face of the cylinder and the end of the barrel, was sometimes liable to flash past the bullets in the neighbouring chambers and ignite their charges, with serious effects to both the weapon and the firer. Gas-seal revolvers overcame this problem by having the rear ends of their barrels slightly coned and the front ends of their chambers correspondingly opened out, so that the one fitted closely over the other; a reciprocating device was, of course, essential, to impart the necessary backward and forward movement to the cylinder in addition to its normal rotation. (The general principles on which this system works are described in the caption for the Lang revolver on the facing page.) The revolver seen here is a robust and well-made arm of service calibre. Like the Baker revolver (above) it was probably made in the mid-1850s, or even later. This particular example has a baize-lined case with a variety of accessories.

Great Britain
PARKER FIELD GAS-SEAL REVOLVER

Length:	12·5" (317mm)
Weight:	38oz (1·08kg)
Barrel:	6" (152mm)
Calibre:	·42" (10·7mm)
Rifling:	24 groove, r/hand
Capacity:	Six
Muz Vel:	c600 f/s (183 m/s)
Sights:	Fixed

This is another example of a gas-seal revolver, bearing the maker's inscription of "PARKER FIELD AND SONS, 233 HIGH HOLBORN, LONDON", a firm well known for the production of weapons of this type. As might be expected, it is a very well-made and finished arm, similar in many respects to the others illustrated on this spread. It has the usual multi-grooved, blued barrel, firmly wedged to the lower edge of the frame and fitted with laterally adjustable sights. The case-hardened cylinder is, however, fluted, giving the weapon a distinctive appearance, and there are flat shields between the nipples to eliminate the risk of multiple discharge. The hammer has the customary three rearward positions, with a safety which locks it securely in the first; the system of rotation and reciprocation is the same as that of the Beattie revolver shown on the facing page (below). The major point of interest in this arm is the existence of a compound rammer below the barrel: when the long arm is pulled down, a horizontal rammer housed in the cylinder below the axis key exerts powerful pressure on the bullet and ensures that it is seated very securely in the chamber. This refinement goes some way toward making the application of the gas-seal principle unnecessary.

Great Britain
LANG GAS-SEAL REVOLVER

Length:	11" (279mm)
Weight:	32oz (·91kg)
Barrel:	4·75" (121mm)
Calibre:	·42" (10·7mm)
Rifling:	24 groove, r/hand
Capacity:	Six
Muz Vel:	c600 f/s (183 m/s)
Sights:	Fixed

As has already been noted, most British gas-seal revolvers bear a strong resemblance to each other; thus, it is almost certain that they have a common ancestry. It is now fairly generally agreed that arms of this type were not developed until after the Great Exhibition of 1851, which gave a considerable impetus to revolving arms of all kinds— and it is possible that the arm seen here may have been the prototype for, although undated, it is certainly early. It has an octagonal, blued, multi-grooved barrel, bearing the inscription "J LANG 22 COCKSPUR ST, LONDON", and is fitted with laterally adjustable sights, the hammer being offset a little to the right in order to facilitate taking aim. The barrel is keyed to the axis pin and has the usual projection engaging with the lower edge of the frame, which makes a good and rigid joint. The cylinder, which is case-hardened, is rebated at the rear, the different diameters being joined by a coned section containing circular depressions for the nipples, which are inclined slightly backwards from the vertical. The frame is of case-hardened iron and is lightly engraved; it has two tangs to hold the finely-chequered butt with the usual cap compartment in the base. The hammer, which is without a safety catch, is slightly unusual in that it has only two rearward positions instead of three: the usual first position, which holds the nose just clear of the caps, is omitted. The action of drawing the hammer back to half-cock allows an internal spring to force the cylinder back sufficiently for the top chamber to clear the barrel cone; while drawing the hammer back to full-cock rotates the cylinder by the necessary amount to bring the next chamber into line. As the trigger falls, a cylindrical metal plug or ram is thrust forward from the standing breech so as to hold the cylinder securely locked to the barrel at the moment of firing. As in many gas-seal weapons, the chambers are somewhat larger in calibre than the bore. This ensures that a ball which loads easily into the chamber is still a good and gas-tight fit in the barrel, which, in conjunction with the gas-seal, gives a considerable improvement to both the range and velocity of the weapon. This is in every sense a sound and reliable arm by a maker whose products we have already seen (pages 50-51); it is plain and almost unadorned, as becomes a practical weapon. Revolvers of this type continued to be made well into the 1860s, at a time when the more modern examples produced by Colt, Adams and others might have been expected to have supplanted them. What is, perhaps, even more surprising is the fact that a much more modern cartridge revolver, the Belgian Nagant which came into use in about 1895, incorporated the same gas-seal principle—and again, it appears, with marked effect on the arm's range and velocity.

KUFAHL'S NEEDLE-FIRE REVOLVER

The needle-fire revolver partially stripped, with the cylinder and axis pin removed. The pawl which engages the ratchet at the rear of the cylinder, causing the whole to rotate, may be seen protruding from the face of the standing breech. The needle would normally be retracted (as explained in the main caption), but it has been placed in the forward position to give an indication of the manner in which the weapon works.

Length:	9·6" (244mm)
Weight:	22oz (·62kg)
Barrel:	3·2" (81mm)
Calibre:	·300" (7·62mm)
Rifling:	5 groove, l/hand
Capacity:	Six
Muz Vel:	c500 f/s (152 m/s)
Sights:	Fixed

A needle-fire weapon is one firing a consumable cartridge in which the cap is immediately behind the bullet; this necessitates a long, needle-like striker which will pierce the base of the cartridge and then pass through the powder charge in order to reach the cap. The earliest of these weapons, a breech-loading rifle, was developed by Johann Nikolaus von Dreyse as early as 1838. It was in many ways an inefficient weapon, but the mere fact that it was a breech-loader, however defective, made it a great asset to Prussia, which was soon to become a

major power in Europe. In 1852, G. L. Kufahl patented in Britain a revolver which worked on very similar principles, but no British maker seemed to be at all interested in it. Kufahl therefore offered it to Franz von Dreyse, son of the inventor of the original needle-gun, who accepted the revolver and put it into production, probably in about 1854, and apparently continued to make it until 1880, long after the development and general introduction of efficient centre-fire metallic cartridges. Kufahl's revolver is also believed to have been made elsewhere on the continent. The specimen seen here has a barrel and frame made out of a single piece of iron, although the top strap, across the cylinder, has been welded on separately. The octagonal barrel is rifled and has a noticeably swamped muzzle. It is fitted with a laterally adjustable foresight; the backsight consists of

a V-notch in the raised part at the rear of the top strap. The butt is a single piece of wood, partially chequered, and is held in place by a screw through the lower tang. The rear trigger-guard is also hooked into this tang, with its front end held in place by a screw. The cylinder is not bored through: instead, there is a small hole at the rear of each chamber to allow the needle to reach the front-loaded consumable cartridge. The cylinder axis pin can be removed by turning it through 90° and drawing it out from the front; a small spring stud on the left side of the frame holds it in place to avoid this process being carried out accidentally. Steady pressure on the trigger first forces the bolt forward and rotates and locks the cylinder; then it allows the needle-holder and needle to go forward and fire the cartridge. Once the trigger is released, the needle

and holder are automatically retracted, thus allowing the cylinder to rotate in readiness for the next shot. The pistol, which is well made and finished, bears the inscription "Fv. V. Dreyse Sommerda" on the top strap. It is numbered "12620" on the left side of the frame; the right side bears the inscription "Cal 0·30" (visible in the photograph), which suggests that this arm was made for the British or American market. An interesting feature of this pistol — although, in view of its date, coincidental — is that it resembles some later revolvers, made specifically to fire self-contained cartridges, at the time when the Rollin-White patent for revolvers with bored-through cylinders was held by the firm of Smith and Wesson. The patent did not expire until 1869. After that date the field was wide open to any maker, and metallic cartridge revolvers appeared in great numbers.

United States of America
TAPE-PRIMER REVOLVERS

Length:	10.5" (267mm)
Weight:	24oz (·68kg)
Barrel:	6" (152mm)
Calibre:	·32" (8·1mm)
Rifling:	7 groove, l/hand
Capacity:	Six
Muz Vel:	c550 f/s (168 m/s)
Sights:	Fixed

In 1851, Colt sued the Massachusetts Arms Company for producing revolvers with mechanically-rotated cylinders in contravention of a patent he had taken out earlier. This event is dealt with at greater length in the caption below; here, it need only be said that the weapon illustrated is one of the modified versions of the revolvers in question, made in the interval between the court case and the expiry of Colt's patent. The barrel of this weapon, which is rifled, is attached to the top of the standing breech by a hinged strap which permits it to be raised to an angle of about 45° in order to remove the cylinder. The latter is mounted on a stout axis pin which protrudes slightly more than 1in (25·4mm) beyond the front face of the cylinder; the object of this extension is to provide a firm locking point for a hook which pivots round the breech end of the barrel, a fitting clearly visible in the illustration. There is a small retaining spring on the end of the axis pin to prevent it being released accidentally. The lock is fitted with a tape-primer (also described in the caption below), which makes possible the use of a single nipple only: the flash is transmitted to the charge by means of a small hole at the rear of each chamber. When the cylinder stop pin (visible in front of the trigger) is pushed, the cylinder may be rotated manually.

Length:	6·6" (168mm)
Weight:	10oz (·28kg)
Barrel:	3" (76mm)
Calibre:	·28" (7·1mm)
Rifling:	7 groove, l/hand
Capacity:	Six
Muz Vel:	c500 f/s (152 m/s)
Sights:	Fixed

The tape primer, which resembled the rolls of caps still used in children's toy pistols, was fitted into the circular depression and its end was fed out over the toothed wheel. The act of cocking the action rotated the wheel and pushed the next cap over the nipple. The fall of the hammer had a sharp enough impact to cut off the surplus paper.

The popularity of Colt's percussion revolvers naturally led to attempts by many manufacturers in the United States and elsewhere to circumvent the patents under which Colt's arms were made. One such manufacturer was the Massachusetts Arms Company (originally the Ames Manufacturing Company) of Chicopee Falls, which was sued by Colt in 1851 for contravention of his patent in respect of a mechanically-revolving cylinder. The Company pleaded that the revolver in question, originally designed by Wesson and Leavitt, made use of a system of bevel gears rather than a pawl and ratchet to rotate the cylinder, and that it was, therefore, not bound by the patent referred to. However, the court found against the Company, which had to pay heavy damages to Colt and also, of course, was forced to cease the manufacture of these particular arms until Colt's patent expired in 1857. The small pocket revolver seen here is one of the pistols modified so as not to contravene the patent. it has several interesting features. The rear end of the top strap, which is integral with the barrel, is hinged to the standing breech in such a way that it can be turned upwards through about 45°, thus allowing the cylinder to be removed by pulling it forward off its axis pin. The length of this is such that, when the cylinder is fully home, about 1in (25·4mm) protrudes beyond its front face; this extension serves as a peg on which is fixed a hook attached to the breech end of the barrel by means of a collar. The hook is held in place by a small press-stud (just visible in front of it, on the lower side of the axis pin). A single nipple is screwed into the top of the breech at such an angle that it is exactly aligned with the vent leading into the rear of each chamber. The use of only one nipple was made possible by the incorporation of a device known as a tape-primer (details are given in the inset).

United States of America
COLT DRAGOON MODEL 1849

Length: 13.5" (343mm)
Weight: 68oz (1.93kg)
Barrel: 7.5" (190mm)
Calibre: .44" (11.2mm)
Rifling: 7 groove, l/hand
Capacity: Six
Muz Vel: c850 f/s (259 m/s)
Sights: Fixed

A brief account of the activities of Samuel Colt is given in the introductory essay to this section, so it is not necessary to refer to them again in detail. The earliest versions of the unusually heavy arm seen here were the Walker or Witneyville-Walker models, which appeared as a result of the increased demand for arms caused by the Mexican War of 1846. These were followed by the Dragoon series, so called because the weapons were primarily used to arm cavalry of that description. This particular specimen is the Colt Dragoon, Model 1849 (although it should be noted that it has the square-backed trigger-guard not often found at such a late date). It has a round barrel with a foresight; the backsight is incorporated into the top of the hammer. The barrel is keyed to the very robust axis pin and is further supported by a solid lug butted to the lower frame. Below the barrel is the arm's very powerful compound rammer, which forced the bullets into the chambers so tightly that neither damp nor the flash from previous shots could enter. This weapon has been over-cleaned, but traces of the engraving showing a Red Indian combat scene remain on the cylinder. The trigger-guard and butt-straps are of brass, and the butt has walnut sideplates. The weapon is numbered 5818; the barrel lug bears the inscription "ADDRESS SAML COLT NEW YORK CITY"; and the frame is marked "PATENT US".

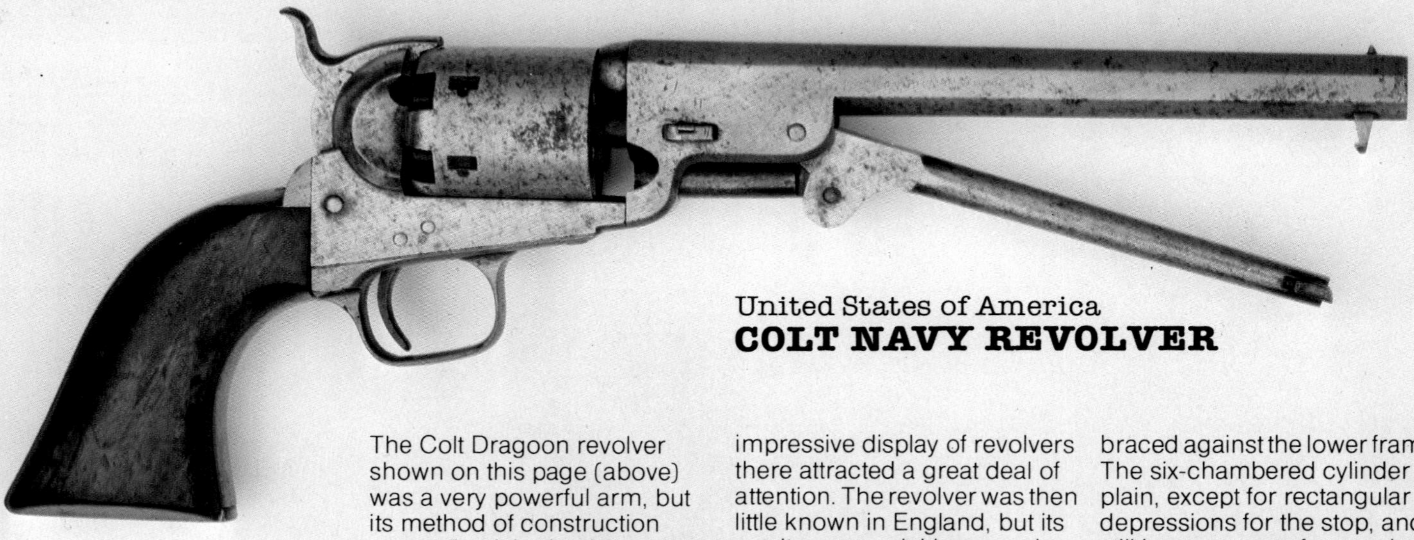

United States of America
COLT NAVY REVOLVER

Length: 12.9" (328mm)
Weight: 39oz (1.1kg)
Barrel: 7.5" (190mm)
Calibre: .36" (9.1mm)
Rifling: 7 groove, r/hand
Capacity: Six
Muz Vel: c700 f/s (213 m/s)
Sights: Fixed

The Colt Dragoon revolver shown on this page (above) was a very powerful arm, but its method of construction meant that it had to be a massive weapon, of dimensions and weight which made it unsuitable as an arm for a man on foot or for a civilian. The next size down was the one illustrated here: the Navy revolver, first introduced in 1851, which was in every respect a more manageable arm than the Dragoon and which very soon became extremely popular. Colt, having begun production at his new factory, decided that the time had come to aim at exporting on a large scale. The Great Exhibition held in London in 1851 provided him with an excellent opportunity for publicity, and his very impressive display of revolvers there attracted a great deal of attention. The revolver was then little known in England, but its merits were quickly appreciated. There were, in addition, one or two excellent British-made arms of similar type on view at the Exhibition, notably the Adams revolver; but these were largely hand-made prototypes and there was little immediate chance of their being made in large numbers, whereas Colt was ready to go into production. The revolver illustrated is of broadly similar type to the Dragoon, although, of course, smaller. It has an octagonal barrel with a bead foresight; the barrel is secured to the frame by means of a wedge through the very stout cylinder axis pin and is firmly braced against the lower frame. The six-chambered cylinder is plain, except for rectangular depressions for the stop, and still bears traces of engraving showing a naval engagement. The revolver has a hemispherical standing breech, in which a depression is located on the right-hand side so as to allow access to the nipples. The revolver was made in Colt's London factory, which was in operation in 1853-57, and is stamped "ADDRESS COL COLT LONDON" on the top barrel flat. Colt Navy revolvers were initially popular with British officers, but it was soon found that although very accurate to long ranges they lacked stopping power against the powerfully-built enemies encountered in colonial wars.

United States of America
REMINGTON ARMY MODEL 1863

Length:	13·75" (349mm)
Weight:	44oz (1·25kg)
Barrel:	8" (203mm)
Calibre:	·44" (11·2mm)
Rifling:	5 groove, r/hand
Capacity:	Six
Muz Vel:	c700 f/s (213 m/s)
Sights:	Fixed

Eliphalet Remington was originally a blacksmith but turned to gun-making fairly early in his career. He at first specialized in military rifles and soon gained an enviable reputation for the quality of the arms he produced. By 1857, he had begun to make a few pocket revolvers to a design made by F. Beals, but it was not until the outbreak of the American Civil War that he began to produce service revolvers in considerable quantity. The example illustrated is the improved Army Model of 1863; it was a fine arm in its day, perhaps its major feature being its solid frame, which gave it great rigidity. It has an octagonal barrel (the top flat inscribed "PATENTED SEP 14 1850 E REMINGTON AND SONS ILLION NEW YORK USA NEW MODEL") which screws into the frame, and a plain, six-shot cylinder with rectangular slots for the stop. The axis pin can be removed by drawing it forward. The lock is of the then customary single-action type and works smoothly; the act of cocking the hammer also rotates the cylinder. The rammer is of orthodox type; except that its lever broadens towards the rear, presumably to prevent it from catching on the holster, and gives it a streamlined appearance. The butt-plates are of very dark walnut. The trigger-guard, which is of brass, is rather small; it would not be easy to operate the trigger while wearing gloves. This handsome, well-made, service arm was used extensively by Union troops in the Civil War and remained popular afterwards.

United States of America
STARR REVOLVER

Length:	13·5" (343mm)
Weight:	48oz (1·36kg)
Barrel:	7·8" (198mm)
Calibre:	·44" (11·2mm)
Rifling:	6 groove, l/hand
Capacity:	Six
Muz Vel:	c700 f/s (213 m/s)
Sights:	Fixed

The Starr Arms Company of New York began to manufacture revolvers of the kind seen here as a result of a patent of 15 January 1856. There were three types: a Navy double-action model of ·36" (9·1mm) calibre; a double-action Army model of ·44" (11·2mm) calibre; and a somewhat heavier, ·44" (11·2mm) calibre, single-action model, like the weapon illustrated here. Unlike the Colts of the period, the Starr has a top strap and the barrel is hinged at the front of the frame. The removal of the screw visible below the hammer nose (a task needing no tools) enables the revolver to be broken (rather like the later Webleys) and stripped for cleaning very easily. This particular arrangement makes it possible to dispense with a cylinder pin: the cylinder is mounted by means of its rear-projecting ratchet and by a forward plug fitting into recesses in the frame. The six-chambered cylinder is plain, except for 12 oval slots for the stop. These slots allow the cylinder to be locked with a nipple on either side of the nose of the hammer, thus eliminating the chance of accidental discharge by a drop or jolt. The rammer is of the powerful type usually found on such weapons. The one-piece walnut butt is held between two tangs. All the metalwork of the pistol is of steel. It has a blade foresight, adjustable laterally; the backsight is formed by a notch on the top of the nose of the hammer. The frame is marked "STARRS PATENT JAN 15 1856" on the right hand side, and "STARR ARMS CO NEW YORK" on the left; while the cylinder is numbered "27479". The letter "C", presumably a viewer's mark, also appears on various components. This is in every respect a robust and well-made arm which saw very extensive use on the Union side in the Civil Car and which was also quite often carried by civilians as a belt pistol. However, as in the case of many other perfectly satisfactory arms, its makers presumably found it difficult to compete with the already well-established and well-advertised range of Colt revolvers; as a result, manufacture ceased completely in 1867. This was a sad end for a very fine revolver; but, perhaps, one made inevitable by the fierce competition from other makers in the extremely revolver-conscious United States of America.

ADAMS POCKET REVOLVER

This photograph shows the left-hand side of the pistol, displaying the rammer patented by a Birmingham gunmaker named Brazier, who also made complete pistols for Adams under contract. The lever of the rammer, which normally lies along the barrel, is here partially raised to show how the curved slot fits over the stud on the rammer head and forces it back into the chambers. This system allowed for the employment of tight-fitting bullets.

Length: 9" (229mm)
Weight: 20oz (·57kg)
Barrel: 4·5" (114mm)
Calibre: ·32" (8·1mm)
Rifling: 3 groove, r/hand
Capacity: Five
Muz Vel: c550 f/s (168 m/s)
Sights: Fixed

It will be apparent that the three pistols illustrated on this spread have a good many characteristics in common. In order to avoid unnecessary repetition, therefore, the three captions should ideally be read in conjunction with each other, so as to obtain a comprehensive account. Adams revolvers were made in three main sizes, of which the earliest, and largest, was the model shown on the facing page (below). It was initially made in 34-bore (about ·51"/12·9mm calibre), but this was fairly soon reduced to 38-bore (about ·49"/12·4mm calibre). These figures refer only to the bores: the chambers tended to be a couple of bore larger, which meant that a bullet comfortably tight in the chamber was very tight in the bore. These large pistols, which are regarded as a single group, are comparable to the Colt Dragoon (illustrated on page 68, above) and are, in fact, sometimes referred to as Adams Dragoons. They are very large and bulky weapons,

primarily intended to be carried by mounted men. The next calibre was the 54-bore (about ·44"/11·2mm). This was of a very convenient size for service use and had ample stopping-power; it was probably the most popular type among officers of the armed services. Specimens are illustrated elsewhere, so there is no need to enter into more detail here. Although a few Adams revolvers were made in 90-bore (about ·36"/9·1mm), and thus approximated to the Colt Navy model, the next and last calibre was of 120-bore (or ·32"/8·1mm). This was essentially a pocket pistol: it really lacked the stopping-power considered necessary for service use. The revolver illustrated here is of this type and, as may be seen, it bears a strong family resemblance to the self-cocking revolver shown on the facing page (below). It has the usual solid frame and octagonal barrel, and the system of mounting the cylinder is also the same: the axis pin (or arbor,

as it is often called) is drawn forward to remove it, and there is a spring pin on the right-hand side of the frame to prevent it slipping out accidentally. The lock is of the self-cocking pattern and the spring safety-plunger can be seen on the left-hand side of the frame. This held the hammer nose clear of the nipple and allowed the pistol to be carried loaded; it had the advantage that it released itself automatically as soon as the trigger was pulled. The most distinctive feature of this weapon is probably the patent Brazier rammer attached to the left-hand flat of the barrel. The system by which this works is described in the inset (above) and need not be repeated here. Joseph Brazier, who patented it in 1855, was a well-known Birmingham gunmaker whose firm was one of those which made Adams revolvers under licence. A number of other licensees, in Britain, on the continent and in the United States, also made revolvers on the Adams pat-

tern, and the weapon illustrated may be the product of one of these firms. Unfortunately, the revolver has been so heavily over-cleaned that it is really almost impossible to speculate on its origin; the cylinder bears London proof marks, but that is all the evidence there is to consider. Revolvers of this type and calibre were neat and compact and very soon became popular as pocket arms for self-defence. As we have seen, the self-cocking lock did not make for long-range accuracy, but this would hardly have been a serious disadvantage in a pocket arm. In 1856, the Deane, Adams and Deane partnership was dissolved: it was replaced by the London Armoury Company, which continued to make Adams-type arms. Among these was a Beaumont-Adams pistol of 120-bore; some examples of this arm were beautifully blued and highly ornamented with gold inlay work. These were, of course, mainly presentation models.

Great Britain
BEAUMONT-ADAMS REVOLVER

Length:	13" (330mm)	**Rifling:**	3 groove, r/hand
Weight:	47oz (1·33kg)	**Capacity:**	Five
Barrel:	7" (178mm)	**Muz Vel:**	c750 f/s (229 m/s)
Calibre:	·49" (12·4mm)	**Sights:**	Fixed

In commercial terms, Colt's revolvers had a considerable advantage over those of Adams, for they were readily available in large numbers and were widely advertised by their inventor, who had an excellent eye for publicity. Adams arms were, however, so obviously of good quality that, as manufacture increased, they began to make ground: although the Colt was probably the more widely-used in the Crimean War of 1854-56, it seems that the balance had swung in favour of the Adams by the outbreak of the Indian Mutiny in 1857. One great improvement to the Adams, which is at once obvious on the revolver seen here, was the addition of a double-action lock, the invention of Lt F. Beaumont of the Royal Engineers. British officers liked fast-shooting arms for use at close quarters, but their heavy trigger pull naturally affected their accuracy at longer ranges. The new lock overcame this disadvantage by giving the firer a choice of single-action or self-cocking, according to the circumstances in which he found himself. The Beaumont-Adams revolver illustrated here has the solid frame and octagonal barrel of the earlier Adams, but the shape of the butt is of more modern appearance and the curve in the trigger is less pronounced. The new mechanism made it possible to place the hammer at half-cock; thus, the spring plug was no longer necessary, but there is a sliding safety on the right-hand side of the frame. This intervenes between a nipple and a partition, thus preventing the cylinder from rotating and making it impossible to draw the hammer back to full-cock. Another very interesting addition is a rammer. The first Adams was loaded with wadded, finger-tight bullets in slightly over-sized chambers; but although this speeded reloading, there was a risk of a bullet slipping forward and jamming the cylinder. A tight bullet also gave better shooting and a good, water-tight seal, so Adams followed Colt's example and fitted a rammer. The lever of the rammer is held against the barrel by light spring pressure against a stud, and when the lever is drawn upwards, the rammer itself is thrust backward with considerable force.

Great Britain
ADAMS SELF-COCKING REVOLVER

Length:	13" (330mm)	**Rifling:**	5 groove, r/hand
Weight:	45oz (1·27kg)	**Capacity:**	Five
Barrel:	7·5" (190mm)	**Muz Vel:**	c700 f/s (213 m/s)
Calibre:	·49" (12·4mm)	**Sights:**	Fixed

It was probably the large and impressive display of Colt's percussion revolvers at the Great Exhibition, held in the Crystal Palace in London's Hyde Park in 1851, which really stimulated interest in this new type of arm. It is true that Colt had then been making revolvers for some 15 years, but almost all of these had been bought and used in the United States. A London gunmaker, Robert Adams, also exhibited a percussion revolver of his own invention at the Exhibition. It was included in a display arranged by the Deane father and son, with whom Adams was in partnership; and, because it appeared to be the most likely rival to the Colt, it attracted a good deal more attention than the exhibitors had perhaps anticipated. As a result of this interest, the revolver was put into production on as large a scale as the firm's resources would allow. The example illustrated here is number 419. Unlike the Colt pistols illustrated earlier, the barrels, frames and butts of Adams' pistols were forged as single entities, which naturally gave them great strength and rigidity. The barrel of this specimen is octagonal and the top flat is engraved with the words "DEANE ADAMS AND DEANE (MAKER TO HRH PRINCE ALBERT) 30 KING WILLIAM ST LONDON BRIDGE". It is rifled and is fitted with a foresight capable of lateral adjustment; the backsight is visible on the frame just in front of the hammer. The plain, five-chambered cylinder, with nipples adequately separated by partitions, rotates on an axis pin and may be removed by drawing the pin forward and clear of the frame. A small, flat spring on the right-hand side of the frame prevents this taking place accidentally. Again unlike the Colt, the lock is of self-cocking type; that is, the pistol can only be fired by steady pressure on the trigger (which is noticeably curved), which causes the hammer to rise and fall. the small, flat spring behind the cylinder is a safety device: there is an inward-facing stud at its top end which, when depressed, holds the hammer clear of the nipples; the slightest pressure on the trigger causes the stud to spring clear, leaving the revolver ready for action, without further manipulation on the part of the firer. The arm has a one-piece butt of chequered walnut, with a cap compartment in the base.

Great Britain
BENTLEY REVOLVER

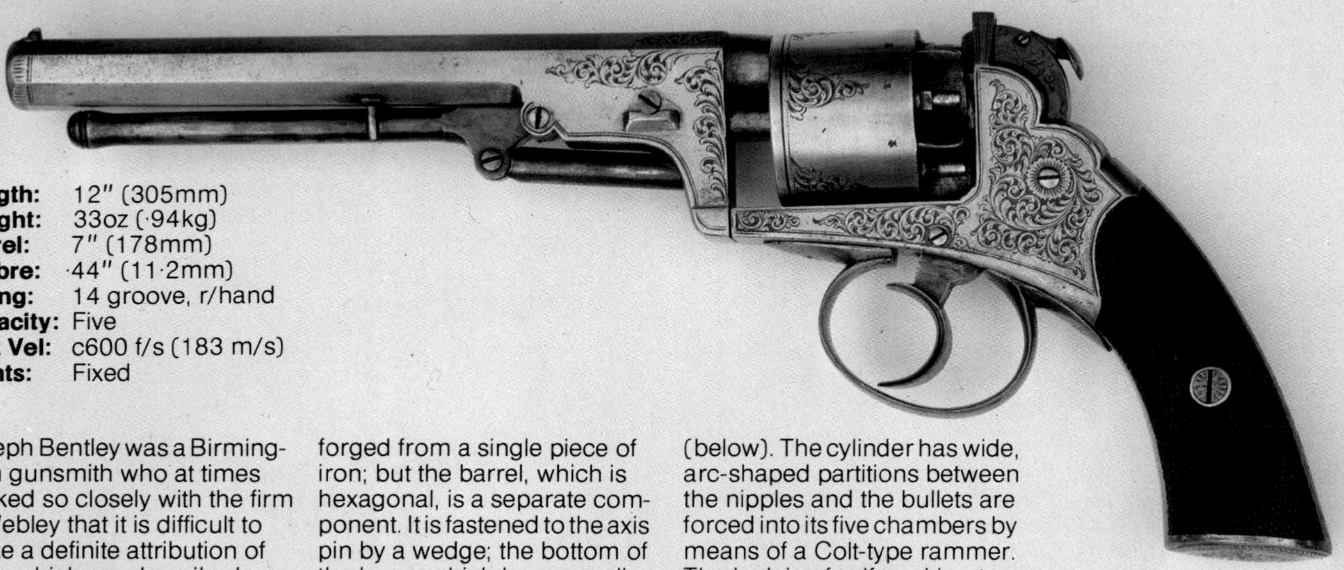

Length:	12" (305mm)
Weight:	33oz (·94kg)
Barrel:	7" (178mm)
Calibre:	·44" (11·2mm)
Rifling:	14 groove, r/hand
Capacity:	Five
Muz Vel:	c600 f/s (183 m/s)
Sights:	Fixed

Joseph Bentley was a Birmingham gunsmith who at times worked so closely with the firm of Webley that it is difficult to make a definite attribution of arms which are described sometimes as Bentley and sometimes as Webley-Bentley. The earliest revolvers of the general type appeared in about 1853, and various modifications were made thereafter to the original design. The arm illustrated here was probably made in about 1857 to a design that remained popular for some years. The frame and butt are forged from a single piece of iron; but the barrel, which is hexagonal, is a separate component. It is fastened to the axis pin by a wedge; the bottom of the lump, which has a small aperture on its inner side, is braced against a corresponding peg in the lower part of the frame. This was an innovation, apparently based on Colt's system, since in earlier models the barrels were screwed to the axis pin and further braced by a thumbscrew; this method, a Bentley invention, was also used on the Longspur revolver (below). The cylinder has wide, arc-shaped partitions between the nipples and the bullets are forced into its five chambers by means of a Colt-type rammer. The lock is of self-cocking type and incorporates a safety device, also a Bentley invention, upon the hammer head: if the trigger is pressed sufficiently to bring the nose of the hammer clear of the frame, the flat stud visible at the back of the hammer can be depressed, causing the hammer's front end to rise so that it fouls the upper edge of the frame and thus is held clear of the nipples. Because this catch is spring-loaded, only a slight pressure on the trigger is required to release the front end and let it drop back flush. The revolver, which is of only moderate quality, bears no mark except "J. PARKINSON, MACCLESFIELD", presumably the retailer.

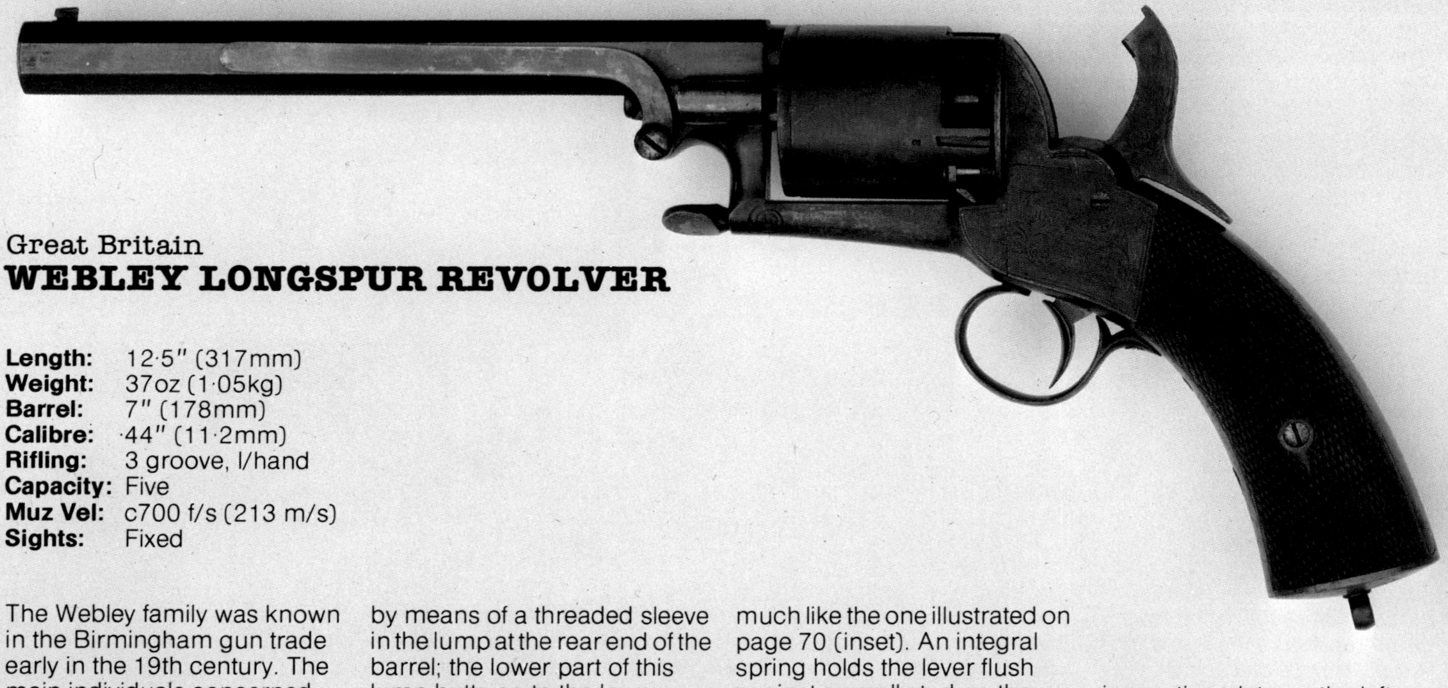

Great Britain
WEBLEY LONGSPUR REVOLVER

Length:	12·5" (317mm)
Weight:	37oz (1·05kg)
Barrel:	7" (178mm)
Calibre:	·44" (11·2mm)
Rifling:	3 groove, l/hand
Capacity:	Five
Muz Vel:	c700 f/s (213 m/s)
Sights:	Fixed

The Webley family was known in the Birmingham gun trade early in the 19th century. The main individuals concerned were James Webley (the inventor of the weapon illustrated here) and his brother Philip; James died in 1856 and Philip carried on the business thereafter. This revolver, known as the "Longspur" from the length of its hammer spur, was patented in 1853; there were various models, of which the one seen here is the third. The frame of the weapon is of malleable iron. the octagonal barrel is a separate component and is attached to the axis pin by means of a threaded sleeve in the lump at the rear end of the barrel; the lower part of this lump butts on to the lower projection of the frame and is attached to it by a thumbscrew, the flat head of which is visible in the photograph. The cylinder, which is case-hardened, has five chambers with horizontal nipples separated from each other by partitions. The first model had a detachable rammer; the second had a simple swivel rammer pivoted back horizontally across the frame below the cylinder; and the one shown has a compound rammer much like the one illustrated on page 70 (inset). An integral spring holds the lever flush against a small stud on the left-hand barrel flat when it is not required for use. Raising the lever thrusts the hollow-nosed rammer into the chamber with sufficient force to allow the use of tight-fitting bullets. The lock is of single-action type and is equipped with a half-cock to hold the hammer nose just clear of the nipples. The trigger is rather small, as it is its almost circular guard. The weapon has a finely-chequered, two-piece butt held by a single screw. The inspection plate on the left-hand side of the frame is visible in the photograph. A foresight and a backsight are provided, the latter being a notch on the top of the hammer. The pistol is blued and lightly engraved, and bears several inscriptions: the inspection plate is marked "WEBLEY'S PATENT"; the strap "BY HER MAJESTY'S ROYAL LETTERS PATENT"; the top flat "MURCOTT AND HANSON" (the retailer); and the underside of the barrel "W G J YORKE" (the owner).

Western Europe
LONGSPUR-TYPE REVOLVER

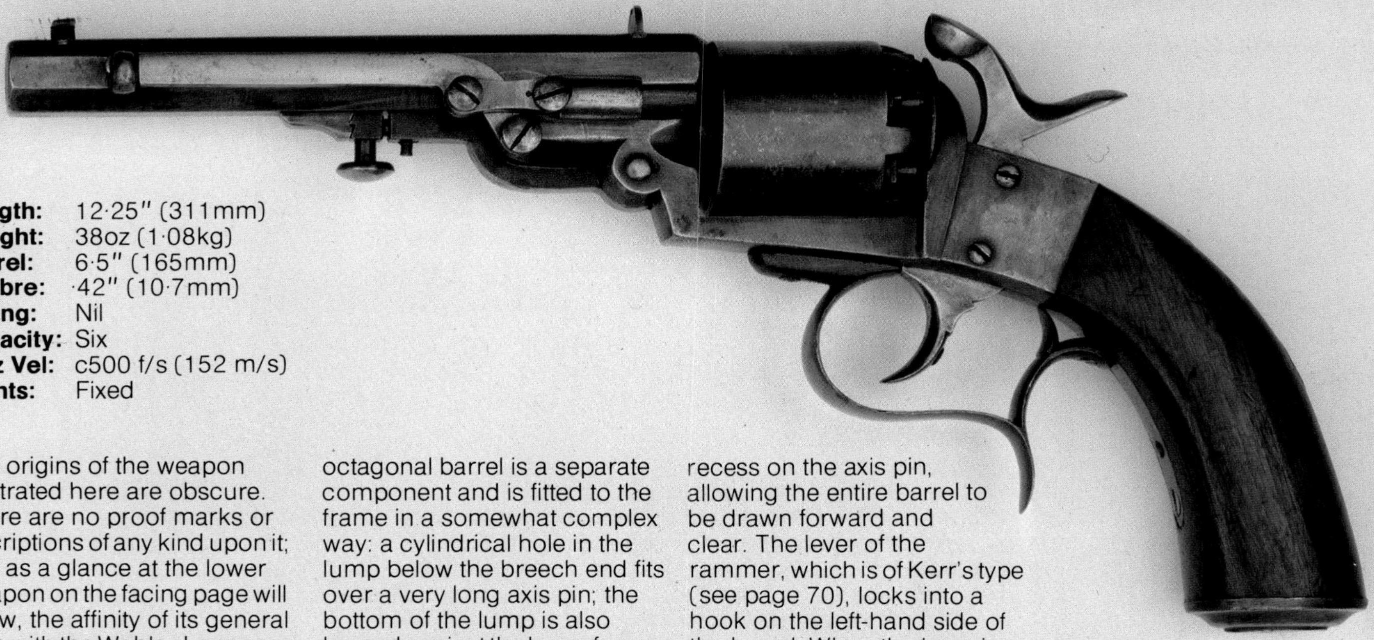

Length: 12·25″ (311mm)
Weight: 38oz (1·08kg)
Barrel: 6·5″ (165mm)
Calibre: ·42″ (10·7mm)
Rifling: Nil
Capacity: Six
Muz Vel: c500 f/s (152 m/s)
Sights: Fixed

The origins of the weapon illustrated here are obscure. There are no proof marks or inscriptions of any kind upon it; but, as a glance at the lower weapon on the facing page will show, the affinity of its general style with the Webley Longspur revolver suggests that it is a continental copy of that arm. The frame is made in one piece, without a top strap, and with a short upper tang and a long lower tang into which is screwed the one-piece walnut butt, with its metal butt-cap. The octagonal barrel is a separate component and is fitted to the frame in a somewhat complex way: a cylindrical hole in the lump below the breech end fits over a very long axis pin; the bottom of the lump is also braced against the lower frame to make a very rigid joint. To remove the barrel it is necessary first to slide back the mushroom-shaped stud below it; then to draw down the lever behind it to the vertical. This disengages a half-round locking pin from its corresponding recess on the axis pin, allowing the entire barrel to be drawn forward and clear. The lever of the rammer, which is of Kerr's type (see page 70), locks into a hook on the left-hand side of the barrel. When the lever is raised vertically, the ram, which has a conical hole in its nose, is forced into the appropriate chamber. The cylinder is plain, with nipple partitions, and the lock is of double-action type. There is no special cylinder stop: the nose of the hammer is so shaped that it fits exactly between two nipple partitions, preventing any rotation of the cylinder. The revolver is plainly constructed, strong and robust; it is quite probable that it was designed for use as a service weapon.

United States of America
LE MAT REVOLVER

Length: 13·25″ (337mm)
Weight: 58oz (1·64kg)
Barrel: 7″ (178mm)
Calibre: ·300″/·65″ (7·62mm/16·5mm)
Rifling: 5 groove, r/hand
Capacity: Nine/One
Muz Vel: c600 f/s (183 m/s)
Sights: Fixed

Jean Alexandre Le Mat was a physician of French birth residing in the state of Louisiana (which was, of course, a French possession until Napoleon sold it to the United States in 1803). In 1856, Le Mat took out a United States patent for a revolver of the type seen here. The weapon is of massive and solid construction. The frame, including the butt, is made in one piece, the lower barrel being an integral part of it. The cylinder is mounted on this lower barrel, which thus doubles as axis pin. The upper barrel is mounted on the lower one by means of a front and rear ring, the latter having an extension which locks firmly on to the lower part of the frame. The lower barrel, which is smooth-bored, is of cylindrical shape; the upper barrel, which is rifled, is octagonal and is fitted with a foresight. The weapon's rearsight was an integral part of the hammer nose, which is, unfortunately, missing in this particular specimen. The revolver is fitted with a rammer of basically similar type to that designed by Kerr and used on the Beaumont-Adams (see page 70) and other British revolvers. When the rammer is not in use, the lever lies along the left flat of the barrel, with its knob in a notch near the muzzle: the size of the knob, together with the natural springing of the steel, holds it firmly in place. The cylinder, which bears English proof-marks, has nine chambers; the nipples, which are in prolongation of the axis, are separated by deep and solid partitions. The nipple for the lower barrel is set in a deep, cylindrical recess on top of the standing breech: when complete, the hammer had a rotatable nose which could be set to fire either the upper or the lower barrel. The lock is of single-action type, access to its mechanism being by means of an inspection plate on the left-hand side of the frame. All parts of the arm are numbered "168" and the top flat of the barrel is inscribed "LEMAT AND GIRARDS PATENT, LONDON". The weapon was never adopted as a service arm by the United States, but was used by the Confederate States Army during the Civil War.

BEAUMONT-ADAMS REVOLVER

Length:	11·75″ (298mm)
Weight:	38oz (1·08kg)
Barrel:	5·75″ (146mm)
Calibre:	44″ (11·2mm)
Rifling:	3 groove, r/hand
Capacity:	Five
Muz Vel:	c550 f/s (168 m/s)
Sights:	Fixed

The original Adams revolvers of 1851 were self-cockers and thus could only be fired by quite heavy pressure on the trigger; this made them fast to use but somewhat inaccurate, except at close range. This deficiency was remedied in 1855 by the adoption of a double-action lock, the invention of Lieutenant F. Beaumont of the Royal Engineers. This allowed preliminary cocking for deliberate shooting, without affecting the rate of fire, and immediately became popular. It appears that only two calibres were made: the massive "Dragoon" arm (illustrated on page 71); and the smaller 54-bore (about ·44″/11·2mm calibre), shown here. This weapon, while still having adequate stopping power, was of more manageable dimensions than the Dragoon, and was thus particularly favoured by unmounted officers, who had to carry their own revolvers. Like all Adams' weapons, the revolver is of strong construction. It has the usual one-piece frame with integral octagonal barrel, which is rifled and bears the foresight; the backsight is a simple notch on the frame above the standing breech. The plain cylinder, with its horizontal nipples separated by partitions, is somewhat longer than those of the original Adams, to allow for a heavier charge, and bears London proofmarks. There is a Kerr-type rammer on the left-hand side of the barrel. The lower frame is marked "B14886" and "Adams Patent No 30550 R", and carries an "L.A.C." (London Armoury Company) stamp near the axis pin.

ADAMS SELF-COCKING REVOLVER

Length:	11·5″ (292mm)
Weight:	30oz (·85kg)
Barrel:	6·5″ (165mm)
Calibre:	44″ (11·2mm)
Rifling:	3 groove, r/hand
Capacity:	Five
Muz Vel:	c550 f/s (168 m/s)
Sights:	Fixed

Adams revolvers attracted considerable attention at the Great Exhibition in London in 1851; mainly, perhaps, because they appeared to offer a viable British alternative to the products of Samuel Colt. the consequent demand may have taken the firm of Deane, Adams and Deane rather by surprise, for it was some time before the various arms came into full production. The original massive "Dragoon" type, 38-bore revolver (illustrated on page 71) was a bulky arm and, although suitable for mounted men, was rather too heavy for a man on foot. The revolver shown here is of the next size down and was of nominal 54-bore (about ·44″/11·2mm calibre). The word "nominal" is used deliberately, because some of the earliest models were, in fact, 56-bore and bear the small number "56" on the front of the frame: the weapon here is one such. It is of the usual strong, one-piece construction and its octagonal barrel is, of course, rifled. It bears the inscription "DEANE ADAMS AND DEANE, 30 KING WILLIAM STT, LONDON BRIDGE", and has London proofmarks. The cylinder, which is bright, has the usual five chambers and horizontal nipples separated by partitions; it bears the usual London proofmarks. It is slightly unusual, in that it rotates in an anti-clockwise direction. The cylinder can be removed by first withdrawing the small plug on the upper end of the vertical spring on the front of the frame, and then drawing the axis pin forward. The lock is of self-cocking type and a safety device to hold the hammer clear of the nipples is located on the left-hand side of the frame (an example is shown and explained on page 71). Comparison with the Beaumont-Adams revolver illustrated above will show that the cylinder is appreciably shorter in this specimen. No rammer is fitted; the bullets had oversized felt wads attached to their bases and were only thumb-tight in the chambers—this made for fast loading.

Belgium
COPY OF ADAMS REVOLVER

Length:	13" (330mm)
Weight:	33oz (·94kg)
Barrel:	6·9" (175mm)
Calibre:	·38" (9·6mm)
Rifling:	8 groove, r/hand
Capacity:	Six
Muz Vel:	c500 f/s (152 m/s)
Sights:	Fixed

Although Adams revolvers were made under licence in Belgium, the name on this pistol —"DAVID H, BREVETTE"—is not that of a licensee. The arm resembles those made by D. Herman of Liège and is probably a pirated copy. The frame is made separately from the octagonal barrel, which is attached to it Colt-fashion by means of a robust cylinder pin and a lump screwed to the lower part of the frame. A rammer, essentially similar to the type used on Beaumont-Adams revolvers, is attached to the left-hand flat of the barrel. The cylinder is of the normal Adams type and bears Liége proofmarks. The lock, too, is of the Adams self-cocking type; on the left-hand side is fitted a spring safety-bolt to hold the hammer clear of the nipples. A flat plate protrudes far enough forward from the top of the frame to cover completely the nipple under the hammer; this is presumably intended to remove any risk of fragments of the copper cap blowing back into the face of the firer. The trigger is of the ring type often found on earlier pepperbox pistols. The one-piece butt, which is held between two tangs, is fitted with a butt-cap of German silver. It contains a percussion cap compartment, with a lid made in the form of a grotesque mask.

Great Britain
DEANE-HARDING REVOLVER

Length:	12" (305mm)
Weight:	41oz (1·16kg)
Barrel:	5·25" (133mm)
Calibre:	·44" (11·2mm)
Rifling:	3 groove, r/hand
Capacity:	Five
Muz Vel:	c550 f/s (168 m/s)
Sights:	Fixed

The Deane of the title of this arm is the older of Adams' two original partners. After severing the partnership, he continued to trade in firearms, and in 1858 began the manufacture of a new revolver patented in that year by William Harding. The weapon shown is of the popular 54-bore service calibre. Perhaps its main point of interest is the manner of its construction: the barrel, barrel lump and upper strap constitute a completely separate component from the frame. In order to strip the weapon, it is necessary first to remove the pin from the hole visible in front of the hammer nose. The barrel is thus pushed downwards to an angle of 45°, which is sufficient to disengage a hook at the bottom of the lump from a corresponding socket in the lower frame. Various types of locking-pin were employed; in this specimen, the pin has been replaced by a screw, but this is a non-standard modification. The barrel group incorporates a rammer, which was also patented by Harding. When the lever below the barrel is released, by means of a spring, and pulled downward, a hook (concealed in the lump) draws the ram into the bottom chamber until the lever is vertically downwards. This method was efficient but is said to have been rather flimsy for service use. The lock is of double-action type, and the whole arm is broadly comparable to the Beaumont-Adams—to which it was clearly intended to be a rival. It is known that the Deane-Adams breakup caused some ill-feeling: Deane, in his *Manual of Firearms* published in 1858, suggested that the addition of the Beaumont lock to Adams' original revolver made it over-complex and liable to derangement; although there seems to have been little truth in this charge. It is difficult to assess the real value of the Deane-Harding revolver: G. N. George quotes Lord Roberts as saying that it could always be depended upon to malfunction at a critical moment. Certainly, it never became popular.

Great Britain
TRANTER REVOLVER, FIRST MODEL

Length:	11·5" (292mm)	**Rifling:**	5 groove, r/hand
Weight:	31oz (·88kg)	**Capacity:**	Five
Barrel:	6·5" (165mm)	**Muz Vel:**	c550 f/s (168 m/s)
Calibre:	·44" (11·2mm)	**Sights:**	Fixed

As the weapons illustrated on this spread form a group, information on the characteristics common to all of them has, to some extent, been dispersed over the various captions in order to avoid unnecessary repetition. Their inventor, William Tranter, was a Birmingham gunmaker of the highest repute. Tranter realized that although self-cocking revolvers were excellent for fast shooting, their heavy trigger pull had an adverse effect for fast shooting, their heavy trigger pull had an adverse effect on accuracy beyond point-blank range. He therefore set to work on a double-action lock and by 1853 had patented the weapon seen here—thus forestalling Beaumont. Pressure on the lower trigger (which is, in effect, a cocking lever) cocks the combless hammer; a very light pressure on the upper trigger is then sufficient to fire the shot. When speed was more important than accuracy, both triggers were pulled together, thus giving the fast shooting needed in a close-quarter mêlée. Tranter's revolvers were all fitted with rammers, and it is by the variations in these that the different models are identified. However, it must be clearly stated that the numbering of the models does not necessarily relate to the strict chronological order of their appearance. The weapon seen here is the first model; it is equipped with a detachable rammer, an example of which is shown below the arm. In order to use the rammer, it is necessary to put the ring on its end over a peg (visible) on the bottom of the frame and then raise the lever so that the ram bears on the bullet and forces it into the chamber. Round the base of each bullet was a cannelure, or groove, which contained a bees-wax mixture: the expansion of the bullet on firing forced bees-wax out into the bore, helping to reduce hard fouling and facilitating cleaning.

Great Britain
TRANTER REVOLVER, SECOND MODEL

Length:	11·5" (292mm)	**Rifling:**	5 groove, r/hand
Weight:	29oz (·82kg)	**Capacity:**	Five
Barrel:	6·5" (165mm)	**Muz Vel:**	c550 f/s (168 m/s)
Calibre:	·44" (11·2mm)	**Sights:**	Fixed

As we have seen, Tranter's revolvers are usually classified by type of rammer. The fully detachable rammer of the first model was satisfactory for target shooting, but on active service it was possible for it to slip through a hole in a pocket or be otherwise mislaid: in view of the tight fit of the bullets, this had the effect of putting the weapon out of action, a risk which no officer cared to run. The rammer on the second model, seen here, therefore represents a compromise: it is so designed that it may be easily enough removed by aligning the recess on its ring with the pin protruding from its anchor peg, on the frame, and lifting it off. On the other hand, the fit was so good that the rammer could be left in position on the revolver without any risk of it falling off. In order to carry the loaded revolver in safety, it was, of course, necessary to keep the nose of the hammer clear of the caps on the nipples—and since the system precluded any use of the normal half-cock, some other device was needed. Tranter's solution was most ingenious: it consists of a spring in the shape of an inverted Y, which can be seen here on the left-hand side of the frame, behind the cylinder. When the hammer is slightly raised, a stud on the inside of the upper arm is interposed between the hammer and the nipples; it remains in position until pressure on the lower trigger brings the hammer back to full-cock, when it is automatically disengaged. This was a simple and effective device which, unlike the similar safety on the Adams, called for no conscious effort on the part of the firer to remove it before beginning to shoot—and it was much preferred to the detachable version. Tranter's revolvers soon became popular with service officers, because they were both mechanically sound and well made. It is true that there were initially some criticisms of Tranter's system; but in practice it proved both fast and simple in operation, and thus remained in service for a long time.

Great Britain
TRANTER REVOLVER, THIRD MODEL

Length:	11·75" (298mm)	**Rifling:**	5 groove, r/hand
Weight:	36oz (1·02kg)	**Capacity:**	Five
Barrel:	6" (152mm)	**Muz Vel:**	c550 f/s (168 m/s)
Calibre:	·44" (11·2mm)	**Sights:**	Fixed

This third and final model of Tranter's double-trigger revolver again differs from the earlier ones because of its rammer, which, as may be seen, is in this arm firmly attached to the frame and is only to be removed by a screwdriver. The reasons for this change from the second model are not clear; it is, perhaps, possible that after long use the second type worked loose, to the stage where there was a risk of it falling off accidentally. It will be observed that in many essential features Tranter's revolvers bear a strong family resemblance to those of Adams. This is not surprising when it is considered that, until 1865, all frames for Tranter's revolvers

were made under licence on an Adams patent, and were stamped accordingly. Tranter considered it essential to have the one-piece, malleable iron frame incorporating the barrel which was a major feature of Adams' arms — and he was content to pay a small royalty on each pistol for the privilege. It is, in fact, believed that Tranter, who was, it will be remembered, already a well-established gunsmith when Adams' revolver appeared, may have had a contract to make frames for Adams; at least, in the early days when Adams himself did not have the manufacturing capacity to cope with the demand. If this was so, the licence arrange-

ment was clearly to Tranter's advantage, for he had the tools and expertise ready to hand in his own factory. When the patent expired in 1865, the system because common property and Tranter was able to continue to use it without further payment of a fee. It will

be seen from the arm illustrated here that the angle of the butt has changed; and this conforms with the change made by Adams at the same time. This particular pistol is provided with a neat case, with bullet mould, lubricating compound and other accessories.

Great Britain
TRANTER REVOLVER, POCKET MODEL

Length:	9·5" (241mm)	**Rifling:**	3 groove, r/hand
Weight:	22oz (·62kg)	**Capacity:**	Five
Barrel:	4·3" (109mm)	**Muz Vel:**	c500 f/s (152 m/s)
Calibre:	·38" (9·6mm)	**Sights:**	Fixed

Tranter's revolvers were made in a considerable variety of calibres to suit all needs. The first model was produced in 38-bore (·500"/12·7mm), 50-bore (·45"/11·4mm), 54-bore (·44"/11·2mm), 80-bore (·38"/9·6mm), 90-bore (·36"/9·1mm), and 120-bore (·32"/8·1mm). (The calibres in inches and millimetres are rounded off to their modern equivalents.) The second and third models appear to have been reduced to the three basic calibres; ie, 38-, 54- and 120-bore. The pistol illustrated here is of 80-bore (·38"/ 9·6mm), and it will be seen that it is the second model, with detachable rammer. Like all Tranter's revolvers in this

series, it conforms closely to the standard design and is fitted with the patent safety device and the usual cylinder axis retaining spring on the right-hand side. Like all Tranter's arms, it bears the inscription "W. TRANTER PATENT" on the upper trigger, just above the guard, and on the rammer, opposite the ram itself. It will be noted that the frame is of the later pattern, with raked-back butt; as it does not bear the words "Adams Patent", it must be presumed to have been made after the patent's expiry in 1865. It bears the usual light engraving on the sides of the frame and at the breech end of the barrel, the top flat of which is engraved "GASQUOINE

AND DYSON, MARKET PLACE, MANCHESTER", this being the name of the retailer. This is in every respect a neat and compact weapon and, although a pocket pistol, it is of sufficient calibre to give it very reasonable stopping-power. A number of Tranter's revolvers were also made in Belgium under licence. Tranter took care to grant such licence only to reputable makers, with the result that the Belgian-made weapons are practically

indistinguishable from the British ones, except that they bear an acknowledgement of the fact that they were made under a Tranter patent. Very occasionally, pocket Tranters may be encountered with a hinged lower trigger, which can be folded forward so as to lie flush outside the guard. It is of interest to note that this refinement is also to be found on one of Lancaster's four-barrelled pistols (illustrated on page 194).

WESTLEY RICHARDS REVOLVER

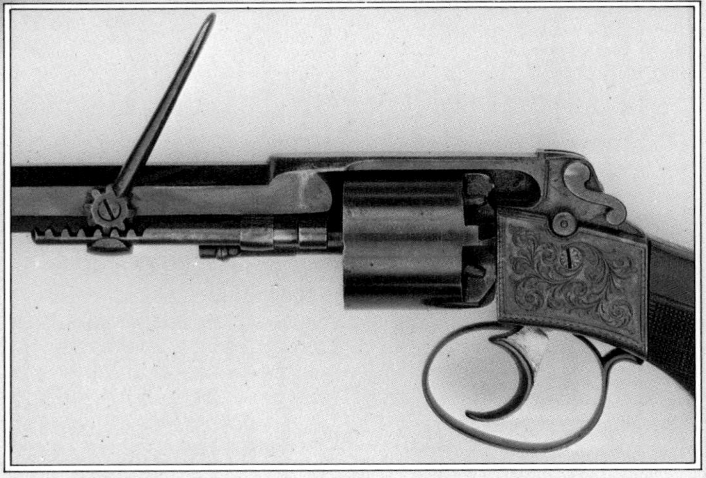

The left-hand side of the revolver, showing the rack-and-pinion rammer. Upward pressure on the lever, which normally lies along the barrel, exerts powerful pressure on the ram. Also visible are the handle of the locking lever and the safety stud mentioned in the main caption.

Length:	12.25" (311mm)
Weight:	39oz (1.1kg)
Barrel:	6" (152mm)
Calibre:	.49" (12.4mm)
Rifling:	12 groove, r/hand
Capacity:	Five
Muz Vel:	c550 f/s (168 m/s)
Sights:	Fixed

The name of Westley Richards has long been a well-respected one in the British gun trade, with a reputation for a wide variety of firearms. Westley Richards revolvers, are, however, comparatively rare. The arm illustrated here, which was made in about 1856, is of unusual design and construction. The barrel and top straps are a completely separate component. The barrel is held to the frame by the combination of two parts: a hook at the rear of the strap engages in the top of the standing breech, where it is locked by means of a rotating pin, the handle of which is on the left-hand side; and a sleeve below the barrel fits over the forward extension of the axis pin. This latter also has a small catch (just visible in the photograph) which engages a slot in the axis pin to prevent accidental removal. The revolver has a double-action lock with a combless side-hammer. As this is positioned off-centre, the nipples are necessarily angled so that the actual chamber is aligned with the bore. There is a push-in safety stud on the left-hand side. The top flat bears the inscription "WESTLEY RICHARDS 170 NEW BOND ST LONDON (PATENTEE)".

Great Britain
WEBLEY DOUBLE-ACTION REVOLVER

Length:	11.5" (292mm)
Weight:	37oz (1.05kg)
Barrel:	6" (152mm)
Calibre:	.44" (11.2mm)
Rifling:	14 groove, r/hand
Capacity:	Five
Muz Vel:	c550 f/s (168 m/s)
Sights:	Fixed

After the Webley Longspur (illustrated on page 72) the firm of Webley, or perhaps Joseph Bentley, produced a series of self-cocking percussion revolvers. These were followed by two types of double-action pistol: one with a solid frame, with a barrel screwed in; the other, the one shown here, of two-piece construction. The octagonal, multi-grooved barrel is made with a top strap and a lump. The rear end of the strap fits into a slot cut across the top of the standing breech above the nose of the hammer; a hole in the lump fits over the front end of the axis pin; and a small stud projects from the lower frame to fit a corresponding hole at the bottom of the lump—thus giving a rigid, three-way locking system. The whole is held firmly together by a Colt-type wedge driven in from the left-hand side and retained by a small grub screw. The thin end of the wedge is visible in the photograph. The cylinder is of the usual Webley type, each chamber being numbered serially from one to five in an anti-clockwise direction. The lock is of double-action type, with a half-cock but no safety catch. The revolver is fitted with a rammer of Colt-type: the lever is held in place below the barrel by a spring catch fastening over a pin on the lower flat. The butt has a cap integral with the tang, and the butt-plates are finely chequered. The entire weapon is well-blued, except for the hammer and trigger, which are bright, and the rammer, which is case-hardened. The top strap is marked "P WEBLEY AND SON, LONDON", which suggests that the firm may have had its own retail outlet in the capital at that time.

Great Britain
KERR REVOLVER

Length:	11" (279mm)	**Rifling:**	5 groove, l/hand
Weight:	42oz (1·19kg)	**Capacity:**	Five
Barrel:	5·75" (146mm)	**Muz Vel:**	c550 f/s (168 m/s)
Calibre:	·44" (11·2mm)	**Sights:**	Fixed

When the partnership of Deane, Adams and Deane was dissolved in 1856, it was replaced by the London Armoury Company, which was able to provide capital for the large-scale manufacture of Adams revolvers to meet military contracts. One of the shareholders was the company superintendent, James Kerr, whose name has been mentioned earlier as the inventor of the rammer used on the Beaumont-Adams revolver. In 1858, Kerr patented a percussion revolver of his own design, one of the very earliest of which (No 27) is illustrated here. Kerr's idea, a very sensible one, was that, however robust a revolver, there was always the risk of breaking a spring. Although this was not necessarily a serious accident in a civilized country where a competent gunsmith might easily be found, it was a grave matter in more remote parts of the world. Kerr therefore designed his new revolver with a detachable lock, which could be removed by two screws, on the assumption that even a primitive blacksmith might be able to replace a spring to which he had easy access. The idea was successful: Kerr's revolvers proved popular in the various British colonies and also as service arms with the Confederate States forces in the American Civil War. The locks of the early models were of single-action type, but double-action locks were sometimes fitted later. This specimen, which is cased, was presumably a presentation model and is well-engraved, but most were plain. More details are given below.

Great Britain
KERR REVOLVER

Length:	10.6" (269mm)
Weight:	34oz (·96kg)
Barrel:	5.5" (140mm)
Calibre:	·44" (11·2mm)
Rifling:	5 groove, l/hand
Capacity:	Five
Muz Vel:	c550 f/s (168 m/s)
Sights:	Fixed

Although the arm illustrated here is a slightly later model of Kerr's revolver, it does not differ significantly from the example shown above. In order not to contravene Adams' patent for a solid frame, Kerr's revolvers had the barrel and top strap forged as a separate component and then fastened to the frame by two screws: one just below the aperture for the hammer nose; the other (the end of which may be seen in the photograph) at the front lower end of the frame. The fit is so accurate that at first sight the revolver could be taken to have a solid frame. This revolver, like all the arms in the series, is fitted with a new type of rammer, also the invention of Kerr. It is centrally placed below the barrel; when not in use, the lever is held between two lugs on the lower side of the barrel by means of a spring catch. Drawing the lever downwards forces the ram (which is concealed in the barrel lump) into the lowest chamber. The central position of the rammer made it difficult to arrange for the cylinder axis pin to be inserted from the front; thus, in this revolver, it is inserted from the rear, the end of it being visible behind the hammer. There is a small spring catch on the left-hand side of the frame to prevent it slipping out accidentally. The main point of interest is, of course, the detachable lock, and in this example it has been removed from the revolver and reversed so as to show its internal mechanism. Unlike the arm shown above, this one has a sliding safety on the lockplate; when pushed forward, it engages a slot at the rear of the hammer and prevents it from being drawn back. Comparison of the two arms will also show a change in the angle of the butt. The right frame bears the inscription "KERRS PATENT 648"; the left side is marked "LONDON ARMOURY" in smaller letters; and the top flat of the barrel is inscribed "LONDON ARMOURY BERMONDSEY". The left top flat is also stamped "LAC", with proofmarks, and the latter are repeated over the chambers. A number of Kerr revolvers were bought and used by the Confederate States during the American Civil War: these examples are now particularly sought after by collectors, but they are extremely hard to identify.

Great Britain
DAW REVOLVER

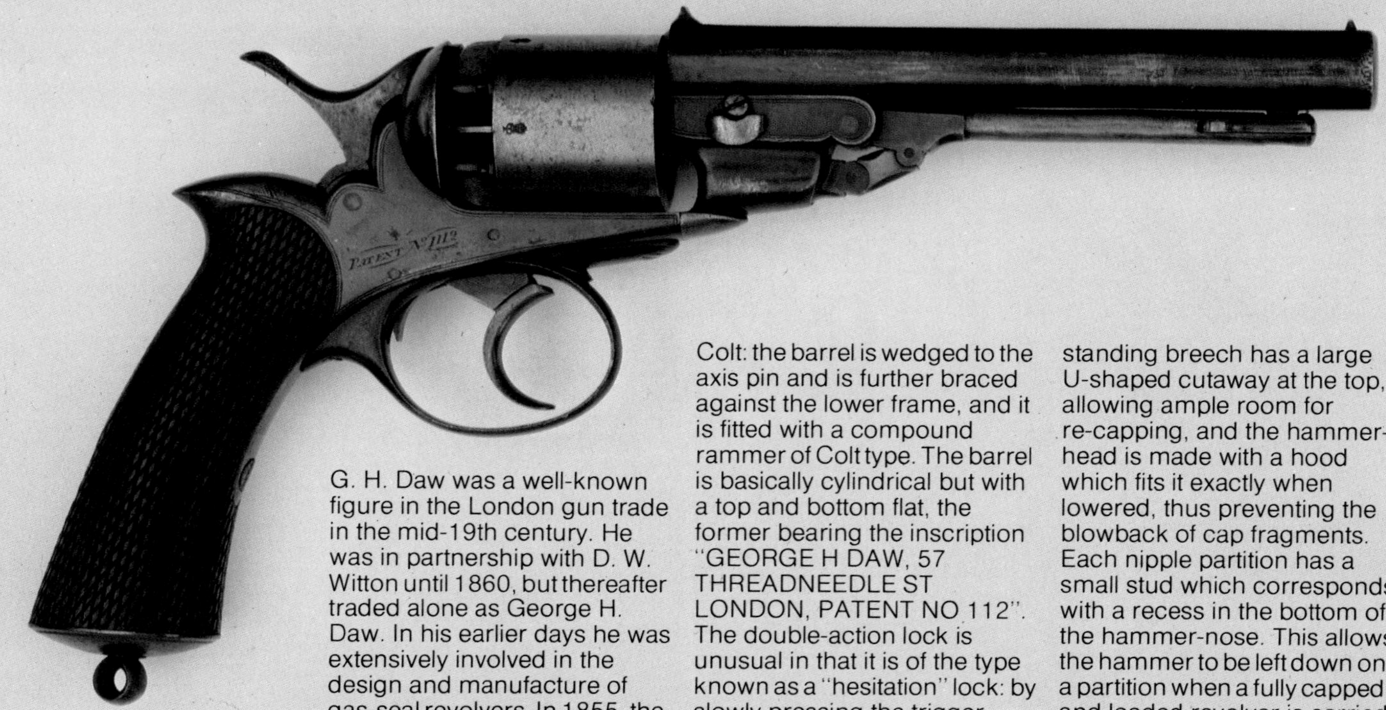

Length: 10·5" (267mm)
Weight: 26oz (·74kg)
Barrel: 5·6" (142mm)
Calibre: ·38" (9·6mm)
Rifling: 5 groove, r/hand
Capacity: Five
Muz Vel: c550 f/s (168 m/s)
Sights: Fixed

G. H. Daw was a well-known figure in the London gun trade in the mid-19th century. He was in partnership with D. W. Witton until 1860, but thereafter traded alone as George H. Daw. In his earlier days he was extensively involved in the design and manufacture of gas-seal revolvers. In 1855, the experienced firm of Pryse and Cashmore patented a double-action lock which Daw took up with enthusiasm; an example of his revolver, incorporating the lock, is seen here. In its general method of construction it may, perhaps, be compared to the

Colt: the barrel is wedged to the axis pin and is further braced against the lower frame, and it is fitted with a compound rammer of Colt type. The barrel is basically cylindrical but with a top and bottom flat, the former bearing the inscription "GEORGE H DAW, 57 THREADNEEDLE ST LONDON, PATENT NO 112". The double-action lock is unusual in that it is of the type known as a "hesitation" lock: by slowly pressing the trigger, the hammer is brought to full-cock, whence a further slight pressure fires it. It can also be cocked manually, and when faster shooting is needed a somewhat stronger pressure on the trigger causes the arm to fire double-action. The

standing breech has a large U-shaped cutaway at the top, allowing ample room for re-capping, and the hammer-head is made with a hood which fits it exactly when lowered, thus preventing the blowback of cap fragments. Each nipple partition has a small stud which corresponds with a recess in the bottom of the hammer-nose. This allows the hammer to be left down on a partition when a fully capped and loaded revolver is carried, without any risk of accident. Hans Busk considered the Daw to be a better weapon than the Adams, but this must be open to considerable doubt. Although very well made and mechanically sound, it seems fragile for service use.

A full-length view of the rifle. No fore-end was needed: the firer's front hand was kept back, round the trigger-guard

Great Britain
WEBLEY REVOLVING RIFLE

Length: 45·5" (1156mm)
Weight: 72oz (2·04kg)
Barrel: 27·75" (705mm)
Calibre: ·500" (12·7mm)
Rifling: 18 groove, r/hand
Capacity: Five
Muz Vel: c800 f/s (244 m/s)
Sights: Fixed

Carbines with revolving chambers were made as early as the 17th century, mainly for use by mounted men. Collier (whose flintlock revolver is illustrated on Page 22) also made a variety of long-arms on the same principle. As with

many other aspects of firearm development, however, it was the introduction of the percussion system in the early years of the 19th century which first made such weapons a practical proposition. Not surprisingly, Samuel Colt, who may fairly be regarded as the father of the modern revolver, was in the field very early, producing revolving rifles from 1836 onwards. However, they were something of a side-line and suffered the inherent defects of the species, discussed below. A number were used in the

American Civil War, but by the end of that conflict effective magazine rifles firing self-contained metallic cartridges had made their appearance and little more was heard of the revolving rifle. The weapon illustrated was made by James Webley in 1853. Although it is, of course, in no sense a pistol, it is included as an extension arm and to demonstrate its very strong family resemblance to the Webley Longspur revolver (page 72). It has a 27in (686mm), octagonal, rifled barrel with a foresight and one

fixed and one hinged backsight; the top flat is inscribed "WILLIAM HENRY FAIRFAX BIRMINGHAM". The barrel lump is hinged to the lower part of the frame, the whole being held rigid by a wedge through the cylinder axis pin. The plain cylinder has five chambers, each serially numbered. The butt is held between two tangs, the upper inscribed "BY HER MAJESTY'S ROYAL LETTERS PATENT"; the removable side-plate on the left of the frame is marked "WEBLEYS PATENT". The butt is fitted with a rectan-

DUAL-IGNITION REVOLVER

Length:	10·8" (274mm)
Weight:	33oz (·94kg)
Barrel:	5·5" (140mm)
Calibre:	·44" (11·2mm)
Rifling:	12 groove, r/hand
Capacity:	Five
Muz Vel:	c550 f/s (168 m/s)
Sights:	Fixed

Apart from some anonymous copies of the early Smith and Wesson cartridge revolver which appeared in Britain in 1860, it is probable that cartridge arms by known makers did not appear until 1863. In the meantime, as had happened during the period of transition from flintlock to percussion arms some 30 years earlier, more conservative users preferred to stick to their well-tried percussion revolvers rather than change. There was, however, a small intermediate category of dual-ignition revolver which, thanks to a certain amount of ingenuity by the makers, could be used either as percussion or cartridge arms, simply by changing the cylinder. The revolver seen here is one such. Its origin is by no means certain: it is of Webley style and is marked "WEBLEYS PATENT"; but since this inscription appears on many arms with little or no connection with the firm, it is not a reliable guide. Webley did make a dual-purpose revolver of similar type, but it had a Kerr-type rammer on the left-hand side.

In fact, the arm shown is probably a hybrid from some unknown workshop. It is of robust construction and the cylinders are easily changed (the cartridge cylinder is, unfortunately, missing from this example). The rammer, the lever of which acts downward, drives a very tight ram into the chambers and is equally effective for loading bullets or ejecting cases, the latter by bearing on their front edges. It was, however, slow to operate, because of the need for absolute alignment of ram and chamber. It has a hinged loading-gate for use with centre-fire cartridges. This type of arm had a short life, for the metallic cartridge was soon in universal use, rendering it obsolete.

gular escutcheon plate and the whole arm is decorated with well-executed scrolls. Because no rammer is provided, the flash of firing was occasionally liable to reach the bullets in the neighbouring chambers and cause a multiple discharge— a fault by no means unknown, even with Colt's rammer. In order to minimise the risk of damage, the barrel lump is grooved so that the mouths of the two chambers are not obstructed; and it was usual for the firer to hold his left hand back, round the trigger-guard.

Cartridge Revolvers

The concept of a made-up cartridge was a very old one—but as long as the flintlock was the only arm available, it was never really possible to load a made-up cartridge intact. If the material of which the cartridge was made was sufficiently robust to stand rough handling, it was, necessarily, also too tough to be penetrated by the flame of the priming. But the perfection of the percussion system, perhaps the most important development in the entire history of firearms, at last made possible the introduction of true, self-contained cartridges—that is, cartridges containing primer, propellant and projectile in a single case—which could be loaded into and fired from breechloading arms without any preliminary opening or tearing of the container.

THE SELF-CONTAINED CARTRIDGE

The earliest experiments in this field tended to be concerned with rifle ammunition, because of the difficulty experienced in forcing a tightly-fitting bullet down a long, rifled barrel from the muzzle end. Some success was achieved, but there was a lingering belief that truly self-contained cartridges were potentially dangerous: it was feared that if a bullet struck a pouch full of such cartridges, the soldier wearing it might be blown apart. This led at first to the appearance of arms known as capping breechloaders, which fired made-up cartridges by means of a separate percussion cap, either of the orthodox copper type or made up into a tape primer. Cartridges for these arms still had to be made of material which was sure to be penetrated by the flash of the cap; which, in practice, made them flimsy. There was also the problem of obturation; ie, the prevention of the escape of the burning gases at the breech end. It was, of course, possible to produce safe breech mechanisms; but it was very difficult to make them fully gas-tight and yet still speedy and simple of operation.

As early as 1812, a Swiss named Jean Samuel Pauly invented a cartridge with a cardboard body and a brass base incorporating a cap. This cartridge, and others like it, achieved some acceptance, particularly by sportsmen, who were always the most ready to experiment. The next step, which was in a sense a divergence from the right line, was taken in the 1840s with the invention of the pinfire cartridge, in which an external brass pin, set at right angles to the base of the metallic case, was driven into an internal cap by means of a hammer. This system proved popular in continental Europe, where revolvers and also sporting guns on the pinfire principle were made in large numbers. An interesting variation was the "Volcanic" hollow bullet, which contained its own propellant and percussion cap. The projectile thus also acted as cartridge case. However, the system was a failure: although it simplified the

Above: *A group of Dodge City "cowboys" in an obviously-posed photograph of c1880. Two of them wear their holstered Colt revolvers—possible supplied by the photographer—in reversed position.*

Below left: *Great men have always feared hand guns because of their potential as easily-concealed assassination weapons. The assailant of this Bulgarian dignitary, in 1891, is armed with a cartridge revolver.*

Below: *This Egyptian gendarme of c1890 has a pinfire revolver, almost certainly of French or Belgian manufacture. There are obvious similarities with the German and French pinfire revolvers which are illustrated on pages 88 and 89.*

Above: *Officers of the Women's Royal Naval Service receive instruction on the Webley and Scott Mark VI revolver. There is no record of women's services actually using revolvers in either World War.*

Left: *A woman agent at practice on the range of the FBI Academy, Quantico, Va., with what appears to be a ·357in Magnum revolver. Note the ear-muffs: high-velocity cartridge noise is likely to damage the hearing without such protection.*

Below left: *British police train their revolvers on a flat in Balcombe Street, London, where gunmen are holding hostages, July 1975. Note the varying types of two-handed grip; one PC grips his wrist; another cups the revolver's butt.*

Below: *Immediately before the invasion of Los Negros in the Admiralty Islands, during the Pacific campaign of 1944, an enlisted man of the US 1st Cavalry runs a cleaning rod down the barrel of his Smith and Wesson ·38in revolver.*

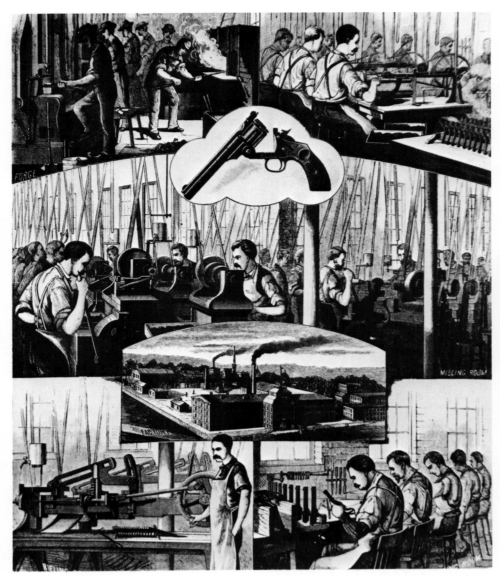

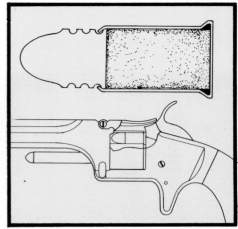

mechanism by dispensing with the need for extraction, it was impossible to use enough powder to give an acceptable velocity to the bullet.

SMITH & WESSON AND COLT

As early as 1857, the American firm of Smith and Wesson, then but little known, acquired the patent for a bored-through revolver cylinder to fire metallic cartridges. The cases were made of copper and the percussion powder was packed round the inside of the rim, where it was detonated by the action of a simple hammer; hence the appellation of rimfire. These revolvers soon became popular, in spite of the fact that the soft copper bases of the cartridges tended to bulge backwards under the force of the exploding powder and prevent the free rotation of the cylinder. This was, however, not a serious problem in arms of relatively small calibre; thus, most rimfire revolvers were pocket models of low power. A version in ·32in (8mm) calibre was extensively carried by Union soldiers in the American Civil War of 1861-65 and proved to be reliable. Like most major conflicts, the Civil War greatly stimulated the development of weapons—and by its end the self-contained cartridge had proved itself

beyond any shadow of doubt. At first, cartridges of copper rimfire type predominated, but these soon gave place to brass cases with a central copper cap in the base. These were sufficiently robust to solve the problem of backward bulging, while the greater elasticity of brass allowed it to expand freely under the pressure of the gases of the explosion, so as to give a perfect gas seal, and then to contract immediately, so as to allow for easy extraction of the case.

As soon as Smith and Wesson's patent expired, many other firms—notably their great rival, Colt—began to make similar revolvers. Most of these had solid frames of the type developed by Robert Adams and incorporated a loading gate as part of the standing breech, along with some kind of sliding rod under the barrel with which to knock out empty cases one by one. Broadly speaking, it may be said of these arms that those made in the United States had single-action locks, while those made in Europe were generally fitted with double-action locks of the Beaumont-Adams type.

In 1870 Smith and Wesson produced a new type of revolver. The frame hinged at the bottom, so that when it was opened the barrel tilted downward,

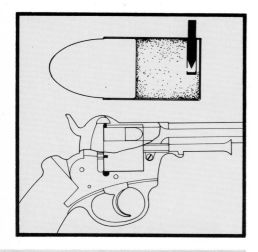

Left: *These diagrams show the principles of the rimfire and pinfire systems. (Extreme left) Rimfire: the percussion compound is packed into the rim of the cartridge, which is made of soft copper so that the hammer is certain to indent it sufficiently. This system was soon abandoned on large-calibre arms, but is still in general use in the case of so-called miniature cartridges. (Left) Pinfire: the hammer is designed to strike vertically downward, thus driving the pin into the internal percussion cap. Pinfire arms never achieved great popularity, and they soon fell out of use and gave place to rimfire and centre-fire weapons. Examples of both rimfire and pinfire rounds are shown with the revolvers illustrated on pages 88-92.*

Far left: *Smith and Wesson's factory in 1880. The revolver inset in the No 3, an excellent arm which failed to gain wide acceptance in the USA, where solid-frame revolvers were preferred.*

Centre: *British troops in Dublin, c1920. The "Black and Tan" auxiliary holds an American-made revolver—probably a Smith and Wesson New Century, made in ·455in calibre for British use.*

Left: *British soldiers training during World War II. The corporal holding the Colt New Service revolver—identifiable by its characteristic foresight—is, in fact, positioned too close to his captive.*

Below left & centre: *"Gun-moll" Bonnie Parker poses with a solid-frame revolver; Bob Ford, assassin of Jesse James, holds a Colt Single-Action Army revolver with a 7·5in (190mm) barrel.*

Below: *This policeman in Bangkok, Thailand, carries his revolver in an open-top, quick-draw holster.*

rather than upwards as in the firm's earlier arms. The new arm incorporated a star-shaped extractor in the base of the cylinder, so that all the cases were ejected simultaneously when the revolver was opened. Smith and Wesson's entire production of the new revolver went to Russia for some years; and although this was profitable in the short term, concentration on a foreign market lost the firm a considerable share of the American one—much of which was taken by Colt. In 1877 the rising British firm of Webley produced a broadly similar hinged-frame model; thereafter, most British revolvers were made to that hinged-frame pattern.

Once the Russian order was completed, Smith and Wesson produced the very similar Model No 3 for the home market. This was a beautiful arm, accurate and well-balanced, and a number of records were set up with it. But in spite of this, it never achieved wide acceptance in the United States, where most people much preferred solid-frame, single-action revolvers as typified by the ubiquitous Colt. Even when Colt did produce a double-action revolver, in 1877, it was not a success.

FURTHER DEVELOPMENTS

A number of British and continental makers produced variations on the basic hinged-frame revolver. All these were designed to achieve the same result—quick and simultaneous extraction and ejection of empty cases—and all worked on broadly similar lines: the cylinder was drawn forward, leaving the cases held in a star extractor whence they could be shaken clear. One such revolver, the invention of Owen Jones, was made at Enfield and issued as the British service revolver; but it was never liked and was soon withdrawn in favour of a reliable model by Webley. The firm of Webley thereafter achieved a near-monopoly of the British market, the greater part of which depended upon military or paramilitary requirements.

In the United States the home market, greatly stimulated by the opening of the vast territories of the West and Southwest, was huge. It remained under the domination of Colt, particularly, perhaps, so far as large-calibre holster pistols were concerned. There were rivals to Colt arms, and some of them, such as the Remington, were of fine quality; but none became universally popular. The only disadvantage of the Colt was the relatively slow system of ejecting empty cases one by one with a rod—and this was remedied in 1887 by the provision of a cylinder on a separate hinged crane, which could be swung out sideways so that the cases were ejected simultaneously by means of a star extractor worked manually by a rod. Smith and Wesson persevered with the No 3 for many years, but by 1896 they

Above left: *At a modern "quick-draw" contest reminiscent of the Old West, the firer "fans" his revolver by knocking back the hammer with the gloved palm of his left hand, to cock the arm.*

Above centre: *A New York policeman with holstered revolver. The unusual shape of the butt suggests that this is a non-standard weapon, with butt specially tailored to the user's requirement.*

Left: *The Balcombe Street siege, July 1975 — Metropolitan policemen with their revolvers in the aiming position.*

had bowed to the inevitable and had begun to make a solid-frame revolver with a hinged cylinder.

Although the revolver market was to a large extent dominated by a few great firms, there was a considerable manufacture by smaller concerns. Hundreds of lesser firms in the United States, Britain, Belgium, France and elsewhere were active in the making of such arms, many of which were obvious copies of the major manufacturers' products. The tendency among the minor makers was to concentrate on fairly small pocket pistols for the cheap end of the market, and these were turned out by the hundred thousand. Their quality and finish varied greatly; many were perfectly safe and reliable weapons, but others were less so, and all now tend to be lumped together under the unkind appellation of "Suicide Specials" or "Saturday Night Specials"—a largely American usage.

A final type of cartridge revolver which must be mentioned is the so-called "automatic revolver" designed by Colonel G.V. Fosbery, VC, and manufactured by Webley at the very end of the 19th century. By this time, self-loading arms in which the recoil of one cartridge was harnessed to load the next had become reasonably well established, so it is perhaps not surprising that the system should also have been applied to a revolver. The Webley-Fosbery handled very much like an orthodox revolver; but an additional feature was that the barrel and cylinder were mounted on a separate frame, thus allowing the recoil of a cartridge to drive them back, cocking the hammer and rotating the cylinder. It was a comfortable weapon to shoot because of the absorption of much of the recoil, but it had to be fired in a target-shooting, straight-arm stance in order to ensure full recoil, and it was also rather more susceptible to malfunction caused by dirt or mud than were orthodox revolvers.

THE MODERN REVOLVER

The development of the revolver was virtually completed by the end of the 19th century, and although many new models and marks have appeared since then, there have been no fundamental changes: improvements have been largely concerned with the use of lightweight metals and new and more powerful cartridges, such as the Magnum.

The introduction of the cartridge revolver also saw the end of the system of describing calibre by reference to the number of spherical balls which could be made from one pound of lead. The advent of the percussion revolver had already made the old system clumsy, for the arm's ability to fire either conical or spherical bullets of the same calibre but different weight caused confusion. Under the new circumstances, there were four basic calibres: ·22in (5·6mm), ·32in (8·1mm), ·38in (9·6mm) and a larger, less clearly defined, one covering ·44in (11·17mm), ·442in (11·22mm), ·45in (11·43mm), ·455in (11·55mm) and ·476in (12·1mm). One or two monsters of ·577in (14·65mm) and even ·6in (15·24mm) were also made, but these must be classed as freaks. There was a degree of interchangeability within the normal

Above: *The equipment of modern police forces reflects the increasing climate of violence in the urban environment. These American policemen are ready for riot duties, with protective helmets and goggles, stout clubs and revolvers (including a Magnum in the holster of the policeman towards the left).*

Right: *Britain's women police now train for the same duties as their male colleagues. A WPC of the Essex Constabulary fires a ·357in Magnum revolver. The two-handed grip gives greater steadiness when firing high-powered cartridges.*

parameters: thus, many British revolvers are marked as ·450/·455in, ·455/·476in, and similar combinations. There was also a good deal of variation in the size of the propellant charge, which in turn affected the length of the cartridge case. Generally speaking, it may be said that in the United States the preference, so far as holster weapons were concerned, was to have a large charge in order to attain good accuracy at long ranges; whereas in Great Britain and the rest of Europe, a man-stopping bullet propelled by quite a moderate charge of powder was the norm. These divergencies naturally led to fairly considerable differences in the length of revolver cylinders.

Revolvers with detachable, rifle-type butts, designed to convert them into carbines, were also made, mainly in the United States, but never found wide acceptance. Such a weapon offered some advantages to a mounted man shooting from the saddle, but excellent purpose-built carbines were so readily available for such use that most people preferred to carry two separate types of arm—

although very often both fired the same cartridge, as was, indeed, desirable.

The future of the revolver seems to lie largely in its use by security forces. Although it is, perhaps, somewhat "old fashioned" in comparison to the self-loading pistol, it is at least holding its own and may even be gaining ground. The revolver has the great advantage of simplicity. It may be carried safely while fully loaded and yet be ready for immediate use by simply pulling the trigger; it is less susceptible to dirt and dust than the self-loader; and, in the event of a misfire (admittedly, a rare event with modern ammunition), the next round is brought under the hammer without delay. The revolver's chief disadvantage is its bulky cylinder, which makes it difficult to carry concealed and which limits its capacity to no more than six rounds.

Right: *A British policeman at London "Spaghetti House" siege, September 1975, wears a flak-jacket and carries a short-barrelled revolver, butt downward in a spring-clip holster for fast drawing.*

Germany
PINFIRE REVOLVER

Length:	11" (279mm)
Weight:	27oz (·76kg)
Barrel:	6" (152mm)
Calibre:	·43" (11mm)
Rifling:	5 groove, l/hand
Capacity:	Six
Muz Vel:	c600 f/s (183 m/s)
Sights:	Fixed

The history of the development of the pinfire cartridge, which this arm and the next seven weapons illustrated in this section were designed to fire, is dealt with below; here, it is necessary only to describe it. A specimen cartridge is shown with the lower revolver on the facing page. From that example, it will be seen that the pinfire cartridge consisted of a rimless, cylindrical, brass case containing the charge; a bullet; and, most important of all, an internal percussion cap inserted into a small compartment in the cartridge's base. The inner end of the small brass-wire pin which gave the cartridge its name rested on this cap. When it was driven inwards by the blow of the hammer, it set off the cap and thus fired the charge. The most interesting aspects of the weapon are the apertures running from the chambers to the rear edge of the cylinder, several of which are clearly visible. To load the revolver, it was necessary to open the top-hinged loading gate; place the hammer at half-cock; and insert the cartridges into the chambers in such a way that the pins protruded from the apertures. The hammer was so shaped that when it fell it struck the outer end of the pin and thus fired the cartridge. The thin brass case expanded at this instant and prevented any rearward escape of burning gases. Then the metal's natural elasticity caused it to contract, so that it could be easily removed by the sliding rod below the barrel. Copper was also used for cases, although it was somewhat less elastic.

France
PINFIRE REVOLVER

Length:	8·4" (213mm)
Weight:	20oz (·56kg)
Barrel:	4" (102mm)
Calibre:	·35" (9mm)
Rifling:	4 groove, r/hand
Capacity:	Six
Muz Vel:	c600 f/s (183 m/s)
Sights:	Fixed

Like a great many other developments in connection with firearms, a practical self-contained cartridge for use in breechloading weapons only became possible as a result of the perfection of the percussion system in the first quarter of the 19th century. A good many previous attempts had been made; but the main and virtually insoluble problem had been that of providing for the direct application of fire to the charge. As soon as the percussion system made it possible to produce such fire by means of a relatively remote blow, the major problem was very largely solved—although, of course, a good deal more experiment was necessary before any really reliable system could be perfected. In particular, there remained the difficulty of obtaining perfect obturation—ie, the prevention of burning gases escaping from the breech at the moment of firing—without making the breech mechanism so complex that it offered little or no advantage over the existing muzzle-loaders. The pinfire cartridge was invented by a Frenchman named Casimir Lefaucheux as early as 1828, and was in quite extensive use, mainly on the continent, before 1840. However, it does not seem to have aroused much interest in Britain until its appearance at the Great Exhibition held in London in 1851, when it was shown in conjunction with an arm of the pepperbox type (like the upper weapon on the facing page). A more modern type of arm was then developed by Casimir's son Eugène, who patented it in Great Britain in 1854. As seen here, the general style of the weapon is clear. It is plain and of robust construction: the octagonal barrel is attached to the axis pin (as in Colt arms) and is further braced against the lower part of the frame, making a reasonably rigid joint. The heavy standing breech is fitted with a top-hinged loading gate with a spring catch, and a simple sliding rod is provided for knocking out the empty cases. The small, square studs on the otherwise plain cylinder engage with the cylinder stop and hold the cylinder rigid at the moment of firing. The weapon has no trigger-guard, and the trigger folds forward, thus making it less bulky for carriage in a pocket.

France
FIST PISTOL

Length:	4.8" (122mm)
Weight:	11oz (.31kg)
Barrel:	1.9" (48mm)
Calibre:	.275" (7mm)
Rifling:	Nil
Capacity:	Six
Muz Vel:	c450 f/s (137 m/s)
Sights:	Nil

This type of pistol is called *coup de poing* in France, where it originated, and the translation "fist pistol" seems to be as appropriate as any. Reference to the earlier section on percussion pistols will show that this is by definition a pepperbox — and it was with a pistol of this type that Casimir Lefaucheux exhibited his new pinfire cartridge at the Great Exhibition of 1851. As will be seen, it is in many ways a rather ugly little weapon. Its long, fluted, pepperbox cylinder is made from a single piece of metal, and the front end of the cylinder axis pin is supported by a bracket screwed to the front end of the lower frame. The standing breech consists of a flat, circular plate: a semi-circular portion is cut out on the right-hand side so that the weapon can be loaded from the breech end. This loading aperture is filled by a bottom-hinged gate fitted with a small stud to give purchase; and its bottom end bears on the small, horizontal, L-shaped spring screwed below it on the frame. There is a further shallow depression, into which the hammer fits, on top of the standing breech. The lock is of self-cocking type and can only be fired by steady pressure on the trigger, which is of the forward-hinged variety and is thus without a trigger-guard. The cylinder is normally free to rotate, but when the trigger is pressed a cylinder-stop rises from the lower frame and engages one of the studs which can be seen on the cylinder. When loaded, the cylinder may be positioned so that there is a pin on either side of the hammer head, thus making it relatively safe to carry the loaded weapon in a pocket. Once the rounds have been fired, the empty cases may be pushed out through the open loading gate by means of a separate extractor pin. This is screwed into the base of the butt when not in use: its end is visible in the arm seen here. Arms of this kind sometimes incorporate a knuckle-duster and dagger; when thus equipped they are known as "Apache pistols", a reference to the denizens of the underworld of 19th-century Paris.

Germany
PINFIRE REVOLVER

Length:	10.4" (264mm)
Weight:	26oz (.73kg)
Barrel:	5.4" (137mm)
Calibre:	.35" (9mm)
Rifling:	6 groove, r/hand
Capacity:	Six
Muz Vel:	c550 f/s (168 m/s)
Sights:	Fixed

This is an attractive arm, strong and well-made, as one would expect of a German weapon, and of unusually good quality and finish. It has a one-piece frame with a top strap and an octagonal barrel, on which the top flat is narrowed to form a distinct rib. It has an unusually high (and thus, perhaps, slightly vulnerable) foresight, while the backsight is a V-shaped notch on the rear of the top strap. The cylinder is unfluted and has long and elegantly-formed projections: these engage against the cylinder stop, which rises from the lower frame when the trigger is pressed. It is fitted with the usual loading gate, with a thumb piece and a spring catch projecting below it. This holds the gate firmly in position, yet allows it to be opened with quite light thumb pressure. The cylinder is removed by pulling forward the axis pin, and on the left-hand side of the frame is a vertical spring and stud which prevents accidental removal. The lock is of double-action type: the arm can be fired either by simple trigger pressure, or by preliminary cocking of the hammer, according to circumstances. There is an upward bulge at the rear end of the top strap to prevent the protruding pins from fouling it when the cylinder rotates, and there is a corresponding notch on the bottom of the frame. The pistol is well blued and engraved, with the exception of the hammer, trigger, foresight and ejector rod, which are of bright steel. The one-piece butt — its shape typical of German arms — is held by two tangs. The top strap bears the inscription "J A COSTER IN HANAU", and there is a gold monogram (apparently C.T.) on the top tang. The pistol was supplied in a baize-lined case complete with a cleaning rod and a bullet mould, so that cartridges could be reloaded with the aid of a small, simple and easily-obtained machine.

France
LEFAUCHEUX PINFIRE REVOLVER

Length:	11.25" (286mm)	**Rifling:**	4 groove, l/hand
Weight:	34oz (.96kg)	**Capacity:**	Six
Barrel:	5.25" (133mm)	**Muz Vel:**	c650 f/s (198 m/s)
Calibre:	.43" (11mm)	**Sights:**	Fixed

The names of Casimir Lefaucheux and his son Eugène have been mentioned earlier in this section (pages 88-89) in connection with the development in the mid-19th century of the pinfire cartridge, in which they were both very closely concerned. The pinfire revolver never really received anything approaching complete acceptance in Great Britain; but matters were very much otherwise on the continent, where it was quite widely used. The French government carried out extensive trials with pinfire weapons in the course of the Crimean War (the other arms concerned were the American Colt and the British Beaumont-Adams; both, of course, percussion arms), and as a result a Lefaucheux pinfire revolver of the type illustrated here was selected in 1856 for use by the French Navy. It is in every respect a well-made and reliable weapon; plain, solid, well-balanced, and worthy of being distinguished as a service arm. It has a round barrel with a lump fitting over the cylinder axis pin and fastened also to the lower frame, to which it is both slotted and screwed to make a rigid joint. It has the usual solid standing breech with a loading gate on the right-hand side. The cylinder revolves freely except at full cock, when a stop protrudes horizontally from the lower part of the standing breech and locks the cylinder by acting on the rectangular blocks between the pin apertures.

France
PINFIRE REVOLVER

Length:	9" (229mm)
Weight:	22oz (.62kg)
Barrel:	4.3" (109mm)
Calibre:	.39" (9.9mm)
Rifling:	9 groove, l/hand
Capacity:	Six
Muz Vel:	c600 f/s (183 m/s)
Sights:	Nil

Apart from the various purpose-built pinfire revolvers for service use, the great bulk of these arms appear to have been self-defence or pocket weapons. As such, they did not get much hard use and, as a result, considerable numbers have survived. Although some of these arms were handsome and well-made (as witness, for example, the lower example on the page 89), it seems fairly certain that most were rather cheap and nasty arms, turned out by a variety of anonymous backstreet makers, mostly in France and Belgium. The example illustrated here may, perhaps, be regarded as a fair example of the type. Its general style can be clearly seen. It has a round barrel, with a lump that appears to have been made separately, which is held on by the usual means of cylinder axis pin and lower frame, the latter being held by a screw. The general construction is flimsy and a good deal of daylight is visible between the face of the cylinder and the breech end of the barrel, which is rifled but lacks sights of any kind. The mechanism is of the self-cocking variety with the hammer head in the form of an animal, possibly a hippopotamus. It has a folding trigger, thus allowing it to be easily carried in a pocket. The crude engraving of the cylinder may have been cast upon it. The frame, loading gate and butt strap are of a brass-type yellow alloy and are also engraved. There is no maker's name nor proof marks—nor, indeed, inscriptions of any kind—visible upon the weapon. However, in spite of these somewhat unkind remarks upon pinfire weapons at the lower end of the scale, it will be clear from what has been said in the other captions dealing with the type that the better pinfire arms, well made and using reliable ammunition, were good enough for all practical purposes. Indeed, they continued to be made well into the 20th century. They were essentially a continental product with manufacture centering on Belgium and France, although some were also produced in Germany. Although Webley's early catalogues list pinfire revolvers, there is no real indication that the firm actually made weapons of this type; although it may well have imported them. Pinfire arms appear never to have been made in the United States: a number were bought by both sides for use in the Civil War, presumably as a matter of hard necessity, but otherwise there was a more or less direct transition from percussion to rim- or centre-fire—as, indeed, there was in Great Britain. Although somewhat outside the scope of this work, it may be noted that pinfire shotguns were for many years made and used in large numbers. A few may still be in service, although pinfire cartridges have been hard to find for some years.

Belgium
CONTINENTAL PINFIRE REVOLVER

Length:	·10" (245mm)	Rifling:	6 groove, l/hand
Weight:	21oz (·59kg)	Capacity:	Six
Barrel:	5·8" (147mm)	Muz Vel:	c550 f/s (168 m/s)
Calibre:	·39" (9·9mm)	Sights:	Fixed

This is a medium-quality pinfire revolver of quite large calibre. Like many of its kind, it is strictly anonymous, bearing no name or markings other than the number (visible in the photograph on the lower part of the frame, just above the trigger) and Belgian proof-marks on the cylinder. It has an octagonal barrel with a very high and somewhat flimsy foresight; the backsight is a simple notch on the top of the hammer nose. The cylinder has long, machined projections, the higher parts being almost level with the pin apertures. These are engaged by a cylinder stop which rises from the lower frame when the trigger is pressed, locking the cylinder when the appropriate chamber is in line with the barrel. The lock is of somewhat later type than on most weapons of this kind, and the hammer may be manually cocked if required. The revolver is fitted with the usual ejector rod—with an additional refinement: it is held by the tension of a small, flat spring which prevents it being pushed into a chamber accidentally and so interfering with the revolution of the cylinder. The arm is blued, with the exception of the hammer, trigger, and ejector rod, and is covered with rather crude engraving. The butt plates are of some black composition, bearing an elaborate pattern, and the weapon is fitted with a lanyard ring, suggesting that it may have been intended for military or paramilitary use.

Spain
PINFIRE REVOLVER

Length:	11·5" (292mm)
Weight:	34oz (·96kg)
Barrel:	6·4" (163mm)
Calibre:	·43" (11mm)
Rifling:	4 groove, l/hand
Capacity:	Six
Muz Vel:	c650 f/s (198 m/s)
Sights:	Fixed

This weapon is very closely based on the Lefaucheux pinfire revolver shown on the facing page (above). The French Navy adopted the Lefaucheux in 1856 and found it sufficiently reliable for its good reputation to spread. It was used principally by boarding- and landing-parties, in conjunction with the cutlass, and proved a handy arm. However, no pistol can hope to compete with a rifle or carbine; so most navies tended to shun the pistol and equip their sailors instead with long arms, which gave a good deal more firepower to a small and possibly isolated landing-party than even the most efficient revolver. But in spite of this, the Italian Navy followed the French example and took into service the Lefaucheux pinfire revolver in 1858. Of course, armies also needed the revolver, and here the pin-fire achieved considerable popularity: it was adopted in one form or another by Norway, Sweden and Spain, as an arm for officers and certain categories of mounted troops. The weapon illustrated here was made by Arriaban and Company of Eibar, probably in the mid-1860s, when Spain first adopted the arm. The Spaniards had a long and honourable history of gun-making. Spanish gunsmiths were particularly noted for their barrels, for the manufacture of which they had considerable deposits of high-grade iron ore in the Biscayan area. Although they were never able to compete in the highly industrialized areas of Northern Europe, they maintained a considerable export trade with their erstwhile colonies in South America, where cheapness was much more important than high quality. Although little is known of the history of the pinfire revolver in South America, it is possible that it was quite widely used. The weapon seen here is of solid construction, with a round barrel fastened to the axis pin and the lower frame. As can be seen, a rearward extension to the barrel lump slides over the lower extension of the frame (to which it is screwed) and fits into a slot in the lower part of the standing breech. The lock is of single-action type and there is a lower spur on the trigger-guard to give added grip for the firer's fingers.

Great Britain
TRANTER RIMFIRE REVOLVER

Length:	12" (305mm)	**Rifling:**	5 groove, r/hand
Weight:	50oz (1·4kg)	**Capacity:**	Six
Barrel:	6·5" (165mm)	**Muz Vel:**	c650 f/s (198 m/s)
Calibre:	·45" (11·4mm)	**Sights:**	Fixed

The name of Tranter has already been mentioned several times in this book (pages 76-77); but always in connection with the early double-trigger percussion revolvers for which he is perhaps best known. Apart from these, however, Tranter also produced a good many double-action percussion revolvers, in a variety of sizes, in order to compete with Beaumont-Adams arms, especially military arms in service calibres. Once the popularity of the new Smith and Wesson breechloading revolvers was assured, Tranter, a competent and enterprising individual, wasted little time: by 1863 he had placed on the market the rimfire revolver seen here. This was the first of its type to be produced (or, it might be safer to say, acknowledged) by a British maker. Reference back to the percussion section will show its continuing strong resemblance to the Adams arms: indeed, Tranter had used the Adams frame, under licence, for his revolvers. The cylinder (which is, of course, bored through) has six chambers instead of the five customary in Tranter's earlier models; and the rear ends of the chambers are recessed to accommodate the rims of the cartridges. There is a bottom-hinged loading gate on the right-hand side of the standing breech. The rammer lever, which is inscribed "TRANTERS PATENT", acts downwards, forcing the ram into the chamber through a sleeve. It is a close fit, in order to push out the cases by their forward edges. This meant that chamber and ram had to be most carefully aligned.

United States of America
ALLEN AND WHEELOCK REVOLVER

Length:	8" (203mm)
Weight:	15oz (·43kg)
Barrel:	4" (102mm)
Calibre:	·32" (8·1mm)
Rifling:	6 groove, l/hand
Capacity:	Six
Muz Vel:	c500 f/s (152 m/s)
Sights:	Fixed

The Allen of this title is the Ethan Allen whose name has been mentioned earlier in this book (page 58) in connection with a pepperbox revolver. When his earlier partner, Charles Thurber, retired in 1856, Allen was joined by Thomas P. Wheelock in a partnership which lasted until 1864. When Smith and Wesson produced their tip-up revolver with the Rollin White bored-through cylinder (see facing page, above) and their own patent rimfire cartridge, both these aspects of the arm were fully protected in the United States. The novelty and obvious utility of such an arm made it extremely susceptible to piracy, and Smith and Wesson spent a good deal of time and trouble in legal actions against various makers who attempted to evade the conditions of the patents. One of these was the Massachusetts Arms Company, whose name has already been mentioned (page 67) in connection with percussion revolvers. Another was Allen and Wheelock, maker of the revolver seen here. Rollin White (who, under the terms of his agreement with Smith and Wesson, was responsible for prosecuting infringements of his cylinder patent) opened proceedings in 1859, but was not successful until 1863. The revolver shown here has a solid frame, including the butt, into which an octagonal barrel is screwed. There are no facilities either for loading the revolver or ejecting the empty cases with the cylinder in position. In order to perform these operations, it is necessary first to remove the large-headed screw below the front frame, which allows the cylinder axis pin to be drawn forward and the cylinder removed. Empty cases may then be punched out by the axis pin; the chambers reloaded, if necessary; and the cylinder replaced. This made the revolver very slow to reload, but it also greatly simplified manufacture and thus made it cheap to produce. The weapon has a single-action lock with an external hammer on the right-hand side, access to the mechanism being gained by way of an oval inspection plate on the left. The trigger is of the variety known as "sheathed"; it has no trigger-guard, and this reduces its bulk and makes it a suitable pocket arm. The barrel and frame are crudely engraved with a standing pugilist on the right side and a kneeling one on the left, with a further motif of boxing gloves on the inspection plate cover. The butt plates are of ivory or bone, probably the latter. The arm is cheap in overall appearance, but is probably sufficiently robust for use as an occasional pocket arm. The left-hand flat of the barrel is marked "ALLEN AND WHEELOCK, WORCESTER, MS US" and "ALLENS PAT'S SEP 7 NOV 9 1858", and the weapon is numbered 444. The perfection of the centre-fire cartridge in the 1860s led to the displacement of the rimfire type, particularly in large-calibre arms, where they had been liable to bulge backwards and prevent the rotation of the cylinder. However, rimfire cartridges remain still in use in a number of arms of small-bore type.

United States of America
SMITH AND WESSON TIP-UP REVOLVER

Length:	10" (254mm)
Weight:	21oz (·6kg)
Barrel:	5" (127mm)
Calibre	·32" (8·1mm)
Rifling:	6 groove, r/hand
Capacity:	Six
Muz Vel:	c600 f/s (183 m/s)
Sights:	Fixed

In 1855 an American inventor named Rollin White patented a revolver with a bored-through cylinder. When the firm of Smith and Wesson began to consider the production of a modern cartridge revolver (which they would be able to do as soon as Colt's patent for a revolving cylinder expired in 1857) they had the good sense to buy this patent. This gave them a monopoly on the system in the United States, although it did not apply to Europe. The first pistols incor-porating the system—of ·22in (5·6mm) calibre, firing copper rimfire cartridges—were on the market in 1858. They quickly became popular and several variations were developed. The revolver seen here is the Model No 2 (Army); this became avail-able in 1861 and was widely purchased as a private arm during the Civil War. The octag-onal barrel is hinged to the front of the top frame, and a retaining catch holds it to the lower frame. When the catch is pushed upward, the barrel can be raised and the cylinder removed, the empty cases being pushed out by means of the pin below the barrel. The cylinder stop is a flat spring on top of the frame; it is held by two pins, and is lifted clear of the cylinder by the hammer nose. The extra forward pin is said to have been added to strengthen the stop: the model is thus usually known as the "three-pin". It was made in a variety of barrel lengths, the longest being six inches (152mm) and the shortest four inches (102mm).

Europe
CONTINENTAL TIP-UP REVOLVER

Length:	10·75" (273mm)
Weight:	32oz (·9kg)
Barrel:	5·5" (140mm)
Calibre	·44" (11·2mm)
Rifling:	7 groove, r/hand
Capacity:	Five
Muz Vel:	c600 f/s (183 m/s)
Sights:	Fixed

The invention of the self-contained metallic cartridge led to a great upsurge of interest in revolvers. The earliest of these new cartridges was, perhaps, the pinfire, to which reference has already been made (pages 88-91). This was soon followed by a cartridge made of copper and having a rim with a compound of fulminate of mercury inserted beneath it. When the outer side of the soft copper base was struck by a hammer, the blow was sufficient to detonate the internal fulminate and fire the charge. This system made possible the development of a self-contained cartridge of material sufficiently elastic for it to be expanded by the pressure of the gases at the instant of firing, thus avoiding the rearward leakage of gases which had been a problem with earlier breechloaders. The cartridge had the added advan-tages of being watertight and having no protruding pin; so it soon became popular. Smith and Wesson patented a ·22in (5·6mm) cartridge of this type in the United States in 1855-56; and it was subsequently pro-duced also in ·32in (8·1mm) calibre, for use in the revolver illustrated at the top of this page. One of the difficulties of Smith and Wesson's patent for a bored-through cylinder was that it was valid only in the United States. Thus, although the patent gave them an American monopoly, the firm had no protection against the cylinder being copied in Europe or elsewhere; as a result, pirated copies soon began to appear. It is generally thought that the firm of Webley was producing such unlicensed copies in the early 1860s; but as these were, of course, unmarked, it is impossible to be certain. The weapon illustrated here is something of a mystery: although obviously of Smith and Wesson type, it bears no name or mark other than the date, 1874, on the left-hand side of the barrel frame, and one or two manufacturing numbers on the cylinder. The major differences (apart from size) from the genuine arm are the provision of a backsight on the top frame; the fact that the cylinder stop rises from the bottom; and the fact that the weapon is of centre-fire rather than rimfire type and is fitted with a sliding safety behind the hammer. The weapon appears to be well made, although it lacks the finish of a real Smith and Wesson. Its size, and the provision of a lanyard ring, suggest that it was intended for use as a military or perhaps paramilitary weapon.

LAGRESE REVOLVER

Length:	11·75" (298mm)
Weight:	28oz (·79kg)
Barrel:	6·25" (159mm)
Calibre:	·43" (10·9mm)
Rifling:	8 groove, l/hand
Capacity:	Six
Muz Vel:	c550 f/s (168 m/s)
Sights:	Fixed

This revolver, made by Lagrese of Paris in about 1866, is well made and finished; but, as may be seen from the photograph, it is of somewhat ornate appearance and extreme complexity. The frame, including the butt, is made in one piece without any top strap; the octagonal barrel is screwed to the front end of the frame, through which also passes the cylinder axis pin. This appears to make a rigid joint and there is no play apparent—although the permanent gap between the barrel and the cylinder is about ·05in (1·3mm), which must have led to a considerable loss of gases. The arrangement of the cylinder is also strange. It is fitted with a separate back plate which incorporates a loading gate. Conical apertures are pierced through the back plate to allow the nose of the hammer to reach the cartridges. In order to load, it is necessary first to put the nose of the hammer into a safety hole in the plate. This holds the plate rigid but allows the gate to be opened and the cylinder to be rotated clockwise. A groove on the right side of the butt allows the rounds to be slid in. The ejection is of percussion rammer type, in which an upward pull of the lever forces the ram backwards into the chamber. The lock is of the self-cocking variety, but there is a basic comb on the hammer which allows it to be drawn back slightly and then lowered into the safety hole mentioned earlier. The arm is lightly engraved but there are no traces of any finish: it is difficult to know whether it was originally bright or has been over cleaned. The barrel is inscribed "Lagrese Bte a Paris". All in all, this is a truly remarkable weapon.

Length:	8" (203mm)
Weight:	19oz (·54kg)
Barrel:	3·5" (89mm)
Calibre:	·32" (8·1mm)
Rifling:	5 groove, r/hand
Capacity:	Seven
Muz Vel:	c550 f/s (168 m/s)
Sights:	Fixed

TRANTER POCKET REVOLVER

William Tranter was a well-known and well-respected member of the Birmingham gun trade for almost the whole of the second half of the 19th century. A number of his products—notably his famous double-trigger percussion revolvers and his service calibre rimfire model—are illustrated and described earlier in this book. Tranter was a flourishing manufacturer of wide interests and, initially at least, revolvers formed only a relatively small, if well-known, part of his business. However, trade fell off badly after the end of the American Civil War in 1865, and it seems probable that Tranter then increased his production of revolvers. In fact, he probably produced more revolvers, particularly pocket revolvers, than almost any other maker in the United Kingdom. The weapon illustrated is, perhaps, typical of Tranter's arms. It has a solid and robust frame, into which the barrel is screwed, and a plain, seven-shot cylinder with recesses to accommodate the cartridge rims. The cylinder is rotated by a pawl, worked by the hammer, acting on a ratchet; the latter is cut out of the actual cylinder instead of attached to it. The cylinder stop rises from the bottom of the frame and engages the rectangular slots towards the front of the cylinder. The cylinder pin is retained by a small, vertical spring: pressure on the bottom end of the spring allows the pin to be withdrawn. The weapon has a bottom-hinged loading gate on the right-hand side of the frame, into which a groove has been machined to allow the copper rimfire cartridges to be inserted. No ejector is fitted: to unload, it is necessary either to use the cylinder pin or to lever the cases out by inserting a knife-point or small screwdriver into the wide slots around the rear edge of the cylinder. This was a somewhat slow method; but presumably it was felt that seven rounds in the cylinder would usually be ample for self-defence. The lock, which is of single-action type, is fitted with a half-cock and is operated by the sheathed trigger usual on pocket arms. The weapon is marked "TRANTERS PATENT" on the frame and is numbered "10719" on the butt cap. The top flat is inscribed with the name of the retailer: "PARKER FIELD AND SONS, HIGH HOLBORN, LONDON". Although the centre-fire cartridge soon ousted the rimfire type in revolvers of service calibre, the older cartridge remained in use for many years in pocket arms and it is still used extensively in small-bore rifles.

ADAMS REVOLVER CONVERSION

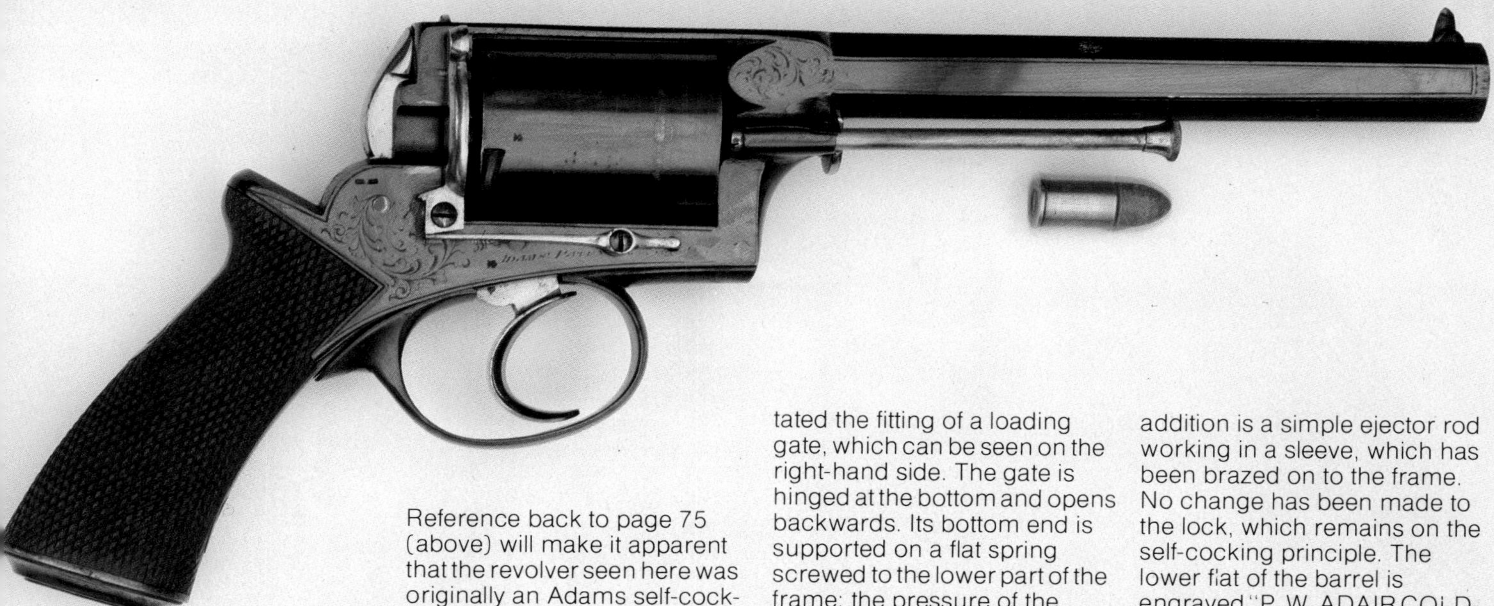

Length:	11·5" (292mm)
Weight:	33oz (·94kg)
Barrel:	6·5" (165mm)
Calibre:	·44" (11·2mm)
Rifling:	3 groove, r/hand
Capacity:	Five
Muz Vel:	c550 f/s (168 m/s)
Sights:	Fixed

Reference back to page 75 (above) will make it apparent that the revolver seen here was originally an Adams self-cocking, percussion arm, and that it has been converted to a breechloader to take centre-fire cartridges. As will be seen by comparison with the earlier weapon, the basic conversion was a fairly simple one. The weapon has been fitted with a bored-through, five-chambered cylinder; this, in turn, necessi-tated the fitting of a loading gate, which can be seen on the right-hand side. The gate is hinged at the bottom and opens backwards. Its bottom end is supported on a flat spring screwed to the lower part of the frame; the pressure of the spring holds the gate firmly open or closed, as required. A piece of metal of the required shape has been screwed to the left-hand side of the frame to prevent the cartridges slipping out, and has been carefully fitted in front of the spring safety which holds the hammer clear of the rounds. The only other addition is a simple ejector rod working in a sleeve, which has been brazed on to the frame. No change has been made to the lock, which remains on the self-cocking principle. The lower flat of the barrel is engraved "P. W. ADAIR COLD-STREAM GUARDS"; an upper flat is engraved "CRIMEA, SEBASTOPOL"—a campaign in which Captain Adair served and in which, presumably, he carried this revolver. He was later in his career appointed Colonel-Commandant of the 4th (Militia) Battalion of the Somerset Light Infantry.

DEVISME REVOLVER

Length:	12·5" (317mm)
Weight:	32oz (·91kg)
Barrel:	5·75" (146mm)
Calibre:	·41" (10·4mm)
Rifling:	4 groove, l/hand
Capacity:	Six
Muz Vel:	c550 f/s (168 m/s)
Sights:	Fixed

The manufacturer of this weapon was F. P. Devisme, a Parisian gunmaker of con-siderable repute, who had produced a self-cocking percussion revolver in limited quantity before 1830. He was also an early experimenter with centre-fire cartridges. The revolver seen here is of the type first shown at the Paris Exhibi-tion of 1867, and it is fairly closely based on an earlier percussion revolver by the same maker. It has a cylindrical steel barrel screwed into a frame which is, in turn, hinged at the bottom of the standing breech, just in front of the trigger-guard. Pressure on the vertical milled lever in front of the frame allows the barrel to drop down to an angle of about 45°, giving access to the cylinder. The locking device is somewhat unusual, for it is based on the cylinder axis pin. The front end of the pin passes through the frame and is attached to the opening lever. The rear end has on it a rectangular stud which enters a corresponding socket on the standing breech when the arm is closed. Returning the opening lever to its normal, vertical position causes the stud to turn in the socket and locks it firmly. The extractor pin sleeve is attached to another sleeve round the barrel: the move-ment of the lever activates a simple rack-and-pinion device which swings the extractor pin out to the right, in readiness to knock out the empty cases one at a time. The lock is of single-action type and is fitted with a half-cock to hold the hammer nose clear of the rounds in the chambers. The weapon is of excellent quality and finish, with barrel and cylinder blued and the remainder case-hardened. The top of the barrel is inscribed "DEVISME a PARIS", and the frame marked "DEVISME BTE".

United States of America
SMITH AND WESSON TIP-UP POCKET REVOLVER

Length:	7" (178mm)	Rifling:	5 groove, r/hand
Weight:	11·5oz (·33kg)	Capacity:	Seven
Barrel:	3·2" (81mm)	Muz Vel:	c500 f/s (152 m/s)
Calibre:	·22" (5·6mm)	Sights:	Fixed

By the mid-1850s, Smith and Wesson had designed a pocket revolver to fire rimfire cartridges and were only awaiting the expiry of Colt's patent for a revolving cylinder to put it on to the market. They also acquired Rollin White's American patent for a bored-through cylinder and agreed to pay him 25 cents thereafter for every weapon of that type made by them. The first, or Model No 1, appeared in 1857. Because the shape of its brass frame made it difficult to machine economically, a second series, of which the weapon illustrated is a specimen, was produced in 1860. The octagonal barrel is hinged at the top of the frame, just above the front of the cylinder, and opens upward when the small catch just below the front of the cylinder is pushed up. The cylinder stop consists of a flat spring on top of the frame. In order to load, or reload, the cylinder is removed and the empty, copper, rimfire cases are pushed out by means of the pin below the barrel. The lock is of single-action pattern and the weapon has a sheathed trigger. The frame is of brass or bronze and was originally silver-plated, although little of this refinement now remains.

United States of America
COLT NEW LINE POCKET MODEL

Length:	5·5" (140mm)
Weight:	8oz (·23kg)
Barrel:	2·2" (56mm)
Calibre:	·22" (5·6mm)
Rifling:	5 groove, r/hand
Capacity:	Seven
Muz Vel:	c500 f/s (152 m/s)
Sights:	Fixed

Although the famous Colt Company had been a leader in the production of what may fairly be described as the modern revolver, Colt's development of revolvers firing metallic cartridges was delayed by the fact that Smith and Wesson had overall rights in Rollin White's patent for bored-through cylinders. This did not expire until 1869. It is improbable that the Colt Company was much disturbed by this delay, for they had established a huge market for their percussion revolvers, and most users of such arms in remote frontier areas preferred to retain them until the new metallic cartridges were universally obtainable. Even after the Rollin White patent had expired, some time was necessary to reorganize. Thus, it was not until 1872 that the Colt New Line series of pocket revolvers came on to the market, in a variety of calibres from ·41in (10·4mm) down to ·22in (5·6mm). The example shown is of the smallest calibre. It has an octagonal barrel complete with foresight, screwed into a solid frame; along the top of the frame runs a long groove to act as a back-sight. The cylinder, which is fluted, is rotated by means of the usual pawl and ratchet and is held steady by a cylinder stop. This projects from the bottom of the standing breech and engages slots cut into the rear of the cylinder between the chambers. The cylinder is removed by pressing a retaining spring on the right-hand side of the frame and drawing forward the axis pin, which may also be used to knock out the empty, copper, rimfire cases. There is no loading gate, but cartridges can be inserted through a small gap in the rear of the frame.

United States of America
ETHAN ALLEN POCKET REVOLVER

Length:	5·5" (140mm)
Weight:	7oz (·2kg)
Barrel:	2·5" (63mm)
Calibre:	·22" (5·6mm)
Rifling:	3 groove, r/hand
Capacity:	Seven
Muz Vel:	c500 f/s (152 m/s)
Sights:	Fixed

The perfection of the rimfire cartridge and the expiry of Smith and Wesson's patent for the bored-through cylinder in 1869 gave rise to a great increase in production of small, cheap, pocket pistols—for which there was apparently an almost insatiable demand in the United States. Ethan Allen continued to manufacture pepperbox pistols for some time, but after his death in 1871 his company switched to pistols of the type seen here. It has an octagonal steel barrel screwed into a gunmetal frame, and a seven-chambered steel cylinder to take rimfire cartridges. In order to load the weapon, it is necessary first to press up the catch under the cylinder axis pin, which can then be drawn out and the cylinder removed. The empty cases are knocked out with the axis pin; this made the weapon relatively cheap to manufacture.

United States of America
SMITH AND WESSON TIP-UP REVOLVER

Length:	6·6" (168mm)	**Rifling:**	5 groove, r/hand
Weight:	9oz (·25kg)	**Capacity:**	Seven
Barrel:	3·1" (79mm)	**Muz Vel:**	c500 f/s (152 m/s)
Calibre:	·22" (5·6mm)	**Sights:**	Fixed

When the American Civil War ended in 1865 there was something of a recession in the United States. In particular, the sales of revolvers fell. Smith and Wesson therefore decided to discontinue their second issue—an example of which is shown on the facing page (top) —and introduce a third issue of more attractive appearance. There was always a demand for pocket pistols in the United States; particularly, perhaps, in the more settled Eastern States where, although fewer people carried a revolver openly, many —both men and women— liked to have one handy in pocket or handbag. The new model did not differ very much mechanically from its predecessor: it had the same tip-up barrel, removable cylinder and single-action lock. However, instead of having a brass frame, like the earlier model, it was made entirely of iron and the whole weapon was plated. The traditional flat-edged butt gave way to the type known as "bird-beak", with walnut side-plates held in place by a screw. The general effect was more eye-catching than previously; and after a slow start in 1868 production rose to 20,000 annually.

Belgium
MINIATURE PISTOL

Length:	4·3" (109mm)
Weight:	6oz (·17kg)
Barrel:	1·6" (41mm)
Calibre:	·22" (5·6mm)
Rifling:	5 groove, r/hand
Capacity:	Six
Muz Vel:	c500 f/s (152 m/s)
Sights:	Fixed

Belgium has a long history of arms manufacture. Until well into the 20th century, much of the country's output came from small, family workshops, staffed by industrious mechanics and capable of producing reasonable weapons much more cheaply than larger manufacturers. Until the later 19th century, few provisions for the control of firearms existed in most countries; any law-abiding citizen could purchase and own firearms almost without restriction; although this freedom was, of course, balanced by heavy penalties in the event of the arms being used for criminal purposes. The tiny pistol seen here is a cheap but well-finished and reliable revolver of the type produced in Belgium in the 19th century. It has a solid frame with integral round barrel, complete with foresight. Its cylinder is chambered to take six, short, copper-cased, rimfire cartridges. It is loaded through a bottom-hinged loading gate, the insertion of the cartridges being facilitated by a groove in the frame; and the chambers are recessed to accommodate the cartridge rims. The ejector rod is housed in the hollow axis pin and can be drawn forward and then swivelled in order to bring it in line with the chamber opposite the loading gate. The double-action lock is activated by a folding trigger. Rather unusually, there is a safety lever on the left side of the frame; when this is pressed down, it prevents the hammer from rising. Apart from the hammer, trigger, ejector and safety, the weapon is blued and bears the appropriate proof marks and the number "8345". At the turn of the century, revolvers like this could be bought in England for about twelve shillings and sixpence (62p), and they were particularly recommended to cyclists.

Belgium
BULLDOG PISTOL

Length:	5·5" (140mm)
Weight:	12oz (·34kg)
Barrel:	1·9" (48mm)
Calibre:	·32" (8·1mm)
Rifling:	5 groove, r/hand
Capacity:	Six
Muz Vel:	c550 f/s (168 m/s)
Sights:	Fixed

In 1878 the British firm of P. Webley and Sons (which had by then begun to establish its excellent reputation for revolvers) introduced a group of weapons under the general title of "British Bulldog". They were solid-frame, five-chambered arms of ·44in (11·2mm) and ·45in (11·4mm) calibre, and were intended primarily as civilian arms. Britain was then a well-settled and generally law-abiding country, but many people liked to keep a pistol handy in the house for protection against aggressive vagrants or burglars. There was also a considerable demand from civilians going out to work in the more remote parts of the British Empire. These reliable Bulldog weapons soon became popular; they were quickly copied in France, Belgium, Germany, Spain— and even in the United States. The weapon illustrated is a Belgian copy of poor quality; with a folding trigger.

Great Britain
THOMAS REVOLVER

Length:	10·75" (273mm)
Weight:	31oz (·88kg)
Barrel:	5·75" (146mm)
Calibre:	·45" (11·4mm)
Rifling:	7 groove, l/hand
Capacity:	Five
Muz Vel:	c600 f/s (183 m/s)
Sights:	Fixed

The process of loading an early cartridge revolver was a slow one. It was thus not long after the introduction of the new system that people started trying to improve it; and in 1869 J. Thomas, a Birmingham gunmaker, patented the revolver seen here. The weapon is of cast steel with a heavy octagonal barrel. Its main features of note are its very long cylinder aperture and the knob beneath its barrel. The revolver is loaded in the normal way, through the loading gate behind the right-hand end of the cylinder, and it is discharged by means of its double-action lock. The real point of interest is the system by which the empty cases are ejected. Pressure on the end of a small spring on the front of the frame releases the barrel catch and allows the barrel to be rotated until the knob (which is there simply to give a firm hold to a hot or oily hand) is uppermost. Then the barrel is drawn forward, taking the cylinder with it to the front of the aperture. A star-shaped extractor is attached to the standing breech, which holds the cases firmly by their rims until they are fully out of the chambers. Then they are thrown clear by a flick of the wrist; the barrel and cylinder are turned back; and the revolver is reloaded in the usual way. What is not apparent from the illustration (although the end of it can just be seen) is the provision on the barrel of a flange working in a slot on the frame. This flange is set at a slight angle to the circumference of the barrel: when the latter is turned it exerts a powerful camming action and draws the cylinder very slightly forward, thus loosening the tightest of cases. The system was effective but was soon overtaken by better ones: thus, revolvers on this system were made in relatively small numbers and are now rare.

Great Britain
HILL'S SELF-EXTRACTING REVOLVER

Length:	7·75" (197mm)
Weight:	15oz (·43kg)
Barrel:	3·75" (95mm)
Calibre:	·32" (8·1mm)
Rifling:	7 groove, r/hand
Capacity:	Six
Muz Vel:	c550 f/s (168 m/s)
Sights:	Fixed

Although the metallic cartridge was a valuable innovation, the system of reloading the earliest types of cartridge revolver was slow. It was necessary first to put the hammer at half-cock; open the loading gate; swing out the pin (if it was not already in alignment); and push out the empty cases one by one before loading fresh rounds. The weapons illustrated on this spread all demonstrate some of the more common attempts to speed up this process. The revolver seen here is of tip-up type, dating from around 1880, but it is more complex than the example shown on the facing page (above), because no special manual operation is necessary to eject the empty cases. There are two hinges: one where the top frame is attached to the standing breech (its pivot pin can be seen); and a second where the barrel joins the frame. The pivot pin of the latter is also visible in the crescent-shaped lever, although the joint itself is concealed behind it. In order to open the weapon, it is necessary first to press the flat lever (just visible) on the lower front corner of the frame and raise the barrel. At this stage, the front hinge remains rigid and only the rear one opens. When the barrel is vertical, the limit of the rear hinge is reached and the crescent-shaped lever also locks. Continued pressure on the barrel causes the front hinge to come into play, allowing the barrel to continue backwards beyond the vertical. Now, the small stud which protrudes from the front of the frame, and is attached to the extractor rod, bears on the front end of the crescent and is thrust downward, so pushing out the star extractor and the empty case. The barrel is marked "HILLS PATENT SELF-EXTRACTOR", although there is some doubt as to whether the Birmingham maker W. J. Hill actually invented it. The same system is to be found on other revolvers, both British and continental in origin.

TIP-UP REVOLVER

Length: 8·5″ (216mm)
Weight: 21oz (·59kg)
Barrel: 4″ (102mm)
Calibre: ·38″ (9·6mm)
Rifling: 5 groove, r/hand
Capacity: Six
Muz Vel: c600 f/s (183 m/s)
Sights: Fixed

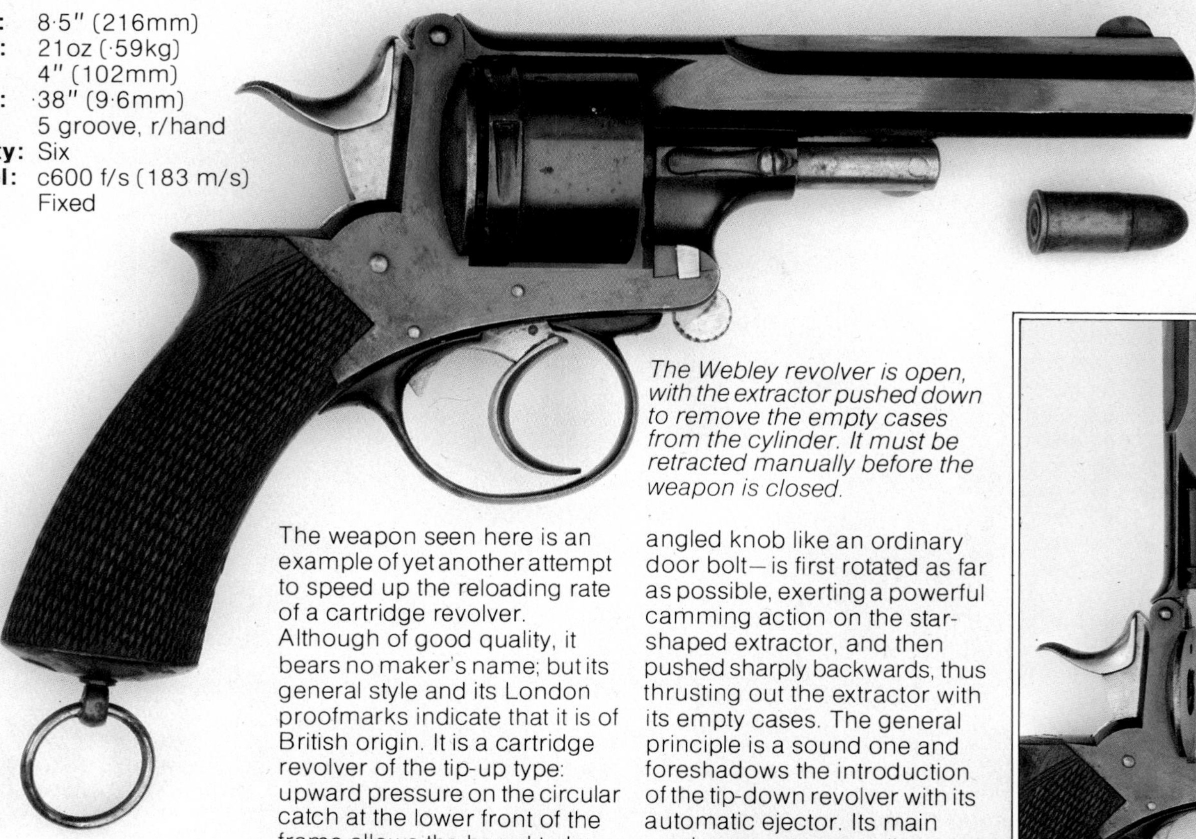

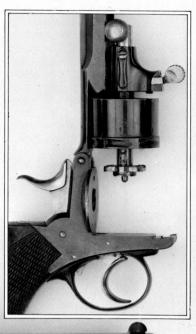

The Webley revolver is open, with the extractor pushed down to remove the empty cases from the cylinder. It must be retracted manually before the weapon is closed.

The weapon seen here is an example of yet another attempt to speed up the reloading rate of a cartridge revolver. Although of good quality, it bears no maker's name; but its general style and its London proofmarks indicate that it is of British origin. It is a cartridge revolver of the tip-up type: upward pressure on the circular catch at the lower front of the frame allows the barrel to be raised to the vertical. Then, the very thick ejector pin—which is, in fact, shaped with a right-angled knob like an ordinary door bolt—is first rotated as far as possible, exerting a powerful camming action on the star-shaped extractor, and then pushed sharply backwards, thus thrusting out the extractor with its empty cases. The general principle is a sound one and foreshadows the introduction of the tip-down revolver with its automatic ejector. Its main weakness appears to lie in the catch, which does not engage deeply with the frame and might open accidentally.

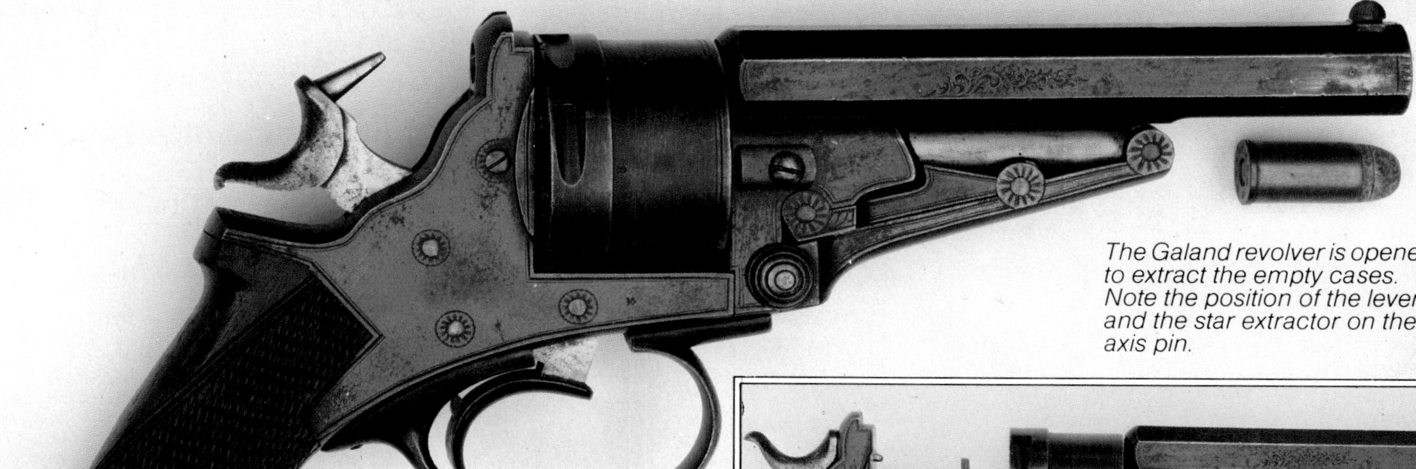

The Galand revolver is opened to extract the empty cases. Note the position of the lever, and the star extractor on the axis pin.

Length: 10″ (254mm)
Weight: 35oz (·99kg)
Barrel: 5″ (127mm)
Calibre: ·45″ (11·4mm)
Rifling: 5 groove, r/hand
Capacity: Six
Muz Vel: c600 f/s (183 m/s)
Sights: Fixed

GALAND AND SOMMERVILLE REVOLVER

Charles François Galand was a gunmaker of Liège in Belgium; Sommerville was a partner in a Birmingham firm. In 1868, they took out a joint patent for a self-extracting cartridge revolver of the general type illustrated, and the arm was made therefore in Birmingham and on the con-tinent. It does not appear ever to have become popular in Great Britain, but a good many revolvers on this principle were made in Europe. This particular specimen is well made but is unnamed, although it carries the name "Wm POWELL of BIRMINGHAM", who was probably the retailer. It bears Birmingham proof marks, and somewhat unusually, an Enfield Small Arms mark of crossed lances with a "B" beneath them. The revolver is opened by gripping the milled studs at the bottom of the frame and drawing them forward. This activates a plunger below the barrel (very like the ram on a percussion revolver) and forces both barrel and cylinder forward, leaving the empty cases held by their rims on the extractor. The partial return of the cylinder to the extractor allows fresh rounds to be loaded.

United States of America
COLT HOUSE PISTOL

Length:	6·75" (171mm)
Weight:	14oz (·4kg)
Barrel:	2·9" (74mm)
Calibre:	·41" (10·4mm)
Rifling:	7 groove, r/hand
Capacity:	Four
Muz Vel:	c450 f/s (137 m/s)
Sights:	Fixed

There was a considerable market for pocket arms in the United States in the second half of the 19th century. Colt entered it fairly early, first with deringers (some of which are illustrated on pages 200-201) and then with a series of so-called House Pistols. The revolver seen here, which appeared in 1871, is one of the earliest of the latter type. As may be seen, it has a solid brass frame into which a steel barrel is screwed. These barrels were made in a variety of lengths, from 1·5in (38mm) to 3·5in (89mm). Perhaps the most interesting aspect of the weapon is its four-chambered cylinder: this has a section shaped like a four-leafed clover, which gave rise to the widely-used nickname of "Cloverleaf Colt". The breech-ends of the chambers are recessed to take the rims of the short, copper-cased, rimfire cartridges. The lock is of single-action type and, as is apparent in the photograph, the comb of the hammer on the earlier models (of which this is one) was almost vertical; in later models, the comb was slanted much farther back. The hammer activates the cylinder stop, which is housed in a long slot below the frame. The trigger is of the sheathed type. There is no loading gate, but the side of the frame is grooved to facilitate loading. A flat fence on the left-hand side of the frame prevents the cartridges from slipping backwards out of their chambers. The rod below the barrel is, in fact, a forward extension of the cylinder axis pin, which is somewhat thicker than the section visible; it may be drawn forward to remove the cylinder. A retaining ring is fitted below the barrel to ensure that the pin cannot be dropped. In order to make the weapon more compact for carriage in a pocket, the cylinder may be partially rotated so that there are two chambers on either side of the frame. When this is done, the nose of the hammer fits into one of the small apertures situated between each chamber: this prevents the cylinder from rotating. The butt is of the type usually referred to as bird-beak. This was a very popular revolver and sold in large numbers in the United States until it was replaced, in 1875, by the Colt New Line pocket revolver (below).

United States of America
COLT NEW LINE POCKET REVOLVER

Length:	6" (152mm)
Weight:	11oz (·31kg)
Barrel:	2" (51mm)
Calibre:	·41" (10·4mm)
Rifling:	7 groove, r/hand
Capacity:	Five
Muz Vel:	c450 f/s (137 m/s)
Sights:	Fixed

The United States has long been a country in which citizens have exercised their long-standing right to bear arms. In the 19th century, in the more remote parts of the South and West of the country, most men carried a belt pistol as a matter of course, while some also favoured a second, smaller, concealed, back-up weapon. Even in the more settled Eastern states, many individuals of both sexes felt a good deal more comfortable if they had a convenient hand gun. This was —and to some extent probably still is— a very understandable memento of the dangerous frontier days of not so long ago.

The Colt House Pistol (illustrated at the top of this page) was succeeded in 1873 by a series of New Line, single-action, pocket revolvers, one of which is seen here. These were made in a variety of calibres from ·22in (5·6mm) to ·41" (10·4mm), including some centre-fire models, and with barrel lengths ranging from 1·5in (38mm) to 3·5in (89mm). The revolver shown is the ·41in (10·4mm) rimfire version with a 2in (51mm) barrel. As may be seen, it is a compact, stream-lined weapon, admirably suited to pocket or handbag. The round barrel, which has a noticeable taper from muzzle to breech, is screwed into a solid iron frame in which is contained a half-fluted, five-chambered cylinder, without recesses for the cartridge rims. The loading gate, on the right-hand side, can be opened with a thumbnail when the revolver is cocked or half-cocked. A corresponding shield is fitted on the left-hand side to retain the rounds in the chambers. Pressure on a small stud at the front of the frame, on the right-hand side, allows the cylinder axis pin to be with-drawn: it is then used to push out the empty cases. The retaining screw of this stud is visible in the photograph. A circular inspection plate on the left-hand side of the frame (the head of its retaining screw can be seen below the cartridge groove) gives access to the lock mechanism. The revolver has the typical bird-beak butt; the only piece of brass in its construction is to be found in the liners for the butt retaining screw. It is marked "COLT NEW LINE" on the left side of the barrel; "·41Cal" on the lower left frame; and is inscribed with the company's name on the barrel.

Great Britain
COPY OF WEBLEY R.I.C. REVOLVER

Length:	8·75" (222mm)
Weight:	30oz (·85kg)
Barrel:	4" (102mm)
Calibre:	·45" (11·4mm)
Rifling:	7 groove, r/hand
Capacity:	Five
Muz Vel:	c650 f/s (198 m/s)
Sights:	Fixed

In 1867, P. Webley and Son placed on the market a new revolver, which was adopted by the Royal Irish Constabu-lary in 1868. It was also adopted by many other colonial military and police forces, and sold widely as a civilian arm. In fact, it was possibly the most popular arm ever made by Webley. There-fore, the model went through many variations and, almost inevitably, was widely copied. As may be seen by comparison with the genuine models illus-trated later in this book (pages 124-125), the weapon shown here is a very close copy of the original: this particular example is based on the Webley No 1 New Model of 1883. (A Belgian copy of the 1880 model is illus-trated on page 109, above.) The weapon has a solid frame; the barrel (unlike that of the original Webley) is integral with it and not screwed in. The barrel is practically cylindrical, but its upper part is drawn to a rib, making it basically ovate in section, with a very slight taper towards the breech-end. The five-chambered cylinder has the half-fluting associated with later Webley models. There is the usual bottom-hinged loading gate on the right-hand side of the frame, with a deep groove to facilitate loading. The extractor pin is normally housed in the hollow cylinder axis pin, but it can be withdrawn and swivelled out to the right so as to align with the chamber opposite the loading gate.

Great Britain
WEBLEY BULLDOG REVOLVER

Length:	5·5" (140mm)
Weight:	11oz (·31kg)
Barrel:	2·1" (53mm)
Calibre:	·32" (8·1mm)
Rifling:	5 groove, r/hand
Capacity:	Five
Muz Vel:	c500 f/s (152 m/s)
Sights:	Fixed

In 1878, P. Webley and Son began to manufacture and sell a range of revolvers under the general name of "British Bull-dog". These were primarily designed for civilian use (although some were used for service purposes) and were plain, robust, reliable arms. The first of the series was a heavy, centre-fire arm in ·442in (11·2mm) calibre; this was followed by others of the same type but in ·44in (11·2mm) and ·45in (11·4mm) calibre, in order to appeal to as wide a market as possible, and then by revolvers in smaller calibres better suited for use as pocket arms. The revolver seen here is the smallest of these pocket types and is classed as the second model, which appeared in about 1880. It is constructed on a solid frame with an integral barrel. This, like the Royal Irish Constabulary model, is of ovate section, with a flat sight plane on its upper surface. The vertical dimension of the barrel at the muzzle is appreciably greater than it is at the breech-end; this gives a markedly tapered effect, even in a very short barrel. As was the universal practice in these early Webley revolvers, the cylinder is plain—except for the slots at its rear end to accommodate the cylinder stop, which rises from the bottom of the frame when the action is cocked. It was origi-nally fitted with a bottom-hinged loading gate (which is, unfortunately, missing from this specimen). The ejector pin is normally housed in the hollow cylinder axis pin; whence it can be withdrawn and swivelled for use. Once this has been done, the cylinder axis pin may also be withdrawn, if required, by means of its flat, milled head; thus, the cylinder may be removed. The mechanism is of double-action type and the arm is designed to take centre-fire cartridges. Rimfire versions were also made, and were so stamped for identification on the frame. Plain but well-finished, the revolver is marked "Webley's No 2, ·320"C.F." on the left side of the frame, which also bears the famous trademark of the flying bullet. Beneath this are the letters "W & S". These stand for Webley and Scott, indicating that the arm was made after 1897, when the amalgamation took place. The Bulldog range was extremely popular and remained in manufacture until 1914. Like many of Webley's products, it was extensively copied in a number of countries.

WEBLEY No 1 REVOLVER

The Webley No 1 revolver, stripped. Note particularly the notched backplate, with expansion holes for the primers, and the axis pin, which is also used as an extractor. It will be obvious from this photograph that reloading was a slow process.

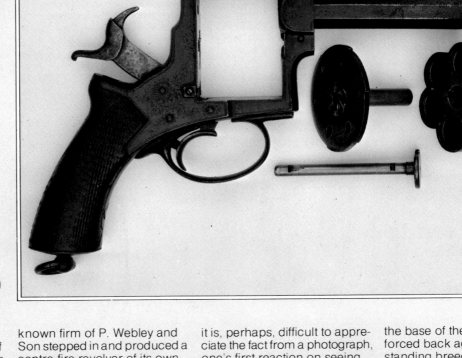

Length:	9·5 (241mm)
Weight:	42oz (1·19kg)
Barrel:	5" (127mm)
Calibre:	·577" (14·6mm)
Rifling:	7 groove, r/hand
Capacity:	Six
Muz Vel:	c600 f/s (183 m/s)
Sights:	Fixed

In 1866 the British government approved the adoption of a breechloading rifle. This was the original Enfield percussion arm, converted by the addition of the Snider breech mechanism. In fact, the rifle caused a good deal of trouble until Colonel E. M. Boxer, Superintendant of the Royal Laboratory at Woolwich Arsenal, produced a workable (although by no means perfect) round for it. This had a cast-iron base, with an aperture for the copper percussion cap, to which was cemented a body of coiled brass foil. Soon after its adoption, the government approved in principle the issue of a revolver to fire a similar type of cartridge. The arm finally selected was invented by John Adams (brother of the more famous Robert) but was not finally adopted until 1872. In the meantime, the well-

known firm of P. Webley and Son stepped in and produced a centre-fire revolver of its own, presumably in the hope of securing the market. Rimfire revolvers made by Tranter and others were already available, but British officers (who in those days bought their own revolvers) naturally liked to keep up-to-date, for their lives might depend on their having the best personal weapon available. Experience during the Indian Mutiny had shown that small, high-velocity bullets lacked the sheer knock-down power necessary to stop a charging fanatic dead in his tracks, so Webley's first centre-fire revolver was designed specifically so that it would not fail its user in that respect. The Webley No 1 revolver, illustrated here, was of ·577in (14·6mm) calibre, exactly the same as that of the service rifle. Although

it is, perhaps, difficult to appreciate the fact from a photograph, one's first reaction on seeing the arm is to wonder at its massive construction. The revolver is built on a robust, solid frame with integral barrel. As in many Webley products of the period, the barrel (although in this example octagonal) is noticeably higher from bottom to top than from side to side. This is particularly true of the muzzle-end; even in a short barrel the taper is quite obvious. The cylinder is fully fluted and the lock is of double-action type. One of the problems connected with the early Boxer cartridge was a marked tendency for the primer to bulge backwards under the force of the explosion. In some forms of breech mechanism, this was not particularly important; but in a revolver of orthodox type – ie, one in which

the base of the cartridge was forced back against a robust standing breech – there was always the risk that a bulged primer would prevent the cylinder from rotating. Obviously, if this should happen at a critical moment it might have very serious results for the user. The Webley No 1 was therefore fitted with a detachable backplate which rotated with the cylinder; it was pierced with holes to accommodate the hammer nose, into which the primers might expand, if necessary, without fouling the mechanism. This was reliable, if slow. The earliest cartridges fired lead balls, but later marks were loaded with elongated bullets with hollow, plugged bases to assist expansion into the rifling. This method had been used successfully in the percussion Enfield rifle and its Snider conversion.

BLAND-PRYSE TYPE REVOLVER

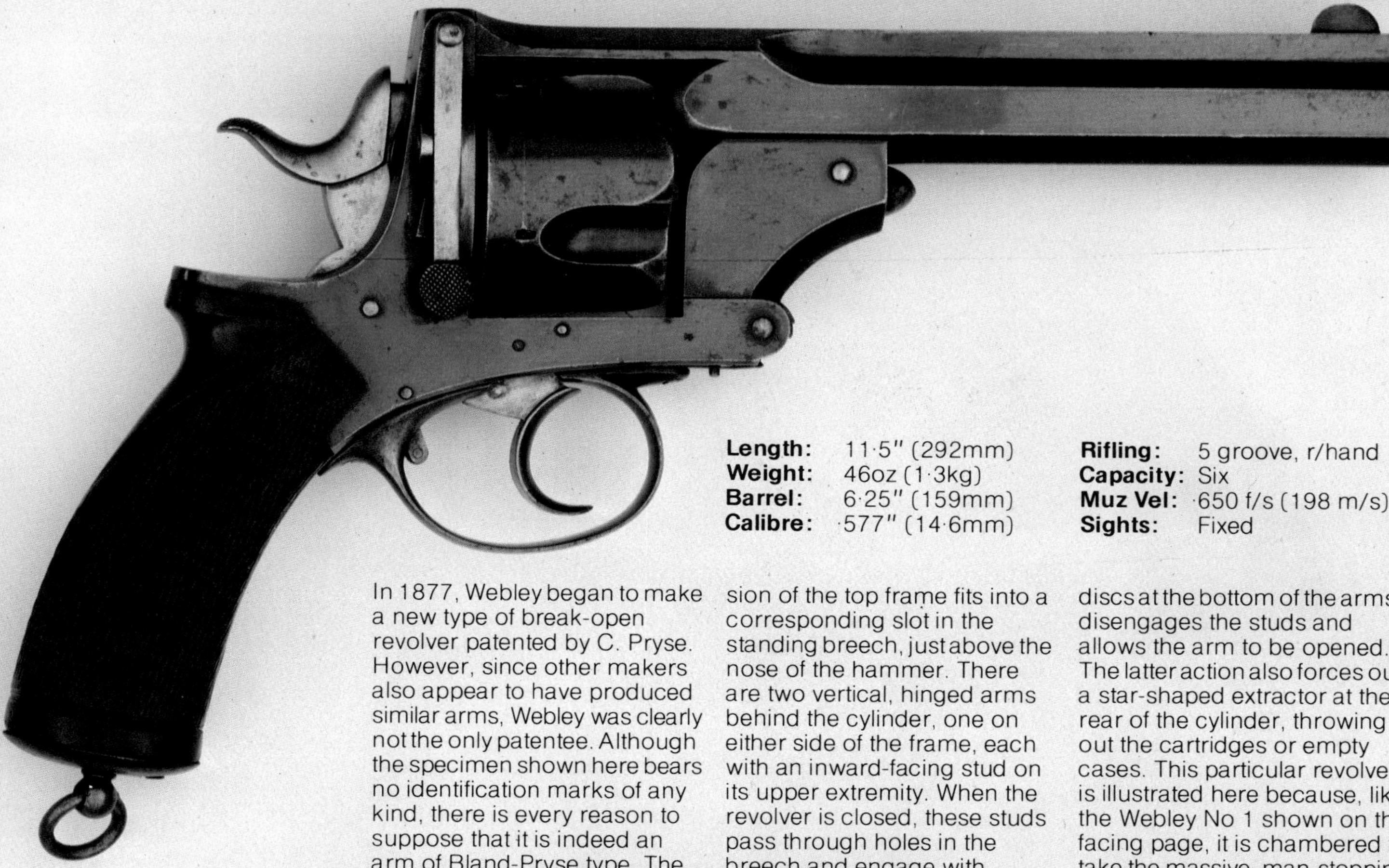

Length:	11·5" (292mm)	**Rifling:**	5 groove, r/hand
Weight:	46oz (1·3kg)	**Capacity:**	Six
Barrel:	6·25" (159mm)	**Muz Vel:**	·650 f/s (198 m/s)
Calibre:	·577" (14·6mm)	**Sights:**	Fixed

In 1877, Webley began to make a new type of break-open revolver patented by C. Pryse. However, since other makers also appear to have produced similar arms, Webley was clearly not the only patentee. Although the specimen shown here bears no identification marks of any kind, there is every reason to suppose that it is indeed an arm of Bland-Pryse type. The weapon is robustly made: there is a hinge at the bottom front of the frame, and a rear exten-

sion of the top frame fits into a corresponding slot in the standing breech, just above the nose of the hammer. There are two vertical, hinged arms behind the cylinder, one on either side of the frame, each with an inward-facing stud on its upper extremity. When the revolver is closed, these studs pass through holes in the breech and engage with recesses on the rear extension, thus holding the arm firmly closed. Pressure on the milled

discs at the bottom of the arms disengages the studs and allows the arm to be opened. The latter action also forces out a star-shaped extractor at the rear of the cylinder, throwing out the cartridges or empty cases. This particular revolver is illustrated here because, like the Webley No 1 shown on the facing page, it is chambered to take the massive, man-stopping ·577in (14·6mm) pistol cartridge, designed to stop any assailant in mid-stride.

Length:	10·2" (259mm)	
Weight:	49oz (1·39kg)	
Barrel:	4·6" (117mm)	
Calibre:	·44"/·65"	
	(11·2mm/16·5mm)	
Rifling:	5 groove, l/hand	
Capacity:	Nine/One	
Muz Vel:	c600 f/s (183 m/s)	
Sights:	Fixed	

LE MAT REVOLVER

This revolver is a cartridge version of the earlier percussion Le Mat illustrated on page 73 (below); it was made in France, probably in about 1868. It is of a somewhat complex, built-up construction, being based on its lower, shot-barrel, which is firmly seated in the standing breech and acts also as an axis pin for the revolver cylinder. The lower frame of the upper barrel has a sleeve which fits over the lower barrel; an extension from this is screwed firmly to the lower

frame, making what appears to be a good, rigid joint. The upper barrel and cylinder (which has nine chambers) allow the arm to be used as an orthodox single-action cartridge revolver, with a loading gate and a sliding ejector rod of Colt type. In order to load the lower shot barrel, it is necessary first to cock the weapon and then open the side-hinged breechblock by manipulating the catch visible behind the cylinder. The breechblock has its own firing pin; in order to

ensure that this is struck, a hinged block on the underside of the hammer is first turned downward. The action of opening the breechblock also activates a semi-circular extractor which engages under the rim of the cartridge case and pushes it clear. This arm is of similar man-stopping type to the others shown on this page: it was used in French penal colonies in the second half of the 19th century, but it does not appear to have been used for military purposes.

Great Britain
TRANTER CENTRE-FIRE REVOLVER

Length:	10.5" (267mm)
Weight:	35oz (·99kg)
Barrel:	5" (127mm)
Calibre:	·45" (11·4mm)
Rifling:	5 groove, r/hand
Capacity:	Six
Muz Vel:	c650 f/s (198 m/s)
Sights:	Fixed

The adoption by the British Army of a breechloading rifle firing a centre-fire cartridge in 1866 soon led to a considerable interest in this type of round — and eventually to the super-session of the rimfire type for service use, although it was still used in pocket pistols. As has already been seen (page 92, above), William Tranter was an early entrant in the field of cartridge revolvers: by 1868 he had produced an up-dated version for use with the new Boxer cartridges. The general appearance of the Tranter revolver illustrated here is familiar, for it is still broadly based on the Adams frame which Tranter had used so successfully in his earlier weapons. The frame is still solid, with an integral, octagonal barrel, and the six-chambered cylinder is plain, except for the slots cut for the cylinder stop. The loading gate has a rearward spring catch; light downward pressure is required to operate it. The lock is of the double-action type. An innovation is the provision of a built-in firing pin on the standing breech; the end of the pin is struck by the hammer (which is cocked in the photograph, to show its flat head). The extractor pin is attached to a swivel mount which allows it to be swung out into line with the right-hand chamber. A small spring catch, visible in the photograph, holds the pin safely in position but allows it to be removed for cleaning. An irregularly-shaped plate on the left side of the frame allows access to the lock mechanism. The frame and ejector pin mount are marked "TRANTERS PATENT" and the revolver is numbered "13061". It bears also the retailer's name.

Belgium
ADAMS CENTRE-FIRE REVOLVER

Length:	11" (279mm)
Weight:	35oz (·99kg)
Barrel:	6" (152mm)
Calibre:	·42" (10·7mm)
Rifling:	6 groove, r/hand
Capacity:	Six
Muz Vel:	c600 f/s (183 m/s)
Sights:	Fixed

By 1868, John Adams, brother of Robert and managing director of the Adams Patent Small Arms Company, had patented and produced a centre-fire cartridge revolver based on — and, indeed, apparently a modification of — the original percussion revolvers produced by Beaumont-Adams a dozen years earlier. The conversion was not, in fact, very difficult: it involved no more than a new bored-through cylinder; a loading gate; and a sliding ejector rod fastened to the right front of the frame, so that it was permanently in line with the chamber opposite the loading gate. A deep groove had to be cut into the frame behind the gate to allow the cartridges free entry. No corresponding addition to the frame was needed on the left side, because none of the chambers was fully exposed; therefore, the cartridges could not fall out. Like other successful revolvers, the new Adams was very quickly copied by Belgian makers — and the weapon seen here is one such copy. Although at first sight it appears to have a solid frame, it is in reality in two parts: there are screws at the bottom front of the frame and by the hammer nose — the construction is, in fact, similar to that of the Deane-Harding percussion revolver illustrated on page 75 (below). The plain cylinder with its top-hinged gate and cartridge groove is, for all practical purposes, identical to the of the original Adams from which it is copied. The only real difference lies in the provision of a Webley-type swivel ejector rod instead of the fixed, sliding model brazed to the original Adams frame. The rod, which is normally housed in the hollow axis pin, pulls forward and swivels. To remove the cylinder, the ejector rod is withdrawn and the small stud visible on the front frame is depressed. Then the milled end of the axis pin is drawn forward.

Germany
MAUSER ZIG-ZAG REVOLVER

Length:	11·75"
Weight:	42oz
Barrel:	6·5"
Calibre:	·43" (10·9mm)
Rifling:	5 groove, r/hand
Capacity:	Six
Muz Vel:	c650 f/s (198 m/s)
Sights:	Fixed

This is an example of a proposed German service revolver of 1878. It was designed and produced by Peter Paul Mauser, a very famous name indeed in the history of gunmaking, although he was, perhaps, better known for rifles than for pistols. The revolver is top-hinged. When a lever on the left-hand side of the frame is pushed upward, it allows the ring in front of the trigger to be pulled downward. This frees the catch and allows the entire barrel and cylinder to be raised just past the vertical, where it locks. Increased pressure on the ring operates a cam which forces a star ejector out of the rear face of the cylinder, throwing the cartridges or empty cases from the chambers. The extractor is then returned to its normal position and the revolver reloaded and closed. Some care must be taken to ensure that the rounds do not slip out of their chambers during the process of reloading. Perhaps the most interesting feature of the weapon is its unusual method of cylinder rotation. When the trigger is pressed, a rod with a stud on its upper surface is forced forward so that its front end protrudes through the barrel catch, ensuring that it cannot be opened by accident. At the same time, the stud engages one of the diagonal slots on the cylinder and thus causes the cylinder to rotate through one-sixth of its circumference. When the trigger is released, the rod is retracted: during this stage, the stud simply rides back along one of the straight grooves of the cylinder. The revolver was never adopted for service use in Germany, for it was considered by the authorities to be too complex.

Great Britain
TIP-UP REVOLVER

Length:	10·5" (267mm)
Weight:	35oz (·99kg)
Barrel:	5·75" (146mm)
Calibre:	·50" (12·7mm)
Rifling:	3 groove, r/hand
Capacity:	Six
Muz Vel:	c600 f/s (183 m/s)
Sights:	Fixed

This is a large and robust revolver by an unknown maker: it has Birmingham proof marks and bears the words "CAST STEEL" on the barrel. It is of tip-up type and is broadly similar in principle to the Mauser revolver shown above—with the important exception of the system of cylinder rotation. When the milled head of an arm attached to the rear part of the trigger-guard is pushed hard over to the left, it not only locks the hammer at half-cock, so as to prevent any accidental discharge, but also unlocks the barrel catch. This allows the barrel and cylinder to be turned over well beyond the vertical, until the top strap rests on the head of the hammer. Increased pressure on the lever forming the front half of the trigger-guard activates a pin attached to a star extractor, forcing it out from the rear of the cylinder to eject the rounds or empty cases from the chambers. When the lever is released, the extractor returns automatically to its original position and the cylinder may then be reloaded. The barrel and cylinder are then returned to the closed position and locked by means of the lever with the milled head. This action also has the effect of freeing the hammer and allowing the double-action lock mechanism to function in the normal way. It is desirable that the pistol should be held horizontally on its side during this process; otherwise, there is a considerable risk that the rounds will fall out of the chambers under their own weight. Unlike the Mauser illustrated above, cylinder rotation in this arm is by the more usual method of pawl and ratchet. Although the principle of this revolver is sound enough, it would have been too complex for a service arm. In particular, the risk of cartridges falling accidentally from the cylinder when reloading in a hurry was considerable.

WEBLEY-PRYSE TYPE REVOLVER

Length: 7·5" (190mm)
Weight: 25oz (·71kg)
Barrel: 3·5" (89mm)
Calibre: ·45" (11·4mm)
Rifling: 3 groove, r/hand
Capacity: Five
Muz Vel: c650 f/s (198 m/s)
Sights: Fixed

In 1876 Charles Pryse patented a type of break-down, self-extracting revolver of the kind seen here. Although many of these arms were made by Webley, there were a number of other licensees for the patent: similar arms were made by Thomas Horsley, Christopher Bonehill and other British makers, and by Belgian manufacturers in Liège. The arm illustrated is marked "T. W. WATSON 4 PALL MALL LONDON" on the top flat of the barrel, but this is almost ·certainly the name of the retailer rather than the maker. It bears London proof marks and has the number "358" on the frame. The revolver is hinged at the lower front of the frame; when the barrel is pushed downward to an angle of about 90°, a star-shaped ejector is forced automatically from the rear end of the cylinder, throwing out the cartridges or empty cases with some force. Two long register pins working in holes in the cylinder are attached to the base of the extractor. The barrel hinge is formed by two lugs on the barrel, with the extractor lever between them, and two outer lugs on the frame; the whole is held by a threaded pin. The locking system consists of two vertical arms, one on either side of the frame; each of these has a flat, milled stud at the bottom and a short bolt on the inner side at the top and is hinged centrally. A rear extension of the barrel enters a slot in front of the hammer; the bolts on the arms pass through holes in the sides of this slot and engage in recesses on the extension, where they are held in place by springs. This would appear to constitute a strong and reliable locking system, but considerable care is needed to ensure that the various holes and apertures for the locking pins are free from grease and dirt. If this precaution is neglected, it is just possible for the weapon to blow open.

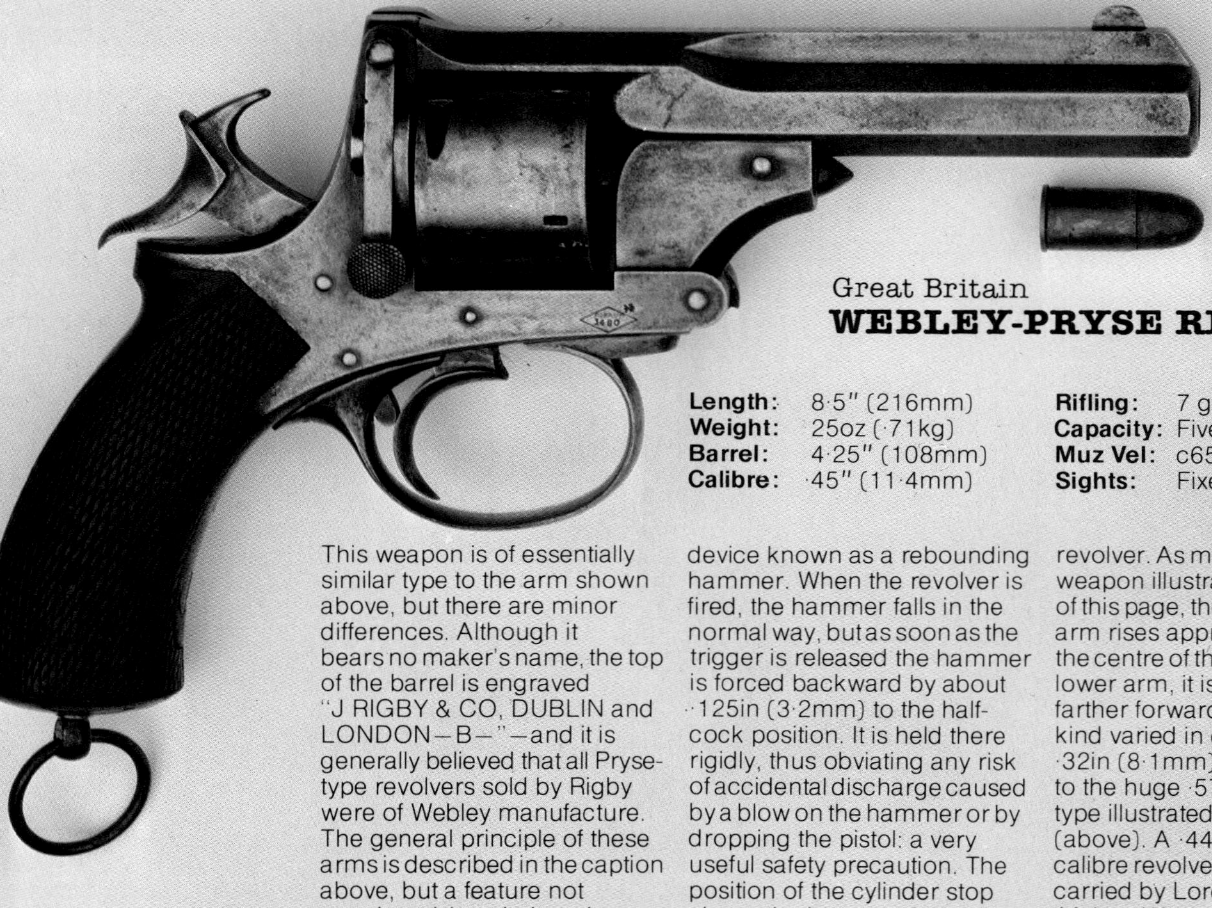

WEBLEY-PRYSE REVOLVER

Length: 8·5" (216mm)
Weight: 25oz (·71kg)
Barrel: 4·25" (108mm)
Calibre: ·45" (11·4mm)
Rifling: 7 groove, r/hand
Capacity: Five
Muz Vel: c650 f/s (198 m/s)
Sights: Fixed

This weapon is of essentially similar type to the arm shown above, but there are minor differences. Although it bears no maker's name, the top of the barrel is engraved "J RIGBY & CO, DUBLIN and LONDON—B—" and it is generally believed that all Pryse-type revolvers sold by Rigby were of Webley manufacture. The general principle of these arms is described in the caption above, but a feature not mentioned there is the existence on all revolvers of this type of a device known as a rebounding hammer. When the revolver is fired, the hammer falls in the normal way, but as soon as the trigger is released the hammer is forced backward by about ·125in (3·2mm) to the half-cock position. It is held there rigidly, thus obviating any risk of accidental discharge caused by a blow on the hammer or by dropping the pistol: a very useful safety precaution. The position of the cylinder stop also varies between the various types and makes of the Pryse revolver. As may be seen, in the weapon illustrated at the top of this page, the stop end of the arm rises approximately below the centre of the cylinder; in the lower arm, it is appreciably farther forward. Arms of this kind varied in calibre, from a ·32in (8·1mm) pocket version to the huge ·577in (14·6mm) type illustrated on page 103 (above). A ·44in (11·2mm) calibre revolver of this type was carried by Lord Roberts in the Afghan War and is now in the Armouries, Tower of London.

France
SERVICE REVOLVER MODEL 1873

Length:	9·5" (241mm)	**Rifling:**	3 groove, l/hand
Weight:	38oz (1·08kg)	**Capacity:**	Six
Barrel:	4·5" (114mm)	**Muz Vel:**	c650 f/s (198 m/s)
Calibre:	·45" (11·4mm)	**Sights:**	Fixed

This was the first centre-fire revolver to be adopted by the French Army and was made at the great factory of St Etienne. It has a solid frame and is very heavy and robust. Its barrel, which is half round and half octagonal, is marked "Mdle 1873" on the top flat; the upper left flat bears the number "H99683" and the upper right flat is inscribed "S1883". The revolver has a Colt-type extractor rod, working in a sleeve. When it is not in use, the front end of the rod is turned under the barrel, where it is held against the end of the cylinder axis rod by light spring pressure. In order to remove the cylinder, it is therefore necessary first to turn down the rod; then loosen the large-headed screw just beneath it; and then draw the axis pin forward. The loading gate is hinged at the bottom and is opened by being drawn backward—as may be seen in the photograph. The lock is of orthodox double-action Chamelot-Delvigne type (so called, although little or nothing is known of its originators). The hammer of the specimen shown here is set at half-cock, with the hammer head held safety clear of the rounds in the chambers. A large, irregularly-shaped inspection plate on the left-hand side of the frame is held by two pins and a screw; the end of the latter is visible at the rear end of the frame, above the butt-plate. The revolver is numbered "H99683" on its main components and "V83" on the minor ones.

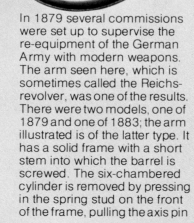

Germany
COMMISSION REVOLVER

Length:	10" (254mm)	**Rifling:**	3 groove, l/hand
Weight:	35oz (·99kg)	**Capacity:**	Six
Barrel:	4·75" (121mm)	**Muz Vel:**	c650 f/s (198 m/s)
Calibre:	·455" (11·5mm)	**Sights:**	Fixed

In 1879 several commissions were set up to supervise the re-equipment of the German Army with modern weapons. The arm seen here, which is sometimes called the Reichs-revolver, was one of the results. There were two models, one of 1879 and one of 1883; the arm illustrated is of the latter type. It has a solid frame with a short stem into which the barrel is screwed. The six-chambered cylinder is removed by pressing in the spring stud on the front of the frame, pulling the axis pin forward, and opening the loading gate. Rather surprisingly, there is no integral system for ejecting rounds or cases; this must be done either with the axis pin or with some improvised implement of suitable dimensions—which must have made it a slow process in action. The breech-ends of the chambers are recessed so that the heads of the cartridges are fully supported—a sensible precaution with most of the earlier metallic cartridges. The lock is of single-action type with a half-cock, and, somewhat unusually in a revolver, there is a safety catch on the left side of the frame. This particular specimen was made at Erfurt in 1894; since this was after the passing of the German Proof Act, the revolver bears a number of proof marks. All major parts are numbered "9775", but the minor components are marked with the last two digits only. The butt-strap is also stamped "30.A.1.53"; probably the mark of an artillery unit.

Austria
GASSER REVOLVER

Length:	14·75" (375mm)	Rifling:	6 groove, l/hand
Weight:	52oz (1·47kg)	Capacity:	Six
Barrel:	9·3" (236mm)	Muz Vel:	c900 f/s (274 m/s)
Calibre:	11mm	Sights:	Fixed

The great Austrian firm of Gasser was founded in 1862 by Leopold Gasser, who patented the revolver seen here in 1870. He died in 1871 and was succeeded by his son, Johann, who continued to manufacture large numbers of revolvers of this or similar types almost until the end of the 19th century. Gasser revolvers were used by the Austro-Hungarian Army and were sold extensively as civilian arms in Austria-Hungary and throughout the Balkans. In common with all original Gasser revolvers, the arm illustrated is an open-frame model with no top strap. Its

basic construction is fairly similar to that of the early Colt, except that there is a threaded hole below the barrel, which screws on to the front end of the axis pin instead of on to the wedge. It has a bottom-hinged loading gate and a sliding ejector rod on the right-hand side; the front end of the rod is cut into an arc of similar diameter to the barrel and fits firmly against it. A small thumb-screw in the sleeve holds the rod firmly in place when it is not in use. The lock is of double-action type and is fitted with a safety device in the form of the flat bar above the trigger-guard.

Internal pins attached to the bar's rear end hold the hammer at half-cock and can only be released by pressure on the trigger. The arm is extensively marked: it bears the inscription "GASSER PATENT, GUSS-STAHL"; an Austrian eagle; and an emblem showing an arrow transfixing an apple, with the words "SCHUTZ MARK". It is a massive weapon, chambered to fire the cartridge originally developed for the Werndl carbine, and is really only suitable for use by mounted men. Even so, it would be hard to use without a detachable butt, which was not fitted.

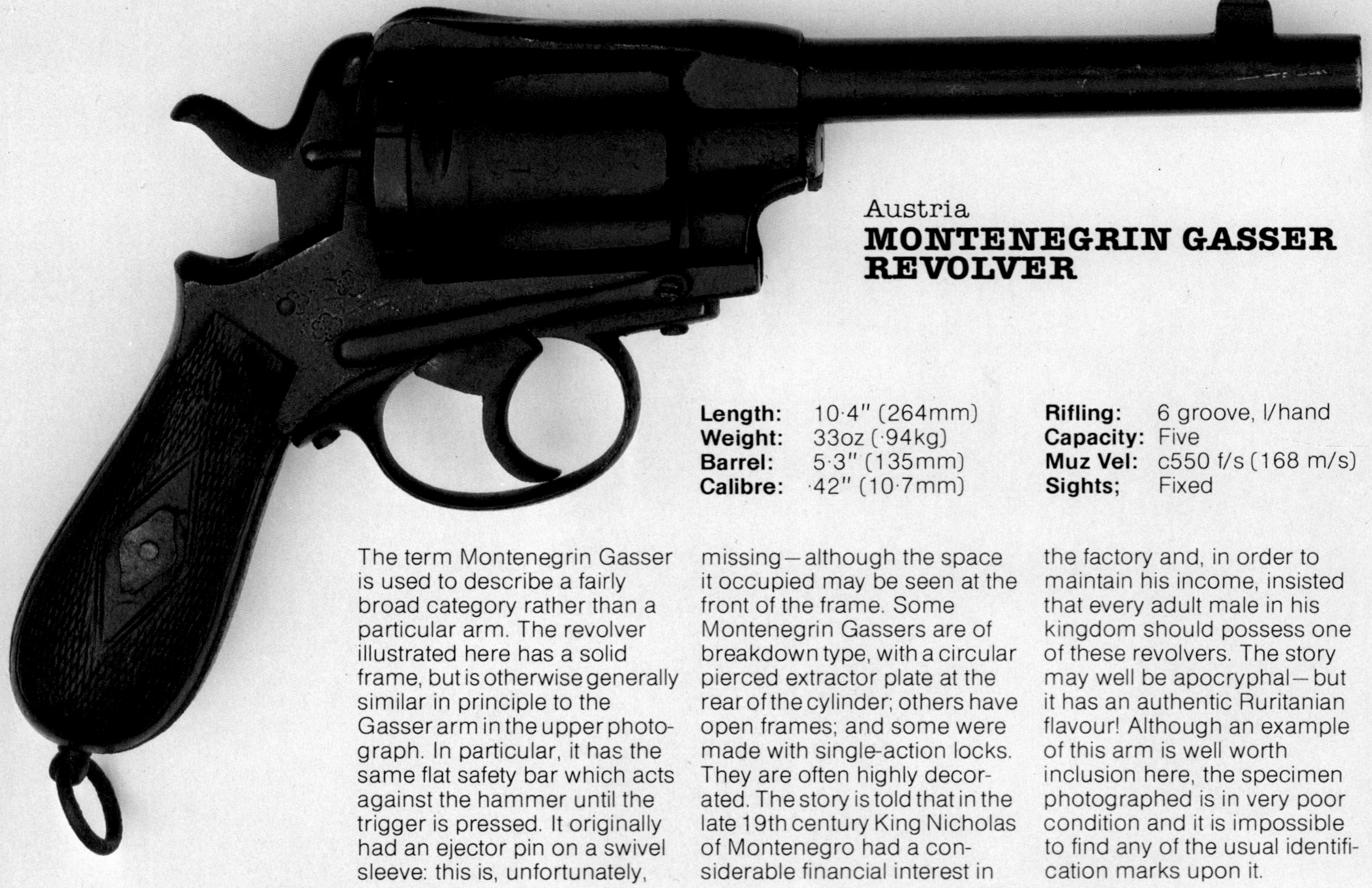

Austria
MONTENEGRIN GASSER REVOLVER

Length:	10·4" (264mm)	Rifling:	6 groove, l/hand
Weight:	33oz (·94kg)	Capacity:	Five
Barrel:	5·3" (135mm)	Muz Vel:	c550 f/s (168 m/s)
Calibre:	·42" (10·7mm)	Sights;	Fixed

The term Montenegrin Gasser is used to describe a fairly broad category rather than a particular arm. The revolver illustrated here has a solid frame, but is otherwise generally similar in principle to the Gasser arm in the upper photograph. In particular, it has the same flat safety bar which acts against the hammer until the trigger is pressed. It originally had an ejector pin on a swivel sleeve: this is, unfortunately,

missing—although the space it occupied may be seen at the front of the frame. Some Montenegrin Gassers are of breakdown type, with a circular pierced extractor plate at the rear of the cylinder; others have open frames; and some were made with single-action locks. They are often highly decorated. The story is told that in the late 19th century King Nicholas of Montenegro had a considerable financial interest in

the factory and, in order to maintain his income, insisted that every adult male in his kingdom should possess one of these revolvers. The story may well be apocryphal—but it has an authentic Ruritanian flavour! Although an example of this arm is well worth inclusion here, the specimen photographed is in very poor condition and it is impossible to find any of the usual identification marks upon it.

Belgium
COPY OF R.I.C. REVOLVER

Length:	8·75" (222mm)
Weight:	24oz (·68kg)
Barrel:	4" (102mm)
Calibre:	·45" (11·4mm)
Rifling:	7 groove, l/hand
Capacity:	Six
Muz Vel:	c650 f/s (198 m/s)
Sights:	Fixed

The original Royal Irish Constabulary revolver was first put on the market by P. Webley and Son of Birmingham in 1867 and proved an immediate success. The force from which its title was derived adopted it in 1868, as did many other colonial forces, both military and police; it also proved extremely popular as an arm for civilian use. The revolver inevitably went through a number of changes in its long history, but its essential characteristics were never really changed. Inevitably, such a popular arm was very widely copied in the United Kingdom (a British copy is shown on page 101, above), on the Continent, and even occasionally in the United States. The quality and reliability of these pirated versions varied considerably. The weapon illustrated here is characteristic of the type: it is a copy of the Webley Model of 1880. It has a solid frame with an octagonal barrel screwed into it; the cylinder is unusual in having elliptical fluting. The lock is of double-action type with a wide hammer comb. The ejector rod is housed in the hollow axis pin. This appears to be one of the better copies, for it is well made and finished, but it bears no marks other than a crown over the letter "R". This is the normal Belgian mark for black-powder revolver barrels which have been tested with a charge 30 per cent above the intended norm.

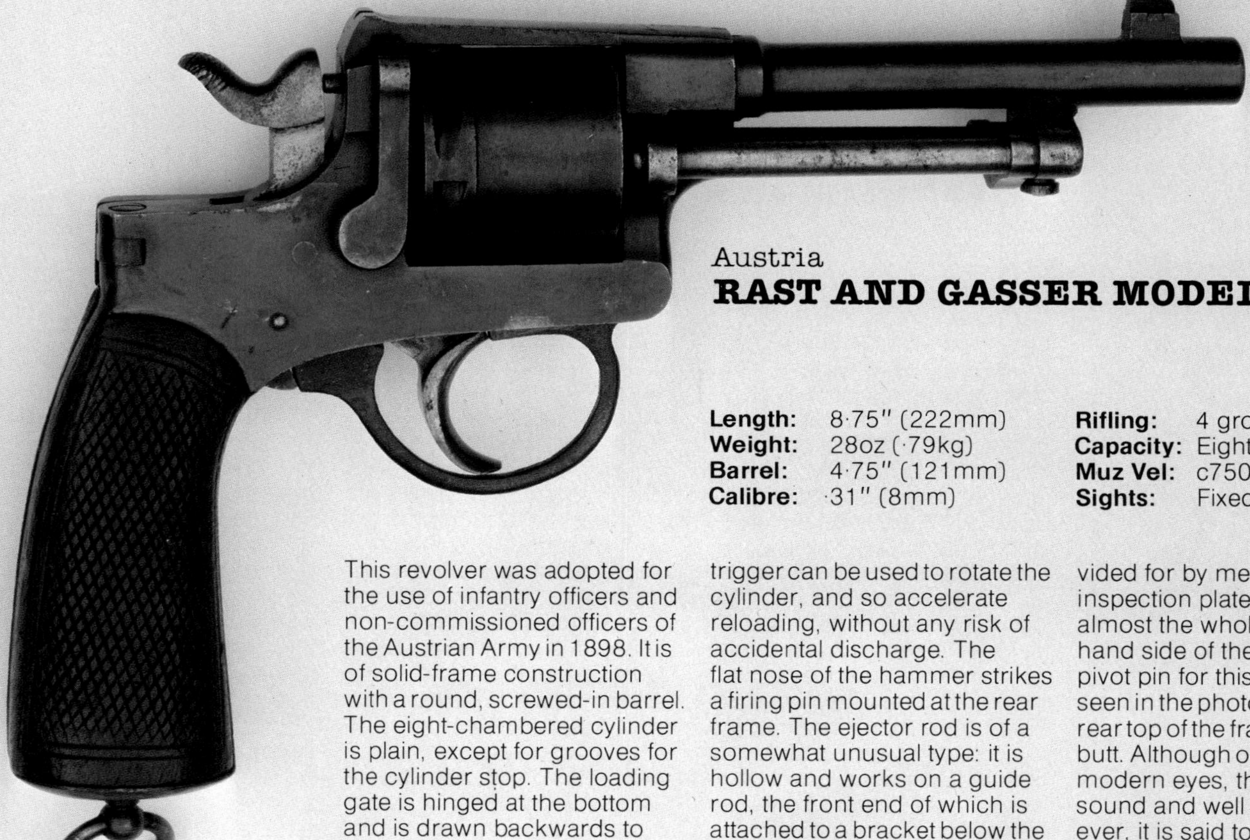

Austria
RAST AND GASSER MODEL 1898

Length:	8·75" (222mm)	**Rifling:**	4 groove, l/hand
Weight:	28oz (·79kg)	**Capacity:**	Eight
Barrel:	4·75" (121mm)	**Muz Vel:**	c750 f/s (229 m/s)
Calibre:	·31" (8mm)	**Sights:**	Fixed

This revolver was adopted for the use of infantry officers and non-commissioned officers of the Austrian Army in 1898. It is of solid-frame construction with a round, screwed-in barrel. The eight-chambered cylinder is plain, except for grooves for the cylinder stop. The loading gate is hinged at the bottom and is drawn backwards to load. While the gate is open, the hammer and trigger are disconnected; thus, the trigger can be used to rotate the cylinder, and so accelerate reloading, without any risk of accidental discharge. The flat nose of the hammer strikes a firing pin mounted at the rear frame. The ejector rod is of a somewhat unusual type: it is hollow and works on a guide rod, the front end of which is attached to a bracket below the barrel near the muzzle. Near-complete access to the double-action lock mechanism is provided for by means of an inspection plate covering almost the whole of the left-hand side of the frame. The pivot pin for this cover can be seen in the photograph—at the rear top of the frame, above the butt. Although oddly-shaped to modern eyes, this revolver is sound and well made. However, it is said to have lacked stopping power, because of its rather poor cartridge—a bad fault in a service arm.

United States of America
COLT SINGLE-ACTION ARMY REVOLVER

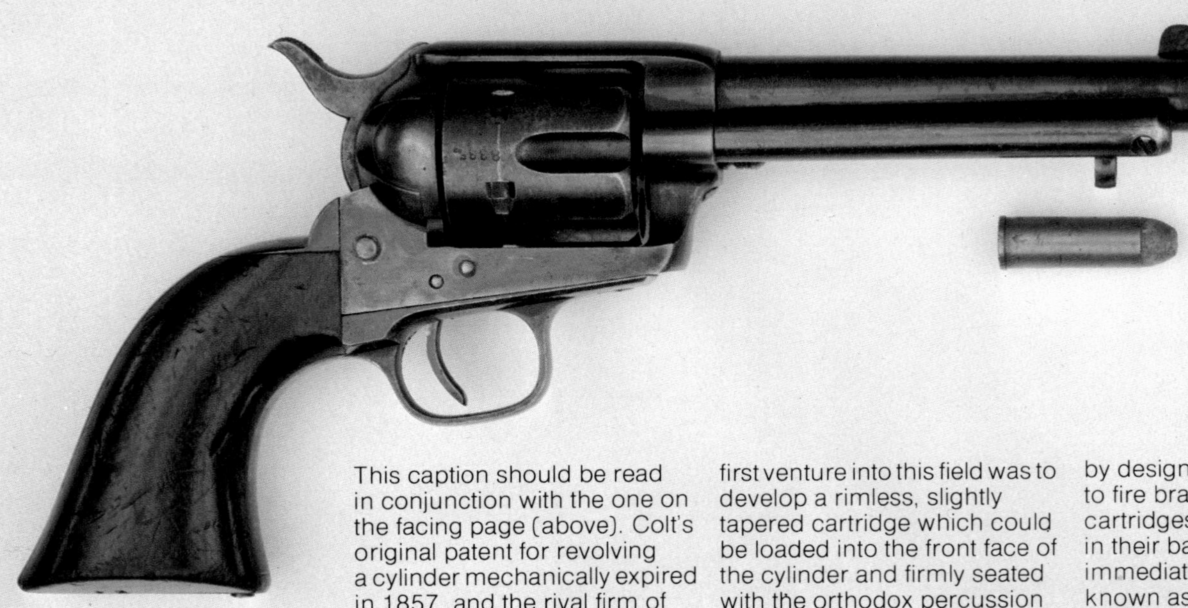

Length: 11" (279mm)
Weight: 35oz (·99 kg)
Barrel: 5·5" (140mm)
Calibre: ·45" (11·4mm)
Rifling: 6 groove, r/hand
Capacity: Six
Muz Vel: c650 f/s (198 m/s)
Sights: Fixed

This caption should be read in conjunction with the one on the facing page (above). Colt's original patent for revolving a cylinder mechanically expired in 1857, and the rival firm of Smith and Wesson had a new version ready by 1856. This was, however, a breechloader of the type already described (page 93, above), and the fact that Smith and Wesson controlled the Rollin White patent for the bored-through cylinder gave them an original monopoly. The early rimfire cartridges proved reliable and gained wide acceptance. Colt's

first venture into this field was to develop a rimless, slightly tapered cartridge which could be loaded into the front face of the cylinder and firmly seated with the orthodox percussion rammer. But this method, known as the Thuer conversion, was only temporary: as soon as possible after the expiry of Smith and Wesson's patent, Colt had a revolver of their own ready to launch on to the market. This arm, which is fully described on the facing page, appeared in 1873 and is sometimes referred to by that date. Colt had gone one step further

by designing the new weapon to fire brass-cased centre-fire cartridges with copper caps in their bases. The arm was an immediate success. It was first known as the "New Metallic Cartridge Revolving Pistol", but was later listed under the more familiar title of the Single-Action Army Revolver. The earliest model was of ·45in (11·4mm) calibre and fired a 235-grain (15 gram) lead bullet by means of 617 grains (40 gram) of black powder, but it was later made in a variety of different calibres and in several barrel lengths.

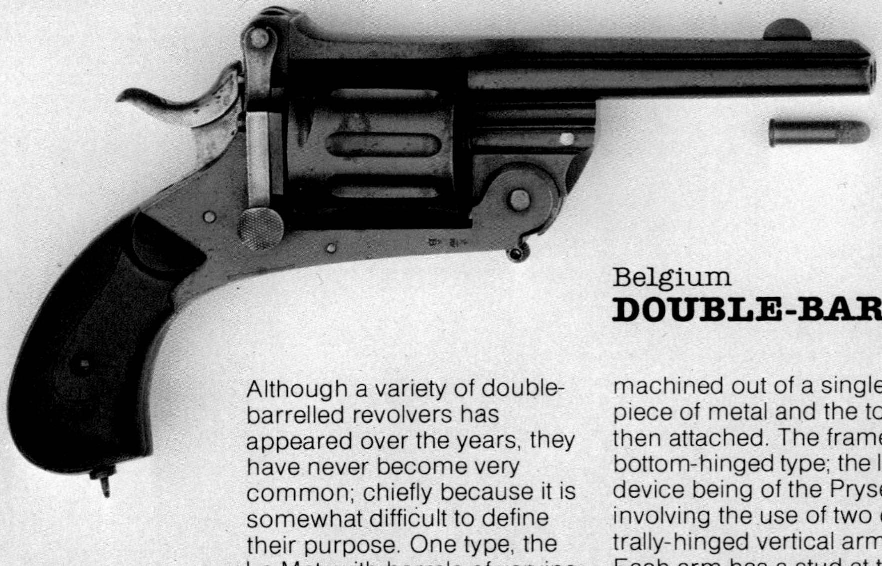

Belgium
DOUBLE-BARRELLED REVOLVER

Length: 7·5" (190mm)
Weight: 18oz (·51kg)
Barrels: 3·75" (95mm)
Calibre: ·22" (5·6mm)
Rifling: 5 groove, r/hand
Capacity: Twelve
Muz Vel: c 650 f/s (198 m/s)
Sights: Fixed

Although a variety of double-barrelled revolvers has appeared over the years, they have never become very common; chiefly because it is somewhat difficult to define their purpose. One type, the Le Mat, with barrels of varying calibres has already been described (page 103, below). Another type, with barrels one above the other, allowed the use of two concentric rings of chambers in a single large cylinder. However, relatively the most common type is that illustrated here, in which two small-calibre barrels are positioned side-by-side and are fired simultaneously. This weapon is of Belgian make and was probably produced towards the end of the 19th century. The barrels, which are round, appear to have been

machined out of a single piece of metal and the top rib then attached. The frame is of bottom-hinged type; the locking device being of the Pryse type, involving the use of two centrally-hinged vertical arms. Each arm has a stud at the top of its inner side; the studs are forced inwards under the pressure of a spring, so that they pass through holes at the top of the standing breech and engage a rearward extension of the top rib. The lock is of double-action type, with a folding trigger which makes the arm convenient for the pocket. The hammer nose is flat and acts on a pair of firing pins mounted in the rear of the standing breech. The fluted cylinder, which is, of necessity, large in relation to the overall dimensions of the weapon, is hollow in the centre

to reduce weight. It is fitted with a star-shaped extractor which automatically throws out the rounds or empty cases when the revolver is opened smartly. The butt is of bird-beak type with wooden side plates. The top rib bears Belgian inspection marks and the frame is stamped with a rampant lion with the letters "RV" beneath it. Overall, the weapon appears to be of good quality and is well finished. It is not, however, very clear what it was meant to achieve—except to hit its victim twice at each discharge. This presumably increased the stopping power of the weapon considerably, but it is likely that a normal six-chambered revolver in ·32in (8·1mm) calibre would have done the job as well, while being less bulky and considerably easier to handle.

United States of America
COLT SINGLE-ACTION ARMY REVOLVER

Length:	13" (330mm)
Weight:	38oz (1·08kg)
Barrel:	7·5" (190mm)
Calibre:	·44" (11·2mm)
Rifling:	6 groove, r/hand
Capacity:	Six
Muz Vel:	c650 f/s (198 m/s)
Sights:	Fixed

The origins of this revolver are described in the caption on the facing page (above). It was available in three barrel lengths: 7·5in (190mm); 5·5in (140mm) and 4·75in (121mm). These were usually referred to as the Cavalry, Artillery and Civilian models respectively; the one illustrated here is the 7·5in (190mm) Cavalry model. Although the arms in the series retained much of their characteristic Colt appearance, there are obvious differences. The frame is solid, with a top strap, the round barrel being screwed into it, and the cylinder is, of course, bored through. The robust, hemispherical standing breech is retained, with a contoured loading gate built into its right side, and ejection is by means of a rod sliding in a sleeve below and to the right of the barrel. The lock is of single-action type. The butt-plates are of walnut on the specimen shown here, but other materials — including hard rubber, ivory and even mother-of-pearl — may be encountered. Production models are usually plainly finished in blue or nickel, but presentation arms may be highly ornate. The arm shown is of ·44in (11·2mm) calibre and is so stamped to the left of the trigger guard. This was a very popular calibre: Winchester's 1873 model rifle was also chambered for the same cartridge, which greatly simplified ammunition supply. A few special models of this revolver with 12in (305mm) barrels were commissioned by a "Western" writer, Ned Buntline, after whom they were named, but these are now rare. This series of revolvers, often known as the "Peacemaker" or "Frontier" models, is still made in various forms.

Length:	13" (330mm)
Weight:	43oz (1·22kg)
Barrel:	7·5" (190mm)
Calibre:	·44" (11·2mm)
Rifling:	6 groove, r/hand
Capacity:	Six
Muz Vel:	c700 f/s (213 m/s)
Sights:	Fixed

United States of America
REMINGTON REVOLVER

It was in 1857, nearly 40 years after he had first set up as a gunmaker, that Eliphalet Remington began making revolvers. Remington's earliest hand guns were all pocket pistols, and it was not until the outbreak of the Civil War in 1861 that large-calibre, service-type revolvers were put into production. Eliphalet Remington died that same year, but his sons continued to develop the business to meet the huge increase in demand for weapons of all kinds. Once the Civil War was over, the great move westward increased tremendously and, as every man was to a large extent his own law, the demand for arms, particularly revolvers, remained fairly high. These revolvers were percussion arms, but the War had seen the rise in popularity of the self-contained metallic cartridge. In the early post-war years, Smith and Wesson had a monopoly in such arms because of their possession of the Rollin White bored-through cylinder patent, but once that had lapsed the field was wide open—and all manufactuers, including Remington, naturally took advantage of this. As may be seen here, the first Remington cartridge revolver, which appeared in 1875, differed very little in general appearance from the firm's earlier percussion arm (illustrated on page 69, above). The major mechanical differences are the bored-through cylinder; the loading gate; and the provision of a Colt-type ejector rod working in a sleeve. The distinctively tapered rammer handle of the earlier arm had, of course, become unnecessary; but, as may be seen, it was replaced by a rib of similar dimensions, thus leaving the silhouette unchanged. The trigger-guard of this model is of steel and the butt is fitted with a lanyard ring. The top of the round barrel is engraved "E REMINGTON & SONS, ILION, NEW YORK, USA". Although the Western scene was largely dominated by Colt arms, the new cartridge Remingtons were excellent weapons—robust, well-made and accurate. A new version appeared in 1891, but by then the Colt had firmly established its dominance. In 1894, Remington reverted to its first interest of long arms, a sphere in which the company still excels, as many modern rifles will bear witness.

United States of America
SMITH AND WESSON NEW MODEL No 3 REVOLVER

Length:	12" (305mm)
Weight:	44oz (1·25kg)
Barrel:	6·5" (165mm)
Calibre:	·32" (8·1mm)
Rifling:	5 groove, r/hand
Capacity:	Six
Muz Vel:	c800 f/s (244 m/s)
Sights:	Fixed

As has already been described, Smith and Wesson were first in the field with an effective cartridge revolver as early as 1857; but it was not until 1870 that they began to make service-type arms of large calibre. The first to be produced was the No 3 First Model American, a bottom-hinged, break-open type with a system of simultaneous extraction. This model attracted the attention of Russia, which was then in the process of re-equipping its Army with modern weapons: by 1871, a contract had been signed for 20,000 revolvers of a type known as Model No 3, Russian 1st Model. There then appeared a second model of similar general type, but with some changes to the frame and with the addition of a finger spur below the trigger-guard. This was followed by a third model, until the order was completed in 1878. Generally similar arms were made in smaller numbers for export to various other countries during this period. The firm then turned to the home market with its New Model No 3, produced from 1878 to 1912, and later with the New Model 3 Frontier. This was intended as a rival to the Colt, but it never became popular and was replaced in its turn by a double-action version. The single-action arm illustrated here first appeared in 1887. It is of broadly similar type to its predecessors, except that the round fore-sight has been replaced by a square-cut bead-type blade pinned into a groove on the top rib. When the milled catch in front of the hammer is pushed upward, the barrel and cylinder can be pushed sharply downward; this causes the star-shaped ejector at the rear of the cylinder to be forced outward, throwing the cartridges or cases clear of the cylinder, a system which allowed for very fast reloading. This specimen, numbered "415", is in ·32in (8·1mm) calibre; a ·38in (9·6mm) calibre arm came into production soon afterwards.

United States of America
SMITH AND WESSON REVOLVING RIFLE

Length:	35" (889mm)
Weight:	80oz (2·27kg)
Barrel:	18" (457mm)
Calibre:	·32" (8·1mm)
Rifling:	6 groove, r/hand
Capacity:	Six
Muz Vel:	820 f/s (250 m/s)
Sights:	200yd (183m)

This rare weapon first appeared in 1879 and by the following year almost the entire batch of 977 had been completed, only six being produced (presumably as a result of special orders) in 1886-87. As may be seen by comparison with the revolvers shown above (left) and on page 114 (above), it is closely modelled on the No 3 revolver, with only minor mechanical differences. The barrel is made in two pieces and is screwed together about 2in (51mm) in front of the breech, although the joint is barely visible. The rifle was made in three barrel lengths: 16in (406mm), of which 239 were made; 18in (457mm), of which 514 were made; and 20in (508mm), of which 224 were made. The one illustrated here is of the middle size and is numbered "222". It has a blued foresight on the top rib and an L-shaped backsight to give two elevations. The aperture back-sight, an optional extra, may be seen on the clamp which holds the rifle butt on to the pistol. The cylinder is six-chambered. The revolver will fire either of the cartridges shown with it here: the standard Smith and Wesson long ·32in (8·1mm) cartridge (below); or a special cartridge in which the bullet is completely contained within the case (above). The grips and fore end are of hard, mottled rubber; the grips are noticeably darker, partly because of wear and partly because of the back escape of gases. The rifle butt, which is clamped to the revolver by means of the milled screw below the backsight pillar, is of fine-quality Circassian walnut and has a rubber butt-plate which, like those on the revolver itself, bears the Smith and Wesson monogram. This arm is an example of a variety of similar types—some of them illustrated elsewhere in this book—which seek to combine the revolver and the rifle. Like most combination weapons, it

WEBLEY-PRYSE REVOLVER No 4

Length:	10·75" (273mm)
Weight:	36oz (1·02kg)
Barrel:	5·75" (146mm)
Calibre:	·476" (12·1mm)
Rifling:	7 groove, r/hand
Capacity:	Six
Muz Vel:	c650 f/s (198 m/s)
Sights:	Fixed

This weapon is one of the early, hinged-frame, self-extracting revolvers incorporating the system patented by Charles Pryse, first put into production by P. Webley and Son in 1877. It was the first revolver to make use of a rebounding hammer; this was automatically lifted back by about ·15in (4mm) when the trigger was released after firing, thus holding the hammer nose well clear of the base of the next cartridge. The fluted cylinder is reliably locked at all times, except when the lock mechanism is actually being operated. This is achieved by means of a double stop worked by the trigger. When there is no pressure on the trigger, the forward stop engages one of the smaller slots; then the trigger is pressed, the cylinder rotates, and the rear part of the stop engages in one of the long, bullet-shaped slots at the rear of the cylinder. The cylinder can be removed by unscrewing a large, milled screwhead to the left of the frame; the end of the screw may be seen immediately below the barrel in the photograph. The cylinder has a star extractor which is forced sharply outward when the revolver is opened; this is done by pressing in the milled discs on the lower ends of the locking arms (one of which is visible), thus disengaging two bolts from a rear extension of the top frame. The extractor is provided with two long register pins which fit into holes in the cylinder. The left side of the frame of this specimen is marked "WEBLEYS NO4 ·476CF"; below this inscription is the famous flying-bullet trademark and the serial number "7546". This particular arm was retailed by the Army and Navy Stores, London. Weapons of this type were popular with British officers: they were reliable and robust and the heavy bullet of ·476in (12·1mm) calibre gave them ample stopping-power. An added attraction was that they could also fire ·45in (11·4mm) and ·455in (11·5mm).

was only moderately successful: it was somewhat muzzle-heavy for use as a revolver and was less accurate than a purpose-built carbine, in which loss of power between the cylinder and the barrel was avoided. It would, however, have been quite a handy arm, easy to carry below the seat of a wagon and with the advantage of being relatively easily concealed. This specimen was captured by British troops in Ireland in 1916 —the year of the Easter Rising— and would presumably have been useful in guerrilla warfare. Most of these arms were sold in the United States: only 137 were exported, and of these 12 were lost at sea. The weapon ilustrated bears no foreign markings and is probably one of those originally sold internally in the United States of America.

United States of America
SMITH AND WESSON MODEL No 3 REVOLVER

Length:	11.5" (292mm)
Weight:	40oz (1·13kg)
Barrel:	6" (152mm)
Calibre:	·44" (11·2mm)
Rifling:	5 groove, r/hand
Capacity:	Six
Muz Vel:	c750 f/s (229 m/s)
Sights:	Fixed

Reference has already been made on page 112 (above) to the early history and development of Smith and Wesson revolvers of this general type, which first appeared in 1870. The arm illustrated here is a New Model No 3 revolver, but, unlike the example shown earlier, this one is chambered to take the ·44in (11·2mm) Russian cartridge. It has a round, tapered barrel with a full top rib, and it is fitted with a target sight instead of the round blade usually found on service models. The revolver is opened by pushing up the milled catch visible in front of the hammer and pushing down the barrel. This automatically forces out the star-shaped ejector, which is mounted on a hexagonal rod and is activated by means of a rack and gear. The six-chambered cylinder is 1·44in (37mm) long: a few later models have cylinders with a length of 1·56in (40mm). The locking device, in itself quite adequate, is further reinforced by the provision of a notch above the hammer nose (visible in the photograph) which engages over a flange on the catch when the hammer is fully down. The lock is of single-action type with a rebounding hammer which, like the trigger and guard, is case-hardened. Although this was a very fine arm and popular with expert target shots, it never really caught on in the United States. American users preferred a more powerful cartridge than was ever considered to be a safe and practical proposition in a break-open arm. Thus, they favoured solid-frame revolvers as a general rule, the only exception being contributed by small, pocket-type arms firing low-powered cartridges.

United States of America
SMITH AND WESSON ·32 SAFETY REVOLVER, THIRD MODEL

Length:	6·75" (171mm)
Weight:	13oz (·37kg)
Barrel:	3" (76mm)
Calibre:	·32" (8·1mm)
Rifling:	5 groove, r/hand
Capacity:	Six
Muz Vel:	c800 f/s (244 m/s)
Sights:	Fixed

The firm of Smith and Wesson first began to make break-open, self-extracting, pocket revolvers in 1880. These were orthodox double-action hammer weapons, usually with 3in (76mm) barrels—although the third model was supplied with a longer barrel if required. The first Smith and Wesson model with a fully-enclosed hammer appeared on the market in 1888 and was a considerable success; in 1902 it was succeeded by a second model, with relatively minor variations. This, in turn, was replaced by a third model, which remained in production until 1937: the revolver illustrated here is one of the third model weapons. The revolver was made in three barrel lengths, 2in (51mm), 3in (76mm), and 3·5in (89mm): this arm has a 3in (76mm) barrel, which is round with a top rib and a round, blade foresight. The foresight was usually forged integrally with the barrel on the 3in (76mm) and 3·5in (89mm) models; however, in the arm seen here the foresight is inserted into a slot in the rib and pinned—a method used on earlier models and also on the 2in (51mm)—barrelled versions of the third model. The revolver is opened by pushing up a T-shaped catch with a knurled knob on either side. This allows the barrel to be forced down and brings the automatic extractor into play. Although weapons of this type are often referred to as "hammerless", this is in a sense a misnomer: they have concealed hammers, which are concealed within the frame. They are, necessarily, self-cockers only; but this is, of course, no disadvantage in a pocket pistol which was intended to be used for quick shooting at close quarters. In order to obviate any risk of accidental discharge by snagging the trigger, the revolver incorporates a reliable safety device in the form of a lever mounted on the back strap. When the butt is properly gripped in preparation for firing, the lever is forced in and allows the lock mechanism to function normally; this makes it an extremely safe weapon. The stocks are of hard, black rubber and are rounded to avoid any risk of catching the lining of a pocket. This particular weapon is nickel-plated, except for trigger, trigger-guard and catch, but blued arms were also available. Access to the mechanism is by an inspection plate on the left side of the frame. This example is inscribed "SMITH AND WESSON SPRINGFIELD MASS USA".

COPY OF SMITH AND WESSON MODEL No 3 REVOLVER

Length:	8" (203mm)
Weight:	22oz (·62kg)
Barrel:	4" (102mm)
Calibre:	·38" (9·6mm)
Rifling:	5 groove, l/hand
Capacity:	Six
Muz Vel:	c740 f/s (226 m/s)
Sights:	Fixed

In 1880 Smith and Wesson introduced a series of double-action, break-open, pocket revolvers in ·38in (9·6mm) calibre. They were useful weapons, for they combined compact dimensions with a cartridge big enough to provide considerable stopping-power; thus, they very soon became popular in the United States and elsewhere. This kind of popularity inevitably led to the pirating of the design, particularly in Belgium, where the revolver seen here originated. The 19th century saw a considerable degree of industralization in that country: in particular, Belgium's capacity to produce small arms of all kinds increased very rapidly as the century progressed. Although there were large factories, a very considerable part of the Belgian output came from small, anonymous, back-street workshops, usually family concerns. The people employed in such workshops were often skilled as well as hard-working; and although some cheap and unreliable arms were produced, most were adequate—and certainly as good as could be expected at the low price charged. The revolver seen here is a close copy of the Smith and Wesson third model, produced from 1884 until 1895, and is of as good a quality as might reasonably be expected, considering its origins. It has a round barrel with a top rib and a round, brass foresight; the backsight is a notch cut in the front of the barrel catch, which is of the usual T-shape. The lock mechanism is of the orthodox double-action type. The weapon is blued and is fitted with either pearl or imitation-pearl butt-plates. It bears Belgian proof marks. It is of a common type, readily available a century ago for a few shillings: there are probably thousands of arms like this one still in existence.

COPY OF SMITH AND WESSON RUSSIAN MODEL

Length:	12·5" (317mm)
Weight:	36oz (1·02kg)
Barrel:	8" (203mm)
Calibre:	·44" (11·2mm)
Rifling:	5 groove, l/hand
Capacity:	Six
Muz Vel:	c700 f/s (214 m/s)
Sights:	Fixed

In 1871 the firm of Smith and Wesson began to manufacture revolvers for the Russian government, which was then in the process of modernizing its army to bring it into line with those of the other major powers of the world. The vast orders involved kept the firm going very happily for seven years, although in the long term it led to a huge loss of business in the United States. This was mainly due to the competition of the Colt company, which seized the opportunity offered it to establish almost complete domination of the great markets opened up in the United States by the mass movement of population to the West and Southwest in the decades following the end of the Civil War. Smith and Wesson's Russian models were fine weapons of their type, and thus they were inevitably copied. As has already been explained, in the caption above, various European countries, and Belgium in particular, were quick to turn out their own versions of any popular arm. These were usually made in small, family workshops, where they could be produced a good deal more cheaply than their more reputable prototypes. Of course, the copies were of varying quality: at best, they never attained the quality of the originals; at worst, they were positively dangerous. The revolver illustrated here, which is based on the various Smith and Wesson Russian models, is of relatively poor quality. Certainly, some corners have been cut in its manufacture. Although it is not possible to assess the quality of the metal, the workmanship and general finish are crude. In particular, it lacks the groove across the top of the hammer which engages a flange on the barrel catch—which is a feature always to be found on the genuine article. The lock is of double-action type; it does not rebound, but is fitted with a manual half-cock. The butt-plates are of bone or ivory, probably the former, and the arm was originally fitted with a lanyard ring, now missing. The barrel is spuriously inscribed "SMITH AND WESSON" and there are Belgian proof marks on the cylinder, enabling its true origin to be established.

United States of America
IVER JOHNSON REVOLVER

Length:	6·5" (165mm)
Weight:	14oz (·39kg)
Barrel:	3" (76mm)
Calibre:	·32" (8·1mm)
Rifling:	5 groove, r/hand
Capacity:	Five
Muz Vel:	c550 f/s (168 m/s)
Sights:	Fixed

In 1871 Iver Johnson and Martin Bye set up a company to make cheap revolvers. These were mostly of pocket type and were produced under a wide variety of trade names. In 1883 Johnson bought out his partner and opened his own company in Worcester, Massachusetts, moving to Fitchburg, in the same state, in 1891. There he made revolvers of a somewhat better quality than before: although still relatively cheap, they were reasonably safe and reliable arms. The revolver seen here is of break-open pattern. It has a round barrel with a rib, the foresight being slotted in. The backsight is a notch on the top extension of the standing breech; and the standing breech itself passes through a rectangular aperture in the top frame, where it is locked. To open the arm, it is necessary first to push up a small, milled catch on the top left side of the frame, which allows the barrel to drop down. The action of opening the revolver also forces out the extractor at the rear of the five-chambered cylinder. The frame of the weapon is nickel-plated, the trigger-guard is blued, and the hammer and trigger are case-hardened. The grips are of hard rubber, with an owl's head in a circular escutcheon at the top of each. The top of the barrel is inscribed "IVER JOHNSON ARMS AND CYCLE WORKS FITCHBURG MASS USA", with a second line of patent numbers, and the number "A7924" is stamped on the bottom of the butt.

United States of America
SMITH AND WESSON HAMMERLESS REVOLVER

Length:	7·5" (190mm)
Weight:	18oz (·51kg)
Barrel:	3·5" (89mm)
Calibre:	·38" (9·6mm)
Rifling:	5 groove, r/hand
Capacity:	Five
Muz Vel:	c625 f/s (190 m/s)
Sights:	Fixed

Smith and Wesson's first revolvers of ·38in (9·6mm) calibre were made in 1876; they were orthodox double-action weapons, mostly of pocket size. Experience showed, however, that the hammer spur tended to catch in the lining of a pocket—a considerable inconvenience if the arm was needed in a hurry, as pocket pistols usually are. So, by 1887, the company had brought out its first safety model, with a completely enclosed hammer which eliminated all risk of snagging at a critical moment. In addition, a grip safety was fitted in the form of a lever on the back strap. This ensured that the lock mechanism was disconnected until the pistol was properly gripped in the palm, when the lever was forced inward and the safety removed, allowing the weapon to be fired. The "hammerless" revolver illustrated here is the fourth model, which was in production from 1898 until 1907. It has a round barrel, with a top rib and a round foresight pinned into a slot; the backsight is formed by a simple notch in the top catch. An interesting feature of this pistol is its lock. As it was strictly a self-cocker, its trigger pull would normally have been quite heavy; but this version was made with a "hesitation" lock. A long initial pull on the trigger brings the concealed hammer back, after which only a light additional pull is needed to fire it. The revolver bears the usual maker's marks, but the left of the frame is also marked "SOLD by WESTLEY RICHARDS AND CO LTD, LONDON".

United States of America
IVER JOHNSON REVOLVER

Length:	7·5" (190mm)
Weight:	15oz (·42kg)
Barrel:	4" (102mm)
Calibre:	·32" (8·1mm)
Rifling:	5 groove, r/hand
Capacity:	Five
Muz Vel:	c550 f/s (168 m/s)
Sights:	Fixed

Some reference to the early history of the firm of Iver Johnson has already been made in the caption on the facing page (above). The Iver Johnson arm illustrated here is a compact and well-made double-action revolver of pocket type. It is opened by lifting the top catch, which causes two parallel projections on the upper part of the standing breech to separate from two corresponding apertures on the top frame. This allows the barrel to be pushed downward and brings the automatic extractor into play. A very interesting feature of this weapon is that it is of the type known as Safety Automatic Double Action; a form of lock mechanism developed by Johnson and others in the 1890s and patented to the Johnson company. The firing-pin was mounted on the standing breech; its rear end was struck by the flat head of the hammer by means of a flat transfer bar, which only rose into position when the trigger was properly pulled. If the bar did not rise, the hammer was held clear of the actual pin by fouling the top of the breech. This was an ingenious and reliable system which remained in use unchanged for many years. The revolver is well finished, with blued trigger-guard and case-hardened lock mechanism, and has the usual hard rubber grips with the familiar owl's head motif.

United States of America
SMITH AND WESSON DOUBLE-ACTION ·38 REVOLVER

Length:	7·5" (190mm)
Weight:	18oz (·51kg)
Barrel:	3·25" (83mm)
Calibre:	·38" (9·6mm)
Rifling:	5 groove, r/hand
Capacity:	Five
Muz Vel:	625 f/s (190 m/s)
Sights:	Fixed

The revolvers of this series, which were classed as "New Model" arms, were first produced by Smith and Wesson in 1880. The specimen illustrated here is an example of the fourth model, which was introduced in 1895 and remained in production until 1909. The model was originally made in four barrel lengths—3·25in (83mm); 4in (102mm); 5in (127mm); and 6in (152mm)—the example shown being of the shortest type; but longer barrels, of 8in (203mm) or 10in (254mm), were introduced in 1888. The finish was in blue or nickel. Special target revolvers, with longer butts and target sights were also available. This specimen has the conventional round sight, pinned into a groove on the top rib; the backsight is a simple V-notch in a raised part of the barrel catch. The earlier models had a rocker-type cylinder stop, which necessitated two sets of notches or grooves on the cylinder; but in the fourth model this was abandoned, so that, as may be seen, only one set of notches was required. In revolvers in the series made after 1889, the notches were lined with a special hard-steel shim to prevent undue wear; but this practice, too, was later discontinued, although the lined notches are present on the model shown. The left side of the frame has an access plate so that the mechanism can be reached. (The unsightly brass screw visible in the photograph is jammed into its aperture—and is due to be removed!) The frame is plated, except for the trigger-guard, and the butt is of the usual hard rubber.

HARRINGTON AND RICHARDSON DEFENDER POCKET REVOLVER

Length:	8·75" (222mm)
Weight:	23oz (·65kg)
Barrel:	4" (102mm)
Calibre:	·38" (9·6mm)
Rifling:	7 groove, r/hand
Capacity:	Six
Muz Vel:	c625 f/s (190 m/s)
Sights:	Fixed

The Harrington and Richardson Company was formed in Worcester, Massachusetts, in 1874, by Gilbert H. Harrington and William A. Richardson. Its stated intention was to produce plain, reliable revolvers at a reasonable price—and this it has always done with great consistency. The company's first models were, of course, solid-frame types, and most of them were pocket pistols, but the success of these caused the company to diversify. Just before the end of the 19th century, Harrington and Richardson produced the first of their break-open "Automatic Ejector" models, which were made in a variety of calibres and barrel lengths; although they still continued to make their well-established solid-frame arms. The weapon illustrated here is of the post-World War II period. It had the trade name of "Defender"; there were, in fact, several versions, with a variety of butts, calibres and barrel lengths: this one is the ·38in (9·6mm) calibre version with a plain butt. The shape of the barrel is some-what difficult to characterize: it is basically round, but has flattened sides and a very solid top rib, with a round foresight slotted in. The weapon is opened in the same way as a Smith and Wesson, by pushing up a T-shaped catch: this allows the barrel to be forced downward and brings the automatic ejector into action. Although basically a pocket arm, it has a very large butt; this, although bulky, provides a very comfortable grip. The butt is of one-piece construction and is held to the weapon by a screw which passes through the back of the butt and into the tang. Overall, the revolver is of plain but robust construction. The top of the barrel is marked "HARRINGTON AND RICHARDSON ARMS CO, WORCESTER MASS USA".

BULLDOG-TYPE REVOLVER

Length:	9" (229mm)
Weight:	29oz (·82kg)
Barrel:	4" (102mm)
Calibre:	·45" (11·4mm)
Rifling:	7 groove, r/hand
Capacity:	Five
Muz Vel:	c600 f/s (183 m/s)
Sights:	Fixed

The earliest Bulldog revolvers were designed, produced and marketed by the Birmingham firm of P. Webley and Son. Although a few were adopted for military or police use, the great bulk of them were sold on the civilian market, as house or self-defence weapons, in the period 1878 to 1914. In the 19th century, few countries had laws for the control of firearms: guns could be freely purchased and owned for lawful purposes. Although Great Britain was well-policed by the middle of the century, burglars and footpads were still active—then, as now—and law-abiding householders, especially those living in more remote areas, often felt rather more secure if they had access to a reliable firearm with which to defend their property. Thus, many revolvers like the one illustrated here were purchased and, because many of them spent their lives lying in readiness in chests or cupboards, but were rarely or never used, they have survived in surprisingly large numbers. This particular specimen has the usual ovate barrel with top rib and is of solid-frame construction. The five-chambered cylinder is plain, except for slots for the cylinder stop, and bears Birmingham proof marks. The ejector is of the usual pin pattern and it is carried inside the hollow cylinder axis pin when it is not in use. In addition, it is fitted with a swivel carrier on the right front of the frame; this allows it to be drawn out and swung over so as to come into line with the chamber aligned with the loading gate. The gate itself is hinged at the bottom and turns down sideways; the usual groove is cut in the frame beside it to facilitate the loading of cartridges into the chambers. The lock is of orthodox double-action type, with a fairly wide, milled comb on the hammer. The arm has a one-piece, wrap-over grip of chequered walnut; this is fastened to the revolver by two vertical screws, one running downward from the rear of the frame behind the hammer, and the other running upward from the butt-plate. The revolver originally had a swivel ring, but this is now missing; such rings were often provided with a short wrist-strap instead of the lanyards usually found on heavier arms of the type. The arm is marked on the top strap with the words "G. E. GIBBS 29 CORN ST, BRISTOL". George Gibbs was a well-known gunmaker in his own right, but in the case of this revolver he will have been only the retailer of the arm.

GALAND-TYPE REVOLVER

Length:	13" (330mm)
Weight:	46oz (1·3kg)
Barrel:	4·8" (122mm)
Calibre:	11mm
Rifling:	10 groove, r/hand
Capacity:	Six
Muz Vel:	c700 f/s (213 m/s)
Sights:	Fixed

Charles François Galand was a well-known Belgian gunmaker during the second half of the 19th century, and he invented and patented a number of improvements to the revolver. He was, perhaps, best known for an improved method of extracting cartridges from the cylinder: a Galand and Sommerville revolver involving this principle has already been referred to (page 99, above). Although Galand made a number of these arms in conjunction with the British maker Sommerville of Birmingham, it is generally true to say that the type was more popular on the continent than in Great Britain; and it was

very rarely found in the United States. The system of operation is fairly simple. The spur on the trigger-guard forms the rear extremity of a long lever hinged to a very long front extension of the cylinder axis pin. When the milled catch at the rear of the trigger-guard is pulled backward, the whole lever can be drawn down to the vertical position. This action draws forward the barrel and cylinder along the axis pin. During the last part of its travel, the rear plate of the cylinder, which is pierced with holes for the cartridges, stops, while the main cylinder goes on for a further ·5in (13mm), leaving the

empty cases behind it on the plate, whence they can be shaken clear. The lock is of double-action type and the weapon is fitted with a folding, skeleton stock (seen here in the folded position); a feature which contributes little, if anything, to the steadiness of the aim taken. The right flat of the barrel is marked "C.F.G." with a crown above; the cylinder carries both a Belgian proof mark and the letter "G" beneath a crown. The weapon is of plain but robust construction; its weakest point is undoubtedly the very flimsy skeleton stock which makes it difficult to grip the butt properly.

R.I.C.-TYPE POCKET REVOLVER

Length:	8" (203mm)
Weight:	28oz (·79kg)
Barrel:	3" (76mm)
Calibre:	·45" (11·4mm)
Rifling:	7 groove, r/hand
Capacity:	Five
Muz Vel:	c600 f/s (183 m/s)
Sights:	Fixed

The Royal Irish Constabulary revolver first appeared in 1867 and it was probably this single, exceptionally-popular arm

which really established the reputation of its manufacturer, P. Webley and Son of Birmingham. As might be expected, such a successful arm was widely copied: it is probable that imitation R.I.C. revolvers greatly outnumbered the originals. Civilian purchasers of weapons were not always very selective; and although a soldier, policeman or traveller, any one of whom might have to depend on his revolver for the preservation of his life, would choose carefully, this was not the case with all users. If a revolver looked effective, and was cheaply priced, this was enough for most civilians. Nor was their trust always misplaced, for many of the R.I.C. copies

were perfectly adequate weapons for household defence. All that can be said is that some were worse than others—and some were very poor indeed. The example illustrated here stands at the lower end of the scale: it was hardly worth the twelve shillings and sixpence (62p, or about $1.40) at which it was probably retailed. In general appearance it resembles the earliest version of the original Webley, with a plain cylinder and the distinctive hump in the top strap just in front of the trigger. It has the usual round, stubby barrel cast integrally with the frame, and it is so badly made that the right barrel wall is appreciably thicker than the left. It bears

Birmingham proof marks and the barrel is stamped "TRULOCK & HARRIS, 9 DAWSON ST DUBLIN". The barrel also bears the inscription "No2450"—and as there is an appreciable gap between the "2" and the "4", the last three figures presumably indicate its calibre. The left side of the frame is stamped "V8958" in unusually large letters, and the letters "T.H." appear on the front of the frame. These initials are possibly those of Trulock and Harris, who may have been both the makers and the retailers of the arm; however, this cannot be established with certainly. In view of the quality of the arm, the uncertainty concerning its maker is not in the least surprising!

Great Britain
TRANTER REVOLVER CONVERSION

Length:	10·25" (260mm)
Weight:	26oz (·74kg)
Barrel:	6" (152mm)
Calibre:	·38" (9·6mm)
Rifling:	5 groove, r/hand
Capacity:	Five
Muz Vel:	c600 f/s (183 m/s)
Sights:	Fixed

The name of William Tranter has been mentioned frequently, both in this section and in the earlier one on percussion revolvers, and a number of his revolvers in both categories have been illustrated. Although he is, perhaps, best known for his double-trigger arms, Tranter also made a number of single-trigger, double-action revolvers from 1856 until 1863. The weapon seen here was originally of that type, although it subsequently underwent the conversion that justifies its inclusion at this point. The perfection of the metallic rimfire cartridge naturally led to a demand for revolvers to fire it, and many existing arms were converted to meet this demand. In this Tranter conversion, the main change has been the provision of a new, bored-through cylinder, with the addition of a loading gate on the right-hand side of the frame and a shield on the left to prevent the cartridges from slipping out. A new hammer, suitable for the firing of rimfire rounds, has also been added. There is no integral ejector, but the empty cases may be pushed out through the loading gate by means of a rod, which screws into the butt when not in use.

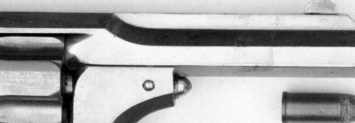

Great Britain
PRYSE-TYPE SERVICE REVOLVER

Length:	8·5" (216mm)	**Rifling:**	5 groove, r/hand
Weight:	29oz (·82kg)	**Capacity:**	Five
Barrel:	4" (102mm)	**Muz Vel:**	c600 f/s (183 m/s)
Calibre:	·455" (11·5mm)	**Sights:**	Fixed

A number of Webley-Pryse revolvers of broadly similar type to this one have already been illustrated. Although the greater number of revolvers on this principle appear to have been made by Webley, from 1877 onwards, the famous Birmingham firm was by no means the only manufacturer to have produced them. Apart from arms produced by British makers, a good many foreign copies are to be found, most of them originating from France or Belgium. The characteristic feature of Pryse revolvers is that they are of break-open type, with a star-shaped ejector at the rear of the cylinder. The action of opening the revolver to the full brings this automatically into play, driving it backwards with some force and thus throwing out the empty cases. After completing this action it snaps back into position under the pressure of a spring. A less obvious feature, but an important one, is the revolver's rebounding hammer. After a shot has been fired, the hammer is taken back about ·125" (3·2mm) to half-cock. Here it is locked rigidly: even a violent blow directly upon it will not drive it forward, so the risk of accidental discharge is very greatly reduced. A third important feature is the system of locking the barrel. A rear extension on the top frame fits into a slot in the top of the standing breech. Two studs, one on the top inner side of each of the vertical arms, pass through holes and engage in recesses on the frame extension, thus holding the frame firmly closed. The studs are released by pressing the lower ends of the vertical arms inward. This particular revolver, which appears to be a version of Pryse's British Army revolver, is British made with Birmingham proof marks. The right side of the frame is marked "Patent 3096" and the left bears the inscription "FIRST QUALITY".

Belgium
CHAMELOT-DELVIGNE SERVICE-TYPE REVOLVER

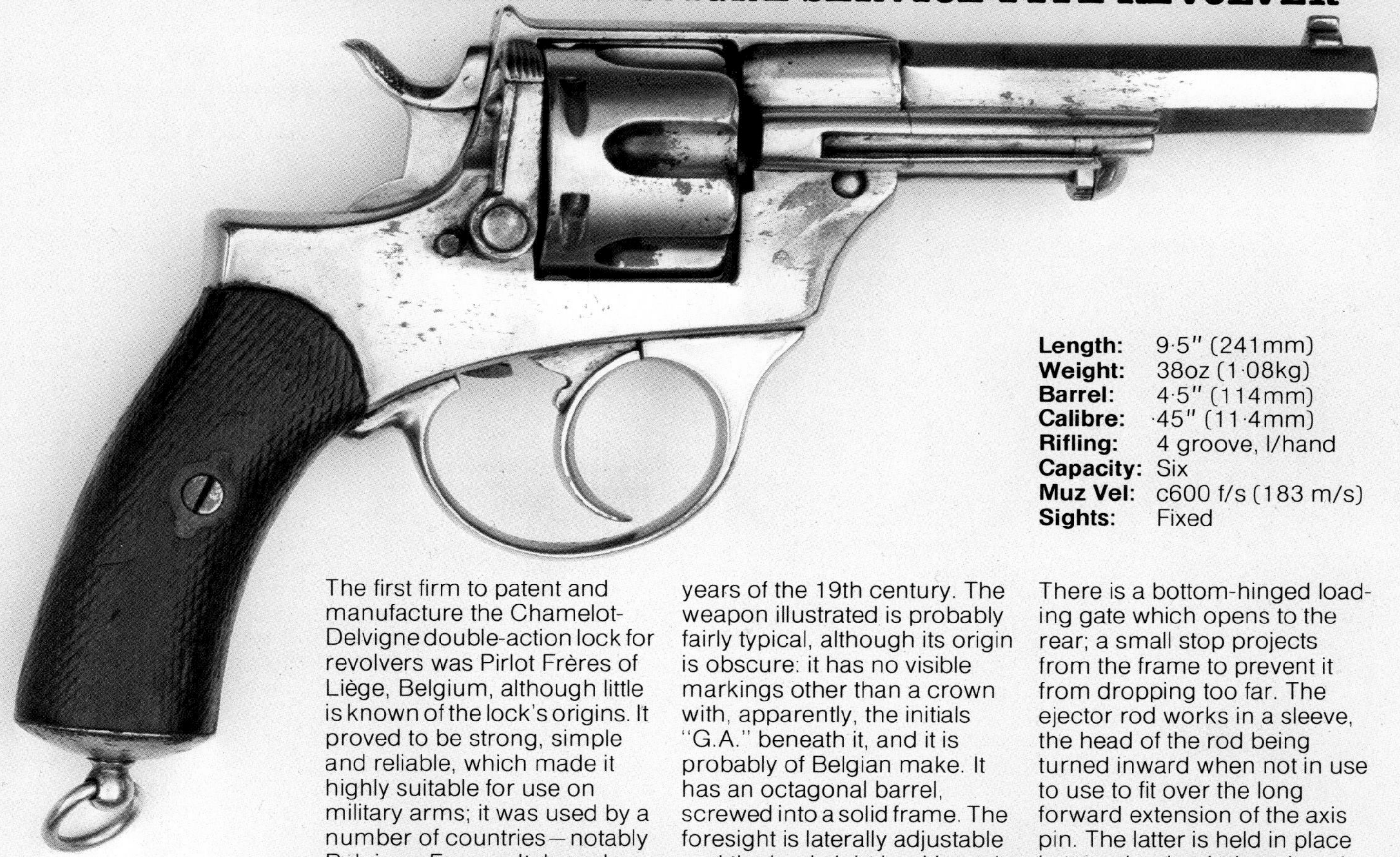

Length:	9·5" (241mm)
Weight	38oz (1·08kg)
Barrel:	4·5" (114mm)
Calibre:	·45" (11·4mm)
Rifling:	4 groove, l/hand
Capacity:	Six
Muz Vel:	c600 f/s (183 m/s)
Sights:	Fixed

The first firm to patent and manufacture the Chamelot-Delvigne double-action lock for revolvers was Pirlot Frères of Liège, Belgium, although little is known of the lock's origins. It proved to be strong, simple and reliable, which made it highly suitable for use on military arms; it was used by a number of countries—notably Belgium, France, Italy and Switzerland—in the last 30 years of the 19th century. The weapon illustrated is probably fairly typical, although its origin is obscure: it has no visible markings other than a crown with, apparently, the initials "G.A." beneath it, and it is probably of Belgian make. It has an octagonal barrel, screwed into a solid frame. The foresight is laterally adjustable and the backsight is a V-notch at the rear of the top strap.

There is a bottom-hinged loading gate which opens to the rear; a small stop projects from the frame to prevent it from dropping too far. The ejector rod works in a sleeve, the head of the rod being turned inward when not in use to use to fit over the long forward extension of the axis pin. The latter is held in place by a spring-loaded stud on the left side of the frame.

Spain
TROCAOLA SERVICE REVOLVER

Length:	10" (254mm)	Rifling:	8 groove, r/hand
Weight:	40oz (1·13kg)	Capacity:	Six
Barrel:	5" (127mm)	Muz Vel:	c650 f/s (198 m/s)
Calibre:	·455" (11·5mm)	Sights:	Fixed

The Spaniards have a long history of making firearms; many of their products are very fine—but some are shoddy, if not actually dangerous. The revolver illustrated here was made by "TROCAOLA, ARANZABAL y CIA, EIBAR, ESPANA", and is so marked along the top rib of the barrel. This firm is believed to have started making revolvers soon after 1900, and almost all its arms were close copies of other manufacturers' designs —principally Colt and Smith and Wesson. However, in the early days, at least, the company's products were of good quality and finish, and in 1915 a quantity of Trocaola arms were bought for use by the British Army, which has always insisted on a high standard. These revolvers, of which the one shown is an example, were given the British designation of "Pistol OP, 5inch Barrel, No 2 Mark 1"; they were not declared obsolete until after World War I. The revolver shown is a close copy of a Smith and Wesson. It has a round barrel with a foresight pinned into a slot on the top rib. The backsight is a notch in the barrel catch, which is of standard T-shape and is opened by upward thumb-pressure on the milled studs above the hammer. When the arm is opened and the barrel pushed smartly downward, the extractor comes into action automatically and throws out the cases. The revolver is blued, except for the case-hardened lock mechanism, and appears to be of sound construction. It is numbered "1389" and the left side of the barrel is stamped with an Enfield inspector's mark of crossed flags. Trocaola's trade mark, visible on the frame below the hammer, is very closely modelled on that of Smith and Wesson—and could easily be mistaken for it at a glance This, it may be supposed, was the maker's intention.

Austria
RAST AND GASSER MODEL 1898

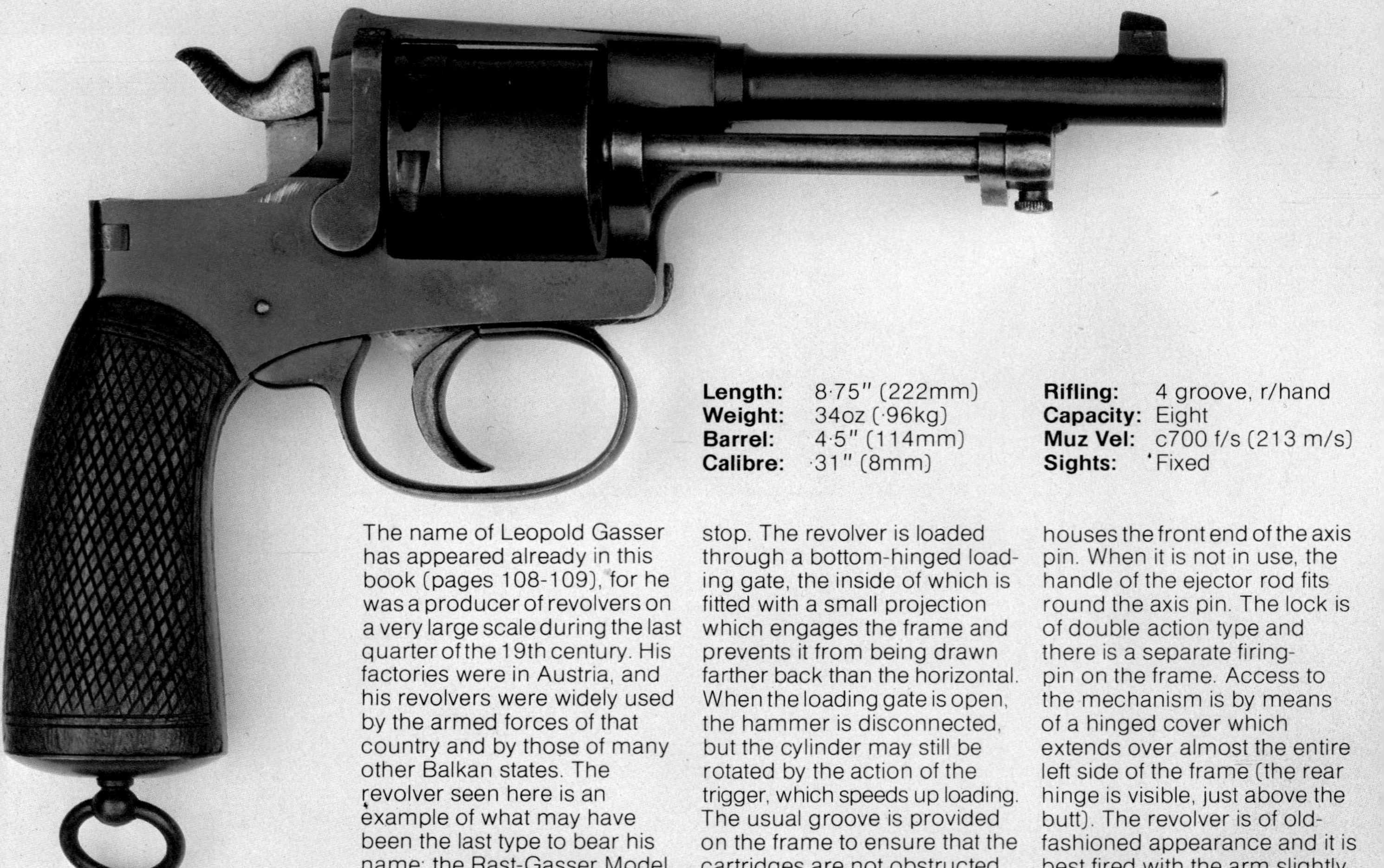

Length:	8·75" (222mm)	**Rifling:**	4 groove, r/hand
Weight:	34oz (·96kg)	**Capacity:**	Eight
Barrel:	4·5" (114mm)	**Muz Vel:**	c700 f/s (213 m/s)
Calibre:	·31" (8mm)	**Sights:**	Fixed

The name of Leopold Gasser has appeared already in this book (pages 108-109), for he was a producer of revolvers on a very large scale during the last quarter of the 19th century. His factories were in Austria, and his revolvers were widely used by the armed forces of that country and by those of many other Balkan states. The revolver seen here is an example of what may have been the last type to bear his name: the Rast-Gasser Model 1898 Austrian Service revolver. It is of solid-frame type, with a round barrel screwed in; its eight-chambered cylinder is plain, except for slots for the stop. The revolver is loaded through a bottom-hinged loading gate, the inside of which is fitted with a small projection which engages the frame and prevents it from being drawn farther back than the horizontal. When the loading gate is open, the hammer is disconnected, but the cylinder may still be rotated by the action of the trigger, which speeds up loading. The usual groove is provided on the frame to ensure that the cartridges are not obstructed on their way in. The ejector rod is hollow and works over a rod which is connected to the projection below the barrel; this projection also houses the front end of the axis pin. When it is not in use, the handle of the ejector rod fits round the axis pin. The lock is of double action type and there is a separate firing-pin on the frame. Access to the mechanism is by means of a hinged cover which extends over almost the entire left side of the frame (the rear hinge is visible, just above the butt). The revolver is of old-fashioned appearance and it is best fired with the arm slightly bent; it is, however, very well made, although the cartridge it fired was too lacking in power to be of very much use for service purposes.

Italy
BODEO MODEL 1889 SERVICE REVOLVER

Length:	10·5" (267mm)	**Rifling:**	4 groove, r/hand
Weight:	32oz (·91kg)	**Capacity:**	Six
Barrel:	4·5" (114mm)	**Muz Vel:**	c650 f/s (198 m/s)
Calibre:	·41" (10·4mm)	**Sights:**	Fixed

The Bodeo revolver took its name from the head of the Italian commission which recommended its adoption in 1889. This recommendation being approved, the Bodeo was put into production; by 1891 it had become the standard Italian service revolver, remaining in service for at least 50 years. The Model 1889 was made in two distinct types: a round-barrelled version, with a trigger-guard; and an octagonal-barrelled version, with a folding trigger. The revolver seen here is of the latter type. Although not an arm of particular distinction, the Bodeo was simple and robust—which is presumably why it lasted so long. The barrel is screwed into the frame, and the cylinder is loaded through a bottom-hinged gate which is drawn backwards to open it. Ejection is by means of a rod which is normally housed in the hollow axis pin. As in the Rast-Gasser revolver, illustrated above, the loading gate was connected to the hammer in such a way that, when it was opened, the hammer would not function, although the action of the trigger still turned the cylinder. This arrangement, which is known as the "Abadie" system, is frequently found on continental weapons. Revolvers of this type were made in a variety of Italian factories, and during World War I a number were also manufactured in Spain for use by the Italian Army. It was officially superseded by a self-loading pistol quite early in the 20th century but, as we have seen, many remained in service up to World War II.

Japan
MEIJI TYPE 26 SERVICE REVOLVER

Length:	9·25" (235mm)
Weight:	32oz (·91kg)
Barrel:	4·7" (119mm)
Calibre:	·35" (9mm)
Rifling:	4 groove, r/hand
Capacity:	Six
Muz Vel:	c600 f/s (183 m/s)
Sights:	Fixed

Many Japanese arms, including the revolver seen here, were dated from the accession of the reigning Emperor. This arm was made in 1893, which was the 26th year of the Meiji Era, and it is therefore known as the Type 26 revolver. At that time, Japan was only just emerging from some three centuries of medieval seclusion; thus, there is little that is original about this weapon. It is, in fact, a quite remarkably composite arm, incorporating a variety of ideas derived from a careful study of Western weapons. The Imperial Japanese Navy had earlier purchased a quantity of Smith and Wesson No 3 Models;

these had been found satisfactory, so it is perhaps natural that the American arm should have formed a basis for this one. In addition, however, there are elements derived from the arms of Galand, Nagant and others. It has an octagonal barrel with a foresight bed into which a sight is pinned; the backsight is incorporated with the top frame. The weapon is opened by lifting the top catch, after which the barrel can be forced down to bring the automatic ejector into action. The lock is of self-cocking variety and, as the mechanism is sluggish, this makes accurate shooting almost impossible.

Access to the mechanism is obtained through a large side plate, similar to the one found on the Rast and Gasser revolver (facing page, above). In view of the fairly primitive state of Japanese industry at the time that this arm was produced, it is not surprising that it is generally of poor material and finish. It was issued quite extensively as a cavalry arm, but its trigger-pull must have made it very ineffective except at point-blank range. It was officially superseded by a self-loading pistol before World War II, but thousands of Type 26 revolvers appear to have remained in service.

Belgium
GALAND VELO-DOG REVOLVER

Length:	4·7" (119mm)
Weight:	10·5oz (·30kg)
Barrel:	1·2" (30mm)
Calibre:	·216" (5·5mm)
Rifling:	4 groove, r/hand
Capacity:	Six
Muz Vel:	c400 f/s (122 m/s)
Sights:	Fixed

As with many other weapons, the term "Velo-Dog" is used to describe a fairly clearly defined group of weapons, rather than one particular arm. Most weapons of this type were cheap pocket revolvers, and they were made in very con-

siderable numbers at the end of the 19th century. They were essentially a continental product, being made in quantity in Belgium, France, Germany, Italy and Spain; the last-named country was particularly prolific. Perhaps their nearest British or American equivalent was the "Bulldog" type of arm, but the comparison is not a very close one. The Velo-Dog was invented by Charles François Galand, whose name has been mentioned earlier in connection with self-extracting revolvers. Galand's first model was of open-frame type, with an orthodox trigger and guard, as on the arm seen here; but later models, wherever produced, tended to have solid frames, completely enclosed hammers and folding triggers. The revolver illustrated is, therefore, a relatively minority type. The earliest Velo-Dogs fired a long 5·5mm cartridge with a light bullet; later they were designed to fire ·22" (5·6mm), 6mm

and 8mm Lebel rimmed cartridges, and even 6.35mm and 7·65mm rimless rounds. According to Hogg and Weeks in *Pistols of the World,* the name was derived from "Velocipede" (the early term for a bicycle) and "Dog", although in view of the arm's geographical origins this seems to be an odd linguistic mixture. There is, however, little doubt that these revolvers were designed principally for the use of pioneer cyclists, who appear to have been much troubled by fierce dogs—and it is of interest to note that the miniature revolver illustrated on page 97 (centre) was advertised as being ideal for the same purpose. Special deterrent, but less lethal, cartridges, loaded with salt, pepper or dust shot, were also supplied. Even so, it seems by modern standards an extreme way of dealing with a nuisance. Arms of this type were still advertised in continental makers' catalogues after World War I.

Great Britain
ENFIELD MARK II SERVICE REVOLVER

Length:	11·5" (292mm)	**Rifling:**	7 groove, r/hand
Weight:	40oz (1·13kg)	**Capacity:**	Six
Barrel:	5·75" (146mm)	**Muz Vel:**	c700 f/s (213 m/s)
Calibre:	·476" (12·1mm)	**Sights:**	Fixed

In the late 1870s, the British government decided to develop a new and more powerful service revolver. Various colonial campaigns during the previous years had shown that the bullet of the standard Adams ·45in (11·4mm) could not always be relied upon to stop a charging fanatic; thus, a new and more powerful round of ·476in (12·1mm) calibre was developed. Because there were doubts, mistaken as it turned out, as to whether a top-break revolver of Webley type could handle such rounds safely, a completely new arm was developed. The designer mainly concerned was a Philadelphian inventor with the very Welsh name of Owen Jones; his revolver was finally approved for service in 1880. As may be seen in the specimen illustrated (which is, in fact, a Mark II), the barrel is hinged to the front of the frame and fastened with a spring catch just in front of the hammer. However, when the revolver is opened and the barrel forced downward, the cylinder remains in the same axis and is simply drawn forward along its pin. This leaves the cases held by their rims in a star-shaped extractor on the standing breech, whence they can be shaken clear. The need for the cylinder to be drawn well forward acounts for the rather ugly bulge below the barrel. The Enfield Mark II was adopted in 1882. Its main points of difference from the Mark I are the provision of a device in the loading gate which prevents the action from working if the gate is open. and vice-versa, and the fitting of a safety catch on the left side of the frame.

Great Britain
WEBLEY R.I.C. REVOLVER No 2

Length:	8·25" (210mm)
Weight:	27oz (·76kg)
Barrel:	3·5" (89mm)
Calibre:	·45" (11·4mm)
Rifling:	5 groove, r/hand
Capacity:	Six
Muz Vel:	c650 f/s (198 m/s)
Sights:	Fixed

The first revolvers of this type were manufactured by P. Webley and Son of Birmingham in 1867. They immediately became popular as robust and reliable service weapons; they were probably the best-known of Webley products and made the firm famous. It is a measure of their quality that they remained in production for more than 30 years. In 1868 the Royal Irish Constabulary was raised. Civilian police were a comparatively new concept in Great Britain (the first such body being the Metropolitan Police of London, founded in 1829), but once established they proved a success and their number rapidly increased. Ireland had always been a troubled country, so the new police force established there was a para-military body, armed with rifles, carbines or revolvers. The first arm adopted was the Webley revolver, which was known thereafter as the Royal Irish Constabulary revolver. The specimen illustrated here is the No 2 Model and was probably made in about 1876.

The barrel is round, although the shape of the top rib gives a distinct impression of taper, and is screwed into the frame. It has a semi-round foresight, slotted in; the backsight is a long, V-shaped groove along the top strap. The six-chambered cylinder is plain except for raised flanges at the rear; the ends of these are held by the cylinder stop, which rises from the lower frame when the trigger is pressed. The extractor pin is housed in the hollow cylinder axis pin when it is not in use, but it can be withdrawn on a swivel in order to align it with the appropriate chamber. Once the pin is drawn, the cylinder may be removed by drawing the axis pin forward by means of its flat, milled head (visible in the photograph). Access to the chambers is by means of a loading gate which is hinged at the bottom and opens sideways against a flat spring. The lock is of double-action type. This particular revolver was carried by Major Webb of the Bengal Cavalry in the Second Afghan War of 1878-88; it is marked "MANTON & CO, LONDON & CALCUTTA" on the strap and was, presumably, purchased in India. The left side of the frame is stamped "WEBLEYS RIC NO 2 ·450 CF", with the flying bullet trademark and it also bears the arm's serial number, which is "10974".

Great Britain
WEBLEY R.I.C. REVOLVER No 1

Length: 9·25" (235mm)
Weight: 30oz (·85kg)
Barrel: 14·5" (114mm)
Calibre: ·45" (11·4mm)
Rifling: 5 groove, r/hand
Capacity: Six
Muz Vel: c650 f/s (198 m/s)
Sights: Fixed

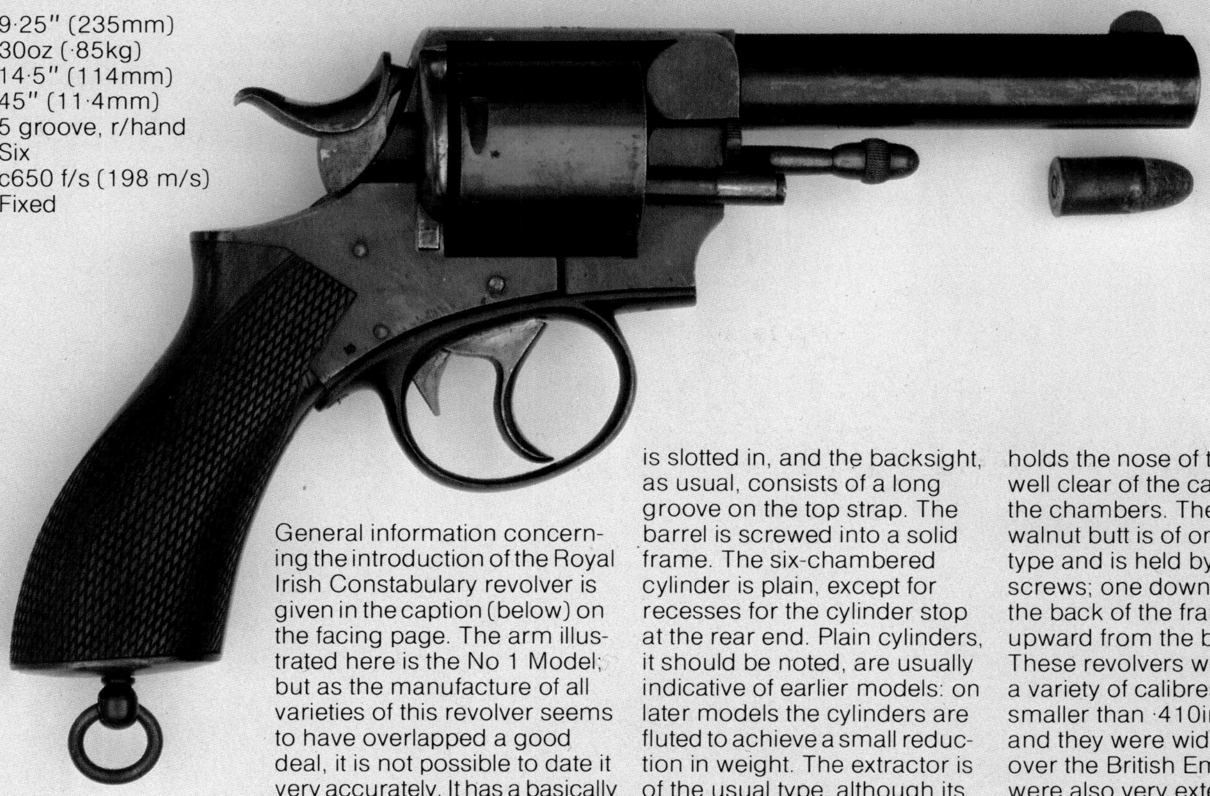

General information concerning the introduction of the Royal Irish Constabulary revolver is given in the caption (below) on the facing page. The arm illustrated here is the No 1 Model; but as the manufacture of all varieties of this revolver seems to have overlapped a good deal, it is not possible to date it very accurately. It has a basically round barrel which is, however, slightly raised on its upper side, on which a flat rib has been machined. The foresight is slotted in, and the backsight, as usual, consists of a long groove on the top strap. The barrel is screwed into a solid frame. The six-chambered cylinder is plain, except for recesses for the cylinder stop at the rear end. Plain cylinders, it should be noted, are usually indicative of earlier models: on later models the cylinders are fluted to achieve a small reduction in weight. The extractor is of the usual type, although its knob is acorn-shaped. The loading gate is standard. The revolver has a double-action lock, with a half-cock which holds the nose of the hammer well clear of the cartridges in the chambers. The chequered walnut butt is of one-piece type and is held by two vertical screws; one downward from the back of the frame and one upward from the butt-cap. These revolvers were made in a variety of calibres, none smaller than ·410in (10·4mm), and they were widely used all over the British Empire. They were also very extensively copied in various European countries; some of these copies have already been illustrated in this section.

Italy
CHAMELOT-DELVIGNE ITALIAN SERVICE REVOLVER

Length: 11·2" (284mm)
Weight: 40oz (1·13kg)
Barrel: 6·25" (·159mm)
Calibre: ·41" (10·4mm)
Rifling: 5 groove, r/hand
Capacity: Six
Muz Vel: c625 f/s (190 m/s)
Sights: Fixed

This is another example of the numerous revolvers fitted with the robust Chamelot-Delvigne double-action lock, first manufactured by Pirlot Frères of Liège, Belgium, which quickly became widely used in Europe after 1870 because of its simplicity and reliability. It was adopted for service weapons by France, Belgium, Switzerland and Italy, among others. The revolver seen here is the Italian version of the Chamelot-Delvigne et Schmidt Model 1872 (Schmidt was a Swiss officer who made some changes in design). There was also a version with a folding trigger—and, therefore, of course, no trigger-guard. The arm is of solid-frame type, with an octagonal barrel which is screwed into the main frame. The foresight is slotted in and the backsight is a U-notch on the lump (visible just in front of the hammer), the top strap also being grooved. The six-chambered cylinder is grooved and has rear notches for the cylinder stop. The ejector rod works in a sleeve; when it is not in use, its head is turned in under the barrel, where it fits over the front end of the cylinder axis pin. In order to remove the cylinder, it is first necessary to turn down the head of the ejector rod and press in a stud on the left front of the frame; this allows the pin to be drawn forward. The spring loading gate is hinged at the bottom and is opened by drawing it to the rear. There is a small stop on the frame, against which the gate rests when in the open position. The lock is of double-action type; very slight pressure on the trigger lifts the hammer to the half-cock position, which allows the cylinder to be rotated for loading. The butt has unchequered side plates and a swivel ring for a lanyard. These revolvers were made in various Italian factories; this one carries the name of the Royal Manufactory of Glisenti, Brescia, on the left of the frame. Versions of the arm were in production until 1930.

WEBLEY-WILKINSON SERVICE REVOLVER

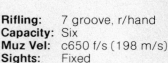

Length:	11" (279mm)	**Rifling:**	7 groove, r/hand
Weight:	38oz (1·08kg)	**Capacity:**	Six
Barrel:	6" (152mm)	**Muz Vel:**	c650 f/s (198 m/s)
Calibre	·455/476"	**Sights:**	Fixed
	(11·5/12·1mm)		

This is a service revolver of a type first produced by Webley in 1892. With one important exception, described below, it is very similar in most ways to the earlier Webley-Pryse model (illustrated on page 113, above). As may be seen, it is a break-open type. Its octagonal barrel has a very high top rib—somewhat higher at the front than the rear—with a bead foresight inset into it. The backsight is a simple U on the barrel catch. This catch is the most interesting feature of the arm: a rear extension on the top strap fits over a raised part of the standing breech and is held in place by a spring top latch (visible in the photograph). This is worked by a lever on the left-hand side (examples on this system may be seen on the weapons illustrated on pages 134-137), and it is very robust and reliable. The revolver cannot be fired when it is open, for unless the latch is fully in position, the upper part of the hammer fouls it and this prevents the hammer nose from reaching the cartridge. When the revolver is opened, a star extractor comes automatically into play and throws out the empty cases.

The one-piece, wrap-round butt is of fine chequered walnut, with an escutcheon plate, and the weapon is particularly well finished. It was made for retail by the famous Wilkinson Sword Company of Pall Mall, London, whose name and address is on the top strap. Wilkinson found it convenient to provide officers with revolvers as well as swords and bought revolvers from Webley for this purpose. Although these arms were standard models, they are distinguished by their fine finish, in keeping with the high reputation of the firm of Wilkinson.

WEBLEY-KAUFMANN REVOLVER

Length:	11" (279mm)	
Weight:	38oz (1·08kg)	
Barrel:	6·8" (173mm)	
Calibre:	·455"/·476"	
	(11·5/12·1mm)	
Rifling:	7 groove, r/hand	
Capacity:	Six	
Muz Vel:	c650 f/s (198 m/s)	
Sights:	Fixed	

Michael Kaufmann was a very talented British inventor of fire-arms. His association with Webley in the period 1878-81 led to the appearance of the revolver seen here, which bears his name and which provided, in effect, the basic design for Webley's famous range of Government (Webley-Green) models, produced from 1882 onward. The Webley-Kaufmann revolver illustrated here has an octagonal barrel with its top flat drawn up into a rib. It is of break-open type, and perhaps its main point of interest is the system by which it is locked. A rear extension on the top strap fits into a corresponding slot in the standing breech, and running through both is a cylindrical hole, with a diameter of about ·16in (4mm), in which the locking bolt works. Pressure on a lever on the left side of the body causes a spring bolt (the milled end of which is visible in the photograph) to be forced outward, thus allowing the revolver to be closed. When the lever is released, the bolt is returned inward, entering the hole in the rear extension. This holds a floating bolt, which is pushed over to the left in order to engage with the far hole on the standing breech, thus providing a very strong locking device indeed. The fluted, six-chambered cylinder is fitted with the usual star extractor, which is forced out automatically when the weapon is opened. The lock is of double-action, rebounding type. The bird-beak butt has two side plates of finely chequered walnut held by a single screw, and the trigger-guard is made integrally with the frame. The frame bears the inscription "MK" in a triangle, together with the number "1228"; on the left side are the words "Webley's patent" and the familiar trade mark of the winged bullet.

WEBLEY-GOVERNMENT (WEBLEY-GREEN) REVOLVER

Length:	11·25" (286mm)	Rifling:	7 groove, r/hand
Weight:	40oz (1·13kg)	Capacity:	Six
Barrel:	6" (152mm)	Muz Vel:	c650 f/s (198 m/s)
Calibre:	·455/·476".	Sights:	Fixed
	(11·5/12·1mm)		

This revolver, frequently known as the "W.G.", is really a development of the Webley-Kaufmann weapon shown on the facing page (below), and was first developed in the period 1882-85. It is of the familiar break-open type, although the barrel is of slightly different section: the lower part is rounded. The six-chambered cylinder is distinctively fluted in the manner sometimes referred to "church steeple", from the very characteristic shape of the flutes, and it is fitted with the usual spring extractor. The system of locking is really the main point of difference between this arm and the Webley-Kaufmann. The top strap of the Webley-Green has a rear extension with a rectangular slot which fits closely over an upper projection from the standing breech. A stirrup-type catch, essentially similar to the one on the Webley-Wilkinson shown on the facing page (above), fits over this whole assembly, and is activated by a lever on the left side. The design is such that, unless the catch is properly home, the nose of the hammer cannot reach the cartridges; this makes it not only strong but also very safe. The lock is of the usual double-action type. The bird-beak butt, which is itself on the small side for a service arm, has plates of a composition that resembles very hard rubber. The left side of the frame is marked "'WG' MODEL, ·455/476", and "WEBLEY PATENT", and the top flat bears the name of the retailer, "ARMY & NAVY CSL" ("Cooperative Society Limited").

WEBLEY Mk I SERVICE REVOLVER

Length:	8·5" (216mm)
Weight:	34oz (·96kg)
Barrel:	4" (102mm)
Calibre:	·455" (11·5mm)
Rifling:	7 groove, r/hand
Capacity:	Six
Muz Vel:	c600 f/s (183 m/s)
Sights:	Fixed

The Enfield revolver (illustrated on page 124, above) was adopted as the British service revolver in 1880. However, after further extensive trials and a good deal of practical use in the field, it was finally felt to be inadequate. Two new weapons were therefore tested: the first was a Smith and Wesson; and the second a Webley revolver of the type shown here. After exhaustive trials, it was decided in 1887 to adopt the British weapon. Since both the arms tested were of break-open type, the principal factor bearing on the decision was the relative reliability of the method of holding the weapons closed; in this respect, in particular, the Webley was considered superior. (The locking system is described in the captions for the other Webley arms on this spread.) Tests found the system to be strong and absolutely safe, for if the stirrup catch was not properly fastened, only two things could happen. Either the projection on the upper part of the catch safely into position, allowing the revolver to be fired; or it fouled the catch and prevented the hammer nose from reaching the cap. As is apparent in the photograph, the Webley Mark I is a stubby, compact weapon, with a short barrel. Its bird-beak butt, of adequate size to afford a good grip, is fitted with plates of brown vulcanite and is provided with a lanyard ring. The horizontal projection visible in front of the cylinder (there is one on the left side also) is a holster guide, designed to prevent the face of the cylinder from catching on the edge of the leather holster. This arm set the style for almost all later Webley service revolvers (see other Webley illustrations).

Great Britain
TRANTER "ARMY" REVOLVER

Length:	11·75" (298mm)	**Rifling:**	7 groove, r/hand
Weight:	36oz (1·02kg)	**Capacity:**	Six
Barrel:	6" (152mm)	**Muz Vel:**	c650 f/s (198 m/s)
Calibre:	·45" (11·4mm)	**Sights:**	Fixed

Numerous references to William Tranter have already been made in this book, many of them in connection with his well-known double-trigger revolvers. He was an enterprising individual who moved with the times: he was, in fact, one of the earliest, if not the earliest, makers of metallic-cartridge revolvers in Great Britain. The obvious advantages of the hinged-frame or break-open revolver — particularly as regards speed of ejection or reloading — were quickly seen by Tranter, who, by 1879, had patented and put into production his own revolver of this type, one of which is here illustrated. It has an octagonal barrel with a raised top rib and a round foresight (the backsight being a groove on the back end of the top strap), and a six-chambered fluted cylinder with an automatic ejector. The cylinder may be removed by first opening the revolver and then pressing the milled catch visible below the barrel; the cylinder may then be lifted off its axis pin. The lock is of double-action type and has a rebounding hammer. The locking system consists of a rear extension to the top strap, with a rectangular aperture which fits over a shaped projection on top of the standing breech. The long, pivoted hook on the left of the frame is basically similar to that on the Webley, but fits over a projection on the top frame. An additional safety device is provided by a slot in the hammer (clearly visible in the photograph) which, when the hammer is fully down in the firing position, engages a corresponding flange on the revolver's strap.

Great Britain
WEBLEY NEW MODEL ARMY EXPRESS

Length:	10·5" (267mm)
Weight:	38oz (1·08kg)
Barrel:	5·5" (140mm)
Calibre:	·45" (11·4mm)
Rifling:	7 groove, r/hand
Capacity:	Six
Muz Vel:	c700 f/s (213 m/s)
Sights:	Fixed

The appearance in 1877 of the new Colt double-action revolver (illustrated on the facing page, above) was quickly followed by that of a new Webley revolver of very similar appearance. Like the Colt, the Webley is a solid-frame revolver, with a loading gate and a sliding ejector rod. Its barrel, which is basically octagonal but with a higher and narrower top flat, is screwed into the frame, although the joint is virtually imperceptible. It has an unusually large trigger-guard, presumably so that it may be used by a man wearing gloves. Its bird-beak butt is somewhat larger than that of the corresponding Colt, and is a good deal more comfortable to handle as a result. The arm was made in one calibre only, nominally ·45in (11·4mm), but, like all Webley service arms of the period, it would accept cartridges of both ·455in (11·5mm) and ·476in (12·1mm) calibre. There was only one standard length of barrel—5·5in (140mm), as seen here—but a few models were made with 12in (305mm) barrels to special orders, and these were supplied with a detachable shoulder stock. The specimen illustrated is numbered "4506" and carries the well-known trade mark of the flying bullet; the top of the frame is marked "ARMY & NAVY C.S.L." and "EXPRESS". In spite of its strong similarity to the new Colt it is, in fact, probable (according to *The Webley Story* by Dowell) that it was based on a prototype designed some ten years earlier to handle the heavy ·577in (14·6mm) pistol cartridge used in the Webley No1 (illustrated on page 102); for it does not seem possible that a completely new arm could have been put into production in the time which elapsed between the appearance of the new Colt and that of the Webley. Unlike its American rival, the Webley turned out to be a very robust and reliable arm. It achieved a wide measure of popularity in the various colonial police forces which were then operative in keeping the peace throughout the British Empire.

United States of America
COLT DOUBLE-ACTION ARMY REVOLVER

Length:	10·25" (260mm)	**Rifling:**	6 groove, r/hand
Weight:	36oz (1·02kg)	**Capacity:**	Six
Barrel:	5·5" (140mm)	**Muz Vel:**	c750 f/s (229 m/s)
Calibre:	·476" (12·1mm)	**Sights:**	Fixed

In 1877 the Colt company added a new revolver to its existing range: the Double-Action Army model, illustrated here. It has the usual solid frame, with a round barrel screwed into it and an ejector rod sliding in a sleeve. The six-chambered cylinder has a loading gate, and a cartridge groove is provided on the right-hand side of the frame. The butt is of the type known as bird-beak and has a swivel for a strap or a flat lanyard. However, the most interesting aspect of the weapon is the fact that it is the first Colt revolver to have been fitted with a double-action lock in place of the popular and well-tried single-action mechanism. It is possible that the United States Cavalry may have expressed a preference for such a weapon, which was faster to operate in a mêlée. The revolver was made in three major calibres—·32in (8·1mm); ·38in (9·6mm); and ·45in (11·4mm)—and in three barrel lengths: 4·75in (121mm); 5·5in (140mm); and 7·5in (190mm). The calibre of the revolver illustrated here is, however, ·476in (12·1mm), which indicates that this parti-cular specimen was probably made for the British market—for this was the standard British service calibre at the time. This attribution is confirmed by the fact that the words "DEPOT 14 PALL MALL LONDON" have been added to the standard inscription on the barrel. This model continued to be made in the United States until 1909, but it never proved popular: it had the reputation of being both badly balanced and mechanically unreliable—remarkable and almost unprecedented allegations to be made against a Colt product.

United States of America
SMITH AND WESSON HAND EJECTOR REVOLVER

Length:	11·75" (298mm)
Weight:	38oz (1·08kg)
Barrel:	6·5" (165mm)
Calibre:	·455" (11·5mm)
Rifling:	6 groove, r/hand
Capacity:	Six
Muz Vel:	c650 f/s (198 m/s)
Sights:	Fixed

Although the Smith and Wesson No 3 revolver (pages 112, above, and 114, above) was in many ways a fine weapon, it never really became popular in the United States, where there was an inherent distrust of the hinged-frame revolver when used with the powerful cart-tridges then popular. It is, indeed, probable that regular use of heavy charges would eventually loosen the frame. Before the end of the 19th century, therefore, Smith and Wesson had bowed to public taste and produced a solid-frame revolver. The principle is simple and reliable: pushing forward a milled catch on the left of the frame allows the cylinder to be swung out to the left a separate yoke. Then, the extractor is manually operated by means of the pin, a method which is only marginally slower than a hinged-frame type. The version seen here first appeared in 1908 and was variously known as the "·44 Hand Ejector First Model"; the "New Century"; the "Gold Seal"; or the "Triple Lock". The latter name came from the fact that the cylinder locked not only at the rear, but also by means of one bolt into the front end of the rod and a second which emerged from the casing below it. The lock is of rebounding, double action type and, as with all Smith and Wesson arms, works very smoothly. The standard calibre for production arms was ·44in (11·2mm), and it was chambered for the special cartridge, but arms in various other calibres were also made. A small number of original ·44in (11·2mm) calibre revolvers were converted to fire the British ·455in (11·5mm) Eley cartridge, mostly at the outbreak of World War I, but later a special version was made and sold to the British Army in some quantity. The specimen shown is one of the latter arms: it bears the serial number "1068" and also has what is apparently a British number on the bottom of the butt-strap, together with London proof marks. It is in every respect a beautiful weapon and is in mint condition.

United States of America
COLT NEW SERVICE REVOLVER

Length:	10·75" (273mm)	Rifling:	6 groove, r/hand
Weight:	40oz (1·13kg)	Capacity:	Six
Barrel:	5·5" (140mm)	Muz Vel:	c650 f/s (198 m/s)
Calibre:	·455" (11·5mm)	Sights:	Fixed

The Colt New Service revolver was one of the modern group of Colt arms designed in the last decade of the 19th century, and it was the largest and most robust of all. It was made in six barrel lengths—4in (102mm); 4·5in (114mm); 5in (127mm); 5·5 (140mm); 6in (152mm); and 7·5in (190mm)—and was used as a United States service arm from 1907 onward, until it was at last superseded by a self-loading pistol. Even after that, however, many continued to be carried privately. The specimen illustrated is of the usual solid-frame type and has a round, 5·5in (140mm) long barrel, with the standard foresight and V-backsight. Access to its six-chambered cylinder is obtained by pulling back a thumb-catch on the left side of the frame; this allows the cylinder to be swung out sideways, to the left, on its separate yoke. Then the manual extractor may be brought into play. The butt is large, providing a comfortable grip, and has chequered plates bearing the word "COLT". The well-known trademark of the rearing horse is borne on the left side of the frame, below the hammer. The revolver was made in a variety of calibres: the one shown here is chambered for the British ·455in (11·5mm) Eley cartridge. This arm bears the additional view marks of the Royal Small Arms Factory, Enfield; showing that it was one of the revolvers imported for use by the British Army in World War I. British proof laws are very strict, and in the absence of any system of government proof in the United States, even the finest products of that country's gunmakers have to be tested on import into Great Britain. The weapons illustrated below and below right are of similar type.

United States of America
COLT NEW SERVICE REVOLVER (CUT-DOWN)

Length:	6·75" (171mm)
Weight:	32oz (·91kg)
Barrel:	1·5" (38mm)
Calibre:	·455" (11·5mm)
Rifling:	6 groove, r/hand
Capacity:	Six
Muz Vel:	Not known
Sights:	Nil

The Colt New Service revolver went into production in 1897 and is still being made. It appeared in a variety of models, with different calibres (but all large) and several different barrel lengths, and was the most massive of what may be termed the modern Colt range of revolvers. At the time of its adoption as a service weapon in 1909, the United States Army and Navy were both using an excellent Colt revolver which was made either in ·38" (9·6mm) or ·41in (10·4mm) calibres. This had proved excellent until the Philippines campaign of 1899-1905, when it was found that the bullets did not have the necessary stopping power to deal with the fanatical Moros, who were fighting-men of savage temperament and great physical strength. It is interesting to compare the experience of the United States Army in the Philippines with the lessons learnt by the British Army in somewhat similar campaigns, against Zulus, Afghans and Dervishes, only a few years previously. The British had found that a large, lead bullet travelling relatively slowly — say at around 600 f/s (183 m/s) — was the most effective, since it tended to expend the whole of its energy within the target, whereas a smaller but higher-velocity bullet simply went through. The weapon seen here has, obviously, been crudely shortened; it was originally a standard Colt New Service model. It is chambered for the British ·455in (11·5mm) Eley cartridge, the word "ELEY" being just visible on the stump of the barrel. Its origins are not known, but it bears British government proof marks and also the double-arrow condemnation mark, which suggests that it saw service (as many of this type did) in World War I. It is in a poor state, and as the cylinder is irretrievably jammed in the frame, it is impossible to acertain its number. The reasons for which it was cut down are not known. It may have had a bulged barrel, or the truncation may have been performed simply to make the arm easier to conceal — although even in its present state it hardly qualifies as a pocket weapon by any stretch of the imagination! The reduction of the barrel to a length of only 1·5in (38mm) must have had a very serious effect on the accuracy of the weapon, except at point-blank range. (It should be noted that this arm was originally identified as being of ·45in (11·4mm) calibre; the round shown is incorrect.)

130

United States of America
COLT POLICE POSITIVE TARGET REVOLVER

Length:	10·25" (260mm)
Weight:	24oz (·68kg)
Barrel:	6" (152mm)
Calibre:	·22" (5·6mm)
Rifling:	6 groove, r/hand
Capacity:	Six
Muz Vel:	c700 f/s (213 m/s)
Sights:	Fixed

The United States has a long history of armed law enforcement services, and the needs of its police have been met with a variety of revolvers. The original Police Positive revolver was produced by Colt in 1905 and was of ·32in (8·1mm) calibre. Two years later a heavier version was produced; it was known as the Police Positive Special and was chambered for the ·38in (9·6mm) special cartridge, which gave it ample power for most purposes. The success of these arms led to a demand for a lighter version for target shooting. In 1910 the Colt Police Positive Target revolver went into production in both ·32in (8·1mm) and ·22in (5·6mm) calibre. An example of the latter is seen here. The larger calibre was discontinued in 1915, but the smaller version remained in production until 1935. The arm has a round barrel with a blade-type foresight, giving a bead in the sight picture, and an adjustable U-backsight. When a catch on the left side of the frame is drawn back, the six-chambered cylinder may be swung out to the left on its hinged yoke, in order to load; the empty cases are ejected manually by means of the extractor pin. The weapon is well finished, as one would expect of a Colt product. The butt-plates are of hard rubber, almost black but with a reddish tinge. The revolver is accurate and reasonably comfortable to fire, although the butt is on the short side for a user with even moderately large hands: in order to get a grip, it is necessary to have the little finger positioned off the end. It was frequently found that the rims of ·22in (5·6mm) cartridges lacked strength if unsupported; in 1932, therefore, the model was changed by the addition of countersinks in the chambers, fully enclosing the rims of the cartridges and thus giving them more support.

United States of America
COLT NEW SERVICE TARGET REVOLVER

Length:	12·75" (324mm)
Weight:	43oz (1·2kg)
Barrel:	7·5" (190mm)
Calibre:	·455" (11·5mm)
Rifling:	6 groove, r/hand
Capacity:	Six
Muz Vel:	c650 f/s (198 m/s)
Sights:	Fixed

Well before the end of the 19th century, the great American firm of Colt had begun to manufacture solid-frame revolvers with swing-out cylinders. The firm did not, of course, abandon its earlier fixed-cylinder type, with loading gate and ejector rod; these arms retained their popularity and are, indeed, still made in large numbers as reproductions of traditional weapons. Although the new models were made in considerable variety, they were all basically built upon four frame sizes only. The last of the frames to appear was also the largest; and it is on this frame that the New Service revolver was built. It first appeared in 1897 and is still manufactured, with only minor changes to its original specification. It has been made in a variety of barrel lengths—from 4in (102mm) to 7·5in (190mm); the weapon illustrated here having a barrel of the latter size — and in numerous calibres. In 1900 a new service target revolver was introduced; the revolver shown here is of this type. It has a rectangular blade foresight, screwed into its bed, and a laterally-adjustable U-backsight at the rear of the frame. The hand-finished lock works very smoothly and the trigger is chequered to prevent the finger from slipping. The butt-plates are of finely chequered walnut with a diamond pattern down the centre; they are unusual in that they do not bear Colt's name or trademark. Although Haven and Belden's *History of the Colt Revolver* states that it was made only in ·44in (11·2mm) Special, ·45in (11·4mm) Colt and ·45in (11·4mm) automatic, this particular weapon is chambered for the British ·455in (11·5mm) Eley cartridge, and is so marked on the left side of the barrel at the breech end. The top strap is marked "WILKINSON of PALL MALL, London".

United States of America
COLT NEW NAVY REVOLVER

Length:	11·25" (286mm)	**Rifling:**	6 groove, r/hand
Weight:	34oz (·96kg)	**Capacity:**	Six
Barrel:	6" (152mm)	**Muz Vel:**	c780 f/s (238 m/s)
Calibre:	·38" (9·6mm)	**Sights:**	Fixed

The New Navy model was one of four new types brought out by Colt in the period 1889-97; it was adopted by the United States Navy in 1892. It was made in both ·38in (9·6mm) and ·41in (10·4mm) calibre, being chambered for both the normal and long cartridge in each case, and in barrel lengths of 3in (76mm), 4·5in (114mm) and 6in (152mm). The revolver illustrated here is of ·38in (9·6mm) calibre and has a round, 6in (152mm) barrel with the typical Colt half-round foresight. The backsight is formed by a notch in the rear of the frame, with a shallow groove along the top strap. The six-chambered cylinder is fluted and has two separate sets of slots for the cylinder stops. When the arm is cocked, the rear stop rises; when the trigger is released, the rear stop drops and a forward stop comes up in its turn to engage the horizontal slots about ·5in (12·7mm) from the back of the cylinder. The thumbcatch, visible in the photograph, is drawn back to allow the cylinder to swing out: the fit between the yoke and the main frame is so good that the joint is difficult to detect, although the vertical line by the hinge is visible at the bottom front of the frame. The lock is of double-action variety. The butt-plates are of some hard rubber composition and bear the trade mark and the word "COLT". This particular arm, numbered "771", has no lanyard ring, although a flat one for a strap was usually fitted. The United States Army adopted this revolver just after the Navy, and it was then also listed as the New Army. A variation, with a butt of different shape and with plain walnut grips, was produced for the United States Marine Corps in the period 1905-10. The Army abandoned this model in 1908 in favour of the New Service, having found that its cartridge, although powerful, lacked immediate stopping-power against savage and fanatical opponents. An officer's target version was brought out in 1904. The revolver was built on the ·41in (10·4mm) frame and, after various changes in title, the frame size finally was designated the Official Police Model, a title it retains to the present day.

United States of America
SMITH AND WESSON BRITISH SERVICE REVOLVER

Length:	10" (254mm)	**Rifling:**	5 groove, r/hand
Weight:	29oz (·82kg)	**Capacity:**	Six
Barrel:	5" (127mm)	**Muz Vel:**	c650 f/s (198 m/s)
Calibre:	·38" (9·6mm)	**Sights:**	Fixed

The heavy-calibre, hinged-frame revolvers made by Smith and Wesson never became really popular in the United States, and before the end of the 19th century the firm had turned to the manufacture of solid-frame arms with swing-out cylinders. The first weapon made in ·38in (9·6mm) calibre, was the Military and Police First Model, which appeared in 1899 and was followed by a series with the same general title but differentiated by model number. After the summer of 1940, Great Britain stood virtually alone against the Axis powers and, as her war economy was not then fully developed, depended largely on the capacity and goodwill of the United States to help keep her supplied with vital arms, ammunition and materiel. Thus, in 1940, Smith and Wesson began production, for the British Army, of a revolver based closely on the Military and Police models the company had been making for so long. Until 1928, the official British service revolver was the Webley and Scott in ·455in (11·5mm) calibre, but in that year a change was made to a ·38in (9·6mm) model made at Enfield. Since the ·38in (9·6mm) Smith and Wesson would take the new British cartridge, no difficulties were experienced in respect of ammunition.

The Smith and Wesson British Service revolver, sometimes known as the "·38/200" (from its 200 grain, 13 gram, bullet) or the Pistol No 2, was of orthodox solid-frame construction. The arm illustrated here has a round barrel with an integral, half-round foresight; the backsight consists of a notch and groove on the top strap. The milled cylinder catch is pushed forward to allow the six-chambered cylinder to be swung out on its yoke. There is a projection below the barrel, with a spring-loaded stud which engages with the end of the ejector pin when the revolver is closed. The lock is of double-action, rebounding type, and the hammer has a separate nose held by a pin (the aperture for which is visible in the photograph). The butt-plates are of chequered walnut, bearing the company's monogram in a small, silvered medallion. The left side of the barrel is marked "SMITH AND WESSON" and the left side of the frame bears the company's trade mark. Later models were less well finished than this example, in brush blue or sandblast blue.

United States of America
COLT ARMY SPECIAL REVOLVER

Length:	11·25" (286mm)	**Rifling:**	6 groove, l/hand
Weight:	35oz (·99kg)	**Capacity:**	Six
Barrel:	6" (152mm)	**Muz Vel:**	c1000 f/s (305 m/s)
Calibre:	·38" Special (9·6mm)	**Sights:**	Fixed

This revolver had its origins in the New Navy double-action arm, which was first patented in 1884 and was brought out five years later, when it was almost immediately adopted by the United States Navy. The United States Army quickly followed suit and large numbers were made. In 1904 a new version, the Officer's Model Target, was introduced. This was essentially similar to the original model, except for a slight difference in the lower front silhouette of the frame and, of course, the addition of adjustable target sights. At the same time, all the ·38in (9·6mm) calibre weapons of the series were chambered to take the ·38in (9·6mm) Special cartridge, firing smokeless powder. In 1908 some changes were made both to the lock mechanism and to the cylinder locking system; the latter was reduced to a single stop, instead of the front and rear alternating stops on the original arm. The revolver illustrated here is of post-1908 pattern: the different arrangement of notches on the cylinder is apparent by comparison with the original New Navy type (facing page). The only other visible differences are the shape of the cylinder release catch and the style of the butt grips. After 1908, this revolver was usually known as the Army Special; then, in 1926, the type became generally classed as Official Police (a version in ·22in (5·6mm) calibre was produced in 1930 and is illustrated on page 131, above). The ·41in (10·4mm) calibre was discontinued at the same time. The ·38in (9·6mm) Special cartridge for which the arm was re-chambered differs considerably from the ·38in (9·6mm) Long Colt for which it was originally intended, principally in power. The Special case is 1·15in (29mm) long, as compared with 1in (25·4mm) for the Long cartridge, and both bullet and case of the Special are somewhat smaller in diameter. The new cartridge also required a throated chamber. Long Colt ·38in (9·6mm) ammunition will fire in the Special revolver, but the arm will not take British cartridges because their cases are of slightly larger diameter.

United States of America
SMITH AND WESSON MODEL 1917 REVOLVER

Length:	9·6" (244mm)	**Rifling:**	6 groove, l/hand
Weight:	34oz (·96kg)	**Capacity:**	Six
Barrel:	5·5" (140mm)	**Muz Vel:**	c700 f/s (213 m/s)
Calibre:	·45" (11·4mm)	**Sights:**	Fixed

The heaviest-calibre revolver normally made by Smith and Wesson was ·44in (11·2mm), which the company considered gave better results than the ·45in (11·4mm). It is true that the firm made various heavy-calibre arms to special order, but it was not until 1908 or 1909 that a few were put into production. These were of No 3 hinged-frame type and usually called Schofield revolvers. Various arms in ·455in (11·5mm) calibre were made by special arrangement from 1914 onward for the British Army. When the United States entered World War I in 1917, she was not well equipped: all available weapons of suitable type had to be pressed into service. It was, however, considered essential to have uniformity of cartridge and, as the standard service pistol was then the Model 1911 Colt self-loader, a considerable number of revolvers were manufactured to take the standard ·45in (11·4mm) ACP rimless round. The revolver illustrated here is a plain, robust arm of handsome appearance. It has the usual solid frame, with a six-chambered cylinder mounted on a separate yoke, or crane, so that it can be swung out to the left after the milled catch below the hammer has been pushed forward. When the cylinder is closed, the end of the extractor pin engages with a spring stud in a lump below the barrel. In order to take a rimless round, the chamber contains a shoulder against which the forward edge of the case rests; this prevents the cartridge from being forced too far in. However, the star extractor will not work with rimless rounds, so the empty cases have to be pushed out with a pencil or some similar instrument. An improvement on this system was to have the cartridges in flat, half-moon clips of three, on which the extractor could grip; these were extensively used. The top of the barrel bears the usual Smith and Wesson inscription; the lower side is stamped "US PROPERTY". The bottom of the butt is marked "US ARMY MODEL 1917" and numbered "50114". The issue models have plain butt-plates, but later commercial versions bear the Smith and Wesson medallion.

Great Britain
WEBLEY-FOSBERY SELF-COCKING REVOLVER

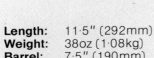

Length:	11·5" (292mm)	**Rifling:**	7 groove, r/hand
Weight:	38oz (1·08kg)	**Capacity:**	Six
Barrel:	7·5" (190mm)	**Muz Vel:**	c650 f/s (198 m/s)
Calibre:	·455" (11·5mm)	**Sights:**	Fixed

Colonel George Vincent Fosbery was a distinguished soldier who won the Victoria Cross in the Umbeyla campaign on the Northwest Frontier of India in 1863. He retired from the Army in 1877 and thereafter devoted his considerable talents to the development of an efficient machine gun. By the end of the 19th century he had also invented a unique revolver, seen here, which made use of recoil to rotate the cylinder and cock the hammer. This revolver, which was made by Webley and Scott, was first demonstrated at Bisley in 1900 and was put into production the following year.

It was of service calibre and handled and loaded in exactly the same way as the standard issue revolver—but with the very important difference that after the first shot the recoil did much of the work: all the firer needed to do was apply light pressure to the trigger, a fact which made for both speed and accuracy. As will be clear from the photograph, the barrel and cylinder were made in such a way that they were free to recoil along guide ribs on the butt and trigger component. On the way back, the cylinder was rotated one-twelfth by the action of a stud working in the zig-zag grooves

on its surface, also cocking the action; going forward, the cylinder turned a further one-twelfth, bringing the next chamber into line with the hammer. The revolver was both fast and accurate: Walter Winans, one of the finest pistol shots of all time, was able to put six shots into a 2in (51mm) bull at 12 paces in seven seconds, which is impressive shooting indeed. The Webley-Fosbery was, however, never really popular as a service weapon: partly because mud and dirt tended to clog the recoiling apparatus, which naturally had to be made to fine tolerances; and partly

because, unless the weapon was fired with an absolutely rigid arm, the recoil was not always sufficient to ensure smooth working. A seven-chambered version in ·38in (9·6mm) calibre was made in small numbers.

Great Britain
WEBLEY AND SCOTT Mk VI (·22in) REVOLVER

Length:	11" (279mm)	**Rifling:**	7 groove, r/hand
Weight:	38oz (1·08kg)	**Capacity:**	Six
Barrel:	6" (152mm)	**Muz Vel:**	c600 f/s (183 m/s)
Calibre:	·22" (5·6mm)	**Sights:**	Fixed

In 1915 there appeared the Webley and Scott Mark VI revolver, perhaps the best known of all British service pistols. It did not vary very much from its predecessors, except that the bird-beak butt of the earlier models was replaced by a standard type with a straight lower edge. This weapon was made in large numbers, Webley having a contract to deliver 2,500 weekly, and it is probable that thousands are still hidden away as souvenirs of World War I, only coming to light when their owners die. It was a solid

and reliable arm, well suited to trench warfare. In order to improve its effectiveness as a close-quarter weapon, a bayonet was developed for it; this was never officially issued, but many were bought privately. In order to give individuals some preliminary practice, a small-calibre version (illustrated here) was made. It fired ·22in (5·6mm) rimfire cartridges, allowing the revolver to be used on indoor ranges, and was economical in ammunition. As may be seen, it bears a strong resemblance to its parent arm (illustrated on page

141, above). The main differences are its round barrel and its stepped cylinder, but its locking system, trigger-pull and method of ejection resemble the orthodox Mark VI. There is a slightly different version, which is sometimes fitted with a shorter cylinder, the barrel then being correspondingly extended to the rear. It is a very accurate and well-balanced weapon and proved to be suitable for introductory practice for beginners; but it was not much instructional value otherwise, because of the complete absence of recoil. And recoil, which tends

to throw the muzzle more or less violently upward, is the chief difficulty for the novice user to overcome when using full-bore ammunition. In service calibre, the Webley and Scott Mark VI remained the standard pistol of the British Army until replaced by an Enfield ·38in in the 1930s.

Great Britain
WEBLEY AND SCOTT Mk V REVOLVER

Length:	11" (279mm)	**Rifling:**	7 groove, r/hand
Weight:	38oz (1·08kg)	**Capacity:**	Six
Barrel:	6" (152mm)	**Muz Vel:**	c650 f/s (198 m/s)
Calibre:	455" (11·5mm)	**Sights:**	Fixed

The first of the Webley series of government service revolvers, the Mark I, is described on page 127 (below). It was replaced in 1894 by a Mark II. This, in its turn, gave place in 1897 to a Mark III, which was chambered to take cartridges of ·45in (11·4mm), ·455in (11·5mm) and ·476in (12·1mm) and had a different system of releasing the cylinder. The Mark IV which followed came into service in 1899; it is very often referred to as the Boer War model, for it was extensively used there by all arms, including Artillery drivers. In December 1913, the Mark V was sealed as the standard

government pistol, but only 20,000 were made before it was superseded in 1915 by the Mark VI (illustrated on page 141, above). Thus, the Mark V is almost certainly the rarest of all the Webley and Scott government series. In general appearance it resembles its predecessors. It has an octagonal barrel with an integral foresight bed, the blade being inserted separately and held in place by a small screw. The locking system remains unchanged from earlier marks, as do the general details of the lock mechanism. The new system of removing the cylinder, first used on the Mark III, was

retained. It consists of a cam (visible below the holster guide), which engages a slot in the front of the cylinder. Loosening the screw allows it to be pushed downwards: the cylinder may then be lifted clear. The butt is of the familiar bird-beak type, and this was the last mark to feature it. Most Mark Vs had 4in (102mm) barrels, but a few —the revolver seen here among them—had barrels that were 2in (51mm) longer. The weapon illustrated bears a most remarkable variety of Government proof and view marks,

many of these being visible in the photograph. In addition, every component is stamped with the broad arrow. This particular mark was fully proved for nitro powder, up to a maximum pressure of six tons to the square inch.

Great Britain
KYNOCH REVOLVER

Length:	11·5" (292mm)	**Rifling:**	7 groove, r/hand
Weight:	42oz (1·19kg)	**Capacity:**	Six
Barrel:	6" (152mm)	**Muz Vel:**	c650 f/s (198 m/s)
Calibre:	·455" (11·5mm)	**Sights:**	Fixed

In 1880 the British Government adopted the Enfield revolver (page 124, above). Further trials, and combat use, showed that the Enfield was not good enough, and a number of makers began to develop models they hoped might replace it. One such arm was the Kynoch revolver, illustrated here. It appears to have been originally patented by a British inventor named H. Schlund in 1885 and 1886, and it was subsequently manufactured in a wide variety of calibres by George Kynoch in his gun factory at Aston Cross, Birming-

ham. The Kynoch revolver illustrated here is a heavy arm of service calibre: it is, in fact, of the type which the maker presumably hoped would be at least in contention as a replacement for the unpopular Enfield. It has an octagonal barrel with a top rib and an integral, half-round foresight. It is of hinged-frame construction, and is opened by pushing forward the catch which can be seen at the rear of the frame. When the weapon is opened thus, the automatic extractor is brought into play. By far the most interesting aspect of the arm, how-

ever, is its lock, which is based closely on the type originally invented by William Tranter (illustrated on pages 76 and 77). Pressure on the lower trigger—which is, in effect, a cocking lever—brings the concealed hammer to full-cock; subsequently, a very light touch on the trigger is sufficient to fire it. A later Kynoch version was made with a much shorter double-trigger, entirely contained within the trigger-guard,

but the type never achieved popularity. After George Kynoch's death in February 1891, manufacture of the revolver bearing his name was soon discontinued.

Great Britain
ENFIELD No 2 Mk 1* REVOLVER

Length:	10" (254mm)	**Rifling:**	7 groove, r/hand
Weight:	27oz (·76kg)	**Capacity:**	Six
Barrel:	5" (127mm)	**Muz Vel:**	c700 f/s (213 m/s)
Calibre:	·38" (9·6mm)	**Sights:**	Fixed

The new Enfield revolver issued in 1932 (Ilustrated on the facing page, above) proved generally popular with the British Army. However, complaints were received from the Royal Tank Regiment (whose personnel carried their revolvers in open-topped holsters) that the hammer spur of the Enfield tended to catch on various fittings in the tanks while they were mounting or dismounting. In 1938, therefore, the Mark I*, seen here, was introduced. As may be seen by comparing this arm with the Enfield No 2 Mark I on the facing page, the two revolvers were essentially

similar: the main functional difference was that the new model had no comb on the hammer. It could thus only be fired by pressure on the trigger, a rather odd reversion to the original Adams revolvers of 1851 (several of which are illustrated in the "Percussion Revolvers" section). As a contribution towards accuracy, the weight of the mainspring was lightened so as to reduce the trigger pull to about 12lb (5·44kg), a reduction of 2lb (·907kg) from the earlier model. Also, the butt-plates were modified by the addition of thumb-grooves to give a

good grip: these were made identical on either side, so that the revolver could be used either right- or left-handed. The end of the screw holding the grips in position fitted into a circular brass disc of ·75in (19mm) diameter, which was sunk into the right grip. The disc was presumably originally intended to bear unit marks and numbers, but these are rarely to be found on extant examples. The self-cocking concept was not popular— imported American revolvers were much preferred—but in spite of this, most of the Mark Is with the original hammers were

gradually called into the work-shops and modified to the new system. A jacketted bullet was introduced in 1938. In 1942, a wartime Mark I** was adopted. It lacked any safety stop on the hammer and could fire acciden-tally if dropped; thus, it did not survive World War II.

Great Britain
WEBLEY ·38in Mk IV REVOLVER

Length:	10" (254mm)	**Rifling:**	7 groove, r/hand
Weight:	27oz (·76kg)	**Capacity:**	Six
Barrel:	5" (127mm)	**Muz Vel:**	c700 f/s (213 m/s)
Calibre:	·38" (9·6mm)	**Sights:**	Fixed

The introduction of the Enfield No 2 revolver in 1932 marked the end of a long line of British service revolvers made by Webley and Scott, who had been virtually sole suppliers to the government since the intro-duction of the Mark I (illustrated on page 127, below) in 1887. However, the firm still had a great many other customers, and in 1923 it produced a Mark IV revolver in ·38" (9·6mm) calibre in order to meet the demands of various military and police forces. It was, like other Webleys, a robust and reliable arm, and

would chamber a variety of ·38in (9·6mm) cartridges, thus making it suitable for world-wide use. The lead bullet originally used in the British Enfield had been abandoned in 1938 because of doubts as to whether it was, in fact, in breach of the St Petersburg convention. (It is amusing to note that when the Commandant at the School of Musketry, Hythe, was asked his views, he replied promptly that the bullet had not been officially tested against flesh!) By the end of World War II, the supply of Enfield revolvers (many of which were, in fact,

made by outside contractors) was beginning to lag; thus, in 1945, the British Government placed a large order with Webley and Scott for the Mark IV. This was not only a reliable arm, but also was so like the Enfield in handling qualities (and, indeed, in appearance; the dimensions differed only slightly) that no retraining was needed; it was, for that reason, a very convenient supplement to exist-ing stocks. It was, moreover, a double-action weapon, which most soldiers preferred. As may be seen from the photo-

graph, the Mark IV was produced with a strictly utility finish and lacked the handsome appearance of Webley's peace-time products. It was, however, a highly effective revolver.

Great Britain
ENFIELD No 2 Mk I REVOLVER

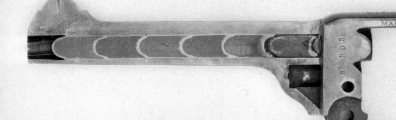

Length:	10" (254mm)	**Rifling:**	7 groove, r/hand
Weight:	29oz (·82kg)	**Capacity:**	Six
Barrel:	5" (127mm)	**Muz Vel:**	c700 f/s (213 m/s)
Calibre:	·38" (9·6mm)	**Sights:**	Fixed

Ever since the first introduction of the revolver, the British Army, accustomed to colonial warfare against enemies of powerful physique and fanatical bravery, had insisted on the need for stopping-power and had preferred a heavy, slow-moving, lead bullet which would expend the whole of its energy in the target. Thus, for many years, calibres of ·45" (11·4mm), ·455in (11·5mm) and ·476in (12·1mm) remained in service and, indeed, proved highly effective. After the end of World War I, however, it was decided that a somewhat smaller calibre would suffice for all contemporary purposes and, after extensive tests, an arm of ·38in (9·6mm) calibre was decided upon. This would be a lighter weapon, making the instructor's task easier, while still retaining the stopping-power considered necessary in a service arm. As will be seen from the illustration, the No 2 Mark I is closely based on the older Webley and Scott Mark VI, with only relatively minor modifications; although it is, of course, considerably lighter and more compact. It has an octagonal barrel with a screwed-in blade foresight. The rectangular backsight is on top of the barrel catch, which is of the usual robust and reliable Webley type. The lock is of double-action, rebounding type, and the hammer is fitted with a separate nose. The revolver bears the full series of Enfield proof and view marks, date "1932" and number "B4447"

United States of America
COLT OFFICIAL POLICE REVOLVER (DAMAGED)

Length:	10·25" (260mm)
Weight:	34oz (·96kg)
Barrel:	5" (127mm)
Calibre:	·38" (9·6mm)
Rifling:	6 groove, l/hand
Capacity:	Six
Muz Vel:	c700 f/s (213 m/s)
Sights:	Fixed

This is one of the revolvers based originally on the 1889 New Navy (illustrated on page 132, above) and known since 1926 as the Official Police. It was purchased by the British Government, together with thousands more, in the course of World War II, during which Colt and Smith and Wesson revolvers were almost as common in the British Army as Enfields and Webleys. It is of orthodox solid-frame construction, with a swing-out cylinder, and is shown here principally as an illustration of what degree of damage a well-made revolver is able to withstand. The damage to this particular revolver was caused by the firing of a weak cartridge, which drove its bullet only sufficiently far foward to lodge in the barrel. (Poor rounds of this kind are, of course, very rare in peacetime; but they are sometimes met with in war, when standards of inspection are less stringent. It may also happen that a once-perfect cartridge deteriorates through having been stored either for too long or in exceptionally bad conditions.) When a second round was fired, its bullet, travelling at normal velocity, struck the one in the barrel and pushed it forward. This probably had no effect on the barrel, partly because of the relatively low velocity of this type of ·38in (9·6mm) cartridge and partly because of the existence of a means of escape for gas between the face of the cylinder and the barrel. The third round, also travelling normally, hit the first two and pushed them a little farther, as did the fourth—but the resistance was, of course, increasing every time: the fifth round hit the solid blockage and caused the barrel to split.

United States of America
FOREHAND ARMS COMPANY REVOLVER

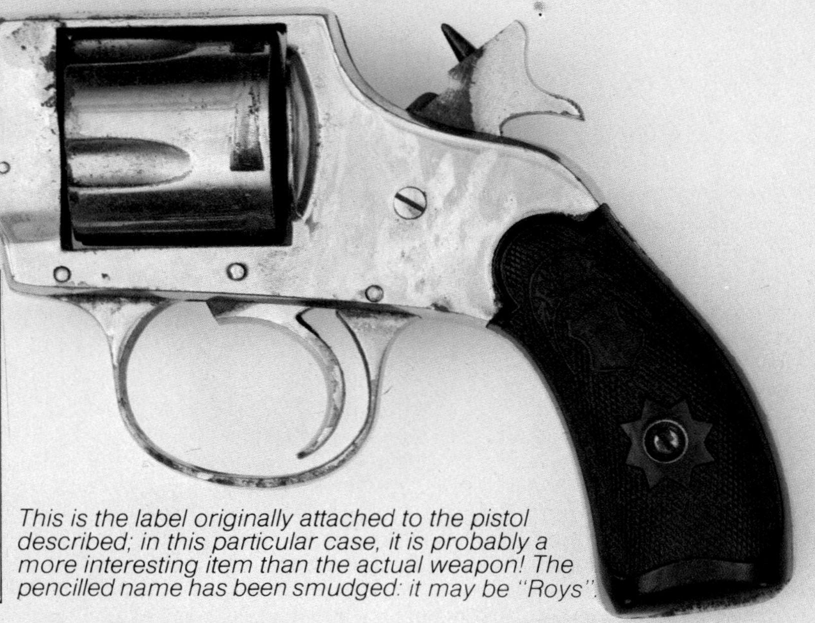

This is the label originally attached to the pistol described; in this particular case, it is probably a more interesting item than the actual weapon! The pencilled name has been smudged: it may be "Roys".

Length: 6·75" (171mm)
Weight: 14oz (·4kg)
Barrel: 2·5" (63mm)
Calibre: ·32" (8·1mm)
Rifling: 5 groove, r/hand
Capacity: Five
Muz Vel: 550 f/s (168 m/s)
Sights: Fixed

Ethan Allen, a well-known American gunmaker whose name is frequently mentioned in the earlier sections of this book, died in 1871. His business then reverted to his daughters, Mrs Forehand and Mrs Wadsworth, and was run by their respective husbands. After Wadsworth left the company in 1890, it was renamed the Forehand Arms Company. In 1898, when Forehand died, the company was bought up by Hopkins and Allen, another well-known firm to which frequent reference has already been made. The arms produced in the period 1871-98 were mainly revolvers in a variety of types and calibres for the cheaper end of the market. The arm illustrated here is inscribed with the words "FOREHAND ARMS COMPANY" on its top strap, together with the address, "WORCESTER MASS", the words "DOUBLE-ACTION", and a patent date of "JUNE 1891"; the last signifying that it is of post-Wadsworth manufacture. In spite of this, however, its butt-plates, which are of black vulcanite, bear the initials "F & W" (ie, Forehand and Wadsworth); so presumably they were old stock. It is a cheap and poorly-finished arm with a solid frame and a five-chambered cylinder without a loading gate: the only provision being a gap left in the shield. In fact, it may with justice be classed as a "Suicide Special" or a "Saturday Night Special". In the summer of 1940, Great Britain lay under threat of imminent invasion by the German Army, which had over-run France and the Low Countries in a lightning campaign during May of that year. Britain was desperately short of weapons and materiel of all kinds and the United States made very considerable efforts (both official and unofficial) to help her. Arms and supplies were hastily gathered together and sent off across the Atlantic — and the revolver illustrated here was one of these.

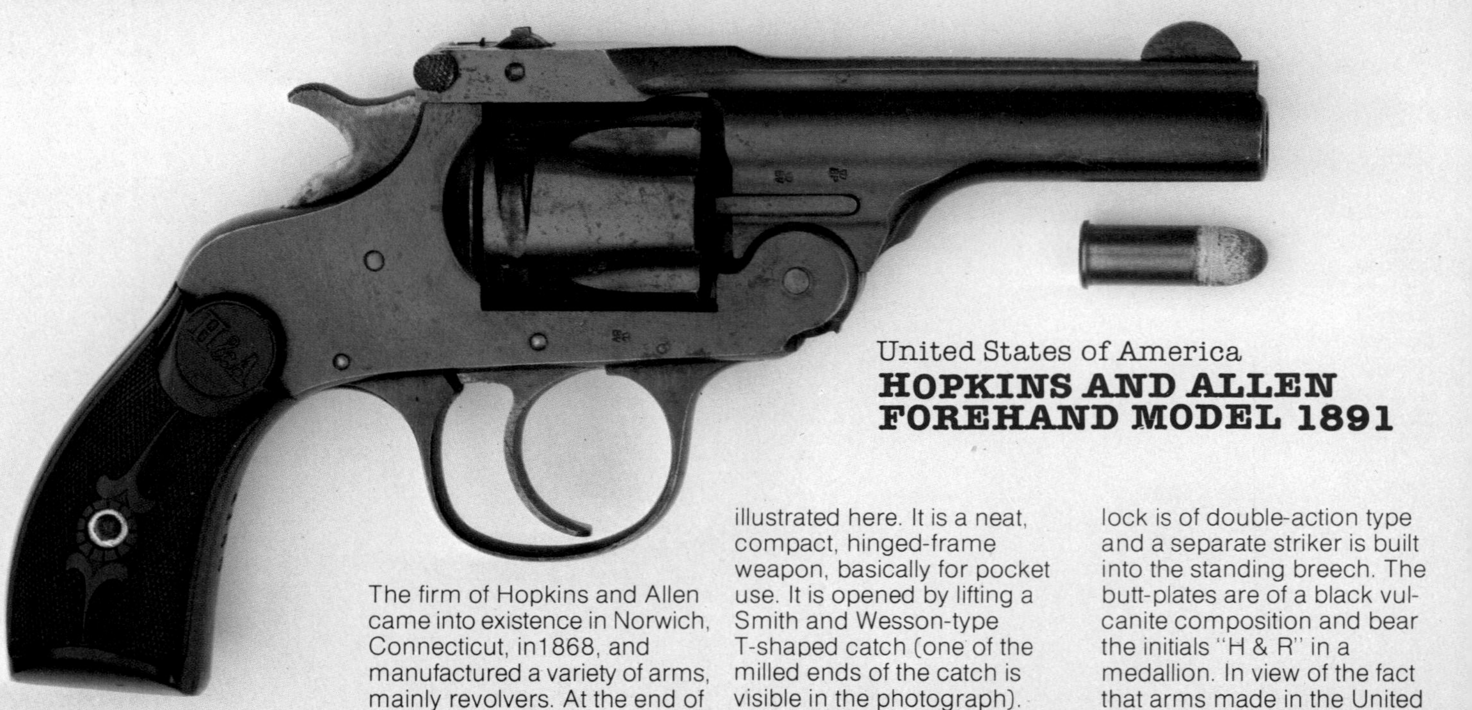

United States of America
HOPKINS AND ALLEN FOREHAND MODEL 1891

Length: 7·5" (190mm)
Weight: 17oz (·48kg)
Barrel: 3·25" (83mm)
Calibre: ·32" (8·1mm)
Rifling: 7 groove, r/hand
Capacity: Five
Muz Vel: c550 f/s (168 m/s)
Sights: Fixed

The firm of Hopkins and Allen came into existence in Norwich, Connecticut, in 1868, and manufactured a variety of arms, mainly revolvers. At the end of the 19th century, it took over the Forehand Arms Company of Worcester, Massachusetts, on the death of its former operator, Sullivan Forehand. Soon afterwards, Hopkins and Allen began to make the so-called Forehand Model 1891, a specimen of which is illustrated here. It is a neat, compact, hinged-frame weapon, basically for pocket use. It is opened by lifting a Smith and Wesson-type T-shaped catch (one of the milled ends of the catch is visible in the photograph). When the barrel is forced downward, a star ejector is automatically brought into play and throws out the cartridges or empty cases. The five-chambered cylinder may be removed from its axis pin by pressing in the front end of the horizontal lever (visible in front of it). The lock is of double-action type and a separate striker is built into the standing breech. The butt-plates are of a black vulcanite composition and bear the initials "H & R" in a medallion. In view of the fact that arms made in the United States bore no proof marks acceptable in Britain, all such weapons imported into the United Kingdom had to be reproofed: this particular revolver bears the marks of the Birmingham Proof House, which indicate that it has been proved for black powder only.

United States of America
IVER JOHNSON HAMMERLESS REVOLVER

Length:	7·75" (197mm)	**Rifling:**	7 groove, r/hand
Weight:	21oz (·59kg)	**Capacity:**	Six
Barrel:	3·25" (83mm)	**Muz Vel:**	c550 f/s (168 m/s)
Calibre:	·32" (8·1mm)	**Sights:**	Fixed

In 1883, Iver Johnson bought out his partner, Martin Bye, with whom he had been associated since 1871, and began manufacture as the Iver Johnson Arms Company in Worcester, Massachusetts. Johnson died 12 years later, but the firm remained in existence. Its earliest revolvers were cheap, solid-frame models, but the range was gradually extended and the quality improved. In 1893, Johnson patented a weapon which he had developed with several other gunmakers; it went into production under the rather cumbersome title of the

Safety Automatic Double-Action Model. This was followed in 1894 by the so-called hammerless version, an example of which is illustrated here. It is opened by lifting the T-shaped catch, which allows two projections on the upper part of the standing breech to separate from a corresponding aperture in the top strap. Then the barrel can be pushed downward, activating a star extractor—the feature from which the word "automatic" in the revolver's title is derived. However, the most important feature of the weapon is the

safety device provided for the prevention of accidental discharge. The firing-pin is mounted separately on the standing breech, so that the rear end of it is struck by the hammer. A transfer bar in the lock mechanism rises to its proper position only when the trigger has been fully and properly pulled; thus, the revolver cannot be fired involuntarily by dropping or some similar mishap. This was an ingenious and reliable invention which greatly improved the company's reputation. The revolver seen here is plated,

except for its trigger and guard, and has hard rubber-composition butt-plates, each with the familiar owl's-head trade mark in a medallion. Since it was imported into Great Britain it bears London proof marks, indicating that it has been proved for use with smokeless powder. The lower right side of the frame is also stamped, just above the trigger, with the minatory legend "NOT ENGLISH MAKE".

United States of America
HARRINGTON AND RICHARDSON REVOLVER

Length:	8·5" (216mm)
Weight:	15oz (·42kg)
Barrel:	5" (127mm)
Calibre:	·22" (5·6mm)
Rifling:	5 groove, r/hand
Capacity:	Seven
Muz Vel:	c500 f/s (152 m/s)
Sights:	Fixed

The well-known firm of Harrington and Richardson was originally formed in 1874 for the manufacture of revolvers. Its first products were of the orthodox solid-frame type, but by 1897 the company was also producing a range of hinged-frame revolvers in a variety of calibres and barrel lengths. The arm illustrated here is well made and finished; reference back to page 112 (above) will show that in terms of general appearance—although not, of course, in scale—it closely resembles the famous Smith

and Wesson No 3 revolver. This weapon has a round barrel with a top rib, the foresight being slotted in; the backsight is a notch in a raised part of the barrel catch. When the barrel catch is raised, the barrel may be forced downward through about 90 degrees, bringing the automatic ejector into action. It has a seven-chambered cylinder which may be removed by opening the revolver, lifting the barrel catch and pressing in a small stud on the left side of the top strap; this allows the cylinder to be lifted

off its axis pin. The lock is of double-action type. The butt-grips are of black vulcanite; both bear the Harrington and Richardson trade mark of a target pierced with five shots. Like all weapons made in the United States (however reputable the company) for sale in United Kingdom it has been re-proofed and bears Birmingham marks. The firm of Harrington and Richardson is still engaged in making good-quality revolvers at a reasonable price at its workshops in Worcester, Massachusetts, USA.

United States of America
COLT OFFICIAL POLICE REVOLVER

Length:	10·25" (260mm)
Weight:	34oz (·96kg)
Barrel:	5" (127mm)
Calibre:	·38" (9·6mm)
Rifling:	6 groove, l/hand
Capacity:	Six
Muz Vel:	c700 f/s (213 m/s)
Sights:	Fixed

This revolver had its origins in the Colt New Navy model (illustrated on page 132, above), which first appeared in 1889. This was later re-classified as the New Army model; a slightly different version being known, later still, as the Army Special (illustrated on page 133, above). In 1926 the name was changed once again—finally, this time—to Official Police. There was very little difference in type, the change being principally made because at that time the United States police forces were markedly better customers than the United States Army. The arm illustrated is of the orthodox solid-frame design, the frame being of the original ·41in (10·4mm) calibre type. The round barrel has an integral, semi-round foresight and a square backsight notch and groove on the top strap; the upper surface of the latter is matted to reduce the shine. The cylinder swings out sideways on its own yoke when a catch on the left of the frame is pulled back; cartridges or cases can then be ejected simultaneously by pushing the pin. The lock is of rebounding, double-action type, with a separate hammer nose, and access to the mechanism is obtained by way of an irregularly-shaped inspection plate on the left-hand side of the frame. The butt-plates are of chequered walnut and bear the famous trademark of a rearing horse in white metal medallions. Large numbers of Official Police revolvers, of which the arm seen here was one, were supplied to the British Army in the course of World War II. It was made also in a ·22in calibre version.

United States of America
SMITH AND WESSON MILITARY AND POLICE FIRST MODEL (CUT-DOWN)

Length:	8" (203mm)
Weight:	28oz (·79kg)
Barrel:	3·25" (83mm)
Calibre:	·38" (9·6mm)
Rifling:	7 groove, r/hand
Capacity:	Six
Muz Vel:	c600 f/s (183 m/s)
Sights:	Fixed

The cut-down revolver seen here had its origins in the Smith and Wesson Military and Police First Model, which first appeared in 1899. Previously the company had pioneered hinged-frame models (several of which are described earlier) but in spite of the excellence of these arms they never became really popular in the United States. The demand there was principally for long-range power and accuracy, which necessitated a very heavy charge of propellant powder in the cartridge, and it was generally believed, probably correctly, that hinged-frame revolvers were unlikely to stand up to the strain. Although it is highly improbable that hinged-frame revolvers would have become truly dangerous in such circumstances, there was the risk that they might become loose, which would have had an adverse effect on accuracy. Smith and Wesson therefore turned to the manufacture of solid-frame revolvers of high quality at about the end of the 19th century. This particular revolver is one of those made for the British Government during World War II, at a time when the hard-pressed British were desperately short of arms and materiel of all kinds. This arm was known variously as the British Service, the Model No 2, or the ·38/200; the latter figure refers to the bullet weight (200 grains, 13 grams) which, by British calculations, provided much the same stopping-power as that fired from the earlier ·455in (11·5mm) calibre Webley service arms (one of which is described on the facing page, above). In fact, the lead bullet of this type had to be abandoned just before World War II because it contravened the international conventions of warfare; it was replaced by a lighter, 178-grain (11·5 gram), jacketed bullet. As may be seen, the weapon is of orthodox solid-frame type; but it is of interest because at some stage of its career its barrel, which will originally have been 5in (127mm) long, has been cut down to 3·25in (83mm) and a ramp foresight added. The work has been quite well done and it is difficult to detect at a glance. It is, however, clear on closer examination: partly from a certain flatness at the muzzle end, and partly because of the position of the words "SMITH AND WESSON" on the left side of the barrel, which are very close to the new muzzle. The reduction has, of course, had an adverse effect on the revolver's accuracy.

Great Britain
WEBLEY AND SCOTT Mk VI REVOLVER

Length:	11" (279mm)	**Rifling:**	7 groove, r/hand
Weight:	37oz (1·05kg)	**Capacity:**	Six
Barrel:	6" (152mm)	**Muz Vel:**	c650 f/s (198 m/s)
Calibre:	·455" (11·5mm)	**Sights:**	Fixed

The famous Birmingham firm of P. Webley and Son (later Webley and Scott) had a virtual monopoly on the supply of British Government revolvers for very many years. The company's last, and probably best-known, service arm was the Webley and Scott Mark VI, seen here. It was officially introduced in 1915 and did not differ very much from its predecessors, except that the earlier bird-beak butt had been abandoned in favour of the more conventional squared-off style. It is of stan-

dard hinged-frame type, with a robust, stirrup-type, barrel catch: a tough and durable arm, and generally well suited to service use. Certainly, it stood up remarkably well to the mud and dirt inseparable from trench warfare in the period 1914-18. In the course of World War I, a short bayonet was designed for the revolver; although it was never officially adopted, it proved effective for trench raids and similar operations, and many officers bought one privately. A detachable

butt, much like those available for the Mauser and Luger self-loading pistols (see pages 152-153), was also provided, but it was not widely used. This model was officially abandoned in 1932 in favour of a similar arm in ·38in (9·6mm) calibre (a specimen of this revolver is described on page 136, below) but many reserve officers still carried Mark VIs in ·455in (11·5mm) calibre when they were recalled in 1939. The model was made in huge quantity, and many still exist.

United States of America
MERIDEN POCKET REVOLVER

Length:	6·5" (165mm)
Weight:	14oz (·4kg)
Barrel:	3" (76mm)
Calibre:	·32" (8·1mm)
Rifling:	5 groove, r/hand
Capacity:	Five
Muz Vel:	c550 f/s (168 m/s)
Sights:	Fixed

The Meriden Firearms Company was one of the many small arms manufacturers which sprang up in the United States of America in the second half of the 19th century, at a time when the cartridge revolver had become popular and modern industrial methods had progressed to the stage where they could be turned out quickly and relatively cheaply. The company operated from about 1895 until World War I, but its origins and ownership are obscure, to say the least. Hogg and Weeks, in their *Pistols of the World,* suggest that Meriden may have been a subsidiary of the famous American mail-order firm of Sears Roebuck; or

part of the Fyrberg; or an off-shoot of the Stevens Arms and Tool Company (some of whose products are described elsewhere in this book): but the history of Meriden remains something of a mystery. The weapons produced by the firm were mostly pocket models, including some hammerless versions; and the revolver shown here can probably be classed as a typical specimen. It is of hinged-frame type with a sprung, T-shaped barrel catch (visible in the photograph), the backsight being a simple V-notch in the raised portion of the catch. It has a round barrel with a top rib of slightly peculiar section: it is wider at the top

than at its junction with the barrel. Perhaps the only feature of the arm that is in any way remarkable is its somewhat unusual foresight, which has a shape reminiscent of an old-fashioned cocked-hat. The lock is of orthodox double-action type, and the butt-grips are of black vulcanite. The top flat of the barrel is marked "MERIDEN FIREARMS CO, MERIDEN, CONN USA", and on the base of the butt is the number "284035" (the figure "8" being stamped upside down on this particular specimen). It is probably not too unfair to say that this weapon may with justice be classed as cheap and nasty. The workmanship is

crude and the components shoddy; but as the price of these revolvers in the early 20th century probably did not exceed a couple of dollars, these low standards are hardly to be wondered at. Such arms, sold extensively by mail order, are often classified as "Suicide Specials" in modern terms. Some arms firms made nothing else, while other, more reputable, companies regarded these weapons as no more than a sideline, and relied on safer and altogether better-quality arms for the bulk of their trade. There is, obviously, still a market for such cheap weapons in the USA, where gun laws are less restrictive.

Brazil
TAURUS MAGNUM MODEL 86

Length:	9·25" (235mm)
Weight:	35oz (·99kg)
Barrel:	4" (102mm)
Calibre:	·357" Magnum (9·06mm)
Rifling:	6 groove, r/hand
Capacity:	Six
Muz Vel:	c1400 f/s (427 m/s)
Sights:	Fixed

The ·357in (9·06mm) Magnum revolver was originally introduced by Smith and Wesson in 1935, the cartridge being designed in co-operation with Winchester. The Magnum cartridge is about ·1in (2·54mm) longer in the case than the ·38in (9·6mm) Special cartridge, and it may be safely fired only in revolvers specially designed for it. It is popular in the United States, particularly perhaps for game shooting, because of its power and flat trajectory, and it is sometimes used as a rifle cartridge. The weapon illustrated was manufactured by Taurus of Brazil, who began to make revolvers of this calibre in 1975. These arms sell well in the United States and are reputed to be of good quality; certainly, the workmanship and finish of the specimen illustrated leaves little to be desired. It is of solid-frame type and has a round barrel with a very wide top rib; the foresight is of ramp type and the arm is fitted with a micrometer backsight, the whole sighting plane being milled to reduce reflection. The cylinder holds six cartridges, the ends of the chambers being recessed to enclose the cartridge heads, and it swings out to the left on its own separate yoke. It has the usual pin-operated extractor; the pin is located in a housing beneath the barrel when the cylinder is in position. There is a separate firing-pin in the standing breech, and the hammer has a wide, flat comb for ease of cocking. The large chequered butt is of two-piece construction and no metal work is visible, except at the back. Small, white-metal medallions in the butt are marked "TAURUS, BRASIL", with a bull's head in the centre. The barrel is marked "FORJAS TAURUS SA P.ALEGRE RCS BRASIL" and is inscribed also "CAL ·357 MAGNUM".

Great Britain
HOME-MADE REVOLVER

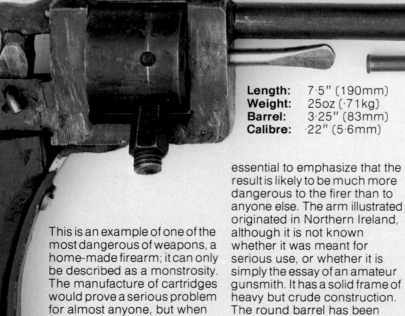

Length:	7·5" (190mm)	**Rifling:**	Nil
Weight:	25oz (·71kg)	**Capacity:**	Six
Barrel:	3·25" (83mm)	**Muz Vel:**	Not known
Calibre:	·22" (5·6mm)	**Sights:**	Nil

This is an example of one of the most dangerous of weapons, a home-made firearm; it can only be described as a monstrosity. The manufacture of cartridges would prove a serious problem for almost anyone, but when factory-made ammunition is obtainable it is not difficult to improvise an instrument with with to fire it. Any person with basic knowledge of metalwork and access to a small workshop can do it—but, this said, it is essential to emphasize that the result is likely to be much more dangerous to the firer than to anyone else. The arm illustrated originated in Northern Ireland, although it is not known whether it was meant for serious use, or whether it is simply the essay of an amateur gunsmith. It has a solid frame of heavy but crude construction. The round barrel has been bored very wide of centre and it is not rifled. The cylinder has a capacity of six and its chambers are counter-sunk to cover the rims of the cartridges. The lump of metal below the cylinder contains a spring plunger; this engages in the circular depressions in the cylinder and thus ensures that the chamber under the hammer is aligned with the barrel. The cylinder itself must be rotated manually. As may be seen, the revolver has no trigger: the hammer is so designed that it must be drawn back by the thumb and then released, when a spring drives it forward with enough force to fire a ·22in (5·6mm) rimfire round. This calibre was presumably chosen because such cartridges are widely used by rifle clubs and are thus relatively easily obtained illegally by unscrupulous persons

Great Britain
WEBLEY Mk IV REVOLVER (DAMAGED)

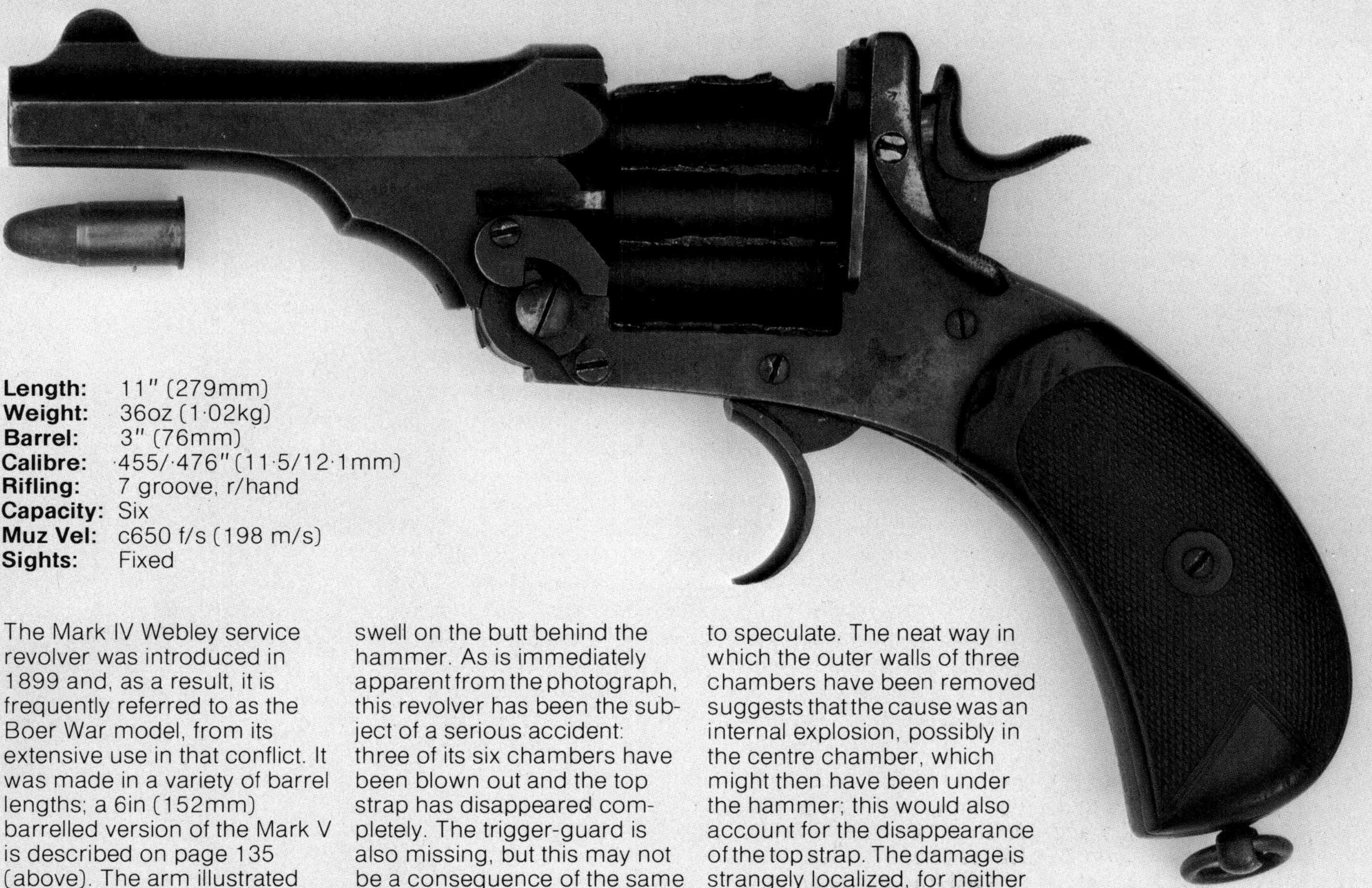

Length: 11" (279mm)
Weight: 36oz (1·02kg)
Barrel: 3" (76mm)
Calibre: ·455/·476" (11·5/12·1mm)
Rifling: 7 groove, r/hand
Capacity: Six
Muz Vel: c650 f/s (198 m/s)
Sights: Fixed

The Mark IV Webley service revolver was introduced in 1899 and, as a result, it is frequently referred to as the Boer War model, from its extensive use in that conflict. It was made in a variety of barrel lengths; a 6in (152mm) barrelled version of the Mark V is described on page 135 (above). The arm illustrated here is the Mark VI with a 3in (76mm) barrel. It bears a strong general resemblance to the Mark I, the chief external difference being the lack of swell on the butt behind the hammer. As is immediately apparent from the photograph, this revolver has been the subject of a serious accident: three of its six chambers have been blown out and the top strap has disappeared completely. The trigger-guard is also missing, but this may not be a consequence of the same mishap: since no positive information regarding the circumstances under which this weapon was damaged can be ascertained, it is necessary to speculate. The neat way in which the outer walls of three chambers have been removed suggests that the cause was an internal explosion, possibly in the centre chamber, which might then have been under the hammer; this would also account for the disappearance of the top strap. The damage is strangely localized, for neither the breech end of the barrel nor the holster guides show any sign of the scars that might be expected from the scale of the damage to the cylinder.

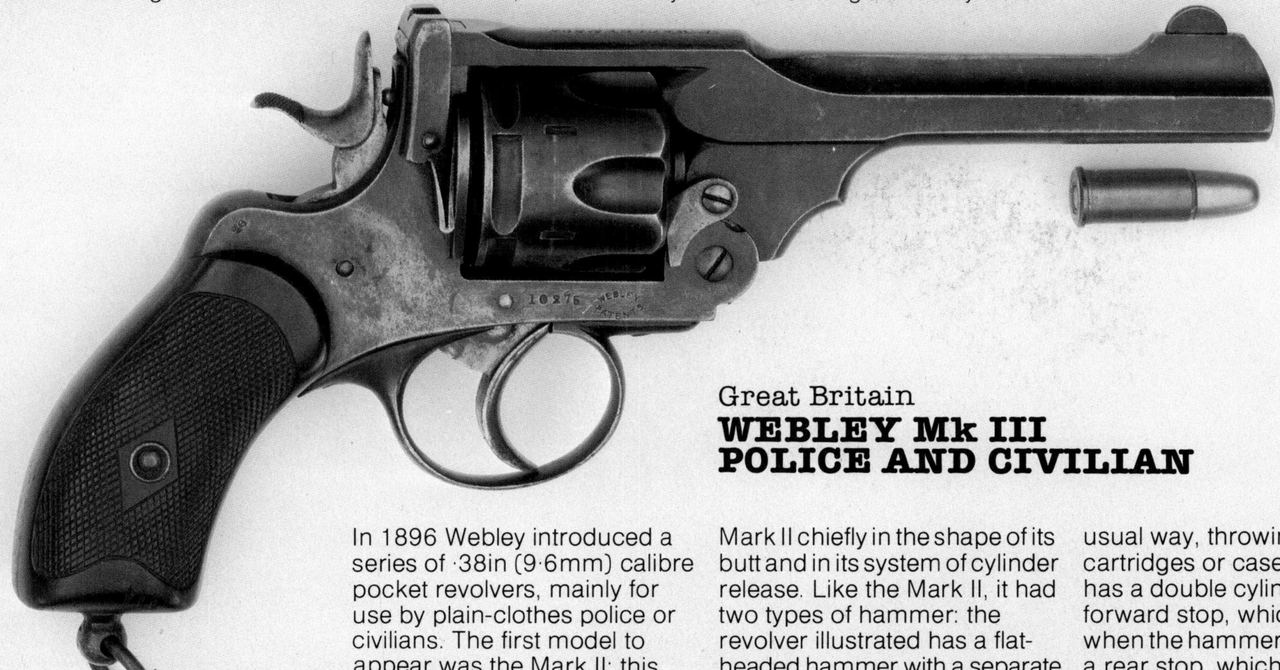

Great Britain
WEBLEY Mk III
POLICE AND CIVILIAN

Length: 8·25" (210mm)
Weight: 19oz (·54kg)
Barrel: 4" (102mm)
Calibre: ·38" (9·6mm)
Rifling: 7 groove, r/hand
Capacity: Six
Muz Vel: c600 f/s (183 m/s)
Sights: Fixed

In 1896 Webley introduced a series of ·38in (9·6mm) calibre pocket revolvers, mainly for use by plain-clothes police or civilians. The first model to appear was the Mark II; this came in two sub-types, one with a fixed hammer and the other with a flat-nosed hammer that fell on to a spring-loaded striker on the standing breech. In terms of style, both sub-types followed the general lines of the ·455in (11·5mm) Government models, being simply scaled down for their reduced calibre. The Mark III, introduced almost immediately, differed from the Mark II chiefly in the shape of its butt and in its system of cylinder release. Like the Mark II, it had two types of hammer: the revolver illustrated has a flat-headed hammer with a separate striker. It has an octagonal barrel with a foresight; the backsight is a V-shaped notch on the barrel catch. The latter is of orthodox type, with a thumb lever on the left side of the frame; the V-spring which takes it forward may be clearly seen in the photograph. When the revolver is opened and the barrel forced down, the extractor comes into action in the usual way, throwing out the cartridges or cases. The arm has a double cylinder stop: a forward stop, which works when the hammer is down; and a rear stop, which operates when the trigger is pressed. It is a compact and handy little weapon and proved popular; its only disadvantage lay in its rather small butt. This fault was rectified in a later model, which first appeared in 1932; this had a very much larger butt and, somewhat unusually, was also fitted with a safety catch, which was positioned on the right-hand side of the frame.

Self-Loading Pistols

When a conventional firearm is discharged the pressure of the expanding gases is evenly distributed in all directions, but naturally follows the line of least resistance by forcing the projectile up the barrel. The only other important direction of pressure is to the rear, where (assuming all the parts of the arm to be locked rigidly in relation to each other) pressure manifests itself in the form of recoil or, as it is popularly called, "kick". The possibility of harnessing this otherwise wasted force was considered very early in the history of firearms, but weapon technology was not then sufficiently advanced to allow the theory to be applied in any practical way. However, the advent of the breech-loading arm firing a self-contained metallic cartridge, in the middle of the 19th century, made it possible to convert theory into practice; and a good many people then began at least to consider how it might be done.

MAXIM'S EXAMPLE

The first to achieve any tangible result was the American inventor Hiram Maxim, who, having first tested out his ideas on a converted Winchester rifle, produced in 1883 a true and highly successful machine gun, which he designed and, largely, manufactured himself. In this arm, the barrel was free to recoil for a short distance while remaining locked to the breechblock, this being necessary to allow the internal pressure to drop to a level where the

case would not rupture. Once the pressure had dropped (which happened very quickly), the breechblock unlocked and continued to move rearwards, extending a powerful fusee spring which duly provided the motive force to complete the forward action of the mechanism. Maxim's arm was a true automatic: it would continue to fire as long as the trigger was pressed and rounds were fed in. It was a revolutionary weapon which was to remain in service for almost a century, without fundamental changes, in many of the armies of the world.

Maxim's first gun used cartridges which fired a plain lead bullet by means of black powder; but soon after its invention there appeared two further important innovations. The first was the general introduction of smokeless propellants, which not only gave greatly increased velocity but were also much cleaner, leaving very little fouling as compared to black powder. The second was the jacketed bullet: it was soon found that the extra heat and power generated by the new propellants was liable to distort and damage an elongated lead bullet—and by the 1890s bullets had been successfully fitted with thin outer jackets of harder metal, which greatly increased their durability. This was found to be particularly necessary in the case of automatic weapons, where the action of the breechblock was more violent than in manually-operated arms. However, a few modern small-bore self-loaders use lead bullets.

Above: *After anti-Chinese demonstrations in February 1975, a young suspect in Phnom Penh, Cambodia (now Kampuchea) is questioned by a policeman armed with a Colt 1911 Government Model self-loading pistol.*

Top: *In a pose reminiscent of many Warner Brothers' movies, a "gun-man" is ready for action with a Colt .38in Pocket Model 1903 (the Sporting Model, with a 6in, 152mm, barrel).*

Centre: *In this scene from an American movie of the 1950s, the soldier carries a Mauser Model 1912 with its holster/stock attached.*

Right: *Close-up of an FN-Browning High Power pistol in a two-handed grip.*

Sir Hiram Maxim (1840-1916) was the pioneer of modern self-loading weapons.

BORCHARDT AND LUGER

The perfection of the small, brass, centre-fire cartridge, with smokeless powder and a jacketed bullet, made possible the reduction of the self-loading system to a scale that could be applied to pistols. Once this appeared to be feasible, several people set to work to make self-loading arms; notably the Austrian inventors Anton Schönberger, in 1892, and Andreas Schwarzlose, in 1893 (see page 154, below).

The first self-loading arm which may reasonably be classed as a commercial success was invented by Hugo Borchardt, an American citizen of German descent, in 1893. It was in many ways a very advanced design. When the first manually-loaded round was fired, the barrel and breechlock recoiled, very much as in the Maxim system, until a toggle joint broke upward and allowed them to separate. The rounds were held in a box magazine in the butt, and when the compressed spring thrust the block forward it stripped the top round from the magazine and chambered it in preparation for the next shot. The main fault of the weapon designed by Borchardt was its clumsy bulk, which made it difficult to fire with one hand. However, it was equipped with a detachable butt which converted it to a carbine, and in this role it could be fired with reasonable accuracy.

Its most notable contribution to the development of self-loading pistols was probably its excellent bottle-shaped cartridge. As we have seen, the relatively violent action of the self-loader tended to distort a plain lead bullet, so that of the Borchardt was jacketed, a practice that became virtually universal. It is a measure of the quality of the original round that it still remains in wide use, with only minor technical changes.

Almost immediately following the Borchardt came the first of a series of pistols by Mannlicher. It was not in itself a great success; but it led to the establishment of a new functional system in which the rearward thrust of the case forced back an unlocked breechblock. In fact, in Mannlicher's first model the

barrel moved forward—but this was a detail: in later models the barrel was fixed and the rate of opening of the breechblock was controlled by its weight and by the strength of the return spring. This system soon gained wide acceptance. It was perfectly reliable, in its simplest form, for pocket pistols firing relatively low-powered cartridges. Where heavier, service-type arms were concerned, various additional features had to be incorporated, either to lock the breech briefly or, at least, to delay its movement until the pressure had fallen to a safe level.

BERGMANN AND MAUSER

Theodor Bergmann first made effective use of this system in a pocket pistol which appeared in 1894; he later produced some military pistols, although these were of the recoiling barrel type. By this time, self-loading arms were coming on to the market in considerable numbers—and the next important arm of the kind was that invented by the German Peter Paul Mauser. He was already well known for his excellent service rifles, which at various times and in various forms armed many of the military forces of the world; and his pistol was also soon to become a household word. It worked on the system of short recoil of the barrel, and although its locking device appeared to be less positive, in theory, than some others, it worked remarkably well in practice. It was patented in 1896 but did not come on to the market until 1898, quickly achieving popularity thereafter. It was heavy and bulky and may fairly be described as awkward to use one-handed. It was, however, mechanically excellent, and the Borchardt cartridge for which it was designed gave it considerable power.

A notable Mauser owner was Winston Churchill, who, as a young cavalry officer, purchased one after an injury to his right shoulder had made it difficult for him to wield a sword effectively. Churchill used his Mauser in the course of the famous charge by the 21st Lancers at the Battle of Omdurman in 1898, and it may have been

instrumental in saving his life when he was surrounded by Dervishes. The Mauser had a magazine capacity of ten rounds, compared to the revolver's six, which made it of particular utility to a mounted man, who would have found difficulty in reloading in the heat of combat.

The Mauser was equipped with a wooden holster which could also be attached as a butt; when used thus as a carbine it shot reasonably well to 200-300 yards (180-270m). It therefore made a reasonably effective weapon for a leader who did not wish to carry a rifle but who wanted a weapon with more claim to long-range accuracy than a revolver. It was used fairly extensively in this role by both sides during the South African War of 1899-1902. Thereafter, it sold well almost worldwide (although in North America the revolver continued to reign supreme) and remained in production for many years.

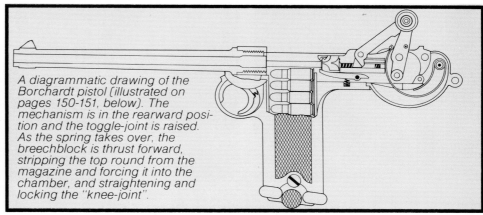

A diagrammatic drawing of the Borchardt pistol (illustrated on pages 150-151, below). The mechanism is in the rearward position and the toggle-joint is raised. As the spring takes over, the breechblock is thrust forward, stripping the top round from the magazine and forcing it into the chamber, and straightening and locking the "knee-joint".

In World War I, the Germans modified large numbers of Mausers to fire the standard, straight-sided, 9mm Parabellum cartridge. When fitted with its detachable butt, the Mauser proved handy for close-quarter trench fighting and it may in some measure be regarded as the tactical predecessor of the Bergmann sub-machine gun, which the Germans had developed by 1918. A fully automatic version of the Mauser pistol was, in fact, made between the two World Wars, chiefly in Spain; but although it was mechanically reliable, its extremely high rate of fire reduced its accuracy very considerably.

It is a significant fact that the early development of the self-loading pistol was mainly a continental phenomenon — Germany being the country chiefly concerned. Until 1871, Germany had not existed as a single state; but after her victory in the Franco-Prussian War, her emergence as a major imperial power

gave a great impetus to industry and manufacture of all kinds — particularly, perhaps, those activities with a military significance.

JOHN BROWNING

In spite of initial indifference in the United States, it was inevitable that sooner or later self-loading arms would be designed and manufactured there. The great John Browning, one of the most famous names in the entire history of firearms, experimented with automatic guns for some time and produced an effective arm by 1890. Unlike Maxim, who harnessed recoil, Browning tapped off some of the gases produced by the explosion of the charge near the muzzle of the weapon and used this pressure to activate the working parts. This action, however, although effective in reasonably long and heavy weapons, proved somewhat too violent in small, hand-held arms; so Browning reverted to the

Top: *In Britain shortly before the D-Day landings of July 1944, a French Master Sergeant of the Regiment de Marche du Tchad cleans his Colt 1911 Government Model self-loading pistol.*

Above left top: *A Chinese Nationalist soldier in Nanking, c1937, armed with a Mauser pistol. This is possibly the Spanish-made, fully-automatic model.*

Above left bottom: *Chinese woman soldier of the 1930s; the pistol she carries is sometimes called the "broom-handle Mauser", from its striated butt.*

Far left: *A British officer with a Mauser pistol has quelled a group of White Russian deserters during the anti-Bolshevik operations of c1918.*

Centre top: *German Waffen SS troops of the "Germania" Regiment, photographed during World War II. The soldier on the left is holding a Luger pistol.*

Centre bottom: *An Eritrean bandit surrenders his Beretta pistol to a British officer, c1947. The pistol's barrel has been unscrewed and drawn forward.*

Above: *A British soldier with a 9mm Browning pistol taken from German possession, 1944; a French Resistance woman with what is apparently a French State Model 1935A (MAB) pistol.*

Far left: *A US Army marksman at practice takes an orthodox straight-arm aiming position with his ·45in Colt Model 1911 pistol (illustrated on page 163).*

Left: *Loading a Smith and Wesson ·22in Model 41 Autoloading target pistol, a specialist weapon for target-shooting (note adjustable sights) introduced in 1957.*

Top right: *A British policewoman sets the sights on a Mauser Model 1912. This weapon is not known to be used by any modern police force.*

Right: *The Russian soldier on the tank holds what is probably a Tokarev, the standard Soviet self-loading pistol at the time—1944.*

concept of recoil. His first pistol of the new type was made in Belgium in 1899—and in 1900 the great American firm of Colt began to manufacture self-loading pistols based on a Browning patent. This utilized the concept of unlocking the barrel from the breech-block by vertical displacement and, since it proved highly successful, it continued in use in almost every pistol made by Colt thereafter. It was also extensively copied elsewhere. The fact that a firm of Colt's repute was making self-loading pistols set a seal of approval on them and ensured their acceptance in the United States—although it is true to say that in spite of this the revolver has retained its great popularity there until the present day.

THE TWENTIETH CENTURY

Great Britain, like the United States, was slow to develop a self-loading pistol, but the firm of Webley and Scott, which had established a virtual monopoly of pistol making in Britain, produced one

in 1904. It was a solid and well-made arm of characteristic shape, but although the final model was adopted by the Royal Navy in 1913, the Army generally much preferred its robust and reliable revolvers by the same maker. One of the firm's most unusual ventures was the odd, but in many ways remarkable, Webley-Mars pistol, which made a brief appearance in 1906. It was a huge and very well-made arm, with a powerful cartridge which necessitated a fully-locked breech; but it was too big and too complex to gain acceptance. The Webley-Fosbery "automatic revolver" is described on page 134, and thus needs only a mention here.

By 1900, Georg Luger had redeveloped the original Borchardt design to the stage where he was able to patent it in his own name. It later achieved fame comparable to that of the Mauser and was used by the German Army, and by many others, in both World Wars.

Although it is not possible to deal with every self-loading pistol developed

in the first few years of the type's history, a number deserve at least a brief mention.

The Glisenti was invented in Turin in 1906 and was adopted as the Italian Army pistol four years later. Certain fundamental weaknesses in its design led to its partial replacement, in the course of World War I, by the Beretta, which had been invented in 1915. This was a simple, reliable, well-made arm, although its short cartridge lacked the requisite power for a military arm. Nevertheless, it continued in service and, in a later version, was in general use in the Italian Army during World War II. Beretta remains a famous name.

The adoption of the Roth-Steyr pistol by the Austro-Hungarian Army in 1907 was the first occasion on which a self-loading arm replaced a revolver in service use. The barrel of the Roth-Steyr recoiled in an outer casing, turning as it did so to unlock the breech. Both the designer George Roth and the firm of Steyr were also involved with other

solving this problem by incorporating a double-action lock with an external hammer, which could be carried safely in the "down" position with a round in the chamber. It proved to be a reliable weapon and was used extensively by German forces in World War II. Many are still to be found.

FUTURE PROSPECTS

There have been few really significant developments since World War II. A number of countries have produced new models, but these are more notable for production refinements—in particular, the use of precision castings and light-weight metals—than for any fundamental advances. The hard fact seems to be that, militarily speaking at least, the pistol is not important enough to warrant very much expenditure on its improvement: it may, therefore, have reached the limit of its practical development in its present-day form.

The recent worldwide upsurge in terrorist activities and armed crime in general has, perhaps, redirected attention to the pistol as a handy weapon for security forces. Although the self-loading type remains popular for this purpose in many countries, it is by no means universally favoured; and in North America the revolver retains its traditional dominance almost unchallenged. In Great Britain, a country with a long tradition of an unarmed constabulary, the need to combat armed crime has inevitably led to the greatly increased use of firearms by the police; but although many police forces have experimented with self-loading arms, an increasing number appear to be reverting to the revolver, with its well-established virtues of robustness, reliability and, as compared to the self-loader, simplicity.

Nevertheless, it is here, perhaps, that the makers of self-loading pistols may hope to gain ground. A compact, large-calibre arm which can be carried in a condition of instant readiness—with the added advantage of a magazine capacity of 12-13 rounds—may yet recapture a reasonable share of the market. The latest products of the great Italian firm of Beretta seem excellent in this respect; and where Beretta leads, other well-known manufacturers are likely to follow.

A NOTE ON TERMINOLOGY

Some readers may consider that the author has been pedantic in using the term "self-loading pistol" throughout this essay; for these arms are now almost universally referred to as "automatic pistols". The present usage has been adopted mainly to ensure clarity and to avoid confusion in cases where reference is also made to true automatic weapons; ie, weapons which continue to fire as long as the trigger is pressed and there is ammunition in the magazine.

arms: a Steyr pistol was adopted by Austria-Hungary in 1911.

The years immediately following World War I saw few advances in weaponry, for most of the major powers were more or less crippled by the war and were concerned with economy and retrenchment rather than innovation. By the 1930s, however, the international situation had once again begun to deteriorate and changes in armaments were increasingly evident. Germany, which had largely pioneered the development of the self-loading pistol, never really lost the lead she had established: the United States continued to produce arms of fine quality—but in Europe, Germany led the field. But German arms, although of excellent quality, were by no means cheap; and this led to extensive copying of German designs. Although Belgium produced cheap arms in considerable quantity, most of them were of fair quality, properly proved and safe to fire: so far as the "Suicide Special" was concerned, the chief pro-

ducer was Spain. Spanish neutrality during World War I had given the country's arms manufacturers a chance to take some of the market in pistols for the combatants; and afterwards Spain continued to turn out inferior arms in large numbers—until the Spanish Civil War brought the trade to an end. Not all Spanish arms fell into the inferior category, but for a relatively short period the Spanish gunmakers' reputation for quality suffered severely.

Probably the major development of the early 1930s was the Browning Hi-Power (GP35) pistol of 1935, made first in Belgium and later in Canada, which was destined to become a standard military arm. The same period saw a new Beretta, the Polish Radom, the French MAS and the Russian Tokarev; and these were soon followed by the German Walther P38. An ever-present problem with earlier self-loading pistols had been the impossibility of carrying them safely at instant readiness: the Walther went a good way towards

Germany
MAUSER MODEL 1898 SELF-LOADING PISTOL

Length:	11·75" (298mm)
Weight:	40oz (1·13kg)
Barrel:	5·5" (140mm)
Calibre:	7·63mm
Rifling:	4 groove, r/hand
Capacity:	Ten
Muz Vel:	1400 f/s (427 m/s)
Sights:	492 yd (450m)

The name of Mauser must be among the most famous in the world as far as firearms are concerned. The first bearer of it to achieve fame was Peter Paul Mauser, who was responsible for the famous German Model 1871 rifle which replaced the needle-gun after the Franco-Prussian War. This was followed by a series of progressively better weapons, culminating in the Model 1898 rifle. It is probably no exaggeration to say that, at one time or another, half the armies of the world have been armed with Mauser's products. Mauser first became interested in pistols in the 1870s, and it is probable that his Model 1878 "Zig-Zag" revolver (a specimen of which is illustrated on page 105, above) was his first successful hand gun. By the 1890s, the principle of using the recoil of one cartridge to operate the mechanism that loaded the next, established by Hiram Maxim, had become fully accepted. It may, perhaps, have been the appearance of the Borchardt pistol (illustrated below) at about that time that inspired Mauser to try his own hand at a similar arm. What is certain is that his new weapon was based on the 7·65mm Borchardt round (the 7·63mm Mauser cartridge is virtually identical). The first Mauser self-loading model appeared in 1896 and, with relatively minor improvements, it developed into the Model 1898 pistol seen here. It operates on the short recoil system: the barrel and bolt recoil locked together for a short distance, after which the

Germany
BORCHARDT SELF-LOADING PISTOL

Length:	13·75" (349mm)
Weight:	46oz (1·3kg)
Barrel:	6·5" (165mm)
Calibre:	7·65mm
Rifling:	4 groove, r/hand
Capacity:	Eight
Muz Vel:	1100 f/s (335 m/s)
Sights:	Fixed

bolt is unlocked and continues its rearward movement, while the barrel stops. The return spring, which is inside the bolt, is compressed during this rearward travel, which also cocks the hammer. As the force of recoil dies, the compressed spring takes over and drives the bolt forward, picking up a cartridge from the magazine and chambering it on the way. The closure of the bolt locks it to the barrel as it drives it forward — and the pistol is then ready to fire its next round. The hammer, which is cocked in the photograph, strikes an inertia firing-pin in the bolt, which fires the cartridge. Initial cocking is, of course, necessary before the first shot: this is achieved by pulling back the milled ears visible at the rear of the frame. The rounds are fed from a box magazine in front of the trigger-guard, which is initially loaded from a ten-round clip of the type shown. When the last round has been fired, the magazine

platform holds the bolt open and thus indicates the need for more ammunition; this system is now the usual one, and the Mauser pistol was the first to feature it. Unlike its predecessor, the Model 1898 is designed to take a stock, which acts also as a holster. It also has an adjustable leaf backsight, which on the weapon seen here is graduated to 450m (492 yds), although the scale on some weapons goes up to 700m (766 yds). Although mechanically reliable, the Mauser never achieved great popularity as a military arm in its early days. Winston Churchill carried one in the Omdurman campaign of 1898, when a shoulder injury prevented him from using a sword effectively, and claimed that it had saved his life, and Mausers were carried by both sides during the South African War of 1899-1902. There, however, long-range rifle fire predominated, and the value of the Mauser was thus limited.

Hugo Borchardt was of German birth but went to work in the United States, where he became a naturalized citizen. In the late 1880s he went back to his native country, where he continued to work on a new self-loading pistol. This weapon, which appeared in 1894, may be classed as having been only moderately successful in the commercial sense. It made use of the principle, firstly clearly defined by Maxim, of harnessing the backward thrust of a fired cartridge to reload and recock the weapon. It fired from a locked breech — a system later made famous by Luger — which worked roughly on the principle of the human knee-joint. When it was straight and locked, it was virtually immovable, but as soon as the joint was pushed upward it opened easily and smoothly. When the cartridge was fired, the recoil drove back the barrel and bolt until lugs on the receiver caused the joint to rise, thus allowing it to break. The barrel then stopped, but the bolt continued to the rear against a spring. When the bolt's rearward impetus was exhausted, the compressed spring drove it forward again, stripping a round from the box magazine in the butt and chambering it ready for the next shot. This was the first time such a principle had been applied to a pistol; it worked well, but the weapon was expensive to make, for it called for fine workmanship and the use of steel of very high quality, especially for the manufacture of the joint pins. The arm was also very bulky, and thus was practically impossible to fire with one hand. To surmount this difficulty, it was provided with a strong and well-fitting stock (which, as may be seen, incorporated a holster): in fact, it seems to have been generally regarded more as a light carbine than as a pistol. Weapons of this type had a certain military value before World War I, since they were suitable for cavalry. The Borchardt fired a powerful cartridge and had a long sight base, which made it reasonably accurate; however, perhaps surprisingly, the backsight was not adjustable. With hindsight, it may be said that what European users really wanted was a weapon constructed on broadly similar principles but small enough to be used as a flat, compact, pocket arm.

LUGER ARTILLERY MODEL 1917

Length:	12·75" (324mm)	**Rifling:**	6 groove, r/hand
Weight:	37oz (1·05kg)	**Capacity:**	Eight (box)/Thirty-two (drum)
Barrel:	7·5" (190mm)	**Muz Vel:**	1250 f/s (380 m/s)
Calibre:	9mm	**Sights:**	875 yd (800m)

The Luger Parabellum self-loading pistol had its origins in the Borchardt, which was developed by Georg Luger. It proved successful and was adopted by the German Army in 1908; this naturally ensured that it would be generally accepted, and its subsequent record in World War I made it a household name: the name of Luger is equally as famous as that of Mauser. A long-barrelled commercial model was produced in 1903-1904, and this was soon adopted as the standard pistol of the German Navy. In 1917, this was followed in its turn by the Artillery Model, illustrated here. Like its parent arm, the Borchardt, the Luger works on a system of short recoil, during which the barrel and bolt remain locked together. The toggle joint then passes over curved ramps and opens upward, detaching itself from the barrel. When the bolt has reached its rearmost position, it is forced forward again by a return spring, stripping a cartridge from the magazine and forcing it into the chamber en route. It then locks, and may be fired again in the normal way. The standard Luger has a box magazine in the butt, but the example seen here is fitted with an extension type, the so-called "snail drum" magazine with a capacity of 32 rounds. A special tool was needed to load this magazine, which tended to jam; this was cured by replacing the original round-nosed bullet with a pointed one. As may be seen, the Luger also had a detachable stock, which converted it into a carbine and made it a very light and handy weapon for local defence. It was originally issued to machine gun detachments and artillery observers in exposed forward positions. As stocks of the arm increased, it was also issued to non-commissioned officers of forward infantry units, where, like the Mauser, it was found to be a very handy arm for such work as night raids. Although Germany cannot really be said to have invented the sub-machine gun, it was probably the success of the German self-loading pistols which encouraged the country to develop the automatic Bergmann.

This photograph shows one of the original Mauser 1912 models, which has been converted to fire the 9mm Para-bellum cartridge. Note the deeply-incised figure "9" on the butt: the grooves of the lettering were filled with red paint, in order to preclude any confusion over ammunition.

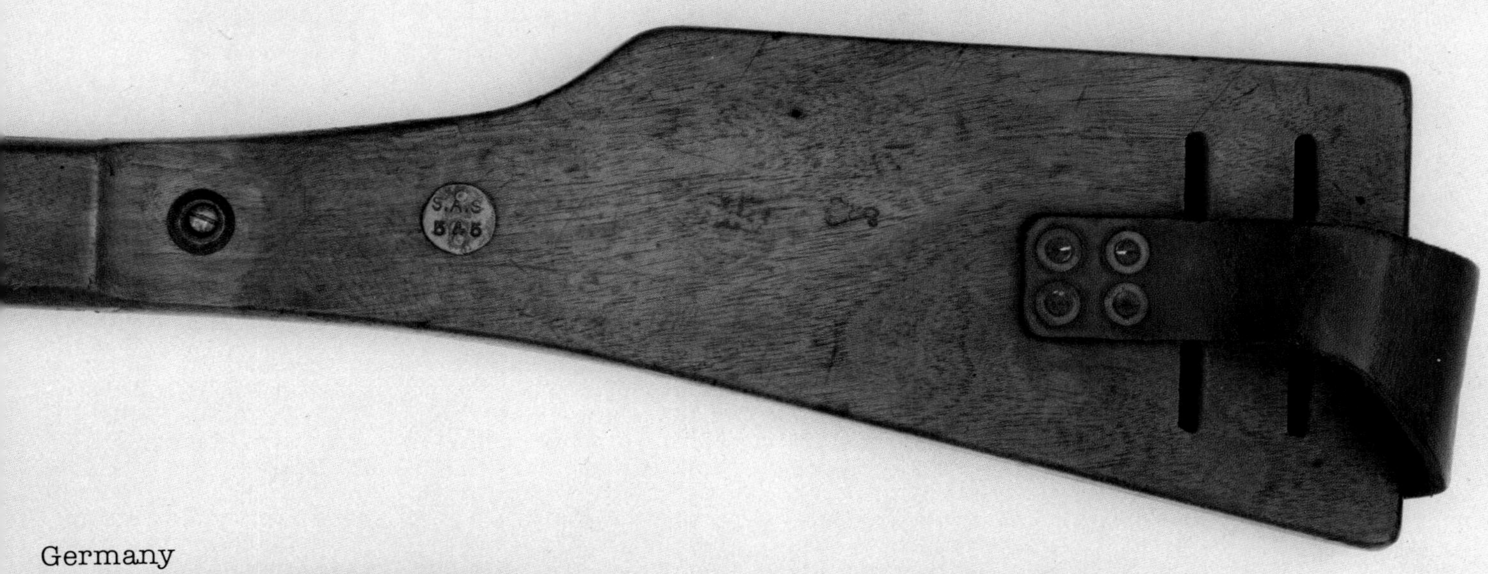

Germany
MAUSER MODEL 1912

Length:	11·75" (298mm)
Weight:	44oz (1·25kg)
Barrel:	5·5" (140mm)
Calibre:	7·63mm
Rifling:	6 groove, r/hand
Capacity:	Ten
Muz Vel:	1400 f/s (427 m/s)
Sights:	1094 yd (1000m)

Some details of the origins and history of the early Mauser pistols have already been given (on pages 150-151, above). The Model 1898 was followed by others in 1903 and 1905; at one time it seemed possible that these would be at last of the series, for Mauser had begun experimenting in other fields. However, his new project was abandoned, and another self-loading pistol, the Model 1912, illustrated here, duly appeared. It did not differ significantly from its predecessor of 14 years before. Weapons of this type were, of course, made by the thousand for use in World War I and, not surprisingly, they are still numerous. In 1916 the German Army had a requirement for Mauser pistols to fire the straight-sided 9mm Parabellum cartridge, and it was quickly realized that conversion of the standard Model 1912 would be relatively simple. The arms thus altered were all distinguished by a large figure "9", cut into the butt-grips and painted red. The Mauser pistol was widely used in World War I because, unlike many earlier 20th-century campaigns, it involved a good deal of close-quarter fighting. The emphasis as far as the infantry was concerned was, of course, on the rifle, light machine gun and medium machine gun; nevertheless, it was found that a Mauser pistol with its shoulder-stock attached was a handy weapon for raids, clearing trenches, and similar operations. It was used in very similar fashion to the sub-machine gun which the Germans finally adopted in 1918. A Mauser-type pistol with a capability for automatic fire was, in fact, made in Spain in the 1930s. However, the combination of a light bolt travelling over a very short distance and a powerful cartridge was not successful, and the arm's rate of fire made it impossible to shoot with very much accuracy.

153

BERGMANN-BAYARD SELF-LOADING PISTOL

Length:	9·9" (251mm)
Weight:	35·5oz (1·01kg)
Barrel:	4" (102mm)
Calibre:	9mm
Rifling:	6 groove, l/hand
Capacity:	Six
Muz Vel:	c1000 f/s (305 m/s)
Sights:	Fixed

Several self-loading pistols produced by the German gun-maker Theodor Bergmann are illustrated in this book, but although Bergmann was responsible for a number of ingenious developments, it is possible that he was himself more of a businessman than an innovator and relied on other people for technical assistance. In 1901 he produced the Bergmann-Bayard pistol seen here. It was designed specifically as a military arm, originally under the trade-name "Mars", and was the first European pistol of its kind to fire a 9mm cartridge, which was a very powerful round. The Spanish Army put in a considerable order, but Bergmann had trouble with contractors and few, if any, pistols were ever actually supplied by him. He eventually sold the rights to Pieper of Liège, who completed the order and also sold some of these arms to the Greek and Danish Armies. Once these orders were completed, Pieper put an improved version on the market as the Bergmann-Bayard. The pistol works on a system of short recoil. The barrel and bolt recoil together for about 0·25in (6mm); the barrel stops; and the bolt is unlocked by being forced downward and continues to the rear, extracting the empty case (if any) and compressing the return spring which is contained within it, coiled round the long striker. On its forward movement, the bolt strips a cartridge from the magazine in front of the trigger-guard and chambers it in readiness for the next shot. The pistol was considered to be clumsy in use, and recoil from its powerful cartridge was considerable. Military models were often fitted with a detachable holster stock of hard leather, to improve long-range accuracy.

SCHWARZLOSE MODEL 1908

Length:	9·2" (234mm)
Weight:	32oz (·91kg)
Barrel:	4·75" (121mm)
Calibre:	9mm
Rifling:	4 groove, r/hand
Capacity:	Six
Muz Vel:	c1000 f/s (305 m/s)
Sights:	Fixed

Andreas Schwarzlose, a German from Charlottenburg, is perhaps best remembered as the inventor of a medium machine gun with a simple but effective blowback action instead of a more complex locked breech. Its reliability was confirmed by its adoption by Austria in World War I and by Italy in World War II. Schwarzlose's real interest, however, was in self-loading pistols, and from 1892 onward he produced a variety of ingenious mechanisms. Perhaps unfortunately for Schwarzlose, the Mauser was fairly well established by the time that his arms appeared, and thus they never really had the success they deserved. However, he persevered, and by 1908 he had produced yet another model, of the type illustrated above. It is, in many ways, a remarkable arm: perhaps its most interesting feature is that the usual blowback system has been replaced by a blow-forward mechanism. The breech-block is an integral part of the frame, but the barrel is mounted on ribs and is therefore free to be forced forward by the explosion of the charge; this leaves the empty case held in an ejector, which throws it clear mechanically. On its forward movement, the barrel stretches a heavy recoil spring; when its forward impetus is exhausted, the spring draws it backward, scooping the next round from the magazine and also cocking the hammer. The metal arm in front of the butt is a grip safety: it must be firmly gripped, in the proper firing position, or the trigger will not function. There is, however, a stud on the left side of the butt which allows the safety to be locked in, if necessary.

BROWNING MODEL 1900 ("OLD MODEL")

Length:	6·4" (163mm)
Weight:	22oz (·62kg)
Barrel:	4" (102mm)
Calibre:	7·65mm
Rifling:	5 groove, r/hand
Capacity:	Seven
Muz Vel:	c850 f/s (259 m/s)
Sights:	Fixed

John Moses Browning is one of the greatest names in the entire history of firearms, and his work on self-loading weapons of all types, ranging from medium machine guns to small pocket pistols, is unsurpassed. His first successful venture was a machine gun made by the Colt company and adopted by the United States Navy in 1898; it was not until two years later that he finally produced a self-loading pistol, of the type shown here. However, after a disagreement with the American gunmaker Winchester, with whom he had worked for some years, Browning came to the conclusion that more interest might be shown in his self-loading pistol in Europe than in the United States—where the revolver was almost universally predominant. In this he was right: the great Belgian firm of Fabrique Nationale ("FN"), Liège, showed immediate interest, and the weapon was soon in production in great quantity. It is robust, reliable and mechanically simple; and although it has not been made since 1912, many are still to be found. The barrel is fastened to the frame; above it is a moving slide which contains the recoil spring. The slide must, of course, be operated manually to load the first round. When this is fired, gas pressure forces the empty case backward, taking with it the breechblock and slide and compressing the recoil spring, which also operates the striker. The spring then takes over and forces the whole assembly forward, stripping a cartridge from the box magazine in the butt and chambering it in preparation for the next shot. Browning continued to design self-loading pistols for many years and, with some wartime exceptions, all bearing his name were made in Belgium.

DANSK SCHOUBOE MODEL 1907

Length:	8·8" (224mm)
Weight:	42oz (1·19kg)
Barrel:	5" (127mm)
Calibre:	11·35mm
Rifling:	6 groove, r/hand
Capacity:	Six
Muz Vel:	c1600 f/s (488 m/s)
Sights:	Fixed

Lieutenant Jens Torring Schouboe was an officer in the Danish Army and also, apparently, a director of the Dansk Rekylriffel Syndikat; he was closely involved with the development of the famous Madsen light machine gun. In 1903, Schouboe patented a self-loading pistol, but although it was well made and reliable, it failed to sell. He therefore decided that what was needed was a heavier arm of the same general type but of service calibre, and this he set out to achieve, the result being the weapon illustrated here. Like his earlier arms, this was of simple blowback design, without any breech-locking mechanism—but while this type of action is easy enough to incorporate into small pocket pistols firing low-powered cartridges, it is very hard to do so in a service-type arm without making it extremely heavy. Schouboe's answer to this problem was to produce a cartridge firing an extremely lightweight bullet which, he reasoned, would not only reduce recoil but would also leave the barrel faster, thus reducing the period of maximum pressure. The bullet was basically a wooden round with a thin metal jacket. Schouboe's solution worked: the weapon was very satisfactory from the purely mechanical point of view — but it had two serious defects as a military arm. The first was that the bullet was too light to have very much stopping-power; the second was that it lost accuracy very quickly, presumably for the same reason. Although Schouboe produced improved versions, it was never popular and ceased manufacture in 1917.

Great Britain
WEBLEY No 1 Mk I

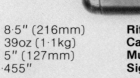

Length:	8.5" (216mm)	**Rifling:**	7 groove, r/hand
Weight:	39oz (1.1kg)	**Capacity:**	Seven
Barrel:	5" (127mm)	**Muz Vel:**	c750 f/s (229 m/s)
Calibre:	·455"	**Sights:**	Fixed

The Webley Model 1904, which is illustrated on the lower part of this page, was followed by some smaller-calibre weapons in ·32in or ·25in calibre; these, being pocket pistols, are dealt with later (see page 169). An intermediate model to take the 9mm cartridge (illustrated on the facing page, above), was also produced, but the next full-bored model was the one shown here. It was developed from about 1906 onward and was officially adopted as the standard pistol of the Royal Navy in 1913. As may be seen from the photograph, it is a

heavy and robust arm with all the Webley characteristics. It works, as usual, by recoil. When a loaded magazine is inserted into the butt and the slide is pulled back and released, a round is chambered and the hammer is cocked. At the moment of firing, the barrel is locked to the slide—a lug on the barrel engaging in a recess in the upper part of the slide—and the two recoil briefly together. Once the gas pressure has dropped to a safe level (a process that is measured in thousandths of a second) the barrel is forced downward by a

cam-way and disengages from the slide, which continues to the rear, cocking the hammer as it does so. The slide's forward movement, under the impetus of the V-spring behind the right butt-plate, strips the top round from the magazine and chambers it. A Mark II version, fitted with a stock was issued to the Royal Flying Corps in 1915 but was withdrawn upon the introduction of the aerial machine gun.

Great Britain
WEBLEY AND SCOTT MODEL 1904

Length;	10" (254mm)	**Rifling:**	7 groove, r/hand
Weight:	48oz (1.36kg)	**Capacity:**	Seven
Barrel:	6.5" (165mm)	**Muz Vel:**	c750 f/s (229 m/s)
Calibre:	·455"	**Sights:**	Fixed

By the end of the 19th century it had become clear that the self-loading pistol had a future. Much of the work of development was done in Western Europe and, initially, neither the United States nor Great Britain showed much interest; both countries preferred to stick to their various revolvers, which had proved to be powerful and reliable weapons. However, the new system could not be ignored completely, and as early as 1898 Webley and Scott

had sought a suitable design. Apart from the Webley-Mars, which is described on the facing page (below), the firm found nothing to its liking until the model illustrated here, which first went on to the market in 1904. As may be seen, it is of the characteristically square style which was later to become a noticeable feature of all Webley and Scott pistols of this type. It fires a powerful cartridge which necessitates a locked breech.

The barrel and breech block remain locked on initial recoil until a vertical bolt drops and allows them to separate. The V-shaped recoil spring is situated under the right butt-plate. Overall, the weapon is of rather complex design; it is, perhaps, *too* well made, and is said to have been susceptible to stoppages caused by dirt. However, it set the general style for Webley self-loaders.

Great Britain
WEBLEY MODEL 1909

Length:	8" (203mm)	**Rifling:**	7 groove, r/hand
Weight:	34oz (·96kg)	**Capacity:**	Seven
Barrel:	5" (127mm)	**Muz Vel:**	c750 f/s (229 m/s)
Calibre:	·38"	**Sights:**	Fixed

In 1908, Webley began work on a pistol of international calibre, to meet the needs of civilian customers who did not require anything quite as powerful as the full-sized ·455in cartridge used in the firm's various military models. The new weapon was on the market by 1909. It was designed principally to handle the 9mm Browning long cartridge, which had been introduced initially for the 1903 Browning pistol made by Fabrique Nationale. This round was of fair velocity and provided adequate stopping-power: it was popular in many parts of the world for civilian and police use, although it was not widely employed in the United States. The round was not sufficiently powerful to necessitate a locked breech, so it was possible for the arm to be of a simple blowback design. The first round must be manually loaded in the usual way, but when it is fired it blows back the slide, cocks the hammer and compresses the recoil spring in the butt. The spring then drives the action forward and strips and chambers the next cartridge. In this model, the barrel is held in position by a lug on top of the trigger-guard, which is pulled forward to strip the weapon. The earliest versions had a safety catch on the left-hand side of the frame, but later examples have a grip safety at the back of the butt, as seen in the photograph. When the safety is out, the sear cannot engage, but when the butt is firmly gripped, the sear is forced into position so that the weapon can be fired. The Model 1909 was adopted by the South African Police in 1920 and production did not end until 1930.

Great Britain
WEBLEY-MARS

Length:	12·25" (311mm)
Weight:	48oz (1·36kg)
Barrel:	9·5" (241mm)
Calibre:	·38"
Rifling:	7 groove, r/hand
Capacity:	Seven
Muz Vel:	1750 f/s (533 m/s)
Sights:	Fixed

The originator of this pistol was Hugh Gabbet-Fairfax, who took out a variety of patents on self-loading pistols in the period 1895-1900. In 1898 he submitted a design to the famous Birmingham firm of Webley and Scott, which was then seeking a suitable design for a self-loading arm. The firm did not wish to adopt this particular model under its own name, but agreed to manufacture it for the inventor, presumably on a commission basis. The British Army tested it in the period 1901-03 but finally did not adopt it. This adverse decision appears to have been due partly to the arm's heavy recoil, and partly to its persistent tendency either to fail to eject empty cases—or to eject them into the firer's face. Although, in 1902, Gabbet-Fairfax decided that the latter fault was due to defective ammunition, and promised a new batch in which this would be rectified, the whole project had to be abandoned. Gabbet-Fairfax, who had borrowed a great deal of money to develop the Mars, then went bankrupt; a new company was formed, briefly and unsuccessfully, in the period 1904-07. The Webley-Mars is a huge arm and was designed to fire a powerful bottle-necked cartridge. Although it is extremely well made, it is mechanically complex, since the cartridge necessitates a robust system of locking the bolt to the barrel at the moment of firing. This is done by arranging for the bolt to turn so that four lugs on it engage in recesses behind the chamber. When a shot is fired, the barrel and bolt at first recoil together, until the latter turns and unlocks itself. The pistol was made in both ·45in and ·38in calibre, and it is now probably the rarest of all self-loading pistols.

BERGMANN 1896 (No 3)

Length:	10" (254mm)
Weight:	40oz (1·13kg)
Barrel:	4" (102mm)
Calibre:	7·63mm
Rifling:	4 groove, r/hand
Capacity:	Five
Muz Vel:	c1250 f/s (380 m/s)
Sights:	Fixed

Theodor Bergmann began experimenting with self-loading pistols at a very early date: his first patent was taken out in 1892, but the pistol to which this referred (which probably was the actual invention of another designer) was never put into production. Several other designs followed, and by 1894, Bergmann had developed a reasonably successful weapon, of which an improved version appeared in 1896: this is the weapon illustrated here. It is a well-made arm of simple blowback type; perhaps its main point of interest (in the early versions) is its complete lack of any mechanical system of extraction or ejection. In fact, the action is so designed that the bolt opens while there is still sufficient gas available to blow the cartridge case out backwards. The case then strikes the next round in the magazine, and, in theory at least, bounces clear — although in practice this process is somewhat unpredictable. A gas escape port in the chamber serves as a safety device should the case rupture under pressure. The early cartridges had no rim of any kind and were quite sharply tapered to avoid any risk of sticking. However, the system was not considered to be reliable, and later versions were fitted with mechanical extractors, necessitating the use of cartridges with grooved rims, like the one shown in the photograph. The pistol is loaded by pulling down and forward on the milled grip by the trigger-guard, which opens the magazine cover. A five-round clip is inserted and the cover is closed. A lifter spring pushes the rounds up under the bolt one by one and the empty clip is finally ejected downwards. Rounds can be loaded without the clip, but the feed system is by no means reliable in this case, since the rounds are liable to become displaced. This pistol is sometimes referred to as the Bergmann "No 3", under a somewhat peculiar system of numbering weapons by calibre, but, on balance, it is less likely to cause confusion if it is characterized by date.

BERGMANN 1897 (No 5)

Length:	10·5" (267mm)
Weight:	26·5oz (·75kg)
Barrel:	4·4" (112mm)
Calibre:	7·63mm
Rifling:	4 groove, r/hand
Capacity:	Five
Muz Vel:	c1100 f/s (335 m/s)
Sights:	765 yd (700m)

Although the 1896 model in the Bergmann series worked fairly well, it did not achieve real popularity; principally, perhaps, because it was somewhat less effective than the Mauser which came on to the market at about the same time. Apart from small, pocket arms, it was by then clear that the main requirement for self-loading pistols would be for military versions — and as these were always required to fire a powerful cartridge, it was necessary that they should fire with the breech locked. If this was not done, the cartridge case would be pushed out of the chamber when gas pressure was still high and, unsupported by the walls of the chamber, it was likely to rupture. In 1897, therefore, Bergmann patented a pistol of the type seen here. In this design the barrel and bolt are locked together at the instant of firing and remain so during the first ·24in (6mm) of recoil. A cam in the frame then forces the bolt slightly sideways and unlocks it from the barrel, which then stops. The bolt continues to the rear, to cock the hammer, and then comes forward, strips a round from the magazine, chambers it, locks on to the barrel, and forces it back to its forward firing position. The magazine is of detachable box type, incorporating its own platform and spring. The pistol may, however, also be loaded through the top of the frame by means of a charger. Much to Bergmann's disappointment, no country adopted this arm, although several experimented with it. Britain rejected it because its bullet weight was considered to be too light — with consequent loss of accuracy and stopping-power — for service use.

MANNLICHER MODEL 1901

Length:	9·4" (239mm)
Weight:	33oz (·94kg)
Barrel:	6·5" (165mm)
Calibre:	7·63mm
Rifling:	4 groove, r/hand
Capacity:	Eight
Muz Vel:	1025 f/s (312 m/s)
Sights:	Fixed

Josef Werndl the Elder founded an arms factory at Steyr in Austria in 1834 and after his death, 11 years later, his family continued to operate the business. His son, also called Joseph, went to the United States just after the outbreak of the Civil War in 1861, to see if he could arrange any contracts for the supply of arms. He was so impressed by American methods of large-scale production by means of sophisticated machinery that, on his return to Steyr, he completely reorganized and modernized his own factory, installing a great deal of new machinery. This made it possible for him to produce good weapons cheaply, and he was soon making military small

arms of all types for the Austrian and other governments. The Steyr factory first made self-loading pistols in 1894, when it produced some made to the design of Ferdinand, Ritter von Mannlicher, a German living in Austria, who is perhaps now best remembered for his excellent military rifles. Several models were made over the next few years; the arm illustrated here is the Model 1901. As is to be expected from a factory with the high reputation of Steyr, the weapon is very well made and finished. It is basically of blowback design, but of the type usually known as retarded blowback. There is no positive locked-breech system: the rearward movement of the

slide is mechanically retarded for a very brief period to ensure that the gas pressure in the barrel falls to a safe level. This system also incidentally permitted the use of a relatively light slide without engendering excessive recoil. Although the magazine is located in the butt — in the style familiar on modern arms — it is not, in fact, a detachable box but an integral part of the arm; and it is loaded from the top by means of a charger. If the user desires to empty the magazine, the slide is drawn back and pressure is put on the small milled catch (visible in the photograph) above the right butt-plate; this allows the magazine spring to force out the unexpended rounds.

MANNLICHER MODEL 1903

Length:	10·5" (267mm)
Weight:	35oz (·99kg)
Barrel:	4·5" (114mm)
Calibre:	7·65mm
Rifling:	5 groove, r/hand
Capacity:	Six
Muz Vel:	c1090 f/s (332 m/s)
Sights:	Fixed

This pistol appeared on the market in 1903, after some years in development, and was the last type of Mannlicher to be produced. Like most other firms concerned with self-loading arms, Mannlicher obviously realized that the future of such weapons lay in the military sphere; thus, development should be concerned with weapons firing powerful cartridges from locked-breech systems. The Mannlicher Model 1903, seen here, is of that type. It is cocked for the first shot by drawing back the bolt by means of the milled

knob visible on top of the frame. When released, the bolt goes forward, stripping a cartridge from the magazine and chambering it. When the bolt is fully forward, a bolt-stop rises from the frame and supports it while the round is fired. Then barrel and bolt recoil for about ·2in (5mm), after which the bolt-stop falls. The barrel now stops, but the bolt continues backward to complete the recocking and reloading cycle in readiness for the next shot. The pistol has an internal hammer which acts on the firing pin; it also has an

external cocking device in the form of the curved lever visible above the trigger. The magazine is of box type and can be removed by pressing in a small catch on the front of the trigger-guard, which allows it to drop down. The small milled catch at the back of the frame is the safety. Perhaps the most remarkable aspect of this weapon is that although it fires a cartridge of the same dimensions as the Mauser, the actual charge is less: thus, the Mannlicher is not considered safe to fire the 7·65mm round used in the Mauser self-loading pistol.

159

BERGMANN SIMPLEX

Length:	7·5" (190mm)
Weight:	21oz (·59kg)
Barrel:	2·75" (70mm)
Calibre:	8mm
Rifling:	6 groove, r/hand
Capacity:	Six or Eight
Muz Vel:	c650 f/s (198 m/s)
Sights:	Fixed

The Bergmann Simplex pistol was patented in 1901. A few were made in Austria, but in 1904 the design was licensed to a company in Belgium, which thereafter turned the arm out in quite large numbers until 1914, when production finally ceased. Although the general shape of the weapon characterizes it as being obviously of Bergmann origin, its scale is much smaller than that of the designer's other weapons: the Simplex was originated strictly as a pocket arm. It fired a specially-designed cartridge (which is no longer available)

and, because it was of low power, it was possible to design the weapon on the blowback principle, with no need for a locked breech. The pistol is cocked by pulling back the bolt by means of the cylindrical cocking-piece, visible just in front of the hammer. When released, the bolt goes forward under its recoil spring, strips a round from the magazine and chambers it ready to fire; after the first shot the process is repeated automatically. The lock is a simple single-action revolver type. The weapon has a detachable box magazine in

front of the trigger in the ortho-dox arrangement: it is removed by pressing the small stud on the front of the magazine hous-ing, which allows it to drop downward. On Belgian-made examples, the barrel is screwed into the frame; whereas the original Austrian arms had their barrels forged integrally. The Bergmann is simple and reliable: it sold well as a pocket pistol, although the fact that it required a special cartridge must have been to some extent a limiting factor. This specimen is marked "PATENT, BREVET DRGM" with Belgian proof marks.

ROTH-STEYR MODEL 1907

Length:	9" (229mm)
Weight:	36oz (1·02kg)
Barrel:	5" (127mm)
Calibre:	8mm
Rifling:	4 groove, r/hand
Capacity:	Ten
Muz Vel:	1090 f/s (332 m/s)
Sights:	Fixed

This pistol first went into full production in 1907, when it was taken into service by the Austro-Hungarian Army, mainly for use as a cavalry arm. This was the first occasion on which any major power adopted a self-loading pistol in place of a revolver. The Roth-Steyr pistol fires from a locked breech — and this mechanism is of a very unusual type. The bolt is very long: its rear end is solid, except for a sleeve for the striker, but its front part is hollow and is of sufficient diameter to fit closely over the barrel. The interior of the bolt has cam grooves cut into it, and the barrel has studs of appro-

priate size to fit the grooves. When the pistol is fired, the barrel and bolt recoil together within the hollow receiver for about ·5in (12·7mm). During this operation, the grooves in the bolt cause the barrel to turn through 90 degrees, after which it is held while the bolt con-tinues to the rear, cocking the action as it does so. On its for-ward journey, the bolt picks up a cartridge through a slot on its lower surface and chambers it, while the action of the studs in the grooves turns the barrel back to its locked position. The magazine, which is in the butt, is an integral part of the weapon and is loaded from a clip.

FROMMER MODEL 1910

Length:	7·25" (184mm)	**Rifling:**	5 groove, r/hand
Weight:	21oz (·59kg)	**Capacity:**	Seven
Barrel:	4·25" (108mm)	**Muz Vel:**	c1100 f/s (335 m/s)
Calibre:	7·65mm	**Sights:**	Fixed

Rudolf Frommer was a talented engineer and designer who worked for the Royal Hungarian Arsenal, Fegyvergyar, for many years. His first pistol appeared in 1903, but it was generally considered to be far too complex for military use. However, he continued to simplify the design, and by 1910 had produced the pistol illustrated here. It is of a most unusual type: it works on the principle of long recoil, in which the barrel and bolt remain locked together for the whole of the rearward phase of movement. Under this system, the barrel only becomes unlocked from the rotating head of the bolt as the barrel resumes its forward movement, the bolt being held briefly to the rear by a stop. Extraction and ejection take place during this forward movement: as the barrel reaches the proper position, it trips the bolt stop and allows the bolt to go forward, stripping a round from the magazine, chambering it, and simultaneously locking back on to the barrel by the rotation of its head. This movement of the barrel and bolt necessitated the incorporation of two separate recoil springs to drive them back into position. The earlier Frommer pistols had integral magazines which were loaded through the top of the frame by means of a clip, but this Model 1910 has a separate, detachable, box magazine. The weapon has a large inspection plate on the left-hand side of the frame: access to the mechanism is obtained by turning and pushing in the circular stud just in front of the hammer, which forces the plate outward. The pistol has a grip safety (seen at the back of the butt).

STEYR MODEL 1911

Length:	8·5" (216mm)
Weight:	35oz (·99kg)
Barrel:	5·1" (130mm)
Calibre:	·357"
Rifling:	4 groove, r/hand
Capacity:	Eight
Muz Vel:	c1100 f/s (335 m/s)
Sights:	Fixed

Some account of the wide-ranging operations of the Steyr factory is given on page 160 (below). As far as hand guns were concerned, Steyr's chief endeavour in the early years of the 20th century appears to have been to produce an acceptable self-loading pistol of military type. This the firm accomplished with the appearance of the Model 1911 pistol illustrated here. It is a solid, square looking arm with some external resemblance to the famous Colt self-loader (see page 163, above) of the same year. It has the same heavy slide, with the barrel inside it, which covers the whole of the frame. When the action is in the forward position, two lugs on the top of the barrel engage in two corresponding slots in the slide. When the slide is drawn back for initial loading, the barrel moves with it for a short distance and is rotated sufficiently to disengage it from the slots. The barrel then stops, but the slide continues to the rear and cocks the hammer. It then moves forward, driven by the recoil spring, stripping a round from the magazine and chambering it. During this forward movement, the barrel rotates back into the locked position in readiness for the next shot. The magazine is in the butt and is loaded by a clip from the top of the frame, with the slide to the rear. This pistol was in Austro-Hungarian service during World War I, until 1918.

Belgium
BROWNING MODEL 1900

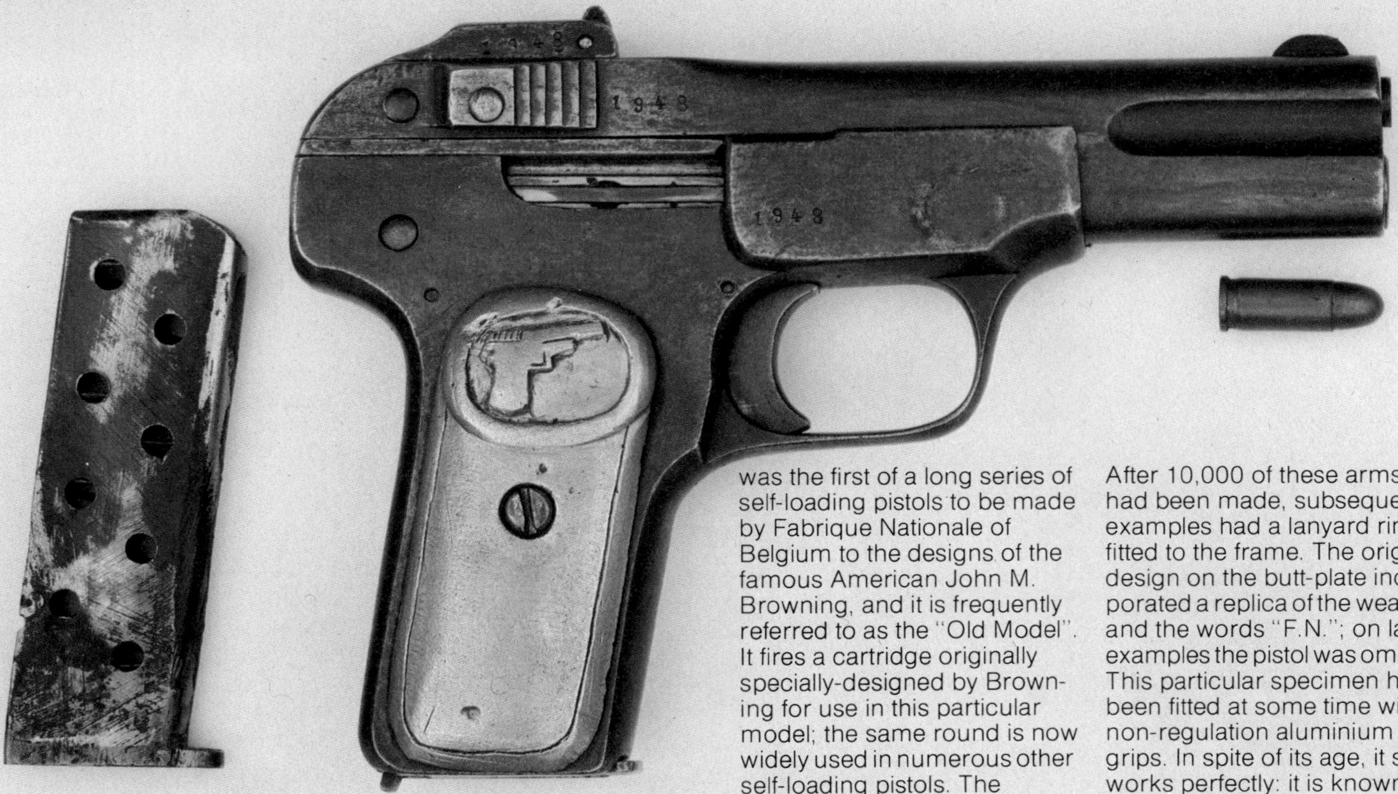

Length: 6·75" (171mm)
Weight: 22oz (·62kg)
Barrel: 4" (102mm)
Calibre: 7·65mm
Rifling: 6 groove, r/hand
Capacity: Seven
Muz Vel: c940 f/s (287 m/s)
Sights: Fixed

A weapon similar to the pistol seen here is illustrated on page 155 (above). This example, however, has some slight variations, and since something is also known of its personal history it has been judged worthy of inclusion. This model was the first of a long series of self-loading pistols to be made by Fabrique Nationale of Belgium to the designs of the famous American John M. Browning, and it is frequently referred to as the "Old Model". It fires a cartridge originally specially-designed by Browning for use in this particular model; the same round is now widely used in numerous other self-loading pistols. The magazine, which fits into the butt, is here shown separately; it will be noted that parts of the zig-zag magazine spring are just visible through the perforations. The pistol is numbered (*not* dated) "1948" and thus must be from one of the very earliest batches produced.

After 10,000 of these arms had been made, subsequent examples had a lanyard ring fitted to the frame. The original design on the butt-plate incorporated a replica of the weapon and the words "F.N."; on later examples the pistol was omitted. This particular specimen has been fitted at some time with non-regulation aluminium grips. In spite of its age, it still works perfectly: it is known to have been carried as a private weapon by a French infantry officer during the Algerian Insurrection of 1954-62. A pistol of this type was used by the student Gavrilo Princip, who assassinated the Archduke Ferdinand and his wife at Sarajevo in June, 1914.

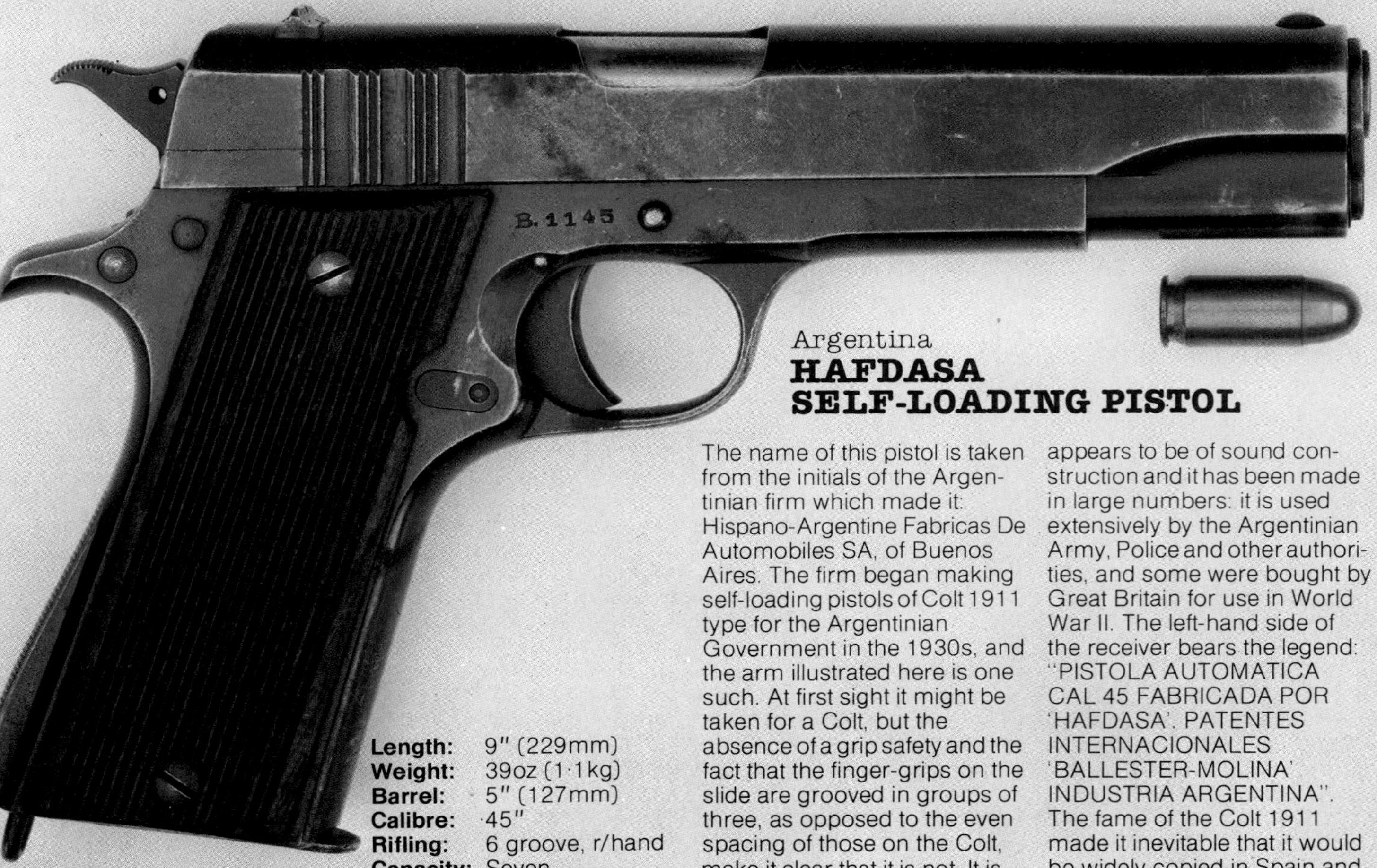

Argentina
HAFDASA
SELF-LOADING PISTOL

Length: 9" (229mm)
Weight: 39oz (1·1kg)
Barrel: 5" (127mm)
Calibre: ·45"
Rifling: 6 groove, r/hand
Capacity: Seven
Muz Vel: c860 f/s (262 m/s)
Sights: Fixed

The name of this pistol is taken from the initials of the Argentinian firm which made it: Hispano-Argentine Fabricas De Automobiles SA, of Buenos Aires. The firm began making self-loading pistols of Colt 1911 type for the Argentinian Government in the 1930s, and the arm illustrated here is one such. At first sight it might be taken for a Colt, but the absence of a grip safety and the fact that the finger-grips on the slide are grooved in groups of three, as opposed to the even spacing of those on the Colt, make it clear that it is not. It is however, mechanically identical to the Colt. The weapon appears to be of sound construction and it has been made in large numbers: it is used extensively by the Argentinian Army, Police and other authorities, and some were bought by Great Britain for use in World War II. The left-hand side of the receiver bears the legend: "PISTOLA AUTOMATICA CAL 45 FABRICADA POR 'HAFDASA'. PATENTES INTERNACIONALES 'BALLESTER-MOLINA' INDUSTRIA ARGENTINA". The fame of the Colt 1911 made it inevitable that it would be widely copied in Spain and elsewhere—and the Hafdasa is one of the better copies.

United States of America
COLT MODEL 1911

Length:	8·5" (216mm)
Weight:	39oz (1·1kg)
Barrel:	5" (127mm)
Calibre:	455"
Rifling:	6 groove, l/hand
Capacity:	Seven
Muz Vel:	c860 f/s (262 m/s)
Sights:	Fixed

Although there was at first little interest in self-loading pistols in the United States, the firm of Colt soon realized that there was to be a future for weapons of the type. By 1898, Colt had produced a prototype which went into limited production as the Model 1900. It was based on the action invented by John M. Browning and was a limited success only. However, the firm persevered and in the next few years produced an entire series of new types which reached culmination in the most famous of all, the Model 1911, a specimen of which is illustrated here. It was designed by Browning, and right from its inception was intended to be a service weapon. The United States Army tested it exhaustively for several years and finally decided on its adoption as the standard service weapon. It is a measure of the US Army's good judgement that the pistol still holds that position at the time of writing, some 70 years later. It has, of course, been to some extent altered and improved, mostly in its earlier years; in 1921, it was redesignated the 1911A1. The example illustrated here was made for use by Canadian forces in World War I, hence its calibre.

United States of America
COLT REMINGTON MODEL 1911A1

Length:	8·5" (216mm)
Weight:	39oz (1·1kg)
Barrel:	5" (127mm)
Calibre:	·45"
Rifling:	6 groove, l/hand
Capacity:	Seven
Muz Vel:	c860 f/s (262 m/s)
Sights:	Fixed

The immediate success of the Model 1911 Colt, followed as it was by World War I, led to an enormous demand for the weapon. As a result, Colt sub-contracted to several other American arms companies of good repute. The pistol illustrated here was made by Remington for use by United States forces during World War II. It is the Model 1911A1, and thus incorporates various improvements over the original Model 1911 Colt, including a longer horn on the grip safety; a slightly shorter hammer; and the chamfering away of arc-shaped grooves behind the trigger—as well as internal differences. But in spite of these, it remains fundamentally the same arm. It consists of three main parts: the receiver; the barrel; and the slide, which works on ribs machined on to the receiver. When the slide is fully forward, the barrel is locked to it by means of lugs on the barrel's upper surface, which engage in slots in the slide. When the slide is forced to the rear—either manually for initial loading or by the cartridges after the first shot—the barrel moves only a very short distance before its rear end drops, disengaging it from the slide which thereafter continues to the rear.

163

Soviet Union
TULA-TOKAREV 1930

Length: 7·7" (196mm)
Weight: 29oz (·82kg)
Barrel: 4·6" (117mm)
Calibre: 9mm
Rifling: 4 groove, l/hand
Capacity: Eight
Muz Vel: c1350 f/s (411 m/s)
Sights: Fixed

This official Russian Government pistol takes the first part of its designation from the state arsenal where it was made and the second part from Feodor Tokarev, a well-known Russian designer from the 1920s onward. It is mechanically a copy of various Colt-Browning types, with one or two modifications to simplify production, and one or two actual improvements in design. In the original version, the barrel locking lugs were machined on to the barrel's upper surface, but for ease of manufacture the lugs were replaced in 1933 by bands which went completely round the barrel. This involved no mechanical changes. On a pistol of this type, the magazine has no lips, a cartridge guide being incorporated into the frame. This is an improvement, for the thin metal of a magazine can become distorted relatively easily. At first sight, it might be thought that this weapon is of hammerless type; in fact, much of the hammer is concealed within the frame: only the cogwheel-type hammer-comb is visible above it, just behind the backsight. Another improvement incorporated in this model is that the entire lock mechanism may be easily removed, greatly facilitating maintenance. There is no safety catch, but the hammer may be placed at half-cock.

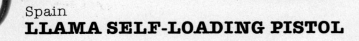

Spain
LLAMA SELF-LOADING PISTOL

Length: 9·5" (241mm)
Weight: 40oz (1·13kg)
Barrel: 5" (127mm)
Calibre: 9mm
Rifling: 6 groove, l/hand
Capacity: Seven
Muz Vel: c850 f/s (259 m/s)
Sights: Fixed

The great success and wide acceptance of the Colt Model 1911 self-loading pistol and its successive variations made it inevitable that the arm should become the subject of extensive copying. In this field, Spanish manufacturers were particularly active. The Spanish firm of Gabilondo y Urresti was originally formed at Guernica in 1904. After the end of World War I, the firm moved to Elgoibar, near Eibar, and began to make pistols under the name of Gabilondo y Cia. In 1931, the firm began to manufacture a new range of Colt-type pistols under the general trade name of "Llama", and these arms have continued in production until the present day. They are, in general, very well-made and reliable weapons and sell in considerable quantities. They have been produced in a wide variety of models and calibres — some of blowback type, some with locked breeches, and yet others with grip safeties — so that individual models are not always easy to identify. The pistol illustrated here appears to be a model produced in c1939. Its general style, which very closely resembles that of the Colt, is clear from the photograph. It is designed to fire the ·38in Colt Super cartridge — a very powerful round, and one which, of course, necessitates a locked breech. This pistol has no grip safety but is fitted with an orthodox safety catch on the left, below the hammer.

Poland
RADOM VIS-35

Length: 8·3" (211mm)
Weight: 37oz (1·05kg)
Barrel: 4·5" (114mm)
Calibre: 9mm
Rifling: 6 groove, r/hand
Capacity: Eight
Muz Vel: c1150 f/s (351 m/s)
Sights: Fixed

The Radom Arms Factory of Poland was set up soon after the end of World War I. It was initially intended principally for the production of military rifles, a few revolvers also being being made, but soon after 1930 it was decided that the Polish Army required a self-loading pistol. After the consideration of various designs, an indigenous model was finally adopted, and by 1935 the VIS, illustrated here, was in extensive production. Like most later self-loading pistols, it is based more or less closely on the basic designs of the American John M. Browning, with some relatively minor changes either for ease of manufacture or in the shape of actual improvements incorporated in the light of experience. The pistol works in the orthodox way: lugs on the upper surface of the barrel engage corresponding slots in the slide when it is locked; the barrel recoils briefly and then drops to disengage when the slide is either drawn to the rear manually or blown back by the gases produced by the explosion of the cartridge. As may be seen, the weapon has a grip safety at the rear of the butt. No manual safety as such as fitted, but the arm incorporates a device for retracting the firing pin, and this allows it to be carried safely with a round in the chamber and the hammer down. This device is activated by the lever below the back-sight; the action of cocking the hammer manually returns the firing pin to its proper position. The markings on the left side of the slide, including the Polish eagle, are clearly visible.

Spain
ECHEVERRIA STAR MODEL B

Length: 8" (203mm)
Weight: 34oz (·96kg)
Barrel: 5" (127mm)
Calibre: 9mm
Rifling: 4 groove, r/hand
Capacity: Eight
Muz Vel: c1100 f/s (335 m/s)
Sights: Fixed

This arm is another of the Spanish self-loading pistols based more or less closely on the Colt Model 1911 and its variants. The firm of Echeverria came into existence in about 1908 in Eibar, and although its later history is somewhat obscure, it appears to have been making self-loading pistols of one kind or another ever since. It has also made submachine guns of various types from time to time. The trade name of "Star" was adopted in 1919 and has been in use ever since on a quite bewildering variety of pistols of various types, sizes, calibres and systems of numbering and classification. The pistol illustrated here is a Star Model B, introduced in about 1928. It is fairly closely based on the Colt, but lacks the grip safety peculiar to that arm. It is a robust and well-made weapon, and since it is chambered for the powerful 9mm Parabellum cartridge it necessarily fires from a locked breech. This works on the well-known Browning principle: after a brief period of recoil, the rear end of the barrel drops, thus unlocking itself from the interior of the slide, which continues to the rear and cocks the hammer. Having done so, it comes forward, chambers the next cartridge, and relocks the breech in readiness for the next shot. This pistol is currently used by the Spanish armed forces.

LUGER PARABELLUM MODEL 1908 (P08)

Length:	8·75" (222mm)
Weight:	30oz (·85kg)
Barrel:	4" (102mm)
Calibre:	9mm
Rifling:	8 groove, r/hand
Capacity:	Eight
Muz Vel:	c1150 f/s (351 m/s)
Sights:	Fixed

The Luger pistol was the logical successor to the original Borchardt (which is described on page 150-151, below). It was basically similar to the Borchardt, the design having been modified and improved by Georg Luger, and was put on to the market at the very end of the 19th century. The manufacturer concerned was the Deutsche Waffen und Munitionsfabrik (usually abbreviated to DWM) of Berlin. After several earlier models, there appeared the pistol illustrated here. It was put into production in 1908 and was almost immediately adopted by the German Army, which was then seeking for a new self-loader to replace its earlier revolver. Of course, this assured the arm's success, as many smaller countries followed Germany's lead and purchased large numbers of Lugers for their armed forces. It served the Germans well during World War I and, like the Mauser, became something of a household word, establishing a popular reputation which is, perhaps, greater than its real merit. After World War I, its manufacture was taken over by Mauser, who continued to make both military and civilian models. This particular example is one of those made by Mauser and is dated "1940". In 1938 the German Army adopted the Walther P38 (facing page, above), but Lugers were in production until 1943.

ČESKÁ ZBROJOVKA MODEL 39

Length:	8·1" (206mm)
Weight:	33oz (·94kg)
Barrel:	4·65" (118mm)
Calibre:	9mm
Rifling:	6 groove, r/hand
Capacity:	Eight
Muz Vel:	c950 f/s (290 m/s)
Sights:	Fixed

An arms manufactory was established at Pilsen in Czechoslovakia, then a newly-founded country, in 1919, and moved to Strakonitz in 1921. It made a wide variety of weapons and accessories for the Czech Army. After World War II, the Ceská Zbrojovka company, like Czechoslovakia itself, came under Communist control; its weapon production was then greatly reduced in favour of other items. Between the two World Wars, however, the company made a whole series of pistols, both small-calibred pocket types for sale commercially and arms of somewhat heavier calibres for military use. The earliest of these fired from a locked breech, but as the short cartridge employed hardly warranted the use of this system, subsequent models reverted to simple blowback. The Ceská Zbrojovka Model 39 pistol illustrated here is very well made and finished, but it was not a success as a military arm. In spite of its weight and bulk, it fires only a low-powered round, and its exposed hammer cannot be cocked: the arm must be fired by a quite heavy pull on the trigger, and this, of course, hardly contributes to its accuracy. It is very easy to strip: forward pressure on a milled catch on the left of the frame allows the slide and barrel to be raised on a rear hinge.

Germany
WALTHER P38

Length: 8·4" (213mm)
Weight: 34oz (·96kg)
Barrel: 5" (127mm)
Calibre: 9mm
Rifling: 6 groove, r/hand
Capacity: Eight
Muz Vel: c1150 f/s (351 m/s)
Sights: Fixed

In the early 1930s, the Carl Walther Waffenfabrik developed two prototype military self-loading pistols, the Models AP and HP. The AP was of hammerless type and the HP had an external hammer; and since the latter arrangement was considered preferable by the German military authorities, the final model was thus equipped. The new arm was easier to manufacture than the Luger 08 (see facing page, above), and by 1943 the P38 had largely superseded the older weapon—although the Luger was still in extensive use at the end of World War II. The type of cartridge used in the P38 made it necessary to employ a locked breech. The lower part of the barrel incorporates a separate locking block, the lugs of which engage in recesses in the slide when the pistol is ready to be fired. When a cartridge is fired, the barrel and slide recoil briefly together, until the lugs are carried out of the slide; then the barrel stops, allowing the slide to continue to the rear to cock the hammer. The slide then travels forward under the pressure of the recoil spring, to continue the cycle by pushing another cartridge into the chamber. The only actions necessary to fire the loaded pistol, therefore, are to push up the safety catch with the thumb to the "fire" position (the position which is shown in the photograph) and then press the trigger.

Germany
LUGER 08/20

Length: 8·75" (222mm)
Weight: 30oz (·85kg)
Barrel: 3·75" (95mm)
Calibre: 7·65mm
Rifling: 8 groove, r/hand
Capacity: Eight
Muz Vel: c1150 f/s (351 m/s)
Sights: Fixed

The aftermath of World War I saw Germany largely disarmed; only a few troops and police were retained for internal security and border patrol duties. Severe restrictions were also imposed on Germany's production of firearms and military equipment of all kinds. However, some degree of manufacture for export was later permitted, and since vast stocks of components were still hidden away in various places a good deal of cannibalization went on, while many salvaged weapons were also reconditioned and found their way on to the world markets. The original title of "Parabellum" for DWM's Model 1908 had by then largely given way to that of "Luger". The demand for this arm was considerable—partly for use and partly because it was a popular souvenir. The pistol illustrated here appears to be one of the post-1918 arms put together by DWM, whose monogram appears on the toggle joint. One way of circum-venting the restrictions imposed by the Treaty of Versailles, which laid down that all weapons made must be of less than 9mm calibre, was to bore 9mm barrel blanks for smaller-calibre rounds. Another was to make the barrels marginally shorter than the maximum of 4in (102mm) specified by the Treaty. Both are used here.

HARRINGTON AND RICHARDSON ·32in

Length:	6·5" (165mm)
Weight:	20oz (·57kg)
Barrel:	3·5" (89mm)
Calibre:	32"
Rifling:	6 groove, r/hand
Capacity:	Six
Muz Vel:	980 f/s (299 m/s)
Sights:	Fixed

The firm of Harrington and Richardson was set up at Worcester, Massachusetts, in 1874 to make revolvers. It has remained in production ever since, and characteristic examples of its earlier arms are illustrated in the section of this book devoted to cartridge revolvers. The company does not appear to have been very interested in self-loading pistols, probably because the revolver long retained its dominance in the United States, but in 1910 it began to manufacture a small self-loader based on a weapon produced by the British firm of Webley and Scott (an example of this pistol is illustrated below). Two or three years later, Harrington and Richardson also put into production a slightly larger self-loading model, illustrated here; this fairly closely resembled the ·32in Webley and Scott pistol illustrated on the facing page (above), although it was by no means an exact copy of it. Its principal external difference is that it lacks the characteristic hammer of the Webley pistol. The slide, too, is of different shape: it has an open top, whereas the Webley's slide has no more than an aperture of sufficient size to allow the empty cases to be ejected. A third difference is the existence on this arm of a grip safety, in addition to an orthodox safety catch. Internally, the weapon is of simple blowback design, but the recoil spring is of the coiled type, while the Webley has a V-spring under the butt plate. The right-hand side of pistol bears the name and address of the company, together with indication that it is made in accordance with patents of 20 August 1907 and 18 April and 9 November 1909. It is, perhaps, not surprising that this particular arm never achieved any real popularity in the United States, where many similar weapons were available. Even so, manufacture continued into the 1920s.

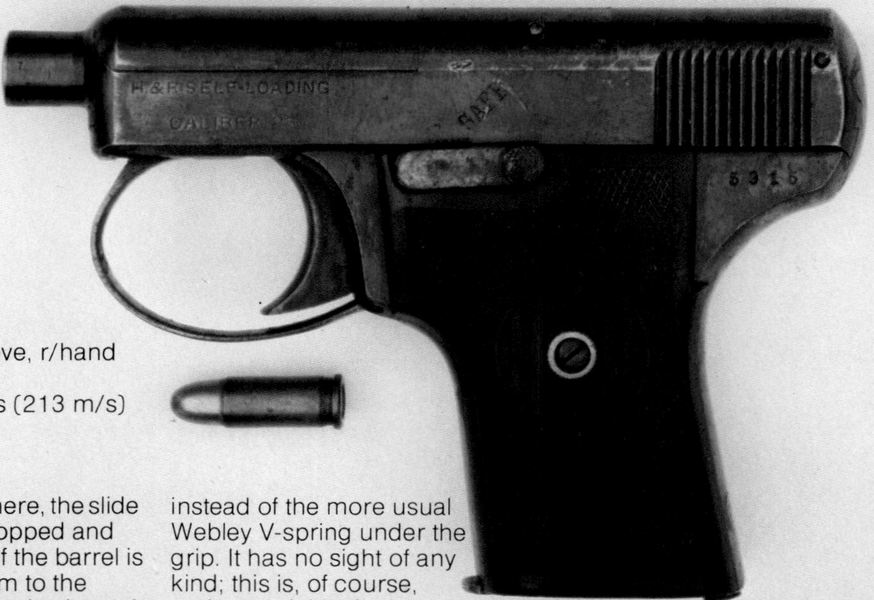

HARRINGTON AND RICHARDSON ·25in

Length:	4·5" (114mm)	**Rifling:**	6 groove, r/hand
Weight:	12·25oz (·35kg)	**Capacity:**	Six
Barrel:	2·1" (53mm)	**Muz Vel:**	700 f/s (213 m/s)
Calibre:	·25"	**Sights:**	Nil

This particular arm was first produced by Webley and Scott in 1909, and was made in the United States by Harrington and Richardson under agreement with the British firm. One of the Webley versions with an external hammer is shown on the facing page (below), and the basic similarity is at once apparent. There were, however, some differences. The Webley arm had a full slide with only an aperture for extraction, whereas, in the pistol seen here, the slide is partially open-topped and the rear section of the barrel is built up to conform to the general shape. The horizontal joint just above the inscription on the slide can be clearly seen; the vertical joint is almost immediately above the front end of the safety catch. Unlike its Webley prototype, however, the US version utilises two parallel coil springs, one on either side of the firing-pin, instead of the more usual Webley V-spring under the grip. It has no sight of any kind; this is, of course, understandable, for it is a low-powered pocket arm. It did not prove popular in the United States and was not manufactured after 1914. The left side of the slide is marked "H & R SELF-LOADING", with the calibre. The right side carries details of the company and patent dates.

Great Britain
WEBLEY AND SCOTT ·32in

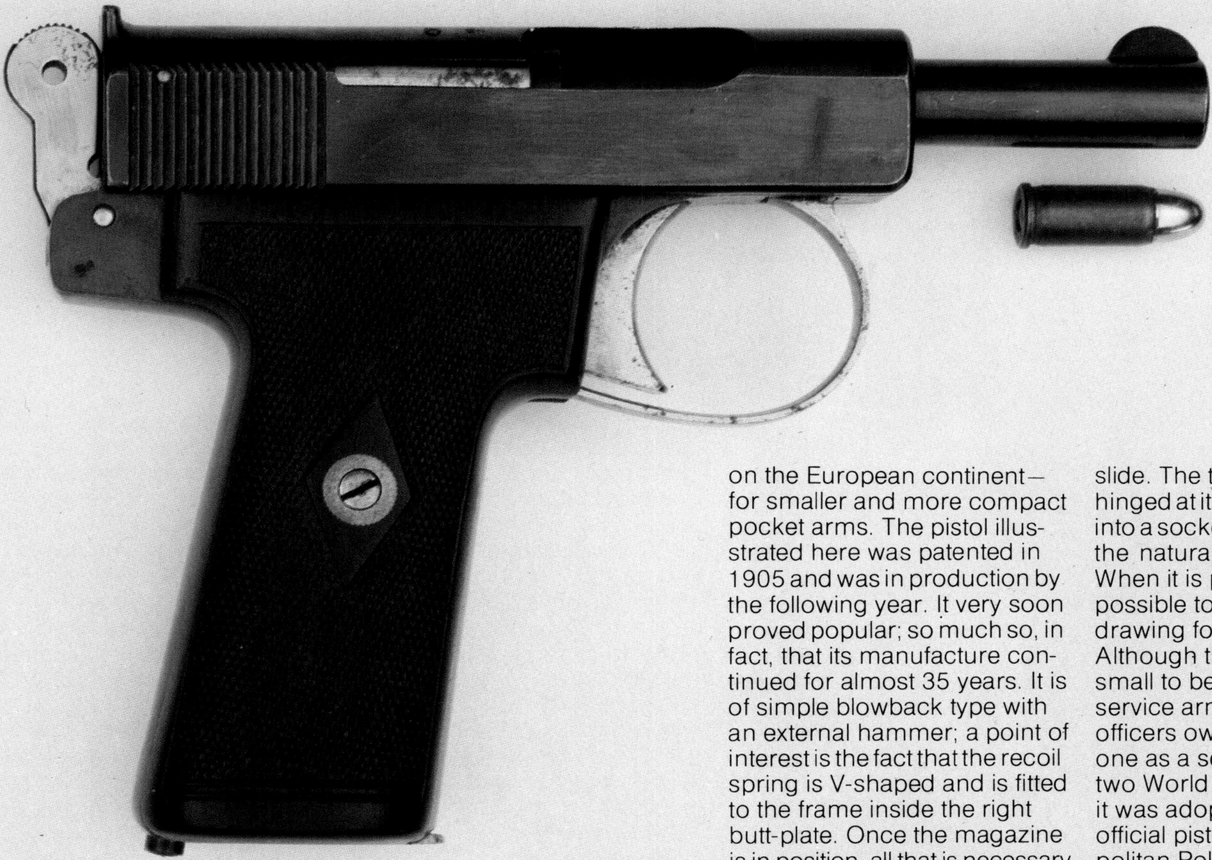

Length:	6·25" (159mm)
Weight:	20oz (·57kg)
Barrel:	3·5" (89mm)
Calibre:	·32"
Rifling:	7 groove, r/hand
Capacity:	Eight
Muz Vel:	c900 f/s (274 m/s)
Sights:	Fixed

A number of Webley and Scott's earlier self-loading pistols have already been discussed (on pages 156-157). These were, in general, heavy-calibre weapons of service type, but there also appeared to be a demand—particularly, perhaps, on the European continent—for smaller and more compact pocket arms. The pistol illustrated here was patented in 1905 and was in production by the following year. It very soon proved popular; so much so, in fact, that its manufacture continued for almost 35 years. It is of simple blowback type with an external hammer; a point of interest is the fact that the recoil spring is V-shaped and is fitted to the frame inside the right butt-plate. Once the magazine is in position, all that is necessary is to pull back the slide by means of the ribbed finger-pieces, push up the safety catch, and fire. The original model had a safety on the left side of the hammer, but most of these pistols, including the one shown here, have the safety situated on the left side of the frame, where it also locks the slide. The trigger-guard is hinged at its top end and is held into a socket at its lower end by the natural spring of its metal. When it is pulled clear, it is possible to strip the pistol by drawing forward the slide. Although this pistol was too small to be considered as a service arm, a good many officers owned and carried one as a secondary arm in the two World Wars. In addition, it was adopted in 1911 as the official pistol of the Metropolitan Police of London: this particular specimen was a police arm, for it is marked with a crown and the letters "MP". Although it is of convenient dimensions to carry concealed, it lacked real stopping-power. For this reason, it was later supplanted in Metropolitan Police service by the revolver concurrently in use.

Great Britain
WEBLEY AND SCOTT ·25in

Length:	4·5" (114mm)	Rifling:	7 groove, r/hand
Weight:	12oz (·34kg)	Capacity:	Six
Barrel:	2" (51mm)	Muz Vel:	750 f/s (229 m/s)
Calibre:	·25"	Sights:	Nil

The Webley and Scott pistol of ·32in calibre described above was closely followed in the same year by an even smaller version of the same type. Since laws for the control of firearms hardly existed in 1906, there appears to have been a very large market for pocket arms of this type. There were, however, numerous makers in Belgium, Germany and elsewhere who were turning out such weapons at competitive prices; thus, it was necessary for the British company to produce its version as cheaply as possible. As is apparent, this pistol is essentially a scaled-down version of the ·32in model. It is well and simply made. Because it is of small calibre and fires a low-powered cartridge, it is of simple blowback design. The main point of difference between this and other Webley self-loaders is that the V-spring under the grip is replaced by two coil springs in the slide, one on either side of the firing-pin. It is fitted with a safety catch and bears the usual Webley markings. It is strictly a pocket pistol, designed to fit into a waistcoat pocket or a lady's handbag, and lacks power and accuracy—although it would have been effective enough at close quarters. The model seen here was followed in 1909 by a hammer-less version.

Italy
BERETTA MODEL 1934

Length:	6" (152mm)
Weight:	23oz (·65kg)
Barrel:	3·75" (95mm)
Calibre:	9mm
Rifling:	4 groove, r/hand
Capacity:	Nine
Muz Vel:	c750 f/s (229 m/s)
Sights:	Fixed

The Beretta company of Brescia has now been in existence for 300 years, during which time it has established a very well-deserved reputation for the excellence of its products. It originally confined its activities to sporting guns and rifles: it was not until the early years of World War I that the company of necessity turned to the manufacture of military weapons of all kinds, including self-loading pistols. The first Beretta self-loader, the Model 1915, was of wartime quality and was designed to take a 7·65mm cartridge; this was soon replaced by a version in 9mm calibre, which was considered more suitable for service use. Development continued after World War I, with a steady improvement in design until 1934, when the weapon illustrated here appeared. Like its predecessors, the Model 1934 works by simple blowback action: thus, although it is of 9mm calibre, it fires a short cartridge in order to keep the gas pressure within safe limits. As may be seen, it has an external hammer: this may be cocked either by the rearward movement of the slide, or manually, and it has a half-cock position. Most examples of the Model 1934 were fitted with a curved lower extension to the magazine (see the arm illustrated below), so as to ensure a firm grip for a user with a large hand, but some (like the example seen here) were fitted with plain magazines. This arm became the standard Italian service pistol in 1935: this particular example is marked with the letters "RE" surmounted by a crown, indicating that it is a military model. During the course of World War II, many British officers acquired Beretta pistols of this model in the expectation that they would be able to fire standard 9mm Parabellum Sten-gun ammunition through them, but they found that this ammunition would not fit the pistol, which takes a 9mm Short cartridge.

Italy
BERETTA MODEL 1935

Length:	6" (152mm)
Weight:	23oz (·65kg)
Barrel:	3·75" (95mm)
Calibre:	7·65mm
Rifling:	4 groove, r/hand
Capacity:	Seven
Muz Vel:	c800 f/s (244 m/s)
Sights:	Fixed

Details of the origin and history of Beretta self-loading pistols are given in the caption above, and need not be repeated here. The Model 1934, illustrated above, was so successful that in the following year the Beretta company produced the Model 1935. It was very similar in all essentials to the earlier weapon, but was of the smaller calibre of 7·65mm. The specimen illustrated is fitted with a spur-shaped extension below the magazine to offer added support for the little finger of the firer's hand. Like the Model 1934, it has a safety catch on the left side of the frame and is usually fitted with a loop for a lanyard on the lower part of the butt. The Model 1935 was extensively issued to the Italian Navy and Air Force and was also used by the Italian police: the specimen illustrated bears the initials "PS" (*Publica Sicurreza*), indicating that it is a police weapon. Like most Berettas of the period, this arm bears details of the calibre on the left side of the slide, which is also dated "1941"; the date is followed by the Roman numerals "XIX", its date in the Fascist Calendar of 1922.

Length:	6·5" (165mm)
Weight:	21oz (·6kg)
Barrel:	3·5" (89mm)
Calibre:	38"
Rifling:	7 groove, r/hand
Capacity:	Seven
Muz Vel:	c900 f/s (274 m/s)
Sights:	Fixed

The Remington Arms Company was founded by Eliphalet Remington in 1816 and thereafter produced a considerable range of rifles, revolvers, pistols and shotguns. Some of its earlier hand guns are described in the sections of this book devoted to percussion revolvers and cartridge revolvers. Remington's first entry into the field of self-loading pistols occurred in 1917, when the company received a contract to manufacture Model 1911 Colts, but this contract was terminated in 1918, at the end of World War I. However, the company had plans for a self-loading pistol of its own, based on the designs of J. D. Pedersen, a well-known and well-respected figure in the world of small arms. This weapon appeared on the market in 1919 as the Model 51. It was made in two calibres—·38in Auto (the arm illustrated here) and, in much smaller numbers, in ·32in. The mechanism is of the type known as delayed blowback. When the cartridge is fired, the slide and its internal breech-block recoil briefly together; the block then stops, allowing the slide to continue to the rear, but after a brief pause the block is released and rejoins the slide. Both then come forward under the influence of the recoil spring, which is fitted round the fixed barrel. The weapon is fited with a grip safety (visible at the back of the butt) and also has a normal safety at the rear left end of the frame. The top of the slide, which is milled to reduce glare, bears the inscription "REMING-TON ARMS UNION METALLIC CARTRIDGE CO INC", with "REMINGTON ILION WKS ILION N.Y. USA, PEDERSENS PATENTS PENDING" beneath it. The Remington Model 51 was an excellent weapon but, because it was expensive to produce—and thus had to be priced accordingly—it never gained the popularity it deserved.

France
MAB MODEL D

Length:	5·8" (147mm)
Weight:	26oz (·74kg)
Barrel:	3·2" (81mm)
Calibre:	7·65mm
Rifling:	7 groove, r/hand
Capacity:	Nine
Muz Vel:	c800 f/s (244 m/s)
Sights:	Fixed

The initials MAB stand for the Manufacture d'Armes de Bayonne, a company which, since 1921, has been chiefly concerned with the manufacture of self-loading pistols of pocket type. The company's products are well made, but most of them are based on the designs of others: the weapon illustrated here, for example, bears a considerable resemblance to the Browning. It was first put on the market in 1933 as the Model C but, enlarged and with a better-shaped butt, reappeared as the Model D—under which designation it is still in production. It is of simple blowback design: when the cartridge is fired, the slide and block are forced to the rear, compressing the coil spring which is located round the barrel. The subsequent forward movement strips a round from the magazine and chambers it ready for the next shot. Access to the recoil spring is obtained by pressing up the rear end of the small bar visible under the muzzle: the nose cap can then be turned and removed, taking the spring with it.

United States of America
SAVAGE MODEL 1907

Length:	6·5" (165mm)	**Rifling:**	6 groove, r/hand
Weight:	20oz (·57kg)	**Capacity:**	Ten
Barrel:	3·75" (95mm)	**Muz Vel:**	c800 f/s (244 m/s)
Calibre:	·32"	**Sights:**	Fixed

The Savage Arms Company was established in 1894 and was principally concerned with the manufacture of good-quality sporting rifles, for which it is still famous. It first produced a self-loading pistol—the arm illustrated here—in 1907, although it is not possible to establish the identity of the weapon's inventor. The Savage Model 1907 pistol is of unusual and interesting design, and it was the subject of a great deal of controversy when it first appeared. The theory of its mechanism is as follows. The slide covers the entire top of the weapon, including the barrel proper (the muzzle of the barrel can just be seen in the photograph). The pistol is loaded in the orthodox way and the slide is pulled back and released to feed the first round into the chamber. A lug on top of the barrel fits into a curved slot on the top of the slide: when the cartridge is fired, the rearward movement of the barrel and slide is briefly checked by the cam, but the barrel overcomes this by twisting slightly until the lug reaches a straight stretch of groove, when the slide is again free to move to the rear. The theory of this arrangement is that the counter-rotation of the bullet in the rifling is sufficient to prevent the barrel from twisting until the bullet has actually left it; at which juncture, of course, the pressure drops instantly. However, this theory has been disputed. The pistol has a safety catch on the left side, just below the serrated cocking piece (visible near the rear end of the slide). The top of the slide is marked "SAVAGE ARMS CO UTICA USA CAL 32", with "PATENTED NOVEMBER 21 9015 — 7·65mm" below.

Czechoslovakia
ČESKÁ ZBROJOVKA MODEL 1924

Length:	6·25" (159mm)	**Rifling:**	6 groove, r/hand
Weight:	24oz (·68kg)	**Capacity:**	Eight
Barrel:	3·5" (89mm)	**Muz Vel:**	c800 f/s (244 m/s)
Calibre:	7·65mm	**Sights:**	Fixed

The pistol illustrated here is the product of a Czechoslovakian manufactory already described (see page 166, below). This arm was developed after World War I and went into production in 1924, principally as a military pistol. At the moment of firing, the barrel and slide are locked. As the slide moves to the rear, it causes the barrel to rotate slightly and to unlock itself, thus allowing the reloading cycle to be completed in the orthodox way. It has an external hammer, the tip of which is just visible, and a safety catch is fitted on the left side of the frame. (This is the small, milled catch visible in the photograph; it is released by pressing the circular stud immediately below it.) The last two digits of the year of manufacture are visible below the sloped ribbing at the rear end of the slide.

Spain
UNCETA VICTORIA

Length: 5·75" (146mm)
Weight: 20oz (·57kg)
Barrel: 3·2" (81mm)
Calibre: 7·65mm
Rifling: 7 groove, r/hand
Capacity: Seven
Muz Vel: c750 f/s (229 m/s)
Sights: Fixed

The arm illustrated here is an example of a fairly cheap, Spanish-made, self-loading pistol. The firm of Unceta y Esperanza was first set up in Eibar in 1908 with the intention of turning out pistols which, although reasonably inexpensive, were to be of good quality — a condition which has been achieved very consistently ever since. This particular specimen is an example of the first pistol of the type made by the firm under the trade name "Victoria" or 1911 Model; a virtually identical type was also produced in 6·35mm calibre. It is a close copy of the 1903 Browning and works on simple blowback, the recoil spring being housed round a rod below the barrel.

When the safety catch, located on the left-hand side of the frame, located on the left-hand side of the frame, is set at "safe", it engages a notch almost in the exact centre of the frame. If the slide is drawn to the rear with the catch still at "safe", a second notch about 30mm (1·2in) farther forward engages the safety and holds the slide to the rear; the barrel may then be removed by rotating it and drawing it forward. The left side of the frame is marked "7.65 1911 MODEL AUTOMATIC PISTOL VICTORIA PATENT" and "MADE IN SPAIN", while the vulcanite grip bears the word "VICTORIA" and the letters "EUC" intertwined. The pistol gained wide acceptance and the company went from strength to strength. It adopted the trade name "Astra" in 1914, but it has also made a variety of pistols under an equal variety of other names. Between the two World Wars, Unceta was one of the companies which took advantage of the serious restrictions imposed on German armaments firms to manufacture a close copy of the Mauser Model 1896; the Spanish arm sold quite well in South America and elsewhere. A good many Spanish armaments companies were closed down after the end of the Spanish Civil War in 1939, but Unceta survived and is still producing weapons, including considerable numbers of arms made for export.

Spain
GABILONDO RUBY

Length: 6" (152mm)
Weight: 30oz (·85kg)
Barrel: 3·4" (86mm)
Calibre: 7·65mm
Rifling: 7 groove, r/hand
Capacity: Nine
Muz Vel: c800 f/s (244 m/s)
Sights: Fixed

The Spanish firm of Gabilondo y Urresti was originally formed in 1904 in Guernica in order to make cheap revolvers, but a small self-loading pistol was soon included in its range of products. In 1914 the firm began to manufacture a pistol of the type shown here under the trade name of "Ruby". It was not a particularly distinguished weapon in any sense of the word, but it appeared on the market at a time when many countries urgently needed arms; thus, a contract for a large number was soon placed by the French Government. The demand was, in fact, so large that Gabilondo was soon forced to put the manufacture of these arms out to sub-contractors. The model was discontinued in 1919, although a smaller version in 6·35mm calibre continued in production under the same name for several years.

Germany
WALTHER PPK

Length:	5·8″ (147mm)
Weight:	20oz (·57kg)
Barrel:	3·15″ (80mm)
Calibre:	7·65mm
Rifling:	6 groove, r/hand
Capacity:	Seven
Muz Vel:	c1000 f/s (305 m/s)
Sights:	Fixed

The famous German firm known as the Carl Walther Waffenfabrik was established in 1886, but it did not begin to make self-loading pistols until 1908. Its first nine models were numbered, but in 1929 it produced a tenth model designed speci- fically for police work, and this was designated the *Polizei Pistole* or "PP". This weapon (an example is illustrated on the facing page, below) was immediately popular, and two years later a smaller version was made for concealed use. It was intended for plain-clothes police work and was known as the "PPK" (the "K" standing, it is said, for *Kriminal*). The Walther PPK pistol, illustrated here, is of blowback type and it has several interesting and important features. The most notable, perhaps, is that it is provided with an external hammer activated by a double-action lock; this allows the pistol to be carried safely with a round in the chamber and the hammer down. Thus, all that is necessary to bring it into action is to push off the safety catch and press the trigger. It also has an indicator pin which protrudes through the top of the slide when there is a cartridge in the chamber—a very useful feature in any self-loading pistol, where the rounds cannot be seen as they can in a revolver. The earliest versions of this pistol had complete butt-frames with a pair of grips, but later examples had a front strap only, with a one-piece, moulded, wrap-round, plastic grip. Most also had a plastic extension on the bottom of the magazine, to increase the area of grip.

Length:	6·75″ (171mm)
Weight:	25oz (·71kg)
Barrel:	3·25″ (83mm)
Calibre:	7·65mm
Rifling:	4 groove, r/hand
Capacity:	Eight
Muz Vel:	c900 f/s (274 m/s)
Sights:	Fixed

Germany
SAUER MODEL 38H

The German firm of J. P. Sauer & Sohn is an old one, with a reputation for producing high-quality weapons. At first, its products were mainly sporting guns and rifles, but the company began to make self-loading pistols in 1913 and continued to do so until after World War II, when it turned to revolvers. The weapon illustrated here is one of Sauer's best products. It was first put on the market in 1938 (hence its Model number), but the outbreak of war soon afterwards restricted its use to German forces—and for some reason manufacture was not resumed afterwards. It works on the blowback principle, having a fixed barrel and an overall slide with the breech-block inside it. It has an internal hammer (hence the "H"—for *Hahn*, hammer— in the Model designation). The first round is chambered in the usual way by the manual operation of the slide, which also cocks the hammer, but thereafter there are various options. If required, the hammer may be lowered by pressing the trigger, with the thumb on the milled catch behind it, and allowing the catch to rise slowly. To fire after this procedure, the pistol can either be cocked by depressing the catch with the thumb, or fired double-action by pressing the trigger.

Hungary
FEGYVERGYAR MODEL 1937

Length:	7·2" (183mm)	Rifling:	6 groove, r/hand
Weight:	27oz (·76kg)	Capacity:	Seven
Barrel:	4·33" (110mm)	Muz Vel:	c900 f/s (274 m/s)
Calibre:	9mm	Sights:	Fixed

The Hungarian firm of Fegyvergyar (Fegyver es Gepgyar Reszvenytarsasag) was established at Budapest in the 19th century and established a reputation for producing good-quality weapons. Its first self-loading pistol appeared in 1903, and there was a variety of later models, including a Hungarian Army pistol. The arm illustrated here, the Model 1937, was the last of the series. It is of blow-back type with a fixed barrel and an overall slide; the recoil spring is situated on a rod below the barrel. The first round is chambered in the normal way by the manual operation of the slide, which also cocks the external hammer. There is a spur on the magazine to extend the butt length. The original version was of 9mm calibre and fired a short cartridge suitable for a blowback pistol; its only safety device was its grip safety. In 1941, however, Germany took out a contract for a 7·65mm version and, apart from the first few made, these were all fitted with a safety catch of orthodox type on the left side of the frame. In this series, the original manufacturer's details on the slide were changed: the new markings were simply "P MOD 37 Kal 7·65". together with the manufacturer's code of "h.v." and the last two digits of the year of manufacture, which was 1943.

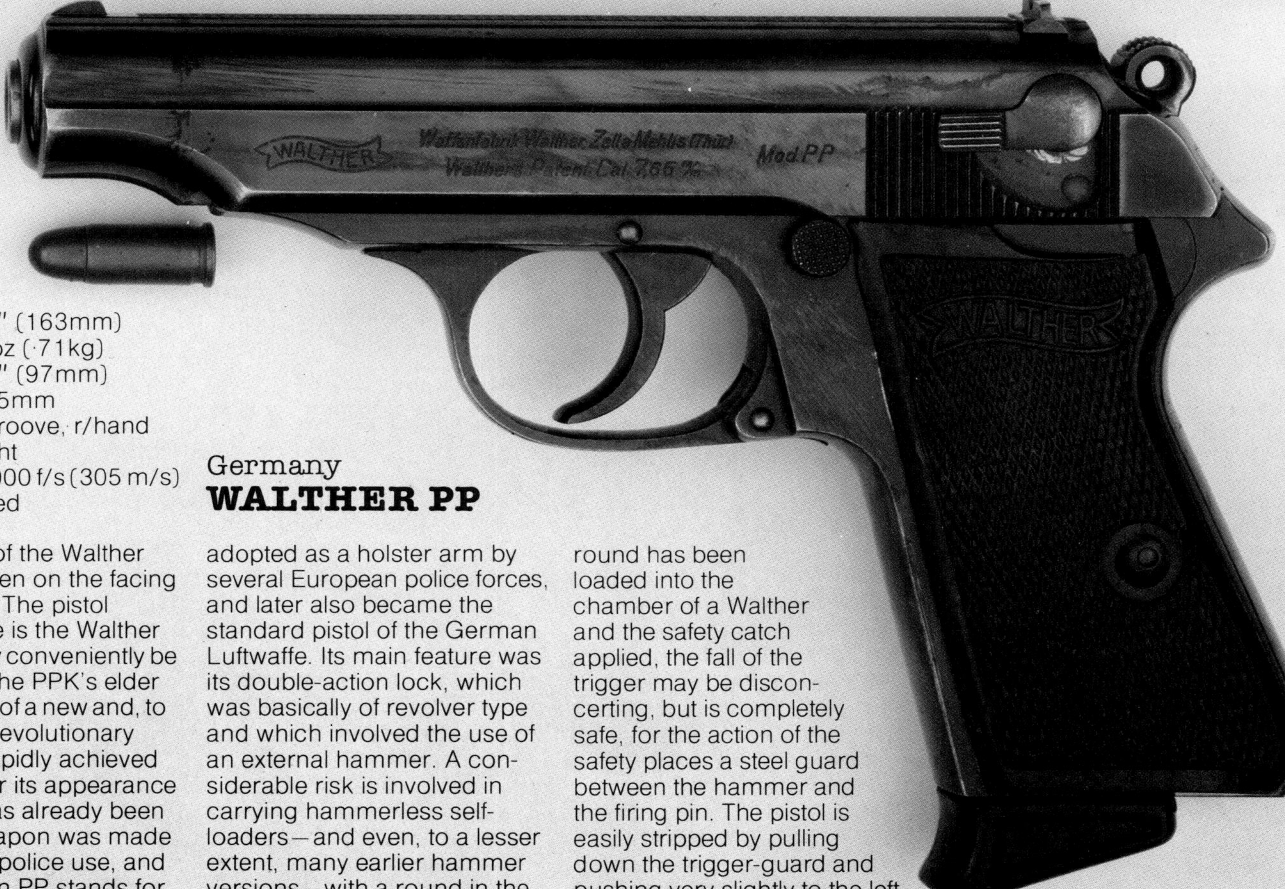

Length:	6·4" (163mm)
Weight:	25oz (·71kg)
Barrel:	3·8" (97mm)
Calibre:	7·65mm
Rifling:	6 groove, r/hand
Capacity:	Eight
Muz Vel:	c1000 f/s (305 m/s)
Sights:	Fixed

Germany
WALTHER PP

Some details of the Walther factory are given on the facing page (above). The pistol illustrated here is the Walther PP, which may conveniently be described as the PPK's elder brother. It was of a new and, to some extent, revolutionary design, and rapidly achieved popularity after its appearance in 1929. As has already been stated, the weapon was made principally for police use, and the designation PP stands for *Polizei Pistole*. It was very soon adopted as a holster arm by several European police forces, and later also became the standard pistol of the German Luftwaffe. Its main feature was its double-action lock, which was basically of revolver type and which involved the use of an external hammer. A considerable risk is involved in carrying hammerless self-loaders—and even, to a lesser extent, many earlier hammer versions—with a round in the chamber. However, when a round has been loaded into the chamber of a Walther and the safety catch applied, the fall of the trigger may be disconcerting, but is completely safe, for the action of the safety places a steel guard between the hammer and the firing pin. The pistol is easily stripped by pulling down the trigger-guard and pushing very slightly to the left, after which the slide is eased off.

France
LE FRANÇAIS MODEL 28

Length:	7·9" (201mm)
Weight:	35oz (·99kg)
Barrel:	5" (127mm)
Calibre:	9mm
Rifling:	6 groove, r/hand
Capacity:	Eight
Muz Vel:	c1100 f/s (335 m/s)
Sights:	Fixed

The Manufacture Française d'Armes et Cycles de St Etienne has a history stretching back to the mid-19th century, but it only began to make self-loading pistols just before the outbreak of the World War I. These arms were all of similar design and of broadly similar type: small-calibre, pocket arms. In 1928, however, the firm produced its Military Model, a specimen of which is illustrated here. Like all the manufacturer's later pistols, the arm is of a very distinctive type. The barrel is hinged at the front end—the pivot pin is clearly visible in the photograph—and when a catch on the frame is pressed, the breech end rises clear of the slide, almost like a modern shotgun. As may be seen, the magazine carries an extra round in its base. When the magazine has been pushed home, this extra round is withdrawn and placed in the breech; then the barrel is closed and the pistol is ready to fire. When the magazine is withdrawn, the breech rises automatically: it is possible, in this model, to withdraw it partially and then load and fire single rounds, leaving the magazine's contents as a reserve. No extractor is fitted: the empty cases are blown clear by the residual gas pressure in the barrel after the shot has been fired. There is no locking system, the pistol functioning by blowback only—and it was probably this factor which doomed it, for the system meant that it must fire a cartridge too weak for service use. It may also happen that a misfired cartridge—admittedly a rare occurrence with modern ammunition—cannot be extracted without the use of some improvised tool. In spite of the eclipse of the Military Model, the smaller-calibre pocket arms produced by the company remained popular.

France
MAS MODEL 1950

Length:	7·6" (193mm)
Weight:	34oz (·96kg)
Barrel:	4·3" (109mm)
Calibre:	9mm
Rifling:	4 groove, l/hand
Capacity:	Nine
Muz Vel:	c1100 f/s (335 m/s)
Sights:	Fixed

The initials that designate this arm are those of the Manufacture Nationale d'Armes de Saint Etienne, a French state factory. The revolvers originally used by the French armed forces (some of which have already been described) all suffered from the defect of firing weak cartridges. After the end of World War I, therefore, France decided to follow the example of virtually every other country on the European continent and change to a self-loading pistol. There followed a period of sporadic and somewhat leisurely experiment—at a time when another war was unthinkable—and it was not until 1935 that a self-loader was adopted. This, the MAS Model 1935, was a very sound and well-made weapon of basic Browning type—but it suffered from the same defect as the French revolvers: its 7·65mm round lacked stopping-power. After 1945, when France embarked on a major rearmament programme, one of the requirements was for a new pistol. The arm chosen was a re-designed Model 1935, capable of firing the standard 9mm Parabellum cartridge. This was a success and at last placed a really good pistol into the hands of French servicemen. It is still in use; some are produced at Châtellerault, as well as at Saint Etienne.

Finland
LAHTI L/35

Length: 9·4" (239mm)
Weight: 44oz (1·25kg)
Barrel: 4·7" (119mm)
Calibre: 9mm
Rifling: 6 groove, r/hand
Capacity: Eight
Muz Vel: c1100 f/s (335 m/s)
Sights: Fixed

This pistol was invented by Aimo Lahti of Finland and was produced by Valtion, the Finnish state factory. It was originally intended to be made in two calibres, 7·65mm and 9mm Parabellum, but the former never got beyond the prototype stage. The arm was adopted as the official pistol of the Finnish armed forces in 1935; it gave good service in the Finnish campaign against the Russians in the early part of World War II, when it was found to be particularly reliable in very low temperatures. Although, as may be seen, it bears a general resemblance to the Luger, this is fortuitous: the two are quite different mechanically. The Lahti fires from a closed breech the bolt being unlocked after a brief rearward travel and going on to complete the usual cycle. The mechanism incorporates a bolt accelerator — a curved arm which is so designed that it increases the rearward velocity of the bolt. A version of the Lahti was also used by the Swedish forces, by whom it was called the M/40. The Swedes had originally settled for the German Walther P38 (see page 167, above), but when war intervened they turned instead to Finland. The Finns supplied some, but later they were made under licence by the Swedish firm of Husqvarna Vapenfabrik. Although the Swedes make excellent weapons, their M/40 was generally considered inferior to its Finnish prototype.

Czechoslovakia
ČESKÁ ZBROJOVKA CZ 1950

Length: 8·2" (208mm)
Weight: 34oz (·96kg)
Barrel: 4·7" (119mm)
Calibre: 7·62mm
Rifling: 4 groove, r/hand
Capacity: Eight
Muz Vel: c1000 f/s (305 m/s)
Sights: Fixed

The firm of Ceská Zbrojovka was formed just after World War I. The self-loading pistol which is illustrated here, however, had its origins after the end of the World War II, when the Czech Army decided that it needed a new pistol. By 1950, the arm seen here was in production. It is basically similar to the German Walther PP (see page 175, below), although there are some manufacturing differences. It was a reasonably effective pistol but, like many European service arms, its calibre lacked the essential stopping-power for service use; therefore, within a very short period, it had been replaced as a military arm, although it continued in use for police purposes. It was replaced by the Ceská Zbrojovka CZ 1952 which, although of the same calibre, fired a much more powerful round from a locked breech, working by means of a roller device similar to that on the German MG 42 machine gun. This pistol was, in its turn, replaced by the Russian Makarov (see page 185, below).

177

BERNEDO 6·35mm POCKET PISTOL

Length: 4·5" (114mm)
Weight: 15oz (·42kg)
Barrel: 2" (51mm)
Calibre: 6·35mm
Rifling: 6 groove, r/hand
Capacity: Six
Muz Vel: c800 f/s (244 m/s)
Sights: Fixed

Vincenzo Bernedo y Cia of Eibar was one of the many small Spanish firms to produce cheap self-loading pistols. During World War I, the company was involved in the manufacture of Ruby pistols (see page 173, below), but after the war had ended, Bernedo developed a new design, a specimen of which is illustrated here. The weapon is of pocket type and of the usual blowback design; as may be seen, the barrel is almost fully exposed, with the slide to the rear of it. A small catch (visible in the photograph) is situated just below the barrel; when the cylindrical part of this is lifted, it may be pushed out through a loop on the lower part of the barrel, and the barrel can then be drawn forward. This is faciliated by the fact that the lower part of the loop has flanges which fit into grooves in the frame of the weapon. The slide bears many Eibar proofmarks, and the butt-grips are marked "V BERNEDO".

WALTHER MODEL 9 POCKET PISTOL

Length: 4" (102mm)
Weight: 9.5oz (·27kg)
Barrel: 2" (51mm)
Calibre: 6·35mm
Rifling: 6 groove, r/hand
Capacity: Six
Muz Vel: 800 f/s (244 m/s)
Sights: Fixed

Carl Walther Waffenfabrik, the well-known German firm whose military arms have already been described, has produced a series of self-loading pistols in the period extending from 1908 to the present day. The first nine models were serially numbered: the arm illustrated here is a specimen of the ninth in the series, the last before the introduction of the famous PP (see page 175, below). It must be one of the smallest and neatest self-loading pistols ever made, well-suited for concealment in a waistcoat pocket or in a lady's handbag. It has a fixed barrel with an open-topped slide and is of simple blowback type. The slide is retained on the frame by a dumbbell-shaped catch at the rear, which is held in place by a small spring catch. When this is raised, the entire assembly is forced out to the rear under the pressure of the striker spring. When the weapon is cocked, the rear end of the striker protrudes slightly through a hole in the upper circle of the catch to indicate that the arm is ready for action. The slide is marked "WALTHER PATENT MODEL 9", with details of the company.

FROMMER BABY

Length: 4.75" (121mm)
Weight: 14oz (·4kg)
Barrel: 2.25" (57mm)
Calibre: 6·35mm
Rifling: 4 groove, r/hand
Capacity: Six
Muz Vel: c800 f/s (244 m/s)
Sights: Fixed

Some account of the Hungarian firm of Fegyvergyar has already been given on page 161 (above). The name of the pistol illustrated here is that of one of Fegyvergyar's designers and engineers, Rudolf Frommer, who was with the firm from 1896 until 1935. This "Baby" of 1912 is basically a smaller type of Frommer "Stop" service pistol of the same year. It works on the system known as long recoil, in which the barrel recoils almost its full length before returning, leaving the breech-block to come forward after it, stripping a cartridge from the magazine and chambering it. This independent movement of barrel and breechblock makes it necessary to have two separate springs, both of which are housed in the separate cylindrical tunnel visible above the barrel.

Germany
LIGNOSE EINHAND MODEL 3A

Length:	4.6" (117mm)
Weight:	18oz (.51kg)
Barrel:	2.1" (53mm)
Calibre:	6.35mm
Rifling:	6 groove, r/hand
Capacity:	Nine
Muz Vel:	c800 f/s (244 m/s)
Sights:	Nil

The pistol illustrated here was originally manufactured by the Bergmann company in about 1917, but the rights were then sold to the Lignose company, under whose name it is better known. A notable problem of the days before self-loading pistols were provided with double-action locks and other refinements, was that it was dangerous to carry such a pistol with a round in the chamber—but, at the same time, it was a relatively slow, two-handed business to prepare it for action. Lignose sought to overcome this problem, and the word *Einhand* (one hand) suggests the method. It will be noted from the photograph that the front end of the trigger-guard is very far forward. This is because the brass section is attached to the slide, which thus can be drawn back by the pressure of the first finger. The finger may then be swiftly moved back to the trigger, to fire.

United States of America
COLT MODEL 1908

Length:	4.5" (114mm)
Weight:	14oz (.4kg)
Barrel:	2.1" (53mm)
Calibre:	.25"
Rifling:	6 groove, l/hand
Capacity:	Six
Muz Vel:	c800 f/s (244 m/s)
Sights:	Fixed

Colt began to make self-loading pistols in 1900, probably its most famous one being the Military Model of 1911. The arm illustrated here is a very small pocket pistol from the other end of the scale. It was designed by John M. Browning and was originally made in Belgium, until Colt bought the patent and made it in the United States. It is of blowback type and orthodox operation; unusually for a pocket pistol, it is fitted with a grip safety in addition to a second safety catch on the frame. The pistol is so small that only the second finger can be placed around the butt—but its recoil is, of course, negligible. It has sights situated in a groove on the top of the slide.

Austria
TOMIŠKA LITTLE TOM

Length:	4.7" (119mm)
Weight:	15oz (.42kg)
Barrel:	2.33" (59mm)
Calibre:	6.35mm
Rifling:	6 groove, r/hand
Capacity:	Six
Muz Vel:	c800 f/s (244 m/s)
Sights:	Nil

Alois Tomiška, a Viennese gunsmith, designed a self-loading pistol which he patented in 1908 as the Little Tom. It has a fixed barrel and an open-topped slide; the recoil spring is contained in a sleeve below the barrel. It has a double-action lock; thus, its external hammer can be cocked either by the rearward movement of the slide or by direct pressure on the trigger. The greater part of the hammer lies within a recess at the rear of the frame, but enough of its milled comb protrudes to make thumb-cocking possible. When the slide is removed, it is possible to gain access to the lock by pushing up the right butt-plate. Pistols of this type appear to have been made by several European factories after the end of World War I, when Tomiška himself worked for Jihočeská Zbrojovka (later Česká Zbrojovka) in Czechoslovakia. Tomiška's long career did not end until 1946.

Italy
GLISENTI 9mm 1910

Length:	8·25" (210mm)
Weight:	29oz (·82kg)
Barrel:	3·9" (99mm)
Calibre:	9mm
Rifling:	6 groove, r/hand
Capacity:	Seven
Muz Vel:	c1000 f/s (305 m/s)
Sights:	Fixed

The Italian company Real Fabbricca d'Armi Glisenti (later Siderurgica Glisenti) began its operations in about 1889. After some earlier experiments with self-loading pistols, the weapon illustrated here was put into production in 1910 and was adopted by the Italian Army. The pistol fires from a locked breech. When the first shot is fired, barrel and bolt recoil briefly together. The barrel then stops in its rearward position, while the bolt, having unlocked itself, continues its travel. As it comes forward, it strips and chambers the next round and drives the barrel forward. As it does so, a wedge rises from the frame and locks the whole into position. The system is complex and not very strong; thus, the cartridge fired is less powerful than the Parabellum of comparable calibre. The pistol's trigger mechanism is peculiar: the striker is not cocked by the moving parts, but by a projection on the trigger; the striker is forced backwards against a spring until it trips and then comes forward to fire the round. This makes the trigger-pull very long. The milled screw at the front of the frame holds in position a plate covering much of the left side; its removal gives access to the working parts. Although it became obsolete in 1934, some were in service in World War II.

Japan
TAISHO 14 (14 NEN SHIKI KENJU)

Length:	8·9" (226mm)
Weight:	32oz (·91kg)
Barrel:	4·75" (121mm)
Calibre:	8mm
Rifling:	6 groove, r/hand
Capacity:	Eight
Muz Vel:	c950 f/s (290 m/s)
Sights:	Fixed

The first self-loading pistol officially adopted by the Japanese Army was the Nambu, which went through various modifications from 1909 onward. The weapon illustrated here represents the final modification; it first appeared in 1925 and remained in service until the end of World War II. When the pistol is fired, the barrel, bolt and receiver all recoil together for about ·2in (5mm). The movement of the barrel causes a block in the receiver to rotate, unlocking the bolt, which continues to the rear. The bolt is then impelled forward by two recoil springs, one on either side of it, and relocks for the round to be fired. The cocking-piece is circular; in early models, there are three grooves around it, but most of these pistols have the knurled type seen here. The magazine catch is a circular stud on the left of the frame, but there is also a small retaining spring in the front strap of the butt (the exterior part is visible in the photograph). An interesting feature is the enlarged trigger-guard; this was a modification introduced as a result of the campaign against the Chinese in Manchuria in 1937, where gloves were found to be essential for winter wear.

Japan
TYPE 94 (94 SHIKI KENJU)

Length:	7·1" (180mm)
Weight:	28oz (·79kg)
Barrel:	3·1" (79mm)
Calibre:	8mm
Rifling:	6 groove, r/hand
Capacity:	Six
Muz Vel:	c950 f/s (290 m/s)
Sights:	Fixed

Until 1934, all self-loading pistols used by the Japanese services had been of the Nambu type shown on the facing page (below), but in that year a new and very different weapon was introduced. This weapon, the Type 94, illustrated here, takes its designation from the last two digits in the year of the Japanese calender in which it was produced: 2594, corresponding to 1934 in the Christian calender. The Type 94 was originally produced commercially, but the demands of the Sino-Japanese War led in 1937 to an increased need for arms, and the Japanese Government purchased this pistol in some quantities, mainly for Army tank crews and aircraft pilots. The weapon is cocked by pulling back the slide (which covers the entire top of the frame and barrel) by means of the milled ears visible at the rear. The breech is locked at the moment of firing by a vertically-moving slide which is cammed in and out of engagement by the brief recoil of the barrel. The trigger mechanism was most unreliable, particularly on later examples made during the course of World War II—when it was so eccentric as to be positively dangerous. The sear bar is exposed on the left-hand side of the frame; it protrudes slightly when the weapon is cocked, making it susceptible to accidental discharge by a blow. It was also possible for the pistol to be fired prematurely, before the breech was locked—and although the cartridge was low-powered, this was obviously a serious fault. This arm may probably be designated as one of the worst service pistols ever made.

Spain
UNCETA ASTRA 400

Length:	9·25" (235mm)
Weight:	38oz (1·08kg)
Barrel:	5·5" (140mm)
Calibre:	9mm
Rifling:	6 groove, r/hand
Capacity:	Eight
Muz Vel:	c1100 f/s (335 m/s)
Sights:	Fixed

The Spanish company of Unceta y Cia of Eibar and Guernica made self-loading pistols almost from the beginning of the 20th century. The firm's early products were mostly pocket pistols, but in 1921 it produced a heavier, service-type pistol of a different design. This was the Astra 400, a specimen of which is illustrated here; it was adopted by the Spanish Army in the same year as it appeared. The pistol has a stepped slide of tubular form: its front end envelops the barrel, while its rear end acts as breechblock. The recoil spring is positioned around the barrel and inside the slide, and is held in place by the bush visible at the muzzle. The pistol has an internal hammer and a grip safety. Probably the main point of interest is that although it fires a cartridge of considerable power, it works on straight blowback, without any form of breech-locking device. This is made possible by the use of a heavy slide and an unusually strong recoil spring, which between them reduce the backward action to within safe limits. This makes the pistol rather heavy and, in spite of the grooved finger-grips on its slide, it is quite hard to cock.

COLT MODEL 1903 POCKET

Length:	6·75" (171mm)	**Rifling:**	6 groove, l/hand
Weight:	24oz (·68kg)	**Capacity:**	Eight
Barrel:	3·75" (95mm)	**Muz Vel:**	c900 f/s (274 m/s)
Calibre:	·32"	**Sights:**	Fixed

Colt's first pocket self-loading pistol appeared in 1903, but it did not prove entirely popular and was replaced in the same year by a new weapon designed by the famous John M. Browning. This was a success—and with various modifications it has remained in production up to the present day. The example of the Model 1903 illustrated here is of post-1911 manufacture: before that date, the barrel, which was rather thin, was held in place by a barrel-bushing which is absent from this specimen. It works by blowback, no locking device being required for the ·32 ACP cartridge, and has a concealed hammer. It is also the first Colt self-loading pistol to be fitted with a grip safety. Most models have vulcanite grips bearing the word "COLT" and the rearing-horse trademark, and it is not clear whether the wooden grips on the arm seen here were optional or are a private replacement. In 1926, a safety disconnector, which separates the sear from the trigger when the magazine is removed, was incorporated into the design, but this feature is not present in the example shown here. This is an unusually handy and well-balanced pistol and well deserves its continuing popularity.

RHEINMETALL 7·65MM DREYSE

Length:	6·25" (159mm)	**Rifling:**	4 groove, r/hand
Weight:	25oz (·71kg)	**Capacity:**	Seven
Barrel:	3·66" (93mm)	**Muz Vel:**	c850 f/s (259 m/s)
Calibre:	7·65mm	**Sights:**	Fixed

The Rheinmetall company of Sommerda, Germany, has been in business (although not under its present title) since 1889. In 1901 it took over Waffenfabrik von Dreyse, the company which had been found in 1841 to manufacture the famous Prussian needle-gun and also needle-revolvers of the type already illustrated on page 66. The pistol seen here is of a type designed by Louis Schmeisser and placed on the market in 1907; it was named Dreyse, although Nikolaus von Dreyse himself had by that time been dead for many years. The pistol is of slightly unusual design. The slide is positioned above the barrel, which lies in a trough in the main frame. At the back of the frame, above the butt, are two parallel rectangular plates, joined at the rear to provide a backsight, but otherwise open to allow the slide to pass between them. The top of the breechblock, which is integral with the slide (but lower, so as to align with the chamber), may be seen between these plates when the slide is forward. When the slide is drawn back to cock the weapon and chamber a round, the breechblock protrudes through the rear of the frame; when the slide goes forward, the end of the striker protrudes slightly as an indication that the arm is cocked. In order to strip the weapon it is necessary to push in the small catch, which is just visible in the illustration, at the rear of the frame; this allows the whole upper part to be pivoted forward on a pin in front of the trigger.

Belgium
BROWNING MODEL 1922

Length: 7" (178mm)
Weight: 25oz (·71kg)
Barrel: 4·5" (114mm)
Calibre: 9mm
Rifling: 6 groove, r/hand
Capacity: Nine
Muz Vel: c875 f/s (267 m/s)
Sights: Fixed

At the end of the 19th century, the Belgium firm of Fabrique Nationale d'Armes de Guerre (FN) purchased several self-loading pistol patents originally taken out by the American designer John M. Browning. These were developed by FN and some of the earlier models are illustrated on pages 155 (above) and 162 (above). In 1910, FN's engineers produced a pistol of new pattern. It had an overall slide with a cylindrical forward end. The recoil spring fitted around the barrel, under the front part of the slide, and was held in place by a nosecap with a bayonet fastening. Twelve years later, this design was modified by making the barrel longer, so as to improve accuracy; in order to avoid lengthening the existing slide, the original nosecap was simply lengthened by the necessary amount. It is removed by pushing forward a small retaining catch on the left side of the slide, which may then be twisted off. Almost immediately, a second version was made to take a 9mm Short cartridge, which was generally considered to be the safe maximum load for a blowback pistol. This arm was adopted by the Belgian Army and others. A modified version of this self-loader is still in production.

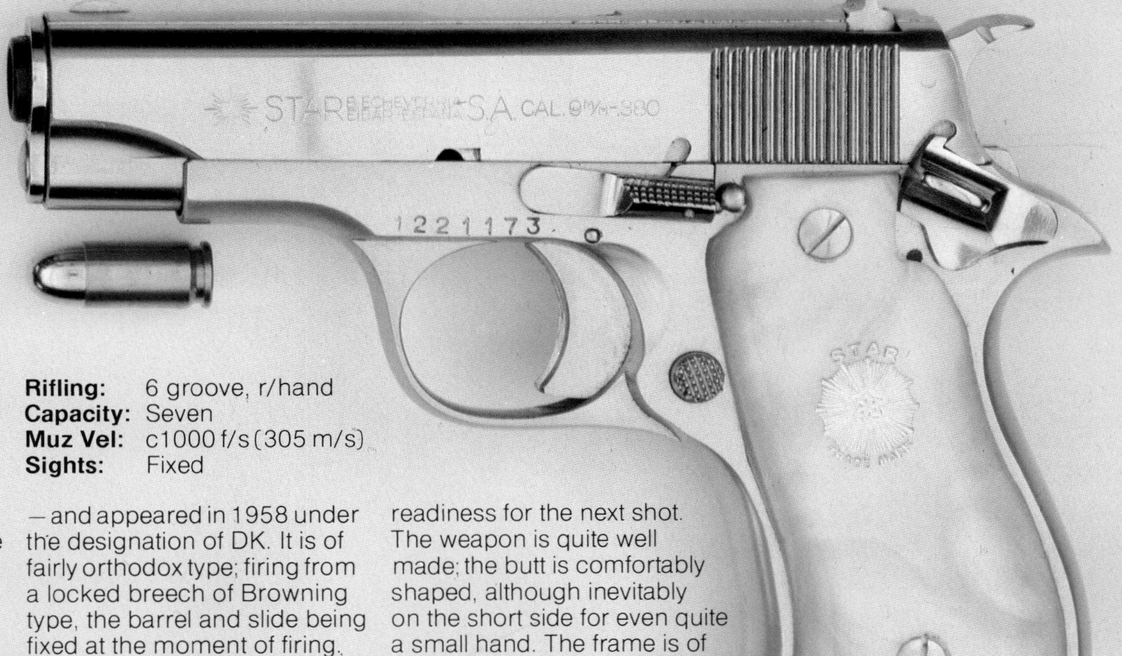

Spain
ECHEVERRIA MODEL DK (STARFIRE)

Length: 5·7" (145mm)
Weight: 15oz (·42kg)
Barrel: 3·1" (79mm)
Calibre: 9mm
Rifling: 6 groove, r/hand
Capacity: Seven
Muz Vel: c1000 f/s (305 m/s)
Sights: Fixed

The Spanish company of B. Echeverria has been in existence for most of the 20th century, although much of its intermediate history remains obscure. The general trade name Star was adopted in 1921, although there was little original in the models bearing this designation: most of them were more or less closely based on the products of other companies. The pistol illustrated here is based on the company's Model D of about 1930 — although the design has been considerably modernized — and appeared in 1958 under the designation of DK. It is of fairly orthodox type; firing from a locked breech of Browning type, the barrel and slide being fixed at the moment of firing. They recoil briefly together until the rear end of the barrel drops, disengages and stops; the slide continues rearward to cock the hammer. It is forced forward again under the influence of the recoil spring (which is located beneath, and parallel to, the barrel), stripping and chambering a cartridge and relocking the breech in readiness for the next shot. The weapon is quite well made; the butt is comfortably shaped, although inevitably on the short side for even quite a small hand. The frame is of some light alloy with a satin finish and the steelwork is bright. This particular specimen, which is known as the Starfire on the United States' market, is supplied in a case with a spare magazine and cleaning rod. It is an attractive enough arm of its kind, and may be said to justify Echeverria's modern reputation for reliability.

Length:	7·75" (197mm)
Weight:	35oz (·99kg)
Barrel:	4·65" (118mm)
Calibre:	9mm
Rifling:	4 groove, r/hand
Capacity:	Thirteen
Muz Vel:	c1100 f/s (335 m/s)
Sights:	Fixed

This is the last of Browning's pistol designs and was introduced in 1935, when it was taken into service by the Belgian Army. It was made in various versions, including one with an adjustable sight and a combined holster/stock of the type found on the original Mausers. When the Germans occupied Belgium in 1940, they continued the manufacture of these weapons—although it is said that various Belgian sabotage operations lowered the quality, sometimes to the point where the arms made were actually dangerous to use. A number of FN engineers went to Britain, taking the drawings with them. In 1942 these were sent to Canada, where the firm of John Inglis put the arms into production for Allied use; the weapon illustrated here is one of this series. After the war, manufacture reverted to the FN factory and the weapon was also put on sale commercially as the Hi-Power. It is currently in use by the British Army and other countries' services.

A stripped Browning pistol. At the top is the slide, with breechblock and striker inside the rear end, by the grooves. The projection below the foresight houses the end of the recoil spring. Next below is the barrel, with its twin lugs which engage with recesses in the upper part of the slide to lock the breech. Below that is the recoil spring, showing the plunger, the end of which engages in a recess below the chamber; the slide locking lever is on the left. At the bottom is the main frame. The hammer is cocked, the horizontal bar in front of it being the ejector.

Czechoslovakia
ČESKÁ ZBROJOVKA CZ 27

Length: 6·25" (159mm)
Weight: 25·5oz (·72kg)
Barrel: 4" (102mm)
Calibre: 9mm
Rifling: 6 groove, r/hand
Capacity: Eight
Muz Vel: c900 f/s (274 m/s)
Sights: Fixed

The Česká Zbrojovka factory was set up just after World War I, when the newly-formed country of Czechoslovakia began to establish the various industries needed by a modern state. Manufacture of self-loading pistols began immediately and still continues. In 1924 there appeared a military-type pistol firing a short 9mm cartridge from a locked breech. The designer, however, considered that a locking system was unnecessary for such a relatively low-powered round, and redesigned the pistol to eliminate this feature. The result was the CZ 27, illustrated here. Externally it appears to be almost identical to the 1924 model, the main apparent difference being that the finger-grooves at the rear of the slide are vertical rather than diagonal. The pistol works on straight blowback, with its recoil spring mounted around a rod situated below and parallel with the barrel. It has an external hammer and there is a magazine safety on the left-hand side of the frame, just above the magazine release stud. In pistols made before 1939, the milled top rib is marked "CESKA ZBROJOVKA AS v PRAZE", together with the serial number. When the Germans occupied Czechoslovakia, manufacture was continued on a considerable scale: weapons made during that period are recognizable by the fact that the inscription reads "BOHMISCHE WAFFEN FABRIK AG IN PRAG". The left side of the slide on this specimen is also marked "PISTOLE MODELL 27 KAL 7·65". Manufacture of this model continued until 1951.

Soviet Union
MAKAROV 9mm

Length: 6·35" (161mm)
Weight: 25oz (·71kg)
Barrel: 3·8" (97mm)
Calibre: 9mm
Rifling: 4 groove, r/hand
Capacity: Eight
Muz Vel: c1075 f/s (328 m/s)
Sights: Fixed

It is very difficult to obtain exact details of the development and production of Russian weapons, because of the almost impenetrable veil of secrecy which surrounds the affairs of all totalitarian regimes, but the following facts are believed to be correct. The Makarov pistol, illustrated here, is thought to date from the early 1960s and it is now the standard pistol for both the Soviet forces and for a variety of their satellites. Externally it is in almost every respect a copy of the German Walther PP (which is fully described on page 175, below). However, there are some mechanical differences: by far the most important of these is the fact that the weapon has no locking system but fires on a simple blowback action. It is loaded in the orthodox way by inserting a magazine and operating the slide manually to chamber a round and cock the action. On firing, the slide is blown back by the rearward movement of the case. In order to avoid excessively stiff springs and heavy slides or breechblocks, the cartridge used is an intermediate one in terms of power, although apparently adequate. The pistol has an external hammer with a double-action lock; this means that it can be carried safely with a round in the chamber and the hammer down. When the pistol has been loaded, the movement of the safety catch—situated on the left rear of the slide, above the buttplate—to the "safe" position allows the hammer to drop safely and also locks the slide. When the last round in the magazine has been fired, the magazine follower rises to such a level that it pushes up the slide stop and holds the slide to the rear, indicating that replenishment is required. To strip the weapon, the magazine is removed and it is ensured that there is no round in the chamber. The front of the trigger-guard is then pulled down and twisted slightly so as to bear on the frame; the slide can now be removed to the rear. There are slight differences between the pistols used by the various Soviet satellite countries, but none is really important. It is not clear why this new design was thought necessary at a time when at least one Soviet-bloc country (Hungary) already had a perfectly adequate self-loading pistol of this type.

This photograph shows the Model 84 stripped to main components. The top one is the slide, the projection below the foresight being the front housing for the recoil spring. Below it is the barrel, and below that, the recoil spring and its guide rod. At the bottom is the main frame, with the magazine and one round.

Length:	6·75″ (171mm)
Weight:	23·5oz (·67kg)
Barrel:	3·75″ (95mm)
Calibre:	7·65mm
Rifling:	6 groove, r/hand
Capacity:	Twelve
Muz Vel:	985 f/s (300 m/s)
Sights:	Fixed

As may be seen from comparison of the photographs, this pistol is virtually indistinguishable at a glance from the Model 84 shown on the facing page (below). This is not surprising, for a good many of the components are identical. The real difference between the two lies in their calibre: the Model 81 is designed to fire the 7·65mm cartridge, as opposed to the 9mm Short cartridge of the Model 84. The only components that differ between the two models are the barrel and the magazine spring and follower, which are necessarily narrower in the Model 81. The same basic magazine is used, but in the Model 81 its internal width is reduced as required by the two long grooves on either side; the magazine has been removed to show these. The weapon is operated in exactly the same way as the Model 84. Its external hammer, which is cocked by the action of the slide, may be lowered quite safely under the pressure of the thumb; thus, the weapon may be carried with a round in the chamber with no risk of accidental discharge. The magazine catch and safety are both reversible, for use by either hand. All these modern pistols are well made and finished, and their anodized aluminium frames make them light. They are reported as being very reliable mechanically, although double-column magazines make them rather bulky. This, of course, is the price which has to be paid for their unusually large magazine capacity.

Italy
BERETTA MODEL 92S

Length:	8·5" (216mm)
Weight:	35oz (·99kg)
Barrel:	5" (127mm)
Calibre:	9mm
Rifling:	6 groove, r/hand
Capacity:	Thirteen
Muz Vel:	c1100 f/s (335 m/s)
Sights:	Fixed

This is the latest Beretta pistol in production at the time of writing (1980) and first appeared in 1976. It is an improved version of the Model 92, which was the 1951 model; this was taken into service by various armies and was also sold commercially under the trade name of "Brigadier". It is initially loaded in the orthodox way by the insertion of a magazine and the manual operation of the slide, which cocks the hammer and chambers the first round. In view of the cartridge used, it necessarily fires from a locked breech. The rearward pressure of the fired case drives back the barrel and slide, which are locked by a block. After travelling about ·3in (8mm), the locking block is pivoted downward and disengages from the slide. The barrel then stops, but the slide continues to the rear to complete the reloading cycle. The chief difference between the Model 92S and and its predecessor, the Model 92, is that the safety catch of the 92S is on the slide instead of on the frame. It has a double-column magazine, which increases capacity but makes the pistol's butt rather bulky.

Italy
BERETTA MODEL 84

Length:	6·75" (171mm)
Weight:	22oz (·62kg)
Barrel:	3·75" (95mm)
Calibre:	9mm
Rifling:	6 groove, r/hand
Capacity:	Thirteen
Muz Vel:	920 f/s (280 m/s)
Sights:	Fixed

This pistol and the Model 81 described on the facing page are very similar: the two captions should be read in conjunction. A good deal has been written about the famous Beretta company earlier in this book (notably on page 170) and need not be repeated here. In 1976, Beretta put the Model 81 and Model 84 pistols into production, together with a more powerful Model 92; all of them share certain characteristics. Unlike the more powerful Model 92, however, the Model 84 is designed to fire the 9mm Short cartridge. As this is a relatively low-powered round, the weapon works on simple blowback, without any requirement for a breech-locking system. Manual retraction of the slide cocks the hammer and chambers a round on its forward motion. The recoil of the fired case thrusts the slide backward, compressing the recoil spring as it does so, and allows the firing cycle to continue. When the slide is forward and the pistol ready to fire, the extractor protrudes slightly from the slide, thus constituting a visual and manual indication of the pistol's state of readiness. There is also a manual safety which is operable either left- or right-handed. The pistol has a double-column magazine which makes the butt rather large. It is regretted that, when this pistol was photographed, the magazine belonging to the Model 81—with its two long grooves—was inadvertently substituted for the magazine of the Model 84.

A Miscellany of Hand Guns

Although the five preceding introductory essays cover the major categories of pistols and revolvers, there are some weapons which cannot be properly placed within any of these classifications.

MULTI-BARRELLED CARTRIDGE ARMS

Most of the hand guns made in the early days of the self-contained cartridge were revolvers; but although these were so popular as to be almost universally used, there were some people who preferred an alternative arm. This may have been caused partly by an inherent distrust of revolvers—perhaps engendered in the individual by the unwise purchase of a cheap and unreliable weapon—but it was probably more often due to the user's need for more stopping power than the ordinary revolver could provide without becoming unwieldy. The heaviest revolvers in use were of about ·577in (14·65mm) calibre, but even these fired a cartridge with a relatively small powder charge and relied mainly on the weight of the bullet for effect.

One of the more popular alternatives to the revolver was the heavy, double-barrelled, cartridge pistol, which was particularly favoured by British sportsmen in India as a back-up weapon with which to finish off a wounded tiger when there was no time to reload a rifle. A good deal of tiger-shooting was done from the backs of elephants; thus, these arms were often called "howdah pistols". They tended to resemble cut-down hammer shotguns, were usually rifled, and fired a somewhat longer cartridge than a revolver of similar calibre. The combination of a large charge with the avoidance of loss of power between the face of the cylinder and the barrel won them a considerable reputation as hard-hitting arms.

A logical development was the four-barrelled pistol produced by the famous British firm of Charles Lancaster. These weapons varied from ·38in (9·6mm) to ·476in (12·1mm) calibre and their general characteristics may be seen in the examples illustrated (pages 194-195). Like howdah pistols, Lancasters were popular among Army officers in the second half of the 19th century, when the adversaries encountered in colonial warfare were frequently men of such powerful physique that it took a good deal to stop them dead in their tracks. By the end of the century, the period of colonial wars was over, and weapons of the Lancaster type had been entirely superseded by the powerful and reliable revolvers of Webley and Scott.

A number of small, multi-barrelled pistols were also made, mainly on the continent. Among the best-known were pepperbox pistols firing pinfire cartridges. These sometimes incorporated a small bayonet and a knuckle-duster butt and were then known as "Apache pistols"—not from the American Indian tribe of that name, but after the denizens

Bottom left: *The US policeman holds (right) a ·38in calibre "fountain-pen" gun and a miniature tear-gas pistol, and (left) a revolver with an integral bayonet.*

Below: *A member of a US Army helicopter transport company in Vietnam, 1964, holds his specially-designed ·22in self-loader, complete with muzzle-brake.*

ECLIPSE.

c VEST POCKET—SINGLE SHOT.

22 Cal., Length of barrel 2½ in., weight 3½ oz , full nickel plated....each. **.68**
32 Cal., Length of barrel 3 in . weight 6 oz.. full nickel plated....... " **$1.06**

Top: *American manufacturer's advertisement of 1884 for a single-shot, waistcoat-pocket pistol of the type generally referred to as a "derringer".*
Bottom: *Smith and Wesson advertisement of 1903 for a combination pistol, firing either single-shot or, with a detachable cylinder, as an orthodox revolver.*

SINGLE SHOT PISTOL

.22, 32 or .38 calibre, 6 inch...........$14 00
.22, .32 " .38   " 8 "............ 14 00
.22, .32 " .38   " 10 "............ 14 00
Combination Revolver and single shot
    pistol complete with case............. 26 00

of the Paris underworld, who were said to use such weapons. Flat arms with the barrels positioned one above the other were also made, in Germany and elsewhere, and, being easily concealed, continued popular until replaced by the pocket self-loader in the 20th century.

SINGLE CARTRIDGE PISTOLS

Another popular pistol of the later 19th century was the single-shot arm. Most of these were designed to fire the cheap and easily available ·22in (5·6mm) rimfire cartridge in its various forms. At one end of the scale were the numerous French and Belgian versions usually classed as "saloon pistols", which fired bulleted caps and were used on indoor ranges where smoke and noise were best kept to a minimum; at the other were the many American (and a few British) arms firing longer and more powerful cartridges, usually of ·22in (5·6mm) calibre, although versions up to ·38in (9·6mm) were also made. These were mainly used for target and small-game shooting and for casual practice at tin cans, bottles and other random targets—a pastime generally referred to in the United States as "plinking". They were usually long-barrelled: 12ins (305mm) was the average, and 20ins (508mm) was not unknown. This gave these arms a good sight base and they shot well, particularly when equipped with a detachable stock. They were manufactured by a variety of makers—notably Harrington and Richardson, Quackenbush, Stevens, Wesson, Webley—and it is probable that many are still in use. They were often designated "bicycle pistols", presumably because they could easily be carried strapped to the crossbar of what was then a novel form of transport. One further development was the version made by Smith and Wesson in 1891-1910, in which the single barrel could be replaced by one with a cylinder attached, making it an orthodox revolver.

An extension of this type which deserves mention was the single-or double-shot pistol, usually designed to fire a ·410in (10·4mm) cartridge. These were made in the United States and Belgium—and are now prohibited in Great Britain. Their unofficial successor is the sawn-off shotgun, which is used almost entirely by criminals.

THE DERINGER

The type of weapon that now bears his name was originally developed by Henry Deringer, a Philadelphia gun-smith. His arms were small, compact, pocket pistols which, when they first appeared in percussion form in the 1830s, differed little from a host of similar weapons. The cartridge version of 1861 was, however, almost immediately popular. Although the inventor strove in the courts to confine the use of his

name to his own products, it was soon applied generically to the type and was extensively used (sometimes spelled as "Derringer") by other makers; thus, in effect, adding a new noun to the English language. These arms (a number of which are illustrated on pages 200-201) were popular because they could easily be carried concealed, and they were often carried thus as secondary weapons. The most distinguished victim of the type was Abraham Lincoln, assassinated by John Wilkes Booth in 1865. Although primarily used in the United States, the deringer sold well in the United Kingdom and was popular as a self-defence weapon for British women in India and the colonies. It was eventually largely superseded by the small self-loader, although modern versions are still made.

SILENT WEAPONS

War is a noisy business and the need for silent arms is limited to special forces engaged in clandestine operations. It is not difficult to silence a weapon so long as the bullet fired from it does not exceed the speed of sound: the method depends on the use of baffle plates of a type broadly similar to those used in motorcycle silencers. If the muzzle velocity marginally exceeds the speed of sound, holes are drilled in the

Above: *Arms captured in a sweep by British troops at Croke Park football ground, Dublin, in November 1920. Then, as now, Irish dissidents carried arms of a wide variety. Note the single-shot pistol with a sheathed trigger on the extreme left: this is probably a blank-firing arm drilled out to fire cartridges. Politically-inspired violence is, sadly, an ever-increasing problem. (Inset) Thus, these may be the weapons needed by the British policeman of the latter 1980s—including a Heckler and Koch VP70 pistol with its holster/butt attached.*

barrel to relieve the pressure behind the bullet by the necessary amount. As far as military pistols are concerned, the best-known silent arm was the Welrod (page 197), which was in limited use by British forces during World War II. This was a purpose-made arm; the alternative being a screw-on silencer.

AUTOMATIC PISTOLS

The term "automatic" is used here in its proper sense: to denote a weapon which will continue to fire as long as the trigger is pressed and there are rounds in the magazine. Most so-called automatic pistols are, in fact, self-loaders, and are referred to as such in this book. The problem inherent in a true automatic pistol (often called a "machine pistol") is that its weight and dimensions cannot be great enough adequately

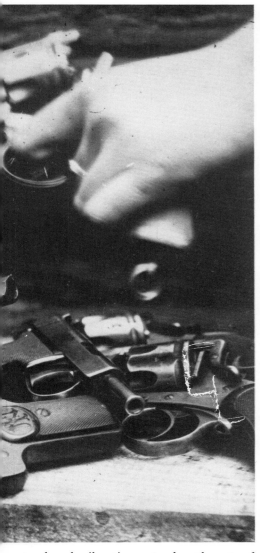

to absorb vibration or to slow the rate of fire; as a result, the weapon becomes virtually unmanageable when fired. A machine version of the Mauser self-loading pistol was made in Spain and Germany in the 1930s but failed to gain acceptance because of the drawbacks described above. Later, during World War II, came the British Machine Carbine Experimental Model (page 196) which, in spite of its name, appears to have been designed originally as a pistol. This suffered from the same defect and was not adopted. Later experiment has been largely concerned with self-loading pistols adapted to fire three-round bursts. This method keeps vibration within reasonable limits and ensures that the bullets are clear of the gun before the muzzle begins to rise.

HOME-MADE PISTOLS

Given a suitable cartridge, it is not too difficult to devise a crude weapon with which to discharge it. It is, however, a dangerous pastime for the amateur, and in many cases the first and only victim of the weapon is likely to be its maker. The only arms in this category which are really worth consideration are the so-called "zip-guns" (pages 196-197), and even these are of limited utility. In the same broad category may

be classed the American Liberator pistol (page 198) which, although factory-made, had most of the characteristics of a do-it-yourself weapon. This was deliberate: the weapon was intended for short-term use and there was no desire that the countries concerned should be flooded with arms after the war.

ROCKET PISTOLS

The Germans experimented with light weapons firing spin-stabilized rockets during World War II. Nothing much was done thereafter until 1960, when M.B. Associates of California produced their Gyro-Jet (page 202). It was a considerable technical achievement to perfect such a small rocket, but the weapon's performance could never really compare with that of orthodox pistols and manufacture soon ceased.

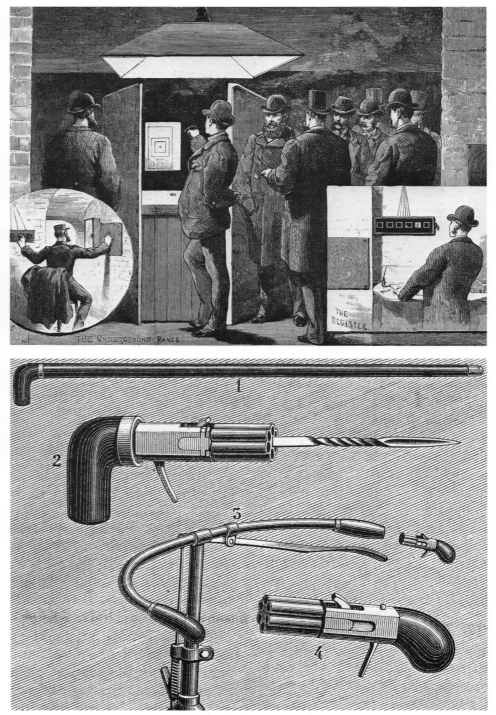

Above: *French "specials" of c1890. (1 & 2) A six-barrelled arm of "pepperbox" type, with a concealed hammer, complete with bayonet. The trigger can be folded flat and the whole assembly fitted into a hollow rod to form the handle of a walking-stick. (3 & 4) This "pepperbox"-type pistol fits into the hollow handlebar of a bicycle. The late 19th-century boom in bicycling gave rise to a number of arms designed specially for protection against tramps and dogs.*

Top: *A London shooting-gallery in the later 19th century. Such establishments, usually in basement premises to minimize noise nuisance, were popular for many years—at least one survived in London's West End into the 1930s—and low-powered "saloon pistols" (see page 193, bottom) were designed to be used by their patrons. This is obviously a well-run gallery; note the steel safety-screens around the firing point, the overhead lighting, and the method of scoring the shots.*

United States of America
BICYCLE "RIFLE"

Length:	15·25" (387mm)
Weight:	25oz (·71kg)
Barrel:	12" (305mm)
Calibre:	·22" (5·6mm)
Rifling:	8 groove, r/hand
Capacity:	One
Muz Vel:	c1100 f/s (335 m/s)
Sights:	100 yd (91m)

Weapons of this type achieved popularity in the United States towards the end of the 19th century, when the bicycle had established itself as a cheap and popular means of transport. The arms presumably got their generic name from the ease with which they could be carried, either assembled or with the wire butt removed, attached to the crossbar of a bicycle. When small game abounded near most country roads, a small, light rifle was a convenient thing to have to hand. The barrel of this specimen is hinged: pressure on the spotted stud below the hammer allows the barrel to drop, giving access to the breech. It was made by the Stevens Company of Chicopee Falls, Massachusetts.

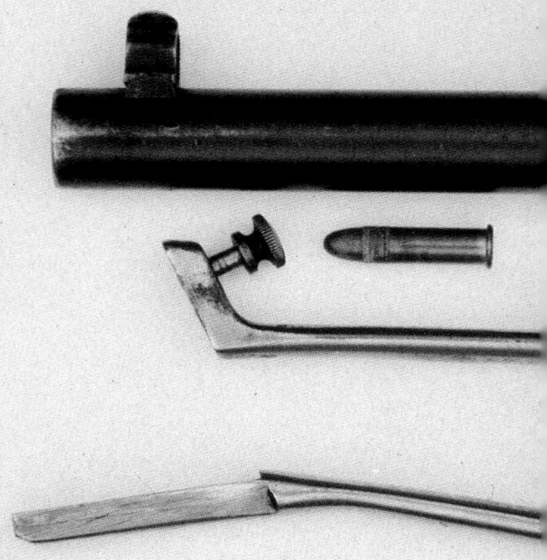

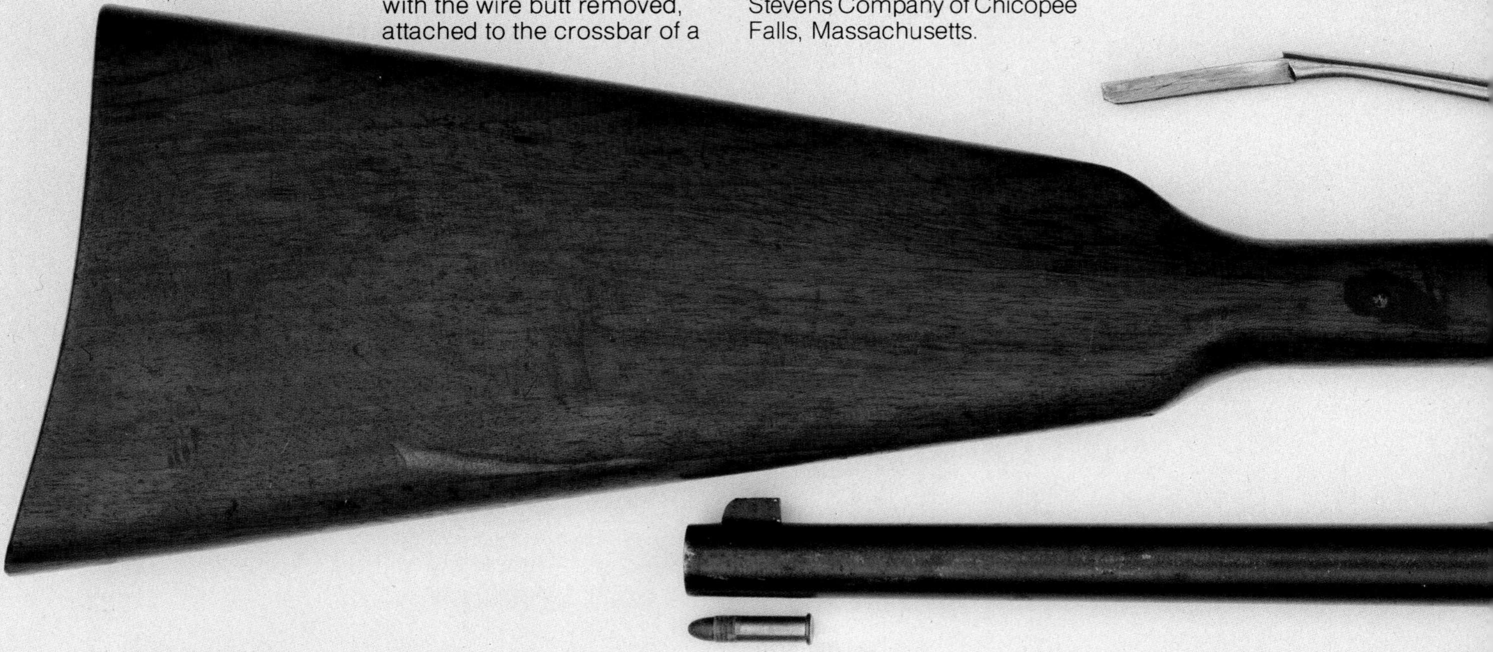

Great Britain
WEBLEY AND SCOTT TARGET PISTOL

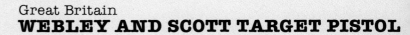

United States of America
SMITH AND WESSON SINGLE-SHOT MODEL 91

This handsome weapon was first produced by the firm of Smith and Wesson in 1891, with the object of providing an accurate and well-balanced target pistol with most of the characteristics of a long-barrelled revolver. The first model was made in three barrel lengths—6in (152mm), 8in (203mm) and 10in (254mm)—and in three calibres—·22in rimfire and ·32in and ·38in centre-fire. It could also be obtained with an interchangeable revolver barrel and cylinder assembly, in ·38in calibre only but with several barrel lengths. This assembly could be mounted on to the existing frame very easily, converting the arm into an orthodox revolver. In 1905 there appeared a Second Model in ·22in calibre, with a 10in (254mm) barrel only, but so designed that the earlier revolver assembly could be fitted to it. The pistol illustrated here is the Third Model, single-shot only. Most arms of this series were blued, but they could be nickel-plated to order—like the specimen illustrated here.

Length:	11·75" (298mm)
Weight:	22oz (·62kg)
Barrel:	8" (203mm)
Calibre:	·32" (8·1mm)
Rifling:	7 groove, r/hand
Capacity:	One
Muz Vel:	c900 f/s (274 m/s)
Sights:	Fixed

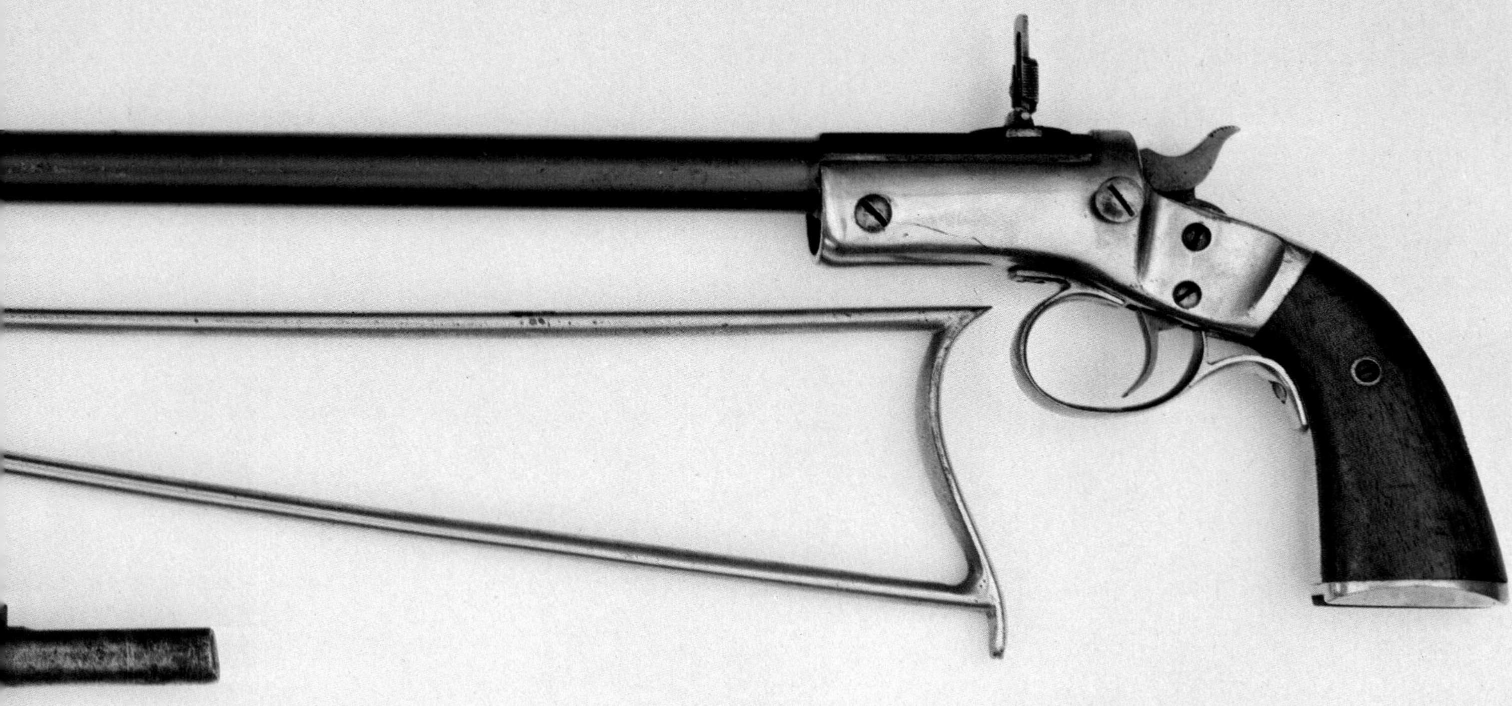

Length:	14·25" (362mm)	**Rifling:**	7 groove, r/hand
Weight:	36oz (1·02kg)	**Capacity:**	One
Barrel:	10·5" (267mm)	**Muz Vel:**	c1100 f/s (335 m/s)
Calibre:	·22" (5·6mm)	**Sights:**	Fixed

This weapon, made in Birmingham by the well-known firm of Webley and Scott, may be taken as the British equivalent of the American "bicycle" arm illustrated above. Britain has long been a relatively crowded country, where the use of rifled arms in or near public roads has been frowned on, if not always deemed illegal. In the more spacious United States, however, the ·22in rifle or pistol was, and still is, a very popular arm, regarded as a suitable first weapon for a boy. But it must be remembered that even in Britain there were no really stringent laws for the control of firearms until well into the 20th century: thus, ordinary citizens were at liberty to purchase and use rifled arms, provided they were handled carefully and employed for lawful purposes. The pistol illustrated here was very much a dual-purpose weapon: when used single-handed, without the butt, it was well balanced and suitable for normal practice; while the addition of the butt at once converted it to a useful arm for small game or vermin. The barrel is hinged and may be lowered to expose the breech by pulling down on the trigger-guard. The action of opening the arm also activates the extractor, which is semi-circular and occupies half of the end of the barrel. There is an inspection plate on the left side of the frame, just below the hammer. The "rifle" butt is attached by pushing its rod portion through a hole in the pistol butt, where it is then held firmly in position by the pressure of a spring stud.

Belgium
SALOON PISTOL

Length:	14·5" (368mm)	**Rifling:**	7 groove, r/hand
Weight:	28oz (·79kg)	**Capacity:**	One
Barrel:	10·1" (257mm)	**Muz Vel:**	c750 f/s (229 m/s)
Calibre:	·22" (5·6mm)	**Sights:**	Fixed

Pistols of this kind were popular for target practice in Europe in the later 19th century. Although duels were by then illegal in Great Britain, they were still quite common on the continent, where young men of fashion considered it prudent to keep in practice in case of a challenge. Small-bore weapons firing bulleted caps were adequate for this kind of exercise; their relative lack of noise and smoke made them eminently suitable for practice in an indoor saloon, hence their name. Although this particular specimen, which is of Belgian origin, bears no maker's name, it is well made and finished. The barrel is hinged and is broken by pressing forward the catch protruding from the frame in front of the trigger-guard. It is provided with an extractor.

LANCASTER FOUR-BARRELLED PISTOL

Length: 11" (279mm)
Weight: 40oz (1·13kg)
Barrel: 6·25" (159mm)
Calibre: ·476" (12·1mm)
Rifling: Oval
Capacity: Four
Muz Vel: c750 f/s (229 m/s)
Sights: Fixed

Charles Lancaster set up as a gunmaker in London in 1826 and achieved a considerable reputation, being appointed gunmaker to His Royal Highness Prince Albert in 1843. He died four years later and was succeeded by his sons, Charles and Alfred. Alfred soon dropped out, but Charles the younger kept up the business. Charles's two great interests were oval-bored rifling and multi-barrelled weapons — and it is for developments in these fields that he is remembered. Instead of having

grooves, the barrels made by Charles Lancaster were very slightly oval in section, although the difference is not immediately perceptible. The oval twisted very slightly as it went down, thus imparting a spin to the bullet; the main advantage of this system was that the absence of grooves made it easier to remove the heavy fouling which always resulted from the use of black powder. Lancaster's multi-barrelled shotguns worked by means of a revolving striker (the mechanism of which is described on the facing page,

above), but were regarded as too heavy and clumsy. When Charles Lancaster died in 1878, the business was bought by his partner, Henry A. A. Thorn, who continued to run it under Lancaster's name. It was Thorn who developed the Lancaster pistol shown here, which he patented in 1881. This new and unusual weapon came at a time when the revolver was well established; it is, at first sight, strange that a weapon which looked back to the multi-barrelled arms of the percussion era (some of which are illustrated between pages 42 and 81 of this book) should have achieved any popularity. The real advantage of the Lancaster pistol, however, lay in its stopping-power. There was of course, no loss of power due to the escape of gas between the face of the cylinder and the end of the barrel, and the new arm was sufficiently robust to handle a cartridge with a heavy bullet and a large charge of powder. In those days of colonial warfare, the British Army was often engaged with more or less savage enemies of great physical strength and courage. Thus, Army officers, usually armed with no more than a light sword, were naturally interested in a pistol which would stop such charging enemies literally dead in their tracks — for it had been found that such adversaries absorbed small-bore bullets without much immediate effect. Therefore, although the orthodox revolver offered one or two extra shots as compared with this four-barrelled arm, a good many officers purchased Lancasters. They saw service notably in the campaigns in the Sudan in 1882-85, which were

waged against as tough and brave an enemy as the British Army had ever previously encountered. Apart from their military use, Lancasters were also popular with big-game hunters. Sportsmen shooting tigers from the backs of elephants found them particularly useful for dealing with wounded beasts which attacked them when their rifles were empty. The general style of Lancaster pistols is clear from the photographs on this and the facing page. The cluster of barrels is hinged at the bottom and is held in place by two hooks engaging over studs on either side of the barrels; one such hook is visible here. Pressure on the side level disengages the hooks, and as the barrels drop a star extractor of revolver type comes automatically into action. The four oval-bored barrels are drilled out of a single block of steel, which gives them great intrinsic strength. The calibre marking and some of the London proof marks are clearly visible in the photograph; the pistol's top rib is marked "CHARLES LANCASTER (PATENT) 151 NEW BOND ST LONDON". One of the disadvantages of the normal lock mechanism of the Lancaster was that it could not be cocked, which made the trigger pull long and heavy. This particular specimen, however, has been fitted with a Tranter-type double-trigger (of the kind seen in the arms illustrated on pages 76-77). Pressure on the lower trigger — which is, in effect, a cocking lever — brings the striker mechanism to the rear, after which a very light touch on the upper trigger, inside the guard, suffices to fire the shot without disturbing the aim.

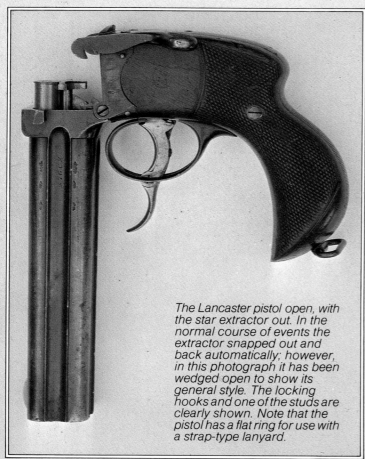

The Lancaster pistol open, with the star extractor out. In the normal course of events the extractor snapped out and back automatically; however, in this photograph it has been wedged open to show its general style. The locking hooks and one of the studs are clearly shown. Note that the pistol has a flat ring for use with a strap-type lanyard.

LANCASTER FOUR-BARRELLED PISTOL

Length:	8·5" (216mm)
Weight:	27oz (·76kg)
Barrel:	4·25" (108mm)
Calibre:	380" (9·6mm)
Rifling:	Oval
Capacity:	Four
Muz Vel:	c625 f/s (190 m/s)
Sights:	Fixed

This arm is essentially similar to the Lancaster opposite. Because most Lancasters were purchased strictly for their stopping-power, for reasons already indicated, the most common calibres were undoubtedly either ·476in (12·1mm) or ·45in (11·4mm) Pistols were, however, made in other calibres to special order: the arm shown here is, presum-

ably, one such. It will be noted that, unlike the pistol shown on the facing page, it is fitted with a single trigger only. On this particular specimen, the butt-plates have been removed in order to show the lock mechanism. Pressure on the trigger causes the vertical hammer-like lever to move to the rear, taking with it the grooved cylinder, which is fitted with a fixed striker on its forward circumference. The cylinder slides along a fixed horizontal rod, the rear end of which can be seen. In the course of its rearward move-ment, the cylinder is turned through 90 degrees by the action of the guide in one of the transverse grooves. When this

cycle is complete, the mech-anism trips, allowing the cylinder to go forward under the impetus of the mainspring. During this forward movement, the guide is engaged in one of the slots parallel to the axis, so that there is no resistance. The striker fires the cartridge and is then revolved through a further 90 degress by the next pressure on the trigger, thus bringing it

into line with the next live car-tridge. The ejector is worked by a transverse arm (part of this arm is visible in the inset photo-graph on the facing page). The lower end of the arm protrudes slightly below the lower pair of barrels: when the barrels are open, this lower end bears on a corresponding projection on the front of the frame, thus lifting the extractor.

LANCASTER DOUBLE-BARRELLED PISTOL

Length:	11" (279mm)
Weight:	26·5oz (·75kg)
Barrel:	6·5" (165mm)
Calibre:	476" (12·1mm)
Rifling:	Oval
Capacity:	Two
Muz Vel:	c750 f/s (229 m/s)
Sights:	Fixed

This is an example of the rela-tively less-known double-barrelled pistol produced by the Lancaster company. Although similar in general principle to the four-barrelled weapons illustrated on this spread, it differs somewhat in detail. The barrels are hinged at the bottom in the same way. The locking system—two hooks engaging over studs on either side of the

upper barrel, controlled by a thumb-lever on the left side of the weapon—is identical; but note the absence in this double-barrelled arm of the small pin on the frame, intended to stop the movement of the lever at the proper position, which is clearly visible on the weapon shown on the facing page. The main difference lies in the system of extraction. In the double-barrelled Lancaster, when the barrels are opened the vertical lever at their breech end initially moves with them, until its lower end catches the horizontal projection just above the trigger. When this happens, the lever stops; but as the barrels continue to move, the

extractor is drawn out by means of a protruding pin which engages in a slot at the upper end of the lever. This particular extractor is not spring-operated: when the barrels are closed, it is pushed back into place by the face of the standing breech, on which it bears. This double-barrelled pistol is, of course, lighter and better balanced than the four-barrelled version. Like most Lancaster pistols, it is fitted with a foresight and a shallow V-backsight. However, the trigger pull is so long and heavy that accurate shooting would have been difficult, except at close quarters—but since these pistols were, in fact, specifically

designed for close action, this was not, perhaps, an important defect. It is of interest to note that the Weapons Museum at the School of Infantry, Warmin-ster, possesses a four-barrelled Lancaster with a rifle butt attached. This conversion is, however, a somewhat amateur effort, and is extremely unlikely to have been carried out by the firm of Lancaster.

Great Britain
ZIP GUNS

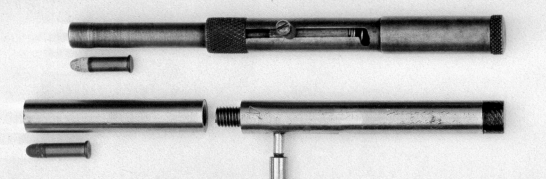

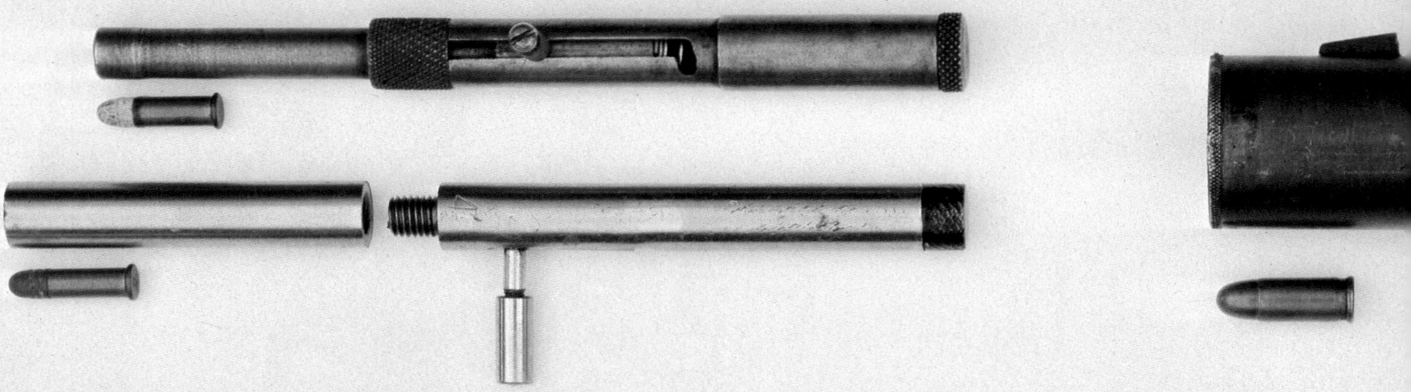

Length: 6" (152mm)
Weight: 4oz (·11kg)
Barrel: 2·5" (63mm)
Calibre: ·22" (5·6mm)
Rifling: Nil
Capacity: One
Muz Vel: c650 f/s (198 m/s)
Sights: Nil

The origins of weapons of this type cannot be established with any certainty, but it seems likely that they first appeared in the ghetto areas of some of the larger cities of the United States. Home-made firearms of various kinds are, however, relatively common—and it is, therefore, difficult to generalize about their genesis. Although the writer has no desire to offer to the public a do-it-yourself guide to the manufacture of illegal firearms, some brief description will not be out of place, since the principles concerned are already so well known that no harm can result. The really difficult thing for an amateur gunsmith to make from scratch is a supply of modern cartridges—but if these can be obtained, it is relatively simple for anyone with some basic skills in the use of metal-working tools to produce a device from which they may be fired. Such improvised weapons are usually of two-piece construction, with a smooth-bored, screw-off barrel; the simple striker mechanism is contained in the handle. Some, however, are more sophisticated: they may be disguised as pens, torches, screwdrivers, or some other apparently harmless piece of equipment. The two specimens illustrated here originated in Ulster, where they were found in about 1976. The data given apply only to the arms shown; naturally, individual weapons vary considerably.

Great Britain
MCEM 2

Length: 14" (356mm)
Weight: 88oz (2·49kg)
Barrel: 9" (229mm)
Calibre: 9mm
Rifling: 6 groove, r/hand
Capacity: Eighteen
Muz Vel: 1200 f/s (366 m/s)
Sights: Fixed

Although the initials by which this weapon is designated stand for "Machine Carbine Experimental Model", it is clear that the original concept was that of a machine pistol; therefore, it has seemed proper to include the arm in this book. Once World War II had ended, the British Government decided that, although the cheap, mass-produced Sten gun had given good service, something better was needed for the post-war Army. Much work on a successor to Sten had, of course, already been carried out by a number of designers, and thus there was no shortage of contenders for the replacement role. All potential successors were given the overall title of MCEM, with a serial number of distinguish them from each other, and it is probable that there was a good deal of rivalry between the various groups involved. The MCEM No 1 was the work of H. J. Turpin, who had been closely concerned with the original Sten, but the No 2, which is illustrated here, was designed by a Polish officer, Lieutenant Podsenkowsky, who, like thousands of his compatriots, had offered his services to Great Britain. The weapon illustrated is less than 15in (380mm) long and its magazine fits into the butt. The bolt is made to what was then an advanced design and consists of a half-cylinder, 8·5in (216mm) long; the striker is at the rear, so that at the moment of firing almost the entire barrel is inside the bolt. There is no cocking handle: the bolt is drawn to the rear by hooking a finger through a slot above the muzzle. Because of the weapon's light weight and rate of fire, vibration was considerable, and eventually a light, rigid-canvas butt was provided; this finally converted it to a true sub-machine gun. Even so, it was never adopted for service use.

Great Britain
WELROD SILENT PISTOL

Length:	12" (305mm)	**Rifling:**	4 groove, r/hand
Weight:	32oz (·91kg)	**Capacity:**	One
Barrel:	5" (127mm)	**Muz Vel:**	700 f/s (213 m/s)
Calibre:	·32" (8·1mm)	**Sights:**	Fixed

There is, perhaps, a certain sinister fascination in the idea of being able to deliver death silently from a distance. Even in the earliest days of gunpowder, men believed that it might be possible to produce a form of it which exploded without noise. However, silent weapons have a limited value in war—there is usually so much noise in battle that one explosion more or less is hardly noticeable—although there is, perhaps, a case to be made for the efficacy of silent sniper weapons in some circumstances. Technically, it is not very difficult to silence a weapon; what is difficult is to make an effective silencer which is not so bulky as to make the weapon hopelessly clumsy in use. There are two problems involved: one is to suppress the noise of the explosion; the other is to conceal what amounts to a sonic boom when the bullet breaks the sound barrier (assuming that it is of such velocity). Many pistol bullets do not exceed the speed of sound, which reduces the problem very considerably —and this was the case with the cartridge fired by the Welrod pistol, illustrated here. The pistol's barrel is relatively short, but the outer casing in front of it is fitted with a series of self-sealing, oil-impregnated, leather washers. These close behind the passage of the bullet and trap the sound; but, of course, they tend to burn out after comparatively few shots. This would, naturally, have been a great disadvantage in a weapon designed for general use. However, in the case of the Welrod, the situation presumably never arose, because it was a weapon for use by special forces only—on operations which sometimes required the silent and surreptitious elimination of an enemy.

Great Britain
HOME-MADE SINGLE-SHOT PISTOL

Length:	13" (330mm)	**Rifling:**	Nil
Weight:	23oz (·65kg)	**Capacity:**	One
Barrel:	8" (203mm)	**Muz Vel:**	c650 f/s (198 m/s)
Calibre:	·22" (5·6mm)	**Sights:**	Nil

Firearms have a certain fascination for many people, but because of the need for strict controls over their ownership and use, relatively few people are able to possess conventional weapons of their own. This leads on occasion to attempts to make them, but although this is to some extent understandable, it is a highly dangerous occupation which has in the past resulted in many cases of death or serious injury. Very few people realize the enormous power concealed in even a small cartridge. A bullet from a ·22in cartridge, propelled by the gases resulting from no more than a pinch of explosive, can kill at ranges in excess of 880 yds (805m): this gives at least some indication of the pressures developed in the breech of a firearm. It will, therefore, be obvious that materials intended to stand such internal stresses must be specially made—and such materials are rarely available to the amateur gunmaker. The fact that a cartridge fits a tube of some kind is no guarantee of that tube's strength: in these circumstances, a home-made weapon becomes as dangerous to the firer as a grenade. The crude weapon shown is, in all essentials, a zip-gun, and its trigger is a dummy.

Great Britain
WEBLEY AND SCOTT SINGLE-SHOT PISTOL

Length:	11" (279mm)	**Rifling:**	7 groove, r/hand
Weight:	25oz (·71kg)	**Capacity:**	One
Barrel:	9" (229mm)	**Muz Vel:**	c1100 f/s (335 m/s)
Calibre:	22" (5·6mm)	**Sights:**	Fixed

This somewhat unusual weapon was produced by Webley and Scott in 1911 to provide a means of cheap target practice for users of the firm's ·32in self-loading pistol (illustrated on page 169, above). Reference to the earlier photograph will show that the arms have a strong similarity in all but barrel length. The frame of the single-shot pistol is the same as that of the self-loader, although modified to accept a different barrel. The single-shot arm was made in two barrel lengths, 4·5in (114mm) and 9in (229mm); the one shown is of the latter type. In order to load the pistol, the slide is drawn back a distance of about 1·75in (44mm) with finger and thumb, thus exposing the breech; this action also cocks the hammer. A cartridge is then pushed into the chamber and, as there is no recoil system, the slide must be pushed forward manually. The pistol is then ready to fire. After the shot has been fired, the slide is again pulled back and the case ejected. This action is performed by a flat ejector bar set on to the upper side of the barrel; at its front end is a milled slide (which is visible in the photograph, just in front of the slide). As with loading, the action must be performed manually. At the moment of firing, the slide is held in position by a very light spring latch, situated on the bottom of the slide, which engages in a groove in the body. There is a machined groove in the bottom of the butt where the magazine opening would normally be; this is intended for the attachment of a rifle-type butt.

United States of America
GUIDE LAMP LIBERATOR

Length:	5·5" (140mm)
Weight:	16oz (·45kg)
Barrel:	3·5" (89mm)
Calibre:	45" (11·4mm)
Rifling:	Nil
Capacity:	One
Muz Vel:	800 f/s (244 m/s)
Sights:	Fixed

In 1942 the United States Government decided that it required a large quantity of cheap arms to drop to various resistance or guerrilla units in occupied territories in the Far East and Pacific theatres. The US Office of Strategic Services (OSS) therefore approached the Guide Lamp division of General Motors, Detroit, to see what could be done—and the company was quickly able to oblige. It knew little of firearms, but it knew a great deal about the mass production of small metal items by the most modern methods, and within about three months it had produced about one million crude pistols of the type illustrated here. According to the calculations of Hogg and Weeks in *Pistols of the World,* this figure entailed the production of a Liberator pistol every 7·5 seconds—which was less time that it took to load the finished product, if, indeed, the term "finished" can be applied to such a device! To load the pistol it is necessary first to pull back the cocking piece and turn it anti-clockwise through 90 degrees, so as to hold it open. The breech is covered by a vertically sliding shutter with a hole for the striker, and is opened by pulling upwards on the back-sight. When this is done, a ·45in ACP cartridge is inserted, the shutter is pushed down, and the cocking piece is returned to its original position; the pistol is now ready to fire. There is, of course, no safety catch, although a pin on the upper part of the cocking piece passes through a hole in the backsight, presumably to ensure that the shutter does not open and foul the striker. Once a shot has been fired, the entire loading process must be repeated; no extractor is fitted, so it is necessary to use a wooden rod or some similar implement to push out the fired case. Although the pistol was strictly of single-shot variety, a few extra cartridges were packed into the butt, access to them being gained through a sliding trap at the base (the catch of which is visible in the photograph). After assembly, the arm was packed into a waterproof bag, together with a sheet of comic-strip type instructions, using no words, and was air-dropped where required. It was never regarded as being much more more than a throw-away assassin's arm, with which a guerrilla fighter might kill an enemy by stealth and afterwards rearm himself with the dead adversary's weapon. At first, the pistol was classed as a "flare projector", for security reasons, but the name Liberator later came into general use. Although the materials used were intentionally cheap and of low quality, it is probable that many of these pistols survive.

Germany
REFORM PISTOL

Length:	5·25" (133mm)
Weight:	12oz (·34kg)
Barrel:	3" (76mm)
Calibre:	6mm
Rifling:	7 groove, r/hand
Capacity:	Four
Muz Vel:	c780 f/s (238 m/s)
Sights:	Fixed

One of the problems associated with the revolver is that, except in very small calibres, the size of its cylinder tends to make it bulky to carry concealed. In the 20th century, this difficulty has, of course, been to a great extent overcome by the development of the medium-calibre, blowback, self-loading pistol, which is flat and inconspicuous; but in the early days of cartridge weapons, before the self-loading arm had been invented, many ingenious attempts were made to solve the problem. The weapon illustrated here was probably developed in the early years of the present century, by August Schuler of Suhl, Germany. Apart from German-made examples, the arm was, almost inevitably, copied in Belgium and Spain. The basic lock mechanism is that of a normal double-action revolver, in which the hammer acts on a firing pin in the frame. The forward end of the frame consists of a pair of parallel side-plates, between which fits a set of four vertically-stacked barrels. These are first loaded and then pressed down like a clip between the plates, where they are held in place by a small spring-loaded stud. The top round is fired first; then, pressure on the trigger raises the block of barrels so that the second cartridge is in line, ready for the next shot. The three lower barrels have small holes drilled on their upper sides to connect each to the barrel immediately above; thus, when the second and subsequent barrels are fired, enough gas passes upwards to blow out the empty case in the barrel above. The comb of the hammer is shaped in such a way as to deflect these ejected cases away from the direction of the firer's face.

Great Britain
HOME-MADE SHOT PISTOL

Length:	9" (229mm)
Weight:	25oz (·71kg)
Barrel:	6" (152mm)
Calibre:	410" (10·4mm)
Rifling:	Nil
Capacity:	One
Muz Vel:	c1000 f/s (305 m/s)
Sights:	Fixed

In the era of muzzle-loading arms, most pistols were smooth-bored, and could, of course, be used to fire either for shot or ball—although the combination of slow-burning black powder and a short barrel probably had an adverse effect on both pattern and velocity. After the introduction of the breech-loader firing self-contained cartridges, however, production of such dual-purpose arms virtually ceased, and specialized types necessarily emerged. One such type was the shot pistol. This was in many ways a useful weapon for what may be classed as casual shooting— for example, at small game or at rats and other vermin—and had the advantage that, unlike a gun, it could be carried conveniently stuck in a belt or inside a large pocket, leaving the hands free. It must also be noted, however, that this ease of concealment made it very suitable as a poacher's arm, so that it was rather disliked by landowners and gamekeepers. Until the Firearms Act of 1937, weapons of this type were obtainable in Great Britain, without formality, over the counters of gunsmiths or country ironmongers, and could be bought for two or three pounds. As may, perhaps, be expected, the main source of these weapons was Belgium, although they were also manufactured in North America and elsewhere. They were often double-barrelled, with external hammers, and varied from ·22in calibre to a maximum of ·410in. The pistol illustrated is home-made, and although a good deal has already been said on the very real dangers involved in making and using home-made firearms, the point may usefully be reiterated here. It will, perhaps, surprise many readers to learn that a diminutive ·410in cartridge of the type shown with this weapon develops appreciably higher pressures than those normally produced by the much larger 12-bore cartridge. The reason for this is that, in order to produce an effective shot pattern, the column of shot in the smaller cartridge has to be very long in relation to its diameter. Sufficient force must then be applied to the very small area at the base of this column of shot to force it from the barrel at a lethal velocity of something in the region of 1200 f/s (366 m/s); thus, the charge must be a comparatively large one. The weapon shown here has been made with the cut-down barrel of a ·410in shotgun, but the locking system is fundamentally weak and the metal used in it is inadequate both in weight and quality. It is probable that a few shots would be enough to destroy it.

Belgium
MINIATURE PISTOL

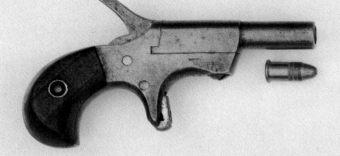

Length:	3·15" (80mm)
Weight:	2oz (·06kg)
Barrel:	1·65" (42mm)
Calibre:	·22" (5·6mm)
Rifling:	Nil
Capacity:	One
Muz Vel:	c700 f/s (213 m/s)
Sights:	Nil

The process of miniaturization has always fascinated designers in many fields, so it is hardly to be expected that the designers of weapons should be exempt from it. The products of this branch of the trade fall into two main categories. In the first place there are so-called apprentice pieces, made by young men in the gunmakers' work-shops to demonstrate their skills. These are often small works of art in themselves. Secondly, we find normal production-line weapons which have simply been made on a reduced scale, but which will fire commercially-available cartridges. The little pistol illustrated is a weapon of the latter type; it was made in Belgium, probably at the end of the 19th century. Although its dimensions are given in the accompanying data table, a better impression of its size may be gained from realization of the fact that the photograph is life-sized. It is of very simple construction, with a single-action hammer and a sheathed trigger. The barrel is mounted on a horizontal pivot, the head of the screw being just visible in the photograph, in the bulge of the front of the frame. In order to load, the hammer is cocked and the breech is swivelled to the right to allow a cartridge to be inserted. As the hammer falls, its nose enters a slot cut in the barrel just above the chamber: this prevents any risk of the barrel turning at the moment of firing. The pistol is smooth-bored and is designed for a bulleted cap, but will chamber a ·22in short cartridge.

United States of America
COLT DERINGER No. 3

Length:	4·8" (122mm)
Weight:	8oz (·23kg)
Barrel:	2·5" (63mm)
Calibre:	·41" (10·4mm)
Rifling:	7 groove, l/hand
Capacity:	One
Muz Vel:	c450 f/s (137 m/s)
Sights:	Fixed

Weapons of this type take their names from Henry Deringer of Philadelphia, who specialized, from the 1830s onward, in the production of small pocket pistols of quite large calibre. These soon achieved popularity in the United States and elsewhere as small and easily-concealed weapons. A pistol of this type was used to assassinate Abraham Lincoln, the President who had led the Northern States during the Civil War. This brought the arm increased fame and led to extensive copying, until eventually the word "deringer" (sometimes spelt incorrectly—or deliberately, by copyists—as "derringer") came to denote a type rather than a trademark. Weapons of this kind were extensively carried in the United States, often as a second, concealed weapon to back up the revolver visible in a holster. They were also popular with ladies, for carriage in handbag or garter (depending on the kind of lady!). The specimen illustrated here was made by Colt in the period 1875-1912, and is classed as the company's Model No 3. It has a brass frame and bird-beak butt. To load the arm, it is necessary to put the hammer at half-cock and swing the breech out to the right in order to insert the cartridge. Then the barrel is swung back and the pistol is cocked. The empty case is ejected automatically when the breech is opened.

United States of America
REMINGTON DERINGER

Length:	4·75" (121mm)
Weight:	7·5oz (·21kg)
Barrel:	2·4" (61mm)
Calibre:	·410" (10·4mm)
Rifling:	5 groove, r/hand
Capacity:	One
Muz Vel:	c450 f/s (137 m/s)
Sights:	Fixed

Some details of the origin of this type of weapon have already been given, in the caption above. Many of the small pocket pistols produced by Remington were designed by William H. Elliott, who became well known for such arms. Some were of "pepperbox" design (like the pistols illustrated on pages 58-61); others had fixed barrels and rotating firing pins; and yet others were of single- or double-barrelled type, in which form they continued to be made until well into the 20th century. The specimen illustrated here is the single-barrelled Remington version of 1867, a simple but quite powerful arm which achieved considerable popularity. It is of very basic construction, since it has, in effect, no breechblock of any kind: the cartridge is held in position at the moment of firing by the heavy hammer. When the weapon is at full-cock, a short rimfire round of ·41in calibre can be inserted. When the hammer falls, a small projection below it engages in front of the sear and holds the round in position to be fired by an integral striker situated on the top of the hammer face.

France
SINGLE-SHOT PISTOL

Length:	5·5" (140mm)
Weight:	3oz (·08kg)
Barrel:	4" (102mm)
Calibre:	·22" (5·6mm)
Rifling:	Nil
Capacity:	One
Muz Vel:	c450 f/s (137 m/s)
Sights:	Fixed

This tiny pistol, like the miniature pistol illustrated on the facing page (top), can be only marginally described as a weapon: it should, strictly, be classified as a dangerous toy. Nevertheless, it is a firearm by definition and has been included accordingly. Although it is thought to be of French origin, the marks on it are so faint that it is impossible to be sure. However, it was probably made towards the end of the 19th century, when it could have been purchased for a few shillings in a gunsmiths or ironmongers without any kind of formality—together with a supply of bulleted caps for which it was designed. These consisted of a short, rimfire case, containing fulminate compound but no powder, with a spherical lead ball as projectile. The round probably equalled the pellet from a modern air-rifle in terms of hitting power. This pistol is now in little better than relic condition.

United States of America
REMINGTON DOUBLE DERINGER

Length:	4·75" (121mm)
Weight:	12oz (·34kg)
Barrel:	3" (76mm)
Calibre:	·410" (10·4mm)
Rifling:	6 groove, l/hand
Capacity:	One
Muz Vel:	c450 f/s (137 m/s)
Sights:	Fixed

This is another of the famous deringer-type weapons designed by William H. Elliott of the Remington company, more details of which are given in the caption for the deringer arm illustrated on the facing page (bottom). This model first appeared in about 1866 and continued to be made almost up to the outbreak of World War II. It is a neat, compact weapon which, in spite of its small size, handles surprisingly well, even though the butt can be gripped only by the second finger. To load the pistol, it is necessary first to turn the lever (visible above the trigger) until it points forward; then the top-hinged barrels can be raised, the cartridges inserted, and the barrels returned to their proper position and locked. The hammer is of single-action type but is, most ingeniously, equipped with a floating nose which fires the top and bottom barrels in succession. The extractor, situated on the left-hand side of the barrels, is worked by the user's thumb.

United States of America
HAMMOND BULLDOG PISTOL

Length:	8" (203mm)	**Rifling:**	5 groove, r/hand
Weight:	24oz (·68kg)	**Capacity:**	One
Barrel:	4" (102mm)	**Muz Vel:**	c500 f/s (152 m/s)
Calibre:	·44" (11·2mm)	**Sights:**	Fixed

Single-shot cartridge weapons of the type broadly classed as deringers became popular during the American Civil War, when many soldiers, particularly on the Northern side, liked to carry a small, concealed pistol as a back-up gun for use in emergency. The weapon illustrated here was produced by the Connecticut Arms and Manufacturing Company, Naubuc, Conn., under a patent dated 25 October 1864. It was generally known under the trade name of Hammond Bulldog. It is a solid, robust arm capable of firing a powerful cartridge. Access to the breech is gained by placing the hammer at half-cock, pressing the top stud, and then pushing the breechblock to the left. The pivot of the block is so arranged that, as the block moves, it also retracts about ·2in (5mm), thus bringing the extractor into play.

United States of America
M.B.A. 13mm GYROJET

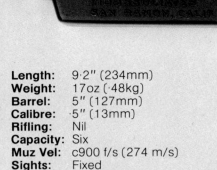

Length:	9·2" (234mm)
Weight:	17oz (·48kg)
Barrel:	5" (127mm)
Calibre:	·5" (13mm)
Rifling:	Nil
Capacity:	Six
Muz Vel:	c900 f/s (274 m/s)
Sights:	Fixed

There have been virtually no significant developments in hand firearms for very many years and it is, therefore, arguable that these arms have reached their full development. In 1960, however, two enterprising Americans, Robert Mainhardt and Art Biehl, found this so hard to accept that they decided to attempt a breakthrough. They produced the weapon illustrated here, which although it looks at first glance very like an orthodox self-loading pistol is, in fact, a rocket-launcher. The rocket is of 13mm calibre: it is about 1·5in (38mm) long, with a solid head as the actual projectile and a tubular body containing a propellant charge. The base is closed but it has four jets to provide thrust; these are also angled to impart spin to the rocket, in order to ensure stability. Once the rocket has been loaded pressure on the trigger causes the hammer to drive it to the rear so that the cap in its base strikes a fixed pin in the breech. The forward action of the rocket recocks the hammer, which lies flat so as not to impede its passage. The weapon lacked both power and accuracy and was not a success.

Germany
HECKLER AND KOCH VP-70

Length:	8·6" (218mm)
Weight:	34·5oz (·98kg)
Barrel:	4·5" (114mm)
Calibre:	9mm
Rifling:	6 groove, r/hand
Capacity:	Eighteen
Muz Vel:	c1100 f/s (335 m/s)
Sights:	Fixed

trated here is the most recent model. The VP-70 is of blowback type, but fires the 9mm Parabellum cartridge of considerable power. The lock is of double-action pattern only, but in order to facilitate deliberate shooting it is fitted with a type of hesitation lock; change lever visible in the photographs is set in the position shown, three-round bursts. The merit of this system is that the bullets are clear of the barrel before the muzzle has a chance to rise, thus removing the basic disadvantage of the so-called machine pistol. The use of the VP-70 as a sub-machine gun is greatly facilitated by the fact that the normal pistol magazine is able to accommodate 18 rounds. Although this can only be achieved by staggering the rounds almost into a double row, it does not make the butt unduly bulky.

The West German firm of Heckler and Koch was established at Oberndorf-Neckar as soon as the manufacture of arms was again permitted in Germany after World War II. It quickly established a reputation for military firearms, and is particularly noted for its famous automatic rifle. The company now also makes service-type pistols, of which the arm illus- this allows a pause between a fairly heavy first-pressure cocking and a much lighter second pressure on the trigger for actual firing. This system makes it safe to carry the pistol with a round in the chamber: a safety catch is not normally fitted. The weapon is fited with a detachable holster-stock; when this is attached, the weapon can be used either for single shots or, when the

Germany
ERMA CONVERSION UNIT

Length: 11·9" (302mm)
Weight: 36·5oz (1·03kg)
Barrel: 7·7" (196mm)
Calibre: 22" (5·6mm)
Rifling: 6 groove, r/hand
Capacity: Five
Muz Vel: c1100 f/s (335 m/s)
Sights: Fixed

When Germany began to rearm in the 1930s, it was decided that there was a requirement for a means of converting the then standard Luger service pistol (see pages 152-153, below) to fire ·22in ammunition, for the purpose of small-range practice. The concept was not, of course, a new one: it had earlier been applied to revolvers — but whereas this end can be accomplished in a revolver by no more than an easily-removed barrel liner and an alternative cylinder, a self-loading pistol, with its very different method of functioning, necessarily requires a more sophisticated arrangement. The solution was provided by the Ermawerke company of Erfurt, which produced a conversion kit. This included an insert barrel, of the type visible in the illustration; a light breech-block containing its own mainspring; a toggle unit; and a magazine of the appropriate size. The kit had been invented by an Ermawerke employee named Kulisch and patented as early as 1927, so there were few delays in putting it into production. The Erma conversion unit was highly effective in transforming a locked-breech arm into a blowback type: the ·22in rifle cartridge was powerful enough to compress the special spring, and the cartridge rims did not, apparently, cause many feed problems. The arm proved very accurate: grouping well up to 55 yards (50m).

France
TURBIAUX PALM-SQUEEZER PISTOL

Length: 4" (102mm)
Weight: 9oz (·26kg)
Barrel: 1·5" (38mm)
Calibre: 6mm
Rifling: 6 groove, r/hand
Capacity: Ten
Muz Vel: c650 f/s (198 m/s)
Sights: Nil

This is a most unorthodox type of pistol: it is held in the palm of the hand, with the barrel protruding between the fingers, and fired by squeezing in a trigger device. It was invented by Jaques Turbiaux, a Parisian, who patented it in 1882. These pistols were briefly popular in Europe; some were made in the United States, but failed to sell. In order to load, it is necessary to remove the top cover and insert the cartridges into the body of the pistol, where they lied radially, bullets outward. The specimen illustrated here is of French origin: American versions had a ring on either side of the barrel for the user's first and second fingers, and a safety.

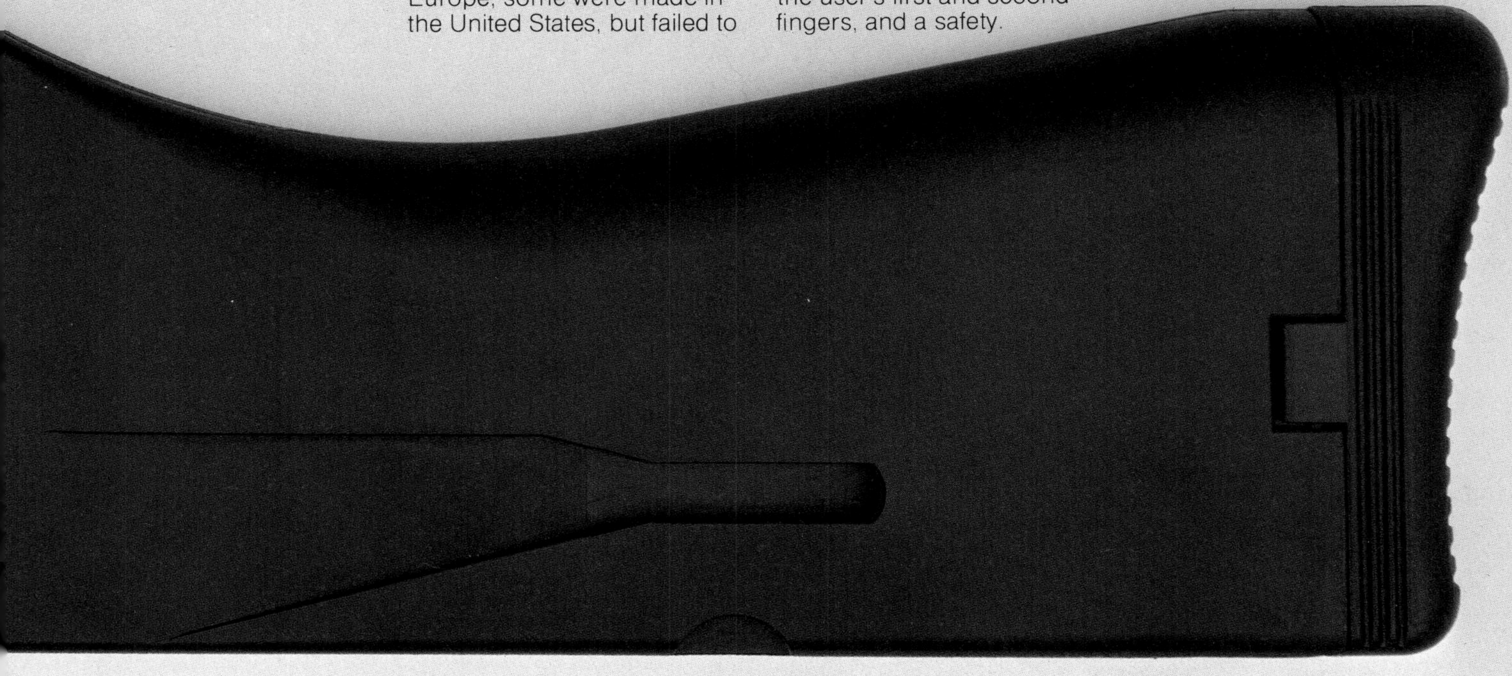

Index

Bibliography

Picture Credits

Title	Author/Editor	Place and year of publication
Cartridges of the World	Barnes	Chicago 1969
British Military Firearms	Blackmore	London 1961
Pistols of the World	Blair	London 1968
United States Firearms	Butler	New York 1971
Adams Revolvers	Chamberlain and Taylerson	London 1976
Manual of Firearms	Deane	London 1858
Georgian Pistols	Dixon	London 1971
The Revolver	Dove	London 1858
The Webley Story	Dowell	Leeds 1962
English Pistols and Revolvers	George	London 1961
The Gun	Greener	London 1881
Remington Historical Treasury of American Guns	Grossett and Dunlap	New York 1966
A History of the Colt Revolver	Haven and Belden	New York 1960
German Pistols and Revolvers	Hogg	London 1971
Illustrated Encyclopedia of Firearms	Hogg	London 1978
Pistols of the World	Hogg and Weeks	London 1978
Treatise on Military Small Arms and Ammunition	HMSO	London 1888
Textbook of Small Arms	HMSO	London 1909
Textbook for Small Arms	HMSO	London 1929
History of Smith and Wesson	Jinks	North Hollywood 1977
Japanese Infantry Weapons of World War Two	Markham	London 1976
Smith and Wesson 1857-1945	Neal and Jinks	New York 1966
Encyclopedia of Firearms	Peterson	London 1964
The Book of the Pistol	Pollard	London 1917
Automatic Pistols	Pollard	London 1920
The British Soldier's Firearms	Roads	London 1964
Two Hundred Years of American Firearms	Serven	Northfield Ill 1975
Book of Pistols and Revolvers	Smith	Harrisburg Pa 1977
Small Arms of the World	Smith and Smith	London 1973
Pistols; a Modern Encyclopedia	Stebbins	Harrisburg Pa 1961
The Inglis Browning Hi-Power Pistol	Stevens	Ottawa 1974
The Revolver 1818-1865	Taylerson, Andrews, Frith	London 1968
The Revolver 1865-1888	Taylerson	London 1966
The Revolver 1889-1914	Taylerson	London 1970
Revolving Arms	Taylerson	London 1967
Luger	Walter	London 1977
Jane's Infantry Weapons 1979-1980	Weeks (Ed)	London 1980
Flintlock Pistols	Wilkinson	London 1969
The Illustrated Book of Pistols	Wilkinson	London 1979
Textbook of Automatic Pistols	Wilson/Hogg	London 1975
Automatic Pistol Shooting	Winans	London 1915
The Art of Revolver Shooting	Winans	London 1901
Early Percussion Firearms	Winant	London 1970
Firearms Curiosa	Winant	New York 1970
Standard Directory of Proof Marks	Wirnsberger	New Jersey 1975

Unless otherwise credited, all pictures in this book were taken by Bruce Scott in the Weapons Museum, School of Infantry, Warminster, Wiltshire; the Pattern Room, Royal Small Arms Factory, Enfield Lock (pages 122-123; 154-155; 176-177; 202-203); and the Armouries, H.M. Tower of London (pages 16-17; 18-19; 20-21; 22-23).

The publisher wishes to thank the following organizations and individuals who have supplied illustrations, here credited by page number (where more than one photograph appears on a page, references are made in the order of columns across the page, and then from top to bottom). For reasons of space some references are abbreviated as follows: Imperial War Museum, London: IWM; Mary Evans Picture Library: ME; Peter Newark's Western Americana: PNWA; BBC Hulton Picture Library: BBC; Mansell Collection: MAN Barnaby's Picture Library: BAR; London News Service: LON; Daily Telegraph Colour Library: DTCL; Pictorial Press: PP.

10: PNWA (2)/ME; 11: Tate Gallery (John Webb); 13: PNWA/ME/ National Maritime Museum; 14-15: MAN (2)/PNWA/BAR; 36-37: BBC/PNWA; 38: MAN; 39: ME/PNWA; 40-41: MAN (2)/PNWA; 52-53: PNWA (3)/Musée de l'Armée, Paris; 54: PNWA/ Smithsonian Institute; 55: PNWA (2); 56-57: Library of Congress/ Terry Gander (4)/PNWA; 82: ME/PNWA/BBC; 83: Federal Bureau of Investigation/Popperfoto/US Army/IWM; 84: PNWA/BBC/PNWA; 85: PP/PNWA/BAR; 86-87: BAR/LON/BAR (2)/DTCL/LON; 144: PNWA/MAN/PP/Popperfoto; 145: US Army; 146: BBC/IWM/PP; 147: PP (2)/IWM; 148: IWM/US Army (3); 149: DTCL/PP; 188-189: BBC/US Army/PNWA; 190-191: Devon News Service/BBC/ME (2).

PRINTED IN BELGIUM BY
proost
INTERNATIONAL BOOK PRODUCTION